Free Justice

JUSTICE, POWER, AND POLITICS

Coeditors

Heather Ann Thompson
Rhonda Y. Williams

Editorial Advisory Board

Peniel E. Joseph
Daryl Maeda
Barbara Ransby
Vicki L. Ruiz
Marc Stein

The Justice, Power, and Politics series publishes new works in history that explore the myriad struggles for justice, battles for power, and shifts in politics that have shaped the United States over time. Through the lenses of justice, power, and politics, the series seeks to broaden scholarly debates about America's past as well as to inform public discussions about its future.

More information on the series, including a complete list of books published, is available at http://justicepowerandpolitics.com/.

Free Justice
A History of the Public Defender in Twentieth-Century America

Sara Mayeux

The University of North Carolina Press CHAPEL HILL

This book was published with the assistance of the Thornton H. Brooks Fund of the University of North Carolina Press.

© 2020 Sara Mayeux
All rights reserved
Set in Merope Basic by Westchester Publishing Services
Manufactured in the United States of America

The University of North Carolina Press has been a member of the Green Press Initiative since 2003.

Library of Congress Cataloging-in-Publication Data
Names: Mayeux, Sara, author.
Title: Free justice : a history of the public defender in twentieth-century America / Sara Mayeux.
Other titles: History of the public defender in twentieth-century America | Justice, power, and politics.
Description: Chapel Hill : University of North Carolina Press, 2020. | Series: Justice, power, and politics | Includes bibliographical references and index.
Identifiers: LCCN 2019052149 | ISBN 9781469656021 (cloth) | ISBN 9781469661650 (pbk.: alk. paper) | ISBN 9781469656038 (ebook)
Subjects: LCSH: Public defenders—United States—History—20th century.
Classification: LCC KF9646 .M39 2020 | DDC 345.73/012630904—dc23
LC record available at https://lccn.loc.gov/2019052149

Cover illustration: Dorothea Lange, *Pulich in Court*, 1957 (A67.137.57136.4). Photonegative, 2.25 × 2.25 in. © The Dorothea Lange Collection, the Oakland Museum of California. Gift of Paul S. Taylor.

Portions of this book were previously published in a different form as "What *Gideon* Did," *Columbia Law Review* 116, no. 1 (January 2016): 15–104.

Contents

Acknowledgments vii

Introduction 1

CHAPTER ONE
Free Justice 24

CHAPTER TWO
From Charity to Right 57

CHAPTER THREE
Democratic Justice 86

CHAPTER FOUR
A Permanent Crisis 117

CHAPTER FIVE
Local Injustice 151

Epilogue 181

Notes 191
Bibliography 241
Index 263

Acknowledgments

I first became curious about this subject in 2008, when I was a student intern at the public defender's office for the City and County of San Francisco (established, as I learned that summer, in 1921). Since then, I have met many public defenders around the country. Some are professional acquaintances I have met only in passing, at conferences or similar events; others are former classmates or personal friends. I did not formally conduct interviews or gather oral histories for this book, which relies mainly on archival and published sources. Nevertheless, my thinking on the subject has surely been informed in some deep sense by my conversations with public defenders over the years and my admiration for their work. I am not entirely sure what they might make of the book, but I wish to thank them for teaching me (probably without realizing they were doing so, in most cases) about their unique role within this experiment we call the United States.

I have the great good fortune to teach at Vanderbilt Law School, where most of the work on this book was completed. Dean Chris Guthrie has cultivated a rigorous, collegial, and relatively low-stress environment for teaching and scholarship—a rare combination in academia. I will refrain from listing all of my colleagues here only because of space limitations, but I am grateful to all of them for contributing to this environment as well, and for their feedback, both formal and informal, on my ideas. Chris Slobogin, my faculty mentor, and Dan Sharfstein, our resident expert on legal history and book writing, provided both moral and other forms of support for this project. Spring Miller and Cara Suvall answered queries about legal ethics and have taught me a lot about the current state of the legal profession; Rebecca Allensworth provided clutch feedback on parts of the final draft. I am also grateful to my colleagues over in the history department for their warm welcome and invitations to collaborate.

Vanderbilt's Criminal Justice Program underwrote a day-long workshop on an early draft of the book manuscript. For giving generously of their time, insights, and careful attention, I am immensely grateful to the scholars who participated: Vanderbilt colleagues Sarah Igo, Nancy King, Dan Sharfstein, Ganesh Sitaraman, and Kim Welch; and three far-flung colleagues who traveled to Nashville for the occasion—Anne Fleming, Joanna Grisinger, and

Danny LaChance. It was an honor to spend the day in the company of this excellent group and receive their input. Thanks are also due to associate dean Jim Rossi, program director Chris Slobogin, and program assistant Quenna Stewart for helping to make the workshop happen, and to my erstwhile faculty assistant, Rae Torres, who coordinated logistics. (And I owe a second thanks to Sarah Igo, who kindly obliged when I requested an additional round of last-minute feedback.)

I received my JD and PhD at Stanford University, where an eclectic group of professors and mentors, in both the law school and the history department, encouraged my interests and provided structure for my intellectually meandering tendencies. From my first semester at Stanford Law School, Bob Weisberg sparked my interest in criminal law and indulged my questions about the deeper stories behind the cases we read in class. George Fisher, Elizabeth Joh, Amalia Kessler, Joan Petersilia, and Norm Spaulding, among many other professors on the faculty, provided encouragement and opportunity for research and writing. By luck, Bob Gordon happened to be visiting during my 2L year, and subsequently decided to return to the Stanford faculty full-time. He became an essential and kindly guide as I sought to understand the history of lawyers and legal culture. Finally, I owe immense thanks and many research debts to Barbara Babcock, for both her personal encouragement and her pathbreaking work on Clara Foltz, without which it would have been impossible to know where to begin this project. Although I arrived at Stanford too late to take a class with Barbara, she was unfailingly supportive of my interest in this subject, whether bequeathing me several boxes worth of research materials that she had gathered or recounting her own memories of working as a public defender in the 1960s.

After law school, I had the unparalleled opportunity to clerk for Judge Marsha Berzon, from whom I learned everything I know about the judiciary and most of what I know about law (with apologies to my professors). From Judge Berzon, I also learned not to give up when you see a problem differently than everyone else does—it might be a sign that you are onto something.

Stanford's PhD program in United States history had that most old-fashioned and (I now think) essential of components—a core curriculum—and I am grateful to all of the professors in the history department who shepherded my cohort through our coursework on the grand sweep of American history, including Gordon Chang, Allyson Hobbs, Richard White, and Caroline Winterer. Most of what I read during those seminars is not cited in this book's bibliography, but the experience crucially formed my understanding both of the modern United States and of the possibilities of history writing. Estelle Freedman should receive some kind of lifetime achievement award for her research seminar, which made explicit so many essential lessons about research and academia that graduate students are too often left to try and piece together on their own. Jack Rakove was an unfailingly incisive interlocutor and an unparalleled teacher of how to read and think about (and teach about) the Constitution. Finally, Jim Campbell welcomed me over to the history department, encouraged this project, prompted me to think about it on a large scale, and shared a lesson that I only later fully understood, about the importance of finding the right characters.

In ways that I did not fully anticipate at the outset, but was thrilled to discover along the way, the background reading for this book enabled me to revisit the great fascination of my college years—the twentieth-century crisis of democracy. When I was an undergraduate, Anthony Grafton introduced me to the many varieties of history, and Anson Rabinbach to the many varieties of fascism and antifascism. I was immensely lucky to study writing with Richard Eder and with the great and good John McPhee, who taught me, along with generations of Princeton sophomores, to diagram a story, describe an object, and recognize that "good writing is where you find it." While I am thanking these people, though, I should also acknowledge the teachers that I had growing up in the Atlanta Public Schools, many of whom exemplified the best potential of public institutions.

Although this book will likely be shelved as legal history, and I think of it also as a kind of cultural history, there is no genre of historical scholarship that I have learned more from, and enjoy reading more, than the so-called new political history. I am grateful to many political historians for their books, articles, conference presentations, and conversations over the years, without which I could not have figured out what I think about law and legal culture (and also without which I would understand a lot less about my own life, and how it has been shaped by political currents). Here, though, I will specifically mention Lily Geismer, who graciously reviewed part of the final draft on a quick deadline and provided late-stage feedback on the framing of this project.

I am fortunate to enjoy scholarly camaraderie with too many far-flung legal historians to list here, across both law schools and history departments. I might have found a different career were it not for the Hurst Institute at the University of Wisconsin, which reminded me at a crucial moment why I became interested in legal history to begin with. For this formative experience, I am grateful to that year's institute leader, Barbara Welke; our

Wisconsin faculty hosts, including Mitra Sharafi and Karl Shoemaker; and my entire cohort of Hurst fellows, whom I am glad to count as friends and whose books I look forward to reading once I am finally done with this one. More recently, I benefited again from legal historians' unique community when I was invited to present a chapter of this book at the American Bar Foundation's legal history roundtable. Thank you to Chris Schmidt for the invitation, to Laura Kalman and Jane Dailey for commenting on my draft, and to everyone in attendance—a literal roundtable of America's top and next top legal historians—for their generous and helpful comments.

Over the years, pieces of this book have benefited from presentations at a number of scholarly conferences and workshops. Here I will name a few recent gatherings that had the most proximate influence on the book. Justin Driver and Aziz Huq kindly invited me to present at the University of Chicago Constitutional Law Workshop; thanks also to John Rappaport for follow-up correspondence about the Sixth Amendment. The parts of this book about the South benefited significantly from feedback from the law school faculty workshops at Emory University, the University of Indiana, and Tulane University, while chapter 3 benefited from a presentation to Vanderbilt's own Americanist seminar. Components of the project were also presented at annual meetings of the American Society for Legal History in 2015 and 2017. Elizabeth Hinton, Mary Dudziak, my various co-panelists, and innumerable audience members raised important questions that helped shape my thinking.

Before I arrived at Vanderbilt, I was blessed to spend two years in the unparalleled legal history community at the University of Pennsylvania, as one of the law school's Sharswood Fellows. Sally Gordon, Sophia Lee, Serena Mayeri, and all of the faculty and graduate students in the "Writer's Bloc(k)" fostered an unusually welcoming and supportive environment, and Sophia served as an incomparable mentor for navigating my next career steps after Penn. Many others at Penn provided feedback and encouragement, including Stephanos Bibas, Jean Galbraith, Dorothy Roberts, participants at the Penn Law Ad Hoc Faculty Workshop, and especially David Rudovsky, who shared his insights and memories about the history of criminal defense in Philadelphia. The Raoul Berger–Mark DeWolfe Howe Legal History Fellowship, at Harvard Law School, also funded a year of research and writing. While at Harvard, I received valuable suggestions on early work toward this project from Tomiko Brown-Nagin, Michael Klarman, Kenneth Mack, Bruce Mann, Michael Willrich, Elizabeth Katz, and other faculty and students who came through the legal history workshop.

Neither this book nor any other book would exist without librarians and archivists. I am grateful to the many at Harvard, Penn, Vanderbilt, Temple, Georgetown, Princeton, UCLA, and Duke who helped me to track down sources, and also to Duke graduate student Siobhan Barco, who provided research assistance. This book hints at some wary sentiments about the Rockefellers, but I am grateful for their foresight when it came to allocating extra mansions to historical preservation; the Rockefeller Archive Center is an unusually pleasant place to page through manuscripts and microfilm, and I am grateful to the archivists for their individualized assistance. I was also delighted to do a bit of research for this book at the Atlanta Historical Society, which is where I first learned to conduct archival research many years ago, back when I was a student at North Atlanta High School. Although I did not conduct formal oral histories, Bruce Jacob, John Cleary, and Judge Harry Pregerson kindly spoke to me over the phone about various people or events encompassed in this book's scope and provided pointers that proved helpful in my research. Pieces of this book were first published, in different form, in my article "What *Gideon* Did" in *Columbia Law Review*; the student editors there provided meticulous editing and cite-checking.

The reviewers lined up by the University of North Carolina Press made this a much better book than it otherwise would have been. They provided expert attention to both the proposal and the eventual manuscript, raised shrewd questions about big-picture questions and small details, and pushed me to articulate what exactly the book was about. I am grateful for the time and care that they gave to this project. I also owe a big thank you to everyone at the press both for their work on this book and for their patience with my protracted tinkering. Brandon Proia expressed confidence in this project early on, provided excellent editorial suggestions, and shepherded it through the logistical pipeline.

During the weeks when I was completing this book, I was listening to a podcast in my car when I heard the following apt quotation, attributed to the filmmaker David Fincher: "Movies aren't finished, they're abandoned, and you have to make peace with that." Mercifully for me, the time has come to abandon this project. Before I do, I have to thank my mother, who made sure that we knew we could do anything, as long as we did our best; my father, who introduced me to books and libraries; and Luke and Ruthie, my first interlocutors about American culture, the concept of fairness, lawyer TV shows, and everything else. As our mom taught us to say at the end of every endeavor: "Good game—what's next?"

Free Justice

Introduction

The Cold War was everywhere in 1955, but where could an American go and see it? Maybe to Korea, or Warsaw, or Bandung. Ellery Cuff was a "Northern California farm boy" who had grown up to become the public defender of Los Angeles County, and he did not think anyone needed to travel so far away. If they wanted to observe firsthand the contrast between democracy and totalitarianism, they needed only to visit his office. Cuff and his deputies provided free legal representation, at public expense, for anyone in Los Angeles who was accused of committing a serious crime and could not afford a lawyer. Cuff believed his work exemplified the "democratic doctrine of the dignity and paramount importance of the individual." Only in a free society, Cuff implied, would the state not only accuse, but also provide a defense for the accused. Under communist rule, "the state is all, the individual nothing." In the United States, public defenders and other protections for the accused instantiated "the profound belief that the individual, his rights and safeguards make up the central nexus of existence, and the state only justifies its existence by protecting these rights and safeguards." "The lot of the public defender is not always a happy one," Cuff acknowledged. But in the public defender's daily activity, visiting jails and arguing in court on behalf of indigent men and women accused of murder and other serious felonies, Cuff found the essence of liberal democracy.[1]

Four years later, the New York lawyer Harrison Tweed expressed a similar view, suggesting that public defenders could help to prove the "workability of our American way of life."[2] A "handsome playboy" from a family of prominent lawyers, Tweed had enrolled in law school as a young man only because his father promised, in exchange, to buy him a polo pony. Now he was a senior partner in the clubby Wall Street law firm that existed primarily to provide legal counsel for the Rockefeller family and that family's prize investment, the Chase Manhattan Bank.[3] Tweed was three thousand miles away from Cuff and many rungs above him in the profession's internal status hierarchy, which tended to peg a lawyer's prestige to the wealth of his clients. But both men spoke the lingua franca of Cold War American liberalism. In a political moment defined by apparent consensus—at least among elites and professionals—liberalism connoted not a partisan platform, but a set of principles ostensibly shared across political, geographic, and class divides: among them, a commitment to individual rights and national unity, and a belief in the uniquely egalitarian potential of American law and legal institutions.[4]

Like all invocations of "the American way," these statements equating the public defender with liberal democracy were arguments, not factual descriptions. In most of the United States, there were no public defenders in the 1950s.[5] In this respect Ellery Cuff's Los Angeles, having established the nation's first public defender decades earlier during the Progressive Era, was unusual. But the landscape would soon change dramatically, now that the public defender had the endorsement of professional leaders like Harrison Tweed. By 1973, nearly two-thirds of Americans lived in an area served by a public defender.[6] That same year, a federal commission recommended that every local jurisdiction maintain "a full-time public defender organization."[7] By the end of the twentieth century, eight out of ten felony defendants in urban counties were represented by a publicly funded lawyer.[8]

Today, public defenders form part of the American way of life in the literal sense. There are thousands of public defenders all around the country, and millions of Americans each year rely on them for legal advice and courtroom advocacy.[9] To be sure, some jurisdictions still do not have full-time public defenders and instead contract out the work piecemeal; other cities have only very recently established public defenders' offices, which remain weakly supported. Nor do public defenders receive material support commensurate with the rhetorical esteem they inspire. Advocates decry public defenders' inadequate budgets and debate whether the federal government should do more to supplement state and local resources for indigent defense. In a moment of widespread concern about mass incarceration, lawyers and legal scholars question whether public defenders can provide meaningful representation or whether defendants' fates are predetermined by draconian sentencing laws, racial bias, and "tough-on-crime" politics.[10] But all of these caveats only confirm that public defenders have grown roots in American legal culture. Only because public defenders are central to the day-to-day operations of the criminal courts do advocates and scholars engage in vigorous debate about how they should be funded and how they fit into larger discussions about criminal law and policy.

However beleaguered, public defenders are now so ubiquitous in American courtrooms that it is easy to forget how recently the legal profession considered their very existence controversial. For much of the twentieth century, elite lawyers did not extol public defenders as exemplars of liberal democracy and "the American way." To the contrary, public defenders remained sparse into the 1950s precisely because many lawyers worried that publicly funded legal assistance threatened the American way of life, which they defined to require free markets, independent professions, and a limited role for government. They regarded the public defender not as a safeguard for individual rights, but as a socialist-style project of coopting lawyers into a centralized government program. When his peers on Wall Street tried to envision the public defender, Tweed explained ruefully, what appeared in their minds instead was the "hobgoblin" of "communism and . . . the socialization of the legal profession."[11]

Tweed observed, correctly, that this strand of professional opposition had waned significantly by the 1950s. Lawyers remained wary of "socialization" and continued to oppose public funding for many types of legal assistance, but were increasingly receptive to public programs in the limited realm of criminal defense.[12] Still, as late as 1956, a federal judge could publish an article in the legal profession's national magazine asserting that "the public defender system" was essentially "totalitarian." The judge offered an illustrative hypothetical: "Put yourself in the place of a poverty-stricken Puerto Rican who does not speak English," and is falsely accused of killing a government agent. "How would you like to be told that another government official would act as your representative?"[13] The very attribute of public defenders that Cuff celebrated as exemplifying democratic regard for the individual—that they were provided by the state—the judge denounced as despotic. Any scenario "where the government, when it prosecutes a man, purports also to defend him," resembled "a police state," with the authorities controlling both sides of what ought to be an adversarial process. Defendants ought to have counsel—but counsel provided by "a free and independent bar," whether through the efforts of individual lawyers or private organizations. The public defender, the judge concluded, "would bring our government so close to the police state that we ought to shun it like the plague."[14]

Earlier in the twentieth century, this preference for private initiative over public provision would not have been an unusual position for a leader of the legal profession. Nor, even in the twenty-first century, would it be considered an extremist view as applied to civil legal aid. By the 1960s, though, such objections as applied to the public defender in criminal cases had become a fringe position. Reminiscing about those old debates, Harrison Tweed felt silly even summarizing the old assertion that public defenders represented "the first step towards communism." Stopping himself, he remarked: "Well, it sounds idiotic."[15]

Precisely because such objections came to seem strange to most lawyers, they present intriguing historical questions. Why did elite lawyers once object so strenuously to the public defender, and what changed? In order to understand these lawyers' eventual embrace of the idea, it is essential first to take seriously their earlier concerns. The association between the public provision of lawyers and socialism was not a redbaiting phantasm; the "free administration of law and the creation of public defenders" was a plank in the Socialist Party platform.[16] Legal elites, whether New Deal Democrats or Rockefeller Republicans, generally fell within the broad liberal middle of twentieth-century politics. This raises the question of how they nevertheless came to embrace a small dose of socialism for their own profession. By the 1970s, the American legal establishment endorsed and promoted publicly funded legal representation within this one particular context, the rights of the criminally accused. Had elite lawyers changed, or had their understanding of the public defender changed, or both?

This book seeks to explain how and why lawyers came to believe in the public defender as a quintessentially American institution, one that ideally should exist in communities all around the country. However, it does not tell this story in the way that bar leaders themselves have often told it. This is not a story of lawyers finding easy consensus around an apolitical, professional commitment to "due process" or the "rule of law." Rather, it is a story of contestation and uncertainty within the legal profession—even within the minds of individual lawyers—over the proper relationship between lawyers, markets, and the modern state.[17] As they puzzled over how to protect the rights of the accused, lawyers confronted in their own professional realm the same dilemmas that confronted America writ large in the twentieth century, as reformers and policymakers sought to accommodate the received legal and political traditions of agrarian settler colonies to an increasingly urban, industrial society and ultimately, a global superpower. If laissez-faire markets could not be trusted to connect lawyers with those in need, what should replace them? Private charity? New public bureaucracies? How could lawyers maintain the profession's independence from the state—which many lawyers guarded jealously—while also meeting the profession's obligations to provide assistance and leadership to the government in carrying out its ever-expanding functions? Rather than a specialized topic of interest only to legal scholars, the public defender merits a place within the mainstream of American political and cultural history. The story of its development into a widespread institution offers insights into the contested meaning of American democracy and the contours and contradictions of twentieth-century liberalism.

More specifically, this book provides a history of the public defender in a particular sense: as a reform project touted as the key to making American courts more just, trials more fair, and the law more equal. One could imagine other fruitful approaches to the subject: a collective biography of lawyers who worked as public defenders, a social history of public defenders' interactions with local communities, an institutional history of particular organizations, a pure political history tracking legislation and policies. Elements of those approaches appear in these pages, but the book's primary endeavor is to explain changes over time in American legal culture—with culture defined as the "values and beliefs that a group or society uses to identify itself."[18] After initially largely rejecting the idea, elite lawyers came to believe, along with Ellery Cuff and Harrison Tweed, that public defenders could help to secure and promote "the American way of life." They came to value the public defender as exemplifying something central about American national identity.

In 1963, the Supreme Court gave its blessing to this view. That year, the Court decided *Gideon v. Wainwright*, which established that criminal defendants have the constitutional right to court-appointed defense counsel. *Gideon* did not expressly require that appointed lawyers be public defenders in the sense that Cuff was a public defender—full-time, government employees who worked solely on court-appointed cases. The Court left open the possibility for local courts to appoint private counsel on a case-by-case basis, as many state courts traditionally had done. But as this book details, *Gideon* was widely interpreted as a mandate for cities and states to establish public defender offices; many lawyers assumed that it would be impossible for local courts to comply with *Gideon* on a mass scale without the services of full-time public defenders. *Gideon*, then, was neither the beginning nor the end of the public defender's history in the United States, but it was crucial in forging lawyers' faith in the public defender. Now that public defender reforms were connected to a constitutional right, it was hard to attack them as creeping bolshevism. In *Gideon*, the Supreme Court, echoing Cuff and Tweed, related the rights of the accused to American national identity: "The right to counsel may not be deemed fundamental and essential to fair trials in some countries, but it is in ours."[19]

It would be a mistake to underestimate the contingency of the public defender. It was not inevitable that this institution would develop at all in the

United States, nor was it predestined to take the form that it does today. As defined in this book, the public defender denotes a lawyer, funded by public appropriations, whose full-time work is to represent individuals accused of violating the criminal law.[20] At first glance, such a public official might seem like an unsurprising offshoot of larger-scale historical developments: industrialization, professionalization, bureaucratization. As the law became more punitive and complex, defendants became more likely to require lawyers; as class divides widened, they became less able to afford lawyers; and with the breakdown of close-knit rural communities, they became disconnected from informal support networks; thus it was only natural that some institutionalized solution would eventually develop. But in fact, the legal profession's embrace of the public defender was exceptional within American legal culture. Outside of the criminal context, lawyers have never reached a similar consensus about the government's role in providing or funding legal services. Individuals entangled in many kinds of high-stakes but noncriminal proceedings—such as immigration, divorce, and employment disputes—cannot rely on any similarly entrenched and widespread public service, and often still muddle through with charitable or volunteer assistance.

If not an inevitable consequence of modernization, it would be equally mistaken to reduce the public defender into an inevitable fulfillment of the text of the Constitution. The federal Sixth Amendment guarantees the "assistance of counsel" in "all criminal prosecutions," and state constitutions have similar provisions. To be sure, the lack of a comparable textual foothold helps to explain why lawyers have remained more divided about the right to counsel in civil proceedings. But these constitutional provisions cannot fully explain why elite lawyers came to endorse the public defender. The Sixth Amendment dates to the eighteenth century, and its interpretation has changed significantly over time. It was originally understood to protect the defendant's freedom to hire a lawyer, if he wanted to. This conception of the right developed in opposition to English law, which historically had prohibited counsel in felony trials altogether, on the theory that defendants should speak for themselves. Only gradually was the right expanded to encompass an obligation to provide counsel for defendants who lacked representation. But even then, the right was not interpreted to require public defenders or even public funding. Traditionally, when local courts appointed counsel for indigent defendants, they often expected those lawyers to serve pro bono. Only in the twentieth century did lawyers associate the Sixth Amendment with a state obligation to provide publicly funded counsel. The public defender should not, then, be understood as simply the modern method of implementing the long-standing right to counsel. Rather, both the modern interpretation of the right to counsel and the public defender as an institution were twentieth-century developments, and they developed in tandem, with doctrine reinforcing institutional reforms and vice versa.[21]

The public defender was a state-building project, albeit a halting and decentralized one: it was a concerted effort to bring the government into an endeavor that was previously the province of private markets and ad hoc benevolence. Like all state-building projects, particularly those carried out within a political culture of ambivalence about government power, the public defender occasioned controversy. Indeed, it combined three issues that have each remained independently controversial in American politics: public assistance for the poor, the rights of criminal defendants, and state intervention into markets for professional services. Yet unlike other forms of public assistance, and unlike state intervention into the medical profession, the public defender became widely endorsed and even celebrated by establishment elites across the spectrum of partisan politics. Even though the public defender's practical implementation has remained contested, lawyers secured a conceptual place for this particular form of public assistance within American political and legal culture.

To explain how this happened, the book's chapters progress through several revealing moments of conflict, when lawyers argued about whether or why to adopt the public defender. Because of the book's focus on the public defender as a reform project, its chapters revolve primarily around places where this project was resisted or threatened, and therefore generated open debate about the values at stake. This approach will take the reader to sites including New York City in the 1910s, where a committee of bar leaders dismissed a public defender proposal as incompatible with professional independence; Boston in the 1930s and '40s, where elite lawyers developed and defended a "voluntary defender" association as a privately funded alternative to the public defender, but were dismayed to receive notice in the 1950s that their own donors now believed a public solution was necessary; the *Gideon* decision in 1963, which enshrined an apparent elite consensus that obfuscated those earlier conflicts in consequential ways; Philadelphia in the late 1960s, where a long-standing voluntary defender transformed into a publicly funded organization, but only after a rocky legal dispute over how to maintain political autonomy from the mayor's office; and south to Mississippi on the cusp of the 1970s, where the public defender as a reform project met with extreme resistance from an insular, local legal elite that viewed outside investment in criminal defense as a threat to white supremacy.

California is less prominent in the book because, paradoxically, it is the state where the public defender has the longest history. Los Angeles established the nation's first public defender in 1914 with relatively little conflict, followed in the 1920s by San Francisco and Alameda County, which encompasses Oakland. By 1957, public defenders had been established in one-third of California counties, covering most of the state's populous urban areas.[22] A history of the public defender told through the California experience would yield a different account, focused more on how public defenders defined their role over time and operated in local communities, and prove less illuminating about the subject that animates this book: debates over whether public defenders should exist at all.

THE PUBLIC DEFENDER, as a solution, eventually became attached to a particular problem, which was labeled, in lawyers' emotionless phrasing, "the problem of the indigent accused." Today the public defender is still understood in this way: as a lawyer who represents people who are poor and cannot afford their own lawyers. This is misleading, insofar as it implies that the public defender is the exception and privately retained counsel is the norm; few criminal defendants can easily afford their own lawyers. That is partly because the criminal law targets the poor, and it is partly because lawyers are so expensive that one need not be destitute to find legal fees daunting. But the public defender has always been most palatable to elite lawyers when framed in this way—as an exception for the indigent, rather than as the norm. It would oversimplify the public defender's history, however, to imagine that the public defender was always framed that way, as if poor people accused of wrongdoing suddenly appeared at a moment in time, and then lawyers muddled their way to the solution of the public defender in response.

Rather, the public defender comported with a pattern that historians have observed time and again: "ideas and problems, solutions and potential crises, circulate remarkably independently through the political stream," and "their futures depend on their finding one another."[23] The public defender as a solution danced, at various times, with many problems: the problem of lawyers' profit motive; the problem of unethical lawyers; the problem of lawyers' narrow conception of themselves as private agents; the problem of lawyers being required to take court appointments without pay; the problem of wrongful convictions; and yes, the problem of the indigent accused, which became the lasting partnership that secured the public defender's future. Throughout the public defender's history, lawyers have contested many specifics: whether public defenders should represent all defendants, or only some; whether they should be elected or appointed; what level of government should provide the funding; whether defenders should be constituted into formally public agencies or maintain fictive independence as nominally private but publicly funded organizations. Thus, the public defender was not a prefabricated policy blueprint whose diffusion can be mapped straightforwardly on a linear timeline. Rather, a major theme in this book is how lawyers periodically redefined what they meant by the public defender, and what goals they imagined that public defenders might achieve.

In the beginning, the public defender idea was not fundamentally a response to poverty or even to conceptual questions about the rights of the accused, but rather, to a bigger and deeper problem that confronted the American legal profession at the turn of the twentieth century. Did modernity require redefining what a lawyer was? American lawyers' traditional understanding of their own profession corresponded to laissez-faire classical liberalism, which idealized the individual pursuit of self-interest in free markets. Individuals out in the world determined their interests, and then hired lawyers in the market to pursue or defend those interests. But by the late nineteenth century, liberalism had begun to morph. The reform liberalism (or "progressivism") that motored American state-building during the Progressive Era and the New Deal sought to accommodate liberalism to industrial capitalism by developing a more active role for the state to regulate the economy at a macro level and to compensate at a micro level for the inequalities that markets produced.[24]

The question, then, was whether the transition from classical liberalism to a more reformist variety, which many lawyers supported in other contexts, should also apply to the legal profession itself. Perhaps lawyers should become subsumed into the expanding government bureaucracy, bringing law into the realm of the "state." Or perhaps they ought to remain apart from it, professionals who organized into private firms and sold their services to paying clients, leaving law in the realm of the "market."[25] In 1914, John Wigmore, the dean of the Northwestern University law school, posed the question directly and provocatively, in an article that asked: "Shall the legal profession be reorganized?" Wigmore observed a proliferation of supposedly "radical" proposals to convert lawyers into "salaried official[s]," although such proposals differed on whether this transformation should apply to the "whole of the bar" or only "a portion." He refused to reject such proposals out of hand. "The state maintains public hospitals," he noted; it was not so "radical," then, to envision public legal clinics. "Justice," he reminded his readers, had become "a state function long before health was."[26]

At the outset of the twentieth century, competing schools of thought implied divergent answers to Wigmore's question. Many strands of "progressivism" implied that the answer was yes: the legal profession should be reorganized, and lawyers should become state officials. Seeking to remediate the miseries of industrial capitalism and impose order upon the nation's fast-growing cities, the generation of thinkers and policymakers who rallied under the progressive banner expanded the state's reach into broad swaths of American life and economy heretofore defined (at least in theory) as private.[27] Believing that the coordinated application of expertise to social problems could solve those problems, and rejecting formalistic boundaries between state and market or public and private, they remade local, state, and federal governments into bureaucratic pyramids of specialized agencies adhering to routinized processes. Through the introduction of professional staffers and new mandates to collect and report and rely upon data, they made over hoary inheritances of eighteenth-century governance like courts and legislatures into, essentially, bureaucratic agencies too.[28] The government now sought to regulate the wages of factory workers and to keep small children in school all day; new types of public officials managed streetcar lines and promoted smallpox vaccinations and lifted birthdates out of family Bibles into the ledger-lines of official registers. Skipping past the old anxieties about defining the proper limits on government, the most enthusiastic reinventors of municipal governance wondered what (if anything) government shouldn't do. Cities now sold water "to ensure the adequacy and purity that private water companies failed to maintain," and designed parks and installed streetlights to promote health and safety, and opened schools "to protect against popular ignorance."[29] In this context, Wigmore and others asked: should cities also hire lawyers to ensure the purity not of water, but of verdicts; to protect not public health, but public confidence in the law?

From this perspective, criminal law seemed among the least controversial targets for further state encroachment. The state—in the course of gradual developments across the eighteenth and nineteenth centuries, of murky origin but unmistakable direction—had already taken over most of the tasks of policing, prosecution, and punishment that ordinary people had once managed among themselves.[30] The idea of replacing criminal defense lawyers with public servants also comported with a related and more specific development in which states, by the late nineteenth century, had converted or begun to convert law enforcement personnel into salaried officials, replacing earlier arrangements in which local functionaries served on a part-time basis and were remunerated through fees for service paid directly by members of the public.[31] Early advocates of the public defender sometimes portrayed criminal defense as the final piece of this unfolding puzzle, the only remaining component of the criminal process where quasi-private, fee-for-service professionals still required conversion into fully public, salaried officials. Some envisioned "compulsory public defense" for all defendants—rich and poor alike.[32]

But many lawyers assumed instead that the legal profession should remain within a different tradition—the school of thought known as "associationalism," which encouraged Americans to address social and even legal problems not by expanding the government, but through private initiative. From this perspective, collective needs should be met by religious charities, professional groups, and voluntary associations, in order to maintain the vibrant, decentralized associational life thought to distinguish American democracy from the sclerotic, statist bureaucracies of the Old World.[33] This school of thought limited and channeled the progressive enthusiasm for state-building. Associationalist reformers often identified as progressive, insofar as they concurred in the importance of applying coordinated expertise to social disorder. But instead of the state doing the coordinating, they envisioned the professions, private philanthropy and civic groups, independent schools and colleges, and even for-profit businesses. The historian Robert Wiebe describes the nuanced sense in which progressivism and associationalism together had remade America by the dawn of the 1920s. "A bureaucratic orientation now defined a basic part of the nation's discourse," channeling both the construction of problems and the engineering of solutions around "values of continuity and regularity, functionality and rationality, administration and management." But the new regime continued to blend public and private initiative. The state expanded but never fully merged with society; instead what resulted was "a society of ceaselessly interacting voluntary groups assisted in their course by a powerful, responsive government."[34]

The national leaders of the American legal profession were enthusiastic associationalists. Indeed, the idea of a singular American legal profession was, itself, an expression of associationalism. In 1878, a small group of prominent lawyers organized themselves into the American Bar Association, under whose name they pretended to speak for lawyers as a whole and promoted their preferred legal reforms. In 1920, only 9 percent of lawyers nationwide were members of the ABA, but they included the top tier of the profession's corporate elite. Meanwhile, at the local level, lawyers organized themselves into proliferating numbers of state and local bar associations, which sought to police entry into the profession, enforce professional standards, engage in various local reform endeavors, and present to the public a unified professional front.[35] Associationalism also pervaded the day-to-day administration of American law. In local criminal courts, private charities and religious groups not only influenced policy but also took part, in many communities, in routine criminal prosecutions. Representatives from private welfare organizations served, in effect, as private prosecutors, social workers, and quasi-probation officers. Their involvement belied the premise of public defender advocates that the defense lawyer was the only remaining private actor in the courtroom.[36]

The legal profession's consolidating elite, dominated by the partners of corporate law firms, did not share Wigmore's equanimity toward "officializing" the legal profession. Elite lawyers worried that transforming some lawyers into salaried state officials might lay the groundwork for transforming *all* lawyers into salaried state officials. This was the dreaded horror of socialization. Even in pockets like criminal law that were already more public than private, elite lawyers maintained that there should remain some breathing space for the pursuit of private interests. Presumably these lawyers did not literally fear the expropriation of the capital owned by Wall Street law firms — at least, not any time soon — but they worried that subsuming any part of the legal profession under the auspices of government would begin a more insidious process of eroding the profession's autonomy. Lawyers could only defend individual rights if they had freedom to challenge the government, which was difficult when the government was also their employer. The issue generated "a great hullabaloo," Harrison Tweed recalled, because lawyers worried "that if you once took public money, then you were obligated to do things the way the source of that money, the city, the state, or national government, wanted you to do it."[37]

Moreover, a core tenet of the American legal profession was that lawyers served as the agents of their clients. They did not pursue their own interests but played an intermediary part in the orderly resolution of the clash of other people's interests and thereby helped to preserve social harmony.[38] Lawyers hired by the government to make arguments on behalf of the government could, albeit with some tension, be accommodated into this model, if "the people" that the government represented were understood as stand-ins for the client. But the public defender caused intolerable conceptual difficulty in this regard, because the task of a criminal defense attorney is to oppose the government. How could a lawyer be hired by the government and also oppose the government in adversarial proceedings?[39] Many lawyers, then, not only initially rejected the public defender but found it baffling as an idea. It surprised them that other lawyers could predict with glee—for instance, in the course of one Chicago lawyer's "argument for the public defender"— that one day "the private bar will be abolished."[40] At the start of the twentieth century, most lawyers regarded even the modern lawyer in the traditional mold: as an independent agent for private interests. *Free Justice* tells how they gradually found a way to accommodate the public defender within that mold.

THE BOOK'S CENTRAL QUESTION—how the public defender became a national ideal—explains certain choices regarding sources and methods. Necessarily, it yields an emphasis on the voices of elite lawyers—men who, like Harrison Tweed, attended prestigious universities and then spent their careers at corporate law firms. This is not because they were uniquely insightful or knowledgeable about the issue. To the contrary, they rarely practiced criminal defense themselves and often had secondhand knowledge, at best, of how criminal courts operated. Nevertheless, they assigned to themselves the power to speak as the nationwide voice of the legal profession and therefore wielded outsized influence over national discourse about legal issues.[41] They led local and national bar associations, served on the boards of legal aid and voluntary defender organizations, joined committees that promulgated professional standards, and collaborated with legal scholars and law professors at the schools they had attended to advocate for reforms and new understandings of law and doctrine. When courts, government agencies, and legislatures introduced legal reforms in the twentieth century, those reforms had often first been developed and recommended by elite lawyers through internal professional initiatives.

That such lawyers arrogated to themselves significant influence over legal policymaking proved consequential to how the public defender developed, in several ways. First, in their own day-to-day work representing business interests and wealthy individuals, such lawyers exemplified the traditional understanding of the lawyer as independent agent of private interests. That understanding fueled their ambivalence about intertwining the profession with the state, leading some lawyers first to object to the public defender altogether and later shaping how lawyers understood the public defender's role. To be sure, many lawyers had different views about the proper balance between state and profession, such as those who founded and joined the leftist National Lawyers Guild, which promoted state-funded legal assistance in a variety of contexts. Such lawyers appear less frequently in this book not because their ideas were uninteresting or unimportant, but because they were less influential (in no small part, because the mainstream bar suppressed them).[42]

Second, for most of the time period covered in this book, the self-defined elite bar consisted of white men who did not expressly frame the public defender as a reform project connected to racial justice. Of course, ideas about race have always shaped American criminal law, with racialized groups targeted disproportionately for punishment, and racial ideology has also operated more specifically as both an implicit and explicit influence upon the development of right-to-counsel doctrine.[43] Even still, elite lawyers often contrived to discuss criminal defendants' rights in ostensibly racially neutral terms well into the early 1960s, long after the civil rights movement had begun to focus national and international attention on Jim Crow injustice. The Constitution ascribed the rights of the accused to formally equal individuals, ostensibly defining all group categories as irrelevant in the criminal courtroom, and elite lawyers adopted this mode of discourse when they debated the public defender and its alternatives.[44] In some ways, Cold War political culture reinforced this tendency, which might seem surprising given that white Cold Warriors were, in other contexts, obsessed with questions of race. They used race as a category of analysis when deliberating over how to manage both the civil rights movement at home and Third World demands for self-determination abroad, and foreign policy officials worried especially that racially motivated miscarriages of criminal justice could tarnish the United States' international image.[45] At the same time, by valorizing national identity and individual dignity in their legal rhetoric, Cold War lawyers often left little conceptual space for connecting formal rights with units of analysis in between the individual and the nation. Beneath the surfaces of white lawyers' discourse about the public defender surely bubbled all kinds of racial ideas, whether the lawyers could have articulated them or not. This book seeks to immerse the reader in those lawyers' often artificial fixation on the individual not in order to endorse that fixation, but to provide some sense of the parameters around the version of the public defender idea that they developed.

Finally, elite lawyers assumed that the organized legal profession was both primarily responsible and best equipped for designing the country's institutions of law and justice. They typically carried out their debates among themselves, on committees and in meetings that consisted almost entirely of other lawyers. For almost all of the time period covered in this book, the lawyers under study made no formal effort to involve members of the general public in their decision-making. They proposed new approaches based on their own suppositions or general impressions about criminal defendants, not based on sustained inquiry into defendants' own views and experiences. Insofar as this book seeks to reproduce the vision of elite twentieth-century lawyers, it also seeks to reproduce for the reader some sense of their myopia; the fact that poor people's voices are absent from many of the conversations recounted in this book is precisely one of the book's points about elite lawyers' approach to reform. Indeed, it was not only the poor who were excluded from their internal discussions but almost anyone who was not a lawyer; and also, for that matter, the vast majority of lawyers—the thousands of lawyers who represented ordinary people in ordinary legal matters, writing up wills, negotiating divorces, filing personal injury lawsuits, challenging traffic tickets, and defending criminal cases. Elite lawyers did include the occasional voluntary or public defender in their discussions about indigent defense, but they tended to view such figures as idiosyncratic members of the profession: honorable and hardworking, and occasionally worth consulting for insights from the trenches, but not blessed with the broad vision required to make policy on a grand scale.[46]

WOVEN THROUGH THIS NARRATIVE, this book advances two arguments. First, the engine that drove elite lawyers' twists and turns on the road to the public defender was their conception of American identity: more specifically, their conception of the United States as a liberal democracy and of lawyers' proper role within such a polity. Liberalism, to be sure, has not remained constant as an ideology, nor have lawyers' conceptions of their role within liberalism. Throughout the changes wrought by the twentieth century, what did remain constant was elite lawyers' concern that the legal profession must be organized in such a way as to maintain the liberal character of American governance, with liberalism defined in contrast primarily to socialism, and later Soviet communism, though also to fascism.[47] This book traces how that orientation translated into debates about the public defender, and thereby shaped the criminal courts that later generations inherited.[48] In the early twentieth century, fear of socialism motivated some elite lawyers to support efforts to provide legal assistance to the poor. As historians of legal aid have observed, elite lawyers hoped that helping the poor to vindicate their interests within the established legal order would forestall the appeal of revolutionary politics.[49] But the specter of socialism also led elite lawyers to prefer that any such assistance was privately funded and organized.[50]

By the 1950s, lawyers had begun to doubt that private initiative alone could meet the need for legal assistance in the criminal courts, particularly once the Supreme Court began to signal that such assistance might be a constitutional requirement. But even as elite lawyers reconsidered their aversion to public funding, the ideal of the United States as a liberal democracy continued to mold their conception of the public defender.[51] Once a socialist harbinger, the public defender was now reimagined as an anticommunist weapon, a means of demonstrating American law's special regard for the rights of the individual.[52] The public defender was now advanced not as a reform of the legal profession but as a mechanism for vindicating the defendant's constitutional rights, including the right to counsel eventually enshrined in *Gideon*. At the same time, the Cold War context placed limits upon both interpretations of the right to counsel and policy justifications for the public defender. Lawyers made clear that the right to state-provided counsel could be justified by unique characteristics of the criminal trial, such as the fact that the state initiated criminal prosecutions, and need not imply any generalizable state obligation to care for the poor.

The book's second, and related, argument is that elite lawyers' eventual embrace of the public defender was deceptively partial. During the Progressive Era, the bar had rejected more capacious versions of the public defender, such as the idea of compulsory public defense for the rich, an idea that was never seriously revisited. By the time of the Cold War, elite lawyers endorsed public defense for the indigent, but they downplayed the significance of the public defender's status as a government official. Instead, they emphasized in a more generic sense the defense of the accused as an essentially American value. Detached from Progressive Era visions of eliminating the private bar, the Cold War public defender was framed in anti-statist terms. The public defender was an adversary of the state just like any criminal defense attorney; it was an incidental detail that he happened to receive his paycheck from the government.

In addition, elite lawyers maintained a significant role for private initiative in the nationwide effort to promote and institutionalize the public defender. In the years immediately following *Gideon*, it was not any level or branch of government that underwrote the initial, nationwide initiative to establish and expand local public defender offices. Rather, it was the Ford Foundation, the largest and most powerful philanthropic organization in the

Cold War United States, which underwrote a dizzying array of projects around the globe under the banner of undermining communism and promoting democracy. Funded with capital generated by the Ford Motor Company, the foundation symbolized the American commitment to both consumer capitalism and public–private governance.[53] Nor did any level or branch of government administer the Ford-supported nationwide defender initiative; it was organized under the auspices of the National Legal Aid and Defender Association, a professional organization with close ties to elite lawyers and the American Bar Association, and its grants were approved by an executive committee consisting largely of elite lawyers—including Harrison Tweed.

By defining counsel as a universal right in criminal cases, *Gideon* sounded the death knell for the hopes of some lawyers that government could be kept out of the profession altogether and the needs of the poor met purely through private charity and pro bono service. But subsequent developments would have equally disappointed those Progressive Era reformers who had once hoped that the public defender would render legal charity obsolete. Ultimately, elite lawyers resolved their old dilemma about how to maintain professional independence by sidestepping it. They combined an affirmative right to counsel with their preferred tradition of governance not by state or society alone, but by an "associational state" at the nexus between them—a partnership between government, professions, and private entities.[54]

That the legal profession's embrace of the public defender was initially ambivalent and finally partial helps to explain two recurring frustrations that Americans have expressed about the public defender, both as an institution and as a reform project, since the 1970s. First are the perennial debates about funding. A stock genre of newspaper exposé reports upon the crushing caseloads, inadequate resources, and brutalizing work conditions of public defenders in a particular local community. Identical articles began appearing in the immediate wake of *Gideon*. Lawyers had reached consensus at a high level of generality in favor of the public defender but had reached no similar consensus about nuts-and-bolts questions of implementation, which would have required confronting more forthrightly the relationship between the profession and the state. They agreed in theory about the need for public funding, but not how much and from what source; they agreed in theory about the need to provide a lawyer for every defendant, but not what the lawyer was supposed to do. Nor had elite lawyers fully confronted how hierarchies within the legal profession, which benefited them, also undermined the profession's stated ideals. Elite lawyers themselves had long defined indigent defense as a low-status role, a legacy at cross-purposes with their newfound campaign to fund and recruit public defenders. In many ways, then, it was elite lawyers who created the conditions for perpetual crisis in the criminal courts—not because they were personally responsible for political battles over funding levels or local scuffles over perceived threats to defenders' autonomy, but because they had left the public defender extremely vulnerable to such skirmishes by failing to reach stronger conclusions about what public defenders were entitled to and how they could enforce those requirements.

Second, this history also helps to explain why *Gideon* did not serve as the opening wedge to a longer list of affirmative rights to public assistance. From the perspective of nonlawyers, the establishment consensus in favor of the public defender can seem puzzling: this consensus undergirds a rare commitment to government aid in a political culture that guarantees few forms of public assistance to anyone. In 1991, a Pennsylvania candidate for the United States Senate highlighted the paradox that Americans had a right to counsel but no right to health care: "The Constitution says that if you are charged with a crime, you have the right to a lawyer," he observed. "But it's even more fundamental that if you're sick, you should have the right to a doctor."[55] The paradox can be resolved by revisiting the particular arguments that convinced elite lawyers to support the public defender, which were explicitly and carefully framed so that they did not imply any broader rights to public assistance. By the early 1960s, lawyers themselves had constructed such arguments in favor of the public defender. Thus, they helped to entrench an enduring American paradox—that the poor enjoy affirmative rights to material assistance from the government primarily when the government is already trying to harm them.

THE CENTER OF GRAVITY for much of *Free Justice* is the period of time between the 1950s and the early 1970s, when elite lawyers came to embrace the public defender. However, to understand this later history, it is first necessary to return to the Progressive Era, when a version of the public defender idea circulated in legal culture but was largely rejected by elite lawyers, particularly in the major Eastern cities. Chapter 1 describes this debate, emphasizing how the public defender imagined by Progressive Era reformers differed from later versions of the idea. Chapter 2 describes the rise and decline of the elite bar's preferred alternative to the public defender: the privately funded voluntary defender. Into the 1950s, some lawyers maintained hope that the expanding jurisprudence of constitutional rights might be combined with the American tradition of associationalism—that voluntary defenders could find a way to provide universal service to all defendants while also remaining privately funded and independent of the state.

By the 1950s, elite lawyers' opposition to the public defender had softened, but the problem remained at a conceptual level: how to endorse an affirmative right to public assistance without falling down the slippery slope to socialism? How to square guaranteed legal representation with an independent legal profession? Chapter 3 traces how the Cold War provided the final impetus (and conceptual resources) needed for elite lawyers to reach consensus in favor of the reimagined, anti-statist public defender. Chapter 4 is about what happened to the public defender once it was no longer a subject of debate within the legal profession, but one of the profession's most visible national reform projects. Almost immediately, lawyers perceived *Gideon* to have generated a "crisis." Although most states theoretically guaranteed counsel in some form prior to the Supreme Court's intervention, many states had no organized, comprehensive method for providing and funding the requisite counsel. Lawyers interpreted *Gideon* as a mandate to build, reorganize, and expand public defender organizations and to lobby for durable public funding streams. The issue of professional independence reappeared, not as a reason to oppose public funding altogether, but as an impetus to develop governance structures that preserved defenders' autonomy.

Chapter 5 covers the same post-*Gideon* timeframe, but digs beneath the familiar story of a funding crisis to describe how post-*Gideon* public defender reforms also provoked a crisis of confidence in American legal culture. Lawyers who observed criminal courtrooms throughout the United States in the late 1960s and early 1970s were disturbed to find that they appeared far more despotic and irrational than was implied by high-level rhetoric. Elite lawyers had endorsed the public defender as a cornerstone of American democracy and a symbol of America's robust commitment to individual rights. That commitment seemed to have been lost in translation somewhere along the way to the nation's local courts, which operated not out of an investment in proving the merits of liberal democracy but according to long-standing hierarchies of local power. In this context, some lawyers began to reimagine the public defender anew, not as a universalistic exemplar of liberal democracy, but as a potential resource within marginalized communities.

This book tells a more complex and open-ended story than the two competing myths of the public defender's history. The first is the *Gideon* myth, which was promulgated by legal elites themselves during the time period covered in this book and has been reproduced for the general public in popular nonfiction, school textbooks, and museum exhibits. In this narrative, the public defender's history revolves around *Gideon v. Wainwright*, which is positioned as both culmination and motor of enlightened progress. Shortly after *Gideon*, Anthony Lewis, the Supreme Court correspondent for the *New York Times*, published a lively, accessible book about the case entitled *Gideon's Trumpet*, which became a staple of reading lists for high schoolers and law students alike. Many states, Lewis's story went, already provided counsel for the indigent prior to *Gideon*. In response to *Gideon*, Lewis assured his readers, the legal profession was already taking steps to ensure that public defenders would become widely available throughout the country.[56] Legal scholars, too, celebrated *Gideon* as a liberal triumph, a bright star in the constellation of Supreme Court decisions during the 1950s and '60s, under the leadership of Chief Justice Earl Warren, that remade America into a more just and equal place.[57]

This narrative positions elite lawyers and institutions—more specifically, legal liberalism as instantiated in the Warren Court—as essentially heroic, committed to equality and willing to pursue large-scale change to make that commitment meaningful. When it became apparent, in the years after *Gideon's Trumpet* was published, that public defenders remained overwhelmed and underfunded, adherents of the myth could point to such conditions as evidence that *Gideon* had been betrayed by villains outside of the legal-liberal fold: by the conservative justices who succeeded Warren and declined to enforce *Gideon* rigorously; by tough-on-crime politicians who expanded the criminal law without any commensurate expansion in the resources required to adjudicate accusations fairly; by state-level politicians who either failed to comprehend the importance of adequately funding indigent defense, or who concertedly refused to fund indigent defense because it was associated with unpalatable beneficiaries. This narrative is encapsulated in the dozens of articles that appear on each anniversary of *Gideon* decrying its "failed promise," or mourning *Gideon*'s trumpet as "muted."[58]

This narrative remains influential in popular understandings, and it is not wrong that subsequent generations of jurists and politicians have proven less than zealous about enforcing and complying with *Gideon*. However, in many ways this narrative has fallen out of step with scholarly currents. An accumulating variety of revisionist accounts have complicated the myth of the Warren Court as a catalyst of liberation in twentieth-century America—arguing, for example, that the capacious rights announced by the Court yielded less than transformative results in practice; or that the Court's rulings replicated public opinion more than they shaped it, and those few that tried to challenge public opinion met with backlash; or more recently, that the Court's criminal procedure rulings did more to structure and thereby legitimate than to curtail the aggressive law enforcement practices that have given rise to a metastatic "carceral state."[59]

Thus, it might be tempting to adopt instead the conspiratorial countermyth provided by an interdisciplinary tradition of critical scholarship on the legal profession. Rather than a story of good intentions later betrayed, this account describes a story of bad intentions successfully and relentlessly carried out. Acerbic chroniclers of the profession portray it as a fundamentally conservative guild whose leaders have consistently abetted social and economic inequality. The profession's best credentialed practitioners gravitate toward lucrative careers at law firms where they help business corporations neutralize regulation and evade redistribution of wealth. Against this dominant tide, the bar's minor and limited attempts to organize legal aid for the poor are a mere "fig leaf."[60] A similar indictment finds expression in a more specialized literature on the public defender, which became an object of fascination to legal scholars and social scientists almost as soon as it became a national reform project. These studies seek to isolate some flaw in the public defender that can explain its failure to provide equality, to locate in the past an origin story that reveals that public defenders were never genuinely intended to provide meaningful defense. Rather, elite lawyers partnered with the state to develop institutions that would provide the illusion of advocacy while actually greasing the wheels of law enforcement, as public defenders collaborated with prosecutors to negotiate as many guilty pleas as possible.[61]

This countermyth positions elite lawyers, the heroes of the *Gideon* myth, instead as villains who paid sham tributes to equality while laboring behind the scenes to build an oppressive machinery of punishment. This account captures elements of an undeniable dynamic: the organized legal profession did orient itself around the needs of corporations, and professional elites did give short shrift to training and providing lawyers to help ordinary people. But if so, then the legal profession's history of debate about the public defender, which is more complex than the countermyth recognizes, only becomes more intriguing as a vehicle for investigating lawyers' contributions to twentieth-century liberalism. It is a safe starting premise that elite lawyers never imagined that the public defender would overthrow the capitalist order, eliminate economic inequality, or dismantle the carceral state (even if more radical lawyers and individual criminal defense attorneys sometimes pursued those goals). Nevertheless, they invested quite a bit of energy and resources into the public defender, which raises the question: what *did* elite lawyers imagine that the public defender could do?

In different ways, both the *Gideon* myth and its critical countermyth lack historical perspective. Each myth begins with a present-day standard and then applies it backward to lawyers in the past, flattening out the process of contestation through which present-day standards themselves developed. Both myths also downplay the genuine challenge that the public defender presented to traditional paradigms of American legal thought. The *Gideon* myth understands elite legal culture as the repository of a continuing immanent logic of progressive enlightenment, making the public defender appear (to lawyers) as an easy and obviously virtuous reform because it would aid the needy. The countermyth posits the legal profession as devoted to a continuing agenda of repression, making the public defender appear (to lawyers) as an easy and obviously virtuous reform because it would expand the state. Lawyers' own writings, correspondence, and debates about the public defender provide a more complex picture of change over time and internal tension within elite legal culture, as lawyers themselves debated the profession's values, how best lawyers could promote the cause of progress, and whether or not, and in what ways, the profession should aid the needy or forge an alliance with the state. Assuming that past lawyers could not have known what their decisions would later yield, this book takes inspiration from another historian of elite lawyers and "tries to see what they were thinking and doing more or less as they themselves saw it," as they pursued both ideals and interests (rather than only one or the other) and "struggl[ed] to work out a relationship between their beliefs and their practices."[62]

Ultimately, the goal of this book is not to provide a substitute myth about the public defender, but rather to encourage a sense of capacious possibility for imagining the proper balance of power in a modern society between lawyers, the individual, and the state. Elite lawyers initially rejected the public defender in part because the public defender's advocates were initially arguing for extreme change. When they came to accept the public defender, they also narrowed its meaning so that even though public defense required significant change of cities and states, it required less rethinking for elite lawyers like themselves about their place in society. Perhaps something was lost with that narrowing. To be clear, this book does not argue that today's injustices derive from some neatly identifiable misstep, or that American courts would work better today if lawyers in the past had adopted some particular plan that they rejected. For instance, some Progressive Era proposals included details that are so incompatible with present-day values that it is not worth seriously contemplating them as proposals that could somehow be revived. But elite lawyers often behaved as if they thought that rejecting particular proposals also required rejecting the whole premise that it was possible to think imaginatively about how to reconfigure the legal profession.

In recent years, the public defender has again become a central figure within legal reform efforts. What the public defender is imagined capable of doing has changed. Rather than proving the "American way" as superior to godless communism, the public defender is now called upon to unwind mass incarceration, promote racial justice, alleviate economic inequality, challenge draconian immigration enforcement, and serve as the vanguard of a twenty-first-century civil rights movement.[63] Such calls, interestingly, tend not to invoke the history recounted in this book—the history of the public defender as an elite reform project. They identify twenty-first-century public defenders with other antecedents in American history: the radical left tradition of labor defense, the long campaign of legal activism against Jim Crow, the history of "cause lawyering" in partnership with grassroots social and political movements, and the 1960s emergence of "poverty lawyering" and strategic litigation in the service of the "public interest."

These multifaceted debates confirm a theme that runs throughout this book: the public defender, as a stand-in for visions of equal justice, has never had a fixed meaning. Those who seek to remake the public defender for the twenty-first century may take inspiration from the history in this book, they may regard it as a cautionary tale, or perhaps some of both. Either way they will have to navigate the parameters and constraints put in place by the history recounted in this book. The processes of policymaking that continue to make and remake the criminal courts remain similar to the post-*Gideon* pattern—lawyers, legal scholars, law schools, and professional organizations collaborate with large philanthropic foundations to embark upon various endeavors described as "bipartisan criminal justice reform," which blend public and private initiative in complex and often obfuscatory ways.[64] These collaborations may (or may not) be broadly liberal in their commitments and aims, but are rarely entirely transparent about those aims, and are certainly not premised on any kind of thoroughgoing confrontation with the deep structures of law and the legal profession.

CHAPTER ONE

Free Justice

"Public Defender Proposed for New York," read the headline, atop a full-page article in the 7 June 1914 *New York Times*. Below the headline appeared a pen-and-ink portrait of the proposal's advocate: Mayer C. Goldman, a Manhattan lawyer wearing a suit, tie, and Teddy Roosevelt-style pince-nez. Readers may have found the term "public defender" unfamiliar. Other than an embryonic office across the country in Los Angeles, no American city had such an official. In an interview with the *Times*, Goldman described a novel type of local functionary: a criminal defense lawyer, but a lawyer employed by the city, on a salaried basis, rather than retained case-by-case by individual defendants. This official would appear in court on behalf of New Yorkers accused of crime and argue the defendant's side of each criminal case free of charge. Such an official was necessary, Goldman argued, to ensure that all defendants received a full defense, especially those who were poor or unfamiliar with the law. Under the existing procedures, if indigent defendants had lawyers at all, they usually had one of two types: either "disreputable attorneys," who promised bargain rates, but were notorious in legal reform circles for engaging in extortionate collection practices; or counsel appointed by the court on an ad hoc basis, who were often "inexperienced" and typically served without compensation. By replacing both kinds of "half-hearted" legal representation, Goldman argued, the public defender would guarantee dignified, capable counsel for every defendant.[1]

Goldman's argument rested, in part, on a simple parallelism. Already, New York provided for district attorneys—public officials who argued the prosecution side of criminal cases and were paid a regular salary rather than case-by-case fees. It was only logical that the state provide the lawyer on the other side, Goldman argued, to ensure that both adversaries appeared in court "on an equal footing." The benefits of such an arrangement would extend beyond individual relief. Because they would be ethical and able public servants, public defenders would raise "the tone" of criminal trials. Removing the issue of lawyers' fees from criminal adjudication would upgrade the unruly courts of the nation's largest city into "dignified and orderly" tribunals befitting a "modern civilization."[2]

Goldman was not the first American lawyer to propose public defense in criminal cases. His most significant predecessor (although he failed to credit her) was Clara Foltz, the first woman admitted to the bar in California, who toured the nation lobbying for public defender legislation beginning in the 1890s.³ Nor was Goldman the only outspoken proponent of the idea during the Progressive Era. Others included Maurice Parmelee, a sociologist who would later abandon academia for an eclectic career in government service and finally for retirement in Florida, where he became an outspoken proponent of nudism.⁴ But between 1914 and his death in 1939, Goldman was the public defender's most relentless promoter, and thus he was eulogized as the idea's "leading proponent."⁵ In addition to his "lifelong fight" for the public defender, Goldman worked for many years as counsel to Bernarr Macfadden, the celebrity bodybuilder and pulp magazine magnate.⁶ All three—Foltz, Parmelee, and Goldman—exemplified the eccentric valence of the public defender idea in its early years, when government-provided criminal defense constituted not legal orthodoxy but a novelty that appealed to outsiders.

Three years after the *New York Times* feature, Goldman reprised his case in a book—really an extended pamphlet—entitled *The Public Defender: A Necessary Factor in the Administration of Justice*. The title encapsulated Goldman's style, which was not to suggest the public defender as a possibly useful incremental reform, but to insist that it was necessary; he described himself as "spread[ing] the gospel."⁷ He repackaged his arguments in a second edition of the book in 1920; in dozens of legal articles and letters to the editor; in a motion picture or "propaganda photoplay"; in an unsolicited letter to the Wickersham Commission, the blue-ribbon panel appointed by President Herbert Hoover to study the problem of crime; and in any number of meetings and debates that he joined through his participation in various bar committees about the problem of indigent defense.⁸

Goldman had to repeat his arguments over and over again for a reason: they kept getting rejected. The lawyers who wielded the most professional clout in New York City—the Wall Street lawyers who dominated local bar associations—dismissed his 1914 proposal and thereafter were never convinced by Goldman's case for detaching the profit motive from criminal defense.⁹ To the leaders of the corporate bar, then in the process of consolidating themselves as the legal profession's public voice, proposals like Goldman's raised the specter of "socialization": government intrusion into the independent and self-regulating legal profession.¹⁰ Notably, Goldman and his interlocutors did not limit their proposals to public defenders for the poor.

Although Goldman's 1914 proposal assumed that wealthy defendants could continue to hire their own lawyers, he and other reformers later began to demand compulsory public defense for everyone accused of a crime, rich and poor alike. Parmelee had always insisted that "no one, not even a rich person, ought to be forced to provide his own defense." If society chose to subject a person to "the humiliation of being prosecuted," then society ought to pay for it.[11]

To many lawyers, such rhetoric sounded outlandish. If criminal defense lawyering could be monopolized by the government, where would it end? To the extent that elite lawyers acknowledged the specific plight of indigent defendants, they favored private alternatives to Goldman's solution. Pro bono service, philanthropy, and voluntary associations could provide legal representation for the poor while leaving undisturbed both the market in legal representation for the rich and the classically liberal justifications upon which that market rested. Yet Goldman remains significant to the history of the public defender. Even though he did not succeed, he provoked from elite lawyers a revealing response—one that illuminates certain enduring parameters of American legal culture. The Wall Street lawyers' differences with Mayer Goldman represented one expression of a deeper fissure over the role of lawyers in the modern industrial city, in which law—and especially criminal law—had become a primary means for regulating day-to-day urban life.[12]

BEFORE THE PUBLIC DEFENDER became a real-world plan, a version of the idea had appeared as an inchoate suggestion in the bestselling novel of 1888, the utopian tract *Looking Backward*.[13] Written by the reclusive Massachusetts journalist Edward Bellamy, *Looking Backward* chronicles the time-travels of a Boston lawyer who falls asleep one night and awakens in the year 2000.[14] He learns that America has transformed into a fully nationalized economy, with no distinction between state and society. The means of production are centrally owned and managed, all citizens supply compulsory labor in the "industrial army," and in return, all receive equal provisions, but enjoy few individual liberties. A Baptist preacher's son flummoxed by the Gilded Age, Bellamy disdained the nouveau riche and feared the working-class masses; though later remembered as an inspiration to American socialists, he refused the label of socialist ("It smells to the average American of petroleum, . . . sexual novelties, and an abusive tone about God and religion"). Instead of a revolution, he dreamed that class struggle might gradually dissolve into a placid, bureaucratic equilibrium.[15] Scholars revisiting *Looking Backward* have expressed alarm at the authoritarian tendencies of an imagined world where labor is mandatory and workers are constantly surveilled.[16] In the 1880s, though, Bellamy's prophecy appealed to tens of thousands of less literal readers attracted in a gauzier sense to the possibility that the inequities produced by industrial capitalism might one day work themselves out.[17]

In one chapter of Looking Backward, the time-traveling lawyer Julian West visits the judiciary of the future. It is an expert bureaucracy without codified laws, defined crimes, juries, or even lawyers—at least, not lawyers as Gilded Age Americans understood them. In the novel's year 2000, there are no criminal courts of the type familiar to nineteenth-century Americans— crowded rooms in which lawyers made emotional speeches and juries issued moralizing judgments, applying legal standards that asked them to consider questions like whether a killer had acted with "malice aforethought" or displayed an "abandoned and malignant heart." Such courts have become unnecessary, because in utopia there are no malignant hearts; without inequality or poverty, most of the behavior once labeled "crime" has also disappeared. This plot point in Looking Backward distilled the emerging, late-Victorian understanding of wrongdoing not as the expression of individual sin, but as behavior conditioned by the social environment.[18]

But occasionally, even in Bellamy's utopia, someone commits something like a crime—now labeled instead an "atavism." When that happens, Bellamy's imagined society responds with "an attitude of compassion." Instead of retributive punishment, the offender is met with "gentle restraint." If the accused insists first upon a trial, then "the judge appoints two colleagues to state the opposite sides of the case." But they are indeed "colleagues," West is told, and not adversaries. They are nothing like the "hired advocates and prosecutors" of old, "determined to acquit or convict" at all costs. Their only goal is to reach a mutual understanding. Each case is tried over and over until both sides agree.[19]

Bellamy imagined a utopia without lawyers because he despised lawyers. He had been a lawyer himself once, but only for two days. When he opened a practice in his hometown of Chicopee Falls, he hoped to debate "great constitutional questions." To his dismay, the available small-town legal tasks consisted mainly of collecting bills and evicting tenants. After handling one such case, he aborted his career.[20] Lawyers, he concluded, amounted to "barbarous" mercenaries, loyal "only to the keeper of the money chest." Every other modern profession, he claimed, had "cut out" this kind of behavior. Only in "the so-called liberal profession of law" did purportedly "honorable men" debase themselves for the highest bidder.[21]

Similarly, Bellamy imagined a utopia without individual rights because he placed little stock in individualism. As political scientist Arthur Lipow observes in an astute analysis of Bellamy's dismissive stance toward the rights of the accused, Bellamy defined progress itself to mean "subordinat[ing] the interests of the individual to the state." Defendants neither required nor deserved special procedural rights, because rights were barriers, and there could be "no barriers" between individual and society. An individual accused by the collective must recognize a moral duty "to place society's interests above his own," and submit willingly to punishment if deserved. This framework further confirmed the need to eliminate lawyers: "no third party, the hired defense lawyer, can be allowed to come between the accused and the state in order to act as the agent for the accused criminal's purely personal or private interests."[22]

After the surprising success of *Looking Backward*, Bellamy's politics softened; he became more of a standard-issue Gilded Age populist reformer. The novel's runaway sales propelled the introverted Bellamy into national fame and a new role that he had not sought, but gradually accepted, as the leader of a mass movement organized under the banner of Nationalism. The thousands of Americans who joined local Nationalist clubs also admired the contemporaneous Populist movement of farmers and workers; they were eager to become involved in present-day change, not content to wait for the eventual nationalization of the economy that *Looking Backward* prefigured. Rather than an inevitable but future evolution, Bellamy's later writings posited that nationalization required the concerted, step-by-step takeover by the state of various sectors and functions—political work that could begin at once.[23]

The newly reformist Bellamy endorsed the public defender not as an incidental detail within a utopian panorama, but as a policy recommendation for the here and now. In his movement's newspaper *The New Nation*, Bellamy promoted "free justice"—by which he meant public defenders—as a step toward bringing the law under the auspices of the state. "If a public prosecutor suffices to protect the interest of the people," he wrote, then "surely" it was reasonable to provide the accused with "a public defender, equally without private interest in the case." Public defense would ensure that "poor and rich" are "equalized before the law," but beyond that, it would detach selfish motives from criminal adjudication. Once public defenders were available, defendants should no longer be permitted to retain their own private counsel even if they preferred to. Poor defendants would enjoy access to a full defense, and rich defendants could no longer hide behind Bellamy's despised mercenaries.[24]

Neither Bellamy nor the Nationalist movement survived the 1890s, but the public defender idea endured and developed thanks to one of Bellamy's many thousands of followers. In the movement's heyday, Clara Foltz had served as the founder and president of her local 600-member Bellamyite Nationalist club.[25] Foltz developed a detailed public defender proposal, blending her intellectual influences with practical insights from her own experiences practicing in the California courts. Foltz criticized what was known as the "assigned counsel" approach, in which judges appointed local lawyers in private practice to represent indigent defendants case-by-case, often without any payment. Well-to-do lawyers rarely showed up to take these cases, notwithstanding the ostensible duty of all lawyers to serve as "officers of the court." The brunt fell upon lawyers like Foltz who had few other options—whether, as in Foltz's case, because of prejudice, or, for others, because they were unscrupulous or underqualified. Foltz sympathized with defendants who found themselves at the mercy of appointed lawyers. She equally sympathized with lawyers like herself who bore the bar's responsibility to the indigent without adequate remuneration.[26] To aid both groups, Foltz proposed salaried "public defenders," "chosen in the same way and paid out of the same fund" as public prosecutors.[27]

Foltz's plan displayed more concern for individual rights than Bellamy's version of the idea, and was more conducive to the existing, adversarial structure of the criminal courts. As her biographer Barbara Babcock has detailed, Foltz did not share the aversion of Bellamy, and of many progressives who later picked up the public defender idea, toward adversarial combat in the courtroom.[28] She envisioned defenders who would fight zealously for their clients and take cases to trial. But she did think that prosecutors had been allowed to become excessively combative. Without upstanding defense counsel to check them, they behaved like "bloodhounds." They distorted the facts in court and cut legal corners, driven by "the mistaken notion that it is the duty of the State to convict whoever is arrested." The public defender, she predicted, would restore balance in the courtroom and induce prosecutors to behave in a "calm and solemn" manner.[29]

At a time when women lawyers remained—in the eyes of men—a curiosity, Foltz's campaign on behalf of her "Defender Bill" met with mixed reactions. After introducing her proposal in a fiery speech at the 1893 Chicago World's Fair, she traveled around the country lobbying on behalf of her model legislation and continued to promote the idea until her death in 1934. Foltz recalled her World's Fair presentation as a "tremendous sensation" and the few women in attendance celebrated her appearance on stage as a stunning triumph, but a male judge grumbled afterward about her "exaggerated" remarks.[30] While some newspapers covered Foltz favorably, others lampooned her campaign as "ridiculous." The *New York Times*, which would later give favorable coverage to Goldman's proposal, dismissed Foltz's defender bill as the "strange project" of a "female attorney."[31]

At this stage, the West proved the most fertile territory for the public defender. Los Angeles County opened the nation's first public defender's office in 1914, providing counsel for the indigent in criminal cases and some types of civil matters.[32] Seven years later, California enacted legislation authorizing counties statewide to follow the Los Angeles example. By the late 1920s, public defenders were up and running in San Francisco and Oakland.[33] In the East and the South, a handful of jurisdictions also eventually established public defenders, although they resembled the specifics of Foltz's plan to varying degrees. These included Connecticut and Rhode Island, which established statewide defenders, and—unusually in the Deep South—Shelby County, Tennessee, whose county seat is Memphis.[34] Through the 1920s, the Los Angeles office remained the best-known example of the public defender in practice and—as Los Angeles mushroomed into the nation's fifth-largest city—the most significant. Culminating this initial period of expansion was Chicago, the nation's second-largest city, whose surrounding jurisdiction, Cook County, established a public defender in 1930.[35]

It was no accident that the public defender took hold first in Los Angeles and Chicago, rather than in New York or Philadelphia. In younger cities filled with new arrivals, lawyers' hierarchies were more fluid and their "brand of professionalism" more "open and inventive," making them more receptive to experiments like the public defender.[36] Midwestern and Western jurisdictions introduced a number of Progressive Era judicial reforms, including the juvenile court (Illinois), the centralized municipal court with specialized branches (Chicago), and the streamlined procedure of initiating prosecutions by "information," a charging document filed by the prosecutor, rather than grand jury indictment (California).[37] Into the 1930s, the public defender could remain a curiosity in the eyes of Eastern elites—an idea with roots in utopian fiction, associated with women and Californians, a regional novelty that might work for some localities but not, as Mayer Goldman tried to sell the idea, a "necessary" modernizing reform.

FAMILY TRAGEDY had brought Goldman to New York in his youth. He was born in New Orleans, in 1874, to two children of German-Jewish immigrants. His mother was Selma Franko, a former child musical star. During the Civil

War, the Franko parents had taken the family back to Germany, where the eight-year-old Selma gained acclaim as a piano and violin prodigy. When the family returned to the United States, Selma and her brothers and sisters began to tour as "The Five Franko Children." According to family lore, the young John Philip Sousa decided to devote his life to music because he was so enchanted by the beauty of a Franko Children concert. Mayer's father was David Goldman, a lawyer and rabbi. Selma, David, and their five children moved first from Louisiana to Kentucky and then to Indiana as David pursued various rabbinical and academic posts. When Mayer was about twelve, and the family was living in Terre Haute, Indiana, his father died unexpectedly. The widowed Selma brought her five children to Manhattan. With money tight, she made the agonizing decision to place two of the children, including Mayer's brother Edwin, in a Jewish orphanage. There, Edwin pursued the study of music; he grew up to become an accomplished cornet player and beloved bandmaster. Mayer instead pursued a legal education, graduating in 1895 with a degree from the Law School of the City of New York.[38]

In the 1890s, when Goldman embarked upon his legal career, Manhattan's low-level criminal courts—and the nearby downtown jail, "the Tombs"—still operated as they had for much of the nineteenth century: essentially as a free-for-all bazaar where money changed hands in exchange for freedom, rights, privileges, decisions of law, and verdicts of innocence. The Tombs replicated, in grotesque caricature, the unregulated free market championed by corporate tycoons and their political sponsors. Each step of the process was linked in a chain of petty transactions, which has been pieced together by historian Timothy Gilfoyle. Upon getting arrested and taken to jail, a detainee would encounter a "confusing array" of so-called "'runners,' 'steerers,' 'drummers,' 'shyster lawyers,' and 'straw bondsmen'" touting their services. Criminal lawyers bribed the jailhouse guards to alert them to potential clients and allow their agents free rein in the jail cells to interview and solicit detainees. Guards equally expected bribes from the inmates themselves, in exchange for "extended visiting hours, longer periods of exercise, free movement within the prison, better food, and clean sheets"; for the privilege of walking freely about the city streets; and also for "sexual favors." Vendors came in and out of the jail selling food.[39] Conditions in the courtroom were hardly more orderly. In the low-level police courts, lawyers screamed at each other's clients and lobbed insults at one another. Defendants, crowded into the courtrooms in large groups, could little follow the proceedings.[40] The occasional defendant who could afford to make bail typically also saw his case dropped altogether, because the district attorney's office was insufficiently organized to follow up and the courts maintained inadequate records.[41]

A niche market developed in lawyers who specialized in navigating the bewildering proceedings. Perhaps Goldman had seen the famous sign that once hung in downtown Manhattan, just across the street from the Tombs. In garish lights the sign spelled out three words that offered inmates hope: *Howe and Hummel*.[42] The lawyers a few blocks away on Wall Street, who made their livelihoods representing corporations and banks, would have thought the sign unethical. Lawyers were gentlemen, and gentlemen did not advertise.[43] But Howe and Hummel advertised, and became household names in Gilded Age New York. They had retainer agreements with many of the city's brothels, fences, and street gangs. Abraham Hummel specialized in business disputes from the theater world, but William Howe made his name in the criminal courts, appearing for the defense in hundreds of murder and manslaughter trials. Decked in brightly colored suits and diamond jewelry and given to lengthy quotations from Shakespeare in lieu of technical legal arguments, Howe "was so often moved to tears by his own oratory that other lawyers suspected him of keeping an onion in his handkerchief."[44]

Howe died in 1902, and Hummel was disbarred, serving a year in jail for suborning perjury, before emigrating to England in 1908.[45] But well into the twentieth century, it was their archetype that preoccupied legal scholars, reformers, and corporate lawyers alike. They resembled the type of lawyer that the attorney general of the United States decades later would label "lawyer-criminals."[46] They had little formal education, and recognized few ethical limits on their tactics—two facts that elite lawyers, who sought to impose heightened credentials for admission to the bar, considered intertwined. In court, they launched vicious insults at crime victims, bamboozled jurors with convoluted lines of questioning, and purchased friendly testimony from professional perjurers. To curry sympathy, they encouraged defendants to bring their children to court to sit on their laps; if a client did not have a child, they lent him one.[47] Such tactics could make a lawyer quite wealthy. As the criminal courts became more professionalized and more punitive, the demand for defense lawyers only grew; and since respectable lawyers had little interest in low-level criminal practice, outsiders rushed in to meet the growing demand. Celebrity lawyers like Howe and Hummel occupied the top of a pyramid. At the bottom were scores of less-successful lawyers who took whatever criminal cases they could find by showing up at jailhouses and tossing a few dollars to the guards for a referral, or setting up shop in courtroom pews to talk up defendants' families and pick up appointed cases from the judge.[48]

Though lumped together by the legal upper crust as an undifferentiated "lower stratum" of the profession, the criminal bar at the turn of the century included a mix of types.[49] Some lawyers, in the image of Clarence Darrow, pursued criminal defense as an adjunct to their politics, a way of dramatizing their opposition to the government. Others had more material aspirations for their careers, but even these ranged on a spectrum. Scam artists targeted immigrant defendants, banking on the fact that they understood neither English nor how the courts worked, and sometimes provided egregiously incompetent trial advocacy.[50] But other lawyers in criminal court were well-meaning novices who were shut out of established law firms because of their race, religion, or gender, and hoped to build a respectable practice on the foundations laid by scraping together criminal cases.[51] In New York, the attorneys derided by elites as bloodsuckers often succeeded at freeing their clients—for instance, through expert use of the state's habeas corpus procedure—given that few prosecutions rested upon satisfactory evidence. A lawyer might charge $25 for a writ of habeas corpus—though the court fee was only 25 cents—but paying the markup was better than spending months in jail.[52]

Different configurations of advocates, reformers, and elites worried about the disorderly state of urban courts and jails, each for their own reasons. Law and order officials fretted that the courts turned too many defendants free. Organized crime rackets hired tricky lawyers to confuse or even literally bribe the jury.[53] Advocates for immigrants and the poor—including the celebrated Darrow—indicted the courts as all too effective at convicting and punishing defendants.[54] By the turn of the twentieth century, large business corporations supplied the most lucrative and, therefore, the most prestigious legal work.[55] Corporate lawyers worried about the criminal courts too, but for yet another reason: they fretted that lawyers who practiced criminal law, along with other low-rent specialties like personal injury and divorce, might tarnish the profession's overall reputation.

Elite lawyers had never taken much interest in low-level criminal cases. Now they also begged out of appointments to murder trials, once the foundation for many a lawyer-statesman's reputation, but now degraded as a chintzy business better left to underworld characters. In an 1896 speech, one of Boston's most prominent lawyers dismissed as an outdated, "chivalrous idea" the notion that all members of the bar were obligated to accept appointments in criminal cases. The law was now "so specialized," he explained, that it was unrealistic to expect corporate lawyers to work outside of their niche.[56] Corporate lawyers did, however, take an interest in criminal defense as an object of regulation. They regarded lawyers who specialized in criminal cases not as solutions to the burgeoning need for legal services, but as a problem in themselves. In the view of the elite corporate bar, criminal lawyers—identified variously as "vampires," "legal vermin," and "harpies"—clogged the courts with nonsensical arguments and delays.[57]

By the 1910s, elite lawyers had codified professional ethics rules and established disciplinary tribunals, run by local bar associations, to police other lawyers' behavior. Bar disciplinarians most zealously targeted personal-injury lawyers, whom they disdained as "ambulance chasers," but their rules equally condemned "Tombs runners," the equivalent epithet for low-status criminal lawyers.[58] In 1908, for instance, the American Bar Association declared it "unprofessional" for lawyers to advertise their services, initiate contact with potential clients, or "remunerate policemen, court or prison officials" for referrals.[59] Trawling courtrooms in search of potential clients and offering jail guards a cut of their legal fees had become standard ways for lawyers to drum up criminal business.[60] These practices appear patently corrupt by latter-day standards, and appeared predatory even to many reformers at the time, but their prevalence was predictable. The ABA canons enshrined the traditional view that it was unseemly for lawyers to go out of their way to solicit clients. Rather, individuals with legal problems should be the ones to seek out lawyers, typically through their social and professional connections. This model was incompatible with realities in the urban criminal courts, where no one appeared voluntarily and few defendants were likely to know any lawyers personally.

Legal academics and their brethren in the fledgling sciences of sociology and criminology had more abstract concerns. Sociology sought to map the novel complexities of modern life, with its thickening weave of organizations and subcultures and differentiated occupations, and to isolate "the causal role of society" in human behavior.[61] Once understood, society could be tinkered with for the better by law and policy. Jurists called for a revitalized, "socialized law" incorporating the new academic insights into how individuals were shaped by their surroundings.[62] The classical modes of legal thought that dominated nineteenth-century jurisprudence imagined judges as having a constrained role: they resolved the disputes that came before them by applying the law to the specific facts of the case. "Socialized" judges would think more expansively, relating individual disputes to broader "social facts" and developing a new "sociological jurisprudence" liberated from rigid formal categories.[63]

Crime, and by extension the criminal law, became a central preoccupation of Progressive Era students of society. Legal reformers regarded the criminal courts as archaic holdovers from the days of rural towns and horse-drawn buggies, in desperate need of modernizing and bureaucratizing.[64] They urged judges to welcome into their courtrooms all of the expert professionals who were using scientific methods to develop specialized techniques for regulating and rehabilitating the poor, the young, the unruly, and the purportedly insufficiently Americanized. Out of this moment emerged the modern criminal justice bureaucracy, with its professionalized police departments, probation and parole agencies, and constellation of allied social workers and clinics.[65] Chicago's newly established Municipal Court was the model "socialized court": less a court in the traditional sense than an agency of social workers, probation officers, church and charity volunteers, psychologists, and other professionals, working together to intervene in city life according to the latest academic research.[66] The authors of these reforms harbored few doubts that the problems they identified could in fact be solved.[67] As historian Michael Willrich has observed, "even the most moderate progressives" were optimistic "that, with the right combination of environmental and eugenic reforms, urban governments might dramatically reduce or even eliminate crime within a generation or two."[68]

In the 1910s and '20s, the public defender idea attracted a new wave of interest from lawyers, academics, and legal reformers, whose discussions shared many premises with the ongoing discourse about "socializing" the law. Debates on the public defender appeared regularly in the influential *Journal of Criminal Law and Criminology*, which featured articles by lawyers, judges, doctors, psychologists, social workers, and sociologists. Between 1910 and 1930, the *Journal* averaged one mention of the public defender idea in every issue, and a full article on the subject in every second or third issue.[69] In 1924, a bibliographer tallied four recent books on the public defender—including Mayer Goldman's—and ninety-one articles in law reviews, academic journals, and popular magazines such as *The Nation*.[70] Like proponents of sociological jurisprudence, public defender advocates imagined the law not as a tradition to maintain, but as a tool to recalibrate to serve changing societal needs. They shared the socializers' confidence that criminal law was a lever for social order and that, with the right laws in place, crime could be virtually eliminated. They agreed that court personnel should collaborate to "treat" criminals rather than compete against each other to win verdicts, and that crime represented not simply an individual failing but a collective responsibility. The public defender "would chiefly affect the needy, the weak, the lowly," one advocate allowed, "but society owes a duty to these because it is chiefly responsible for their existence."[71] In the words of another proponent, public defense was a logical component of the ongoing transition toward accepting "social responsibility for the failings of individuals."[72]

Goldman became a well-known participant in this Progressive Era wave of the public defender movement. What concerned Goldman was not only inequality—the many ways in which the wrath of the criminal courts fell especially harshly upon the poor—but also the pecuniary corruption of legal advocacy. Goldman's insistence upon public defenders boiled down to a provocation: maybe lawyers should not be bought and sold like fish at market. It was not only that markets disadvantaged the poor; there was something inherently corrosive about a market in criminal defense, which was essentially a market in chances at acquittal and freedom. Courts, Goldman insisted with simplistic zeal, were supposed to find the "truth."[73] Lawyers-for-hire distorted the truth-seeking process at both ends of the economic spectrum. Among the poor, innocent defendants risked wrongful conviction because they could not afford skilled counsel. Among the rich, guilty defendants wrongfully evaded punishment because they could afford to pay for devious counsel. As a result of this market, not only did the courts fail to distinguish between the innocent and the guilty, but lawyers themselves lost sight of their obligation to serve justice.

If elite lawyers responded to the tensions inherent in fee-for-service advocacy by purporting to improve professional ethics, or by rehearsing elaborate accounts of how the pursuit of private interests served societal well-being in the aggregate, Goldman and others offered a more straightforward solution: simply eliminate fee-for-service advocacy. Subsume lawyers into the state. For a generation of middle-class professionals for whom an expert civil service meant progress, this solution had obvious appeal. Maurice Parmelee, as a young sociology professor at the University of Missouri, posited public defense as the "final" step in the "historical evolution" of the criminal trial. To Parmelee this step made perfect sense. Private victims no longer managed prosecutions. Instead, public prosecutors filed criminal charges on behalf not of individual victims but of society as a whole. It was only reasonable to convert the defense of the accused into a wholly public function as well. Out of all the other judicial reforms bandied about, public defense, Parmelee predicted, might prove "the most important" reform of all, for it would complete the heretofore uneven conversion of the criminal process into a state-managed endeavor. The collection of data, the development of specialized expertise and efficient procedures, the elimination of private interest from decision-making would all follow. The conversion to public defense would enable "a new system of criminal procedure" based not upon inherited traditions, but upon "the modern science of criminology."[74]

Other reformers echoed this view that once prosecution had been taken over by the state, it was logical that defense too should be administered by the state. If the state had a duty "to punish the guilty," then surely it had an equal duty "to shield the innocent."[75] One Chicago lawyer described public defense in terms reminiscent of Taylorization. In cities with large populations, public defense amounted to the "systemizing of the double function of the state in dealing with crime"—that is, the prosecution and the defense functions. Bringing criminal defense under the control of the government would enable the same type of centralized management and "division of labor" advocated by management scientists like Frederick Winslow Taylor. Just as Taylorized factories produced better widgets more quickly, Taylorizing the courts would yield "greater efficiency and precision" in the adjudication of criminal cases, "with less waste and at smaller cost."[76]

WHEN PROGRESSIVE ERA reformers endorsed the public defender, they were imagining a type of lawyer quite different from the public defenders that later became widespread in American courtrooms. They shared many premises with other reformers of their era, and some of those premises in turn influenced later developments, such as the idea of using scientific expertise to inform criminal punishment. But they took those premises in a different direction, imagining a version of the public defender that, in retrospect, appears out of joint with subsequent developments in twentieth-century legal history. For this reason, their writings have proven somewhat inscrutable or even offensive to latter-day readers. Yet it is also for this reason that Progressive Era public defender proposals are rich historical sources, capturing configurations of thought that later became less available to American lawyers. Examining the Progressive Era public defender idea is important not because present-day public defenders are its direct descendants, but precisely because, despite the shared name, they are not.

Two strange threads united Progressive Era public defender proposals, which otherwise differed in their specifics. First, the Progressive Era public defender tended to be modeled after the public prosecutor, rather than the private defense attorney. Advocates imagined the public defender as "the complement to the district attorney": both a counterweight and a mirror image to the public prosecutor, with similar hiring standards, resources, and duties.[77] As one New York lawyer put it, "the present system is *side heavy*." Prosecutors had "all the money, the detectives, the process servers, the majesty and the awe connected with the public office representing the state."[78] To correct this imbalance, "[t]he public defender ought to be in the Police Court; he ought to be at the Police Station; he ought, in short, to be wherever the district attorney is."[79] While private lawyers carried none of "the dignity of office" enjoyed by district attorneys, public defenders would be government officials and therefore, presumably, "as able, as honest and as diligent as the district attorney is now."[80]

Most controversially, Progressive Era advocates applied to the public defender the same ethical obligation thought to define the prosecutor in American legal culture: the duty to seek justice. An attorney hired by a private individual was understood not as a minister of the state, but as an agent for his client. Within the bounds of ethical and legal limits on legitimate advocacy (themselves, of course, the subject of fierce debate), the attorney's aim was straightforward: to pursue the client's interests.[81] Prosecutors were an exception to this norm. They did have a client, in a way—the government—but the government was no ordinary litigant; in a democracy, it represented in turn the sovereign people. To represent the government, then, required pursuing the interests of the people as a whole, not of any particular individual or group. In the Supreme Court's formulation, the prosecutor's proper aspiration in any given criminal case was not to win for the sake of winning, "but that justice shall be done." This "peculiar" role necessitated that prosecutors adopt not a single goal, but a "twofold aim": "that guilt shall not escape," but also that "innocence [not] suffer."[82]

Progressive Era advocates imagined the public defender in this same mold. Unlike private lawyers who owed a duty only to their clients, public defenders, as "quasi-judicial officers," would also "owe a duty . . . to the state."[83] They would endeavor not "to defeat the ends of justice—but rather to co-operate with the District Attorney." They would zealously defend the innocent, but would limit their services for the guilty to "obtaining a just and fair punishment."[84] Echoing the prosecutor's twofold aim, Goldman explained that the public defender would not seek "to defeat justice by securing the acquittal of a guilty defendant any more than it is the function of the district attorney to convict an innocent man." Rather, "[i]t should be the duty of both officials to work harmoniously, with the sole purpose of bringing out the facts and the law in a given case, and to strive for the highest ideals in the administration of justice."[85]

Second, as a result of the defender's redefined role as a public official, criminal trials would change in a number of ways. For one thing, there would be fewer of them. The public defender would advise defendants to plead guilty in cases where the evidence was overwhelming, and a trial would be "foolish." In such cases, trials benefited hired defense lawyers—because they earned exponentially larger fees for trials—but not defendants. The public defender would have no pecuniary incentive to drag out proceedings any longer than necessary. This approach would likely save money for the criminal courts, but even if not, it would yield other "advantages to the individual, to society, and to the law."[86] One lawyer imagined public defenders as "men of wide experience in the criminal field," who "would be well grounded . . . in the broad principles of the law," unlike "their predecessors" in the private criminal bar who fixated on "petty quibbles." Public defenders "would be alert, intelligent, [and] capable of taking advantage of every honorable means to the exculpation of their client," but would not resort to dishonorable means.[87] Goldman offered a similar litany of benefits sure to flow from the public defender, including "more honest and ably presented" cases, with fewer "perjured and unscrupulous defenses"; speedier trials; improvements in the ascertainment of "the truth in any trial"; and reduced judicial expenses. Last but not least, "the whole tone of a criminal trial and of the criminal courts [would] be elevated by a higher ideal of justice."[88]

Some lawyers read public defender proposals with bemusement: they fixated on how silly it seemed for the state to pay to keep criminals out of jail. For the public defender's advocates, that fixation represented a total misunderstanding of the reform they were proposing. One New York attorney, for instance, assumed that, just like a paid lawyer, a public defender would "assert every technicality . . . which may tend to acquit his guilty client," and questioned whether it was "expedient to champion, at the public expense, every red-handed malefactor."[89] But in the reformers' view, helping "guilty persons escape punishment" was precisely what private counsel did; such attorneys respected no limits because they viewed their clients, "rather than truth and justice, as master."[90] Public defenders "would serve [both] the State, and the individual," rather than "the individual alone."[91] Given "the nature of [public] office," they could not "act so rabidly" on behalf of their clients as could a "private attorney." In fact, reformers insisted, the public defender, having little incentive "to fabricate a defense" or to suborn perjury, might reduce the number of "scoundrels [who] go scot free."[92]

The image of public defenders as public officials modeled after prosecutors flowed from a larger critique of the adversarial tenor of criminal adjudication.

Too often, in the view of Progressive Era public defender advocates, adversarial trials obscured rather than clarified the truth. Relying on private lawyers to test the state's evidence rendered trials overly susceptible to manipulation by the rich, even as it rendered the poor disproportionately vulnerable. This critique anticipated an enduring scholarly debate about whether Anglo-American adversarial procedures are inferior to the European-style inquisitorial process, in which the court itself independently investigates the facts.[93] Progressive Era reformers, however, tended not to attribute the flaws they identified with American trials to the adversarial format itself; they typically continued to assume that two opposing advocates, rather than a neutral party, would investigate and present the facts. Rather, they blamed the way that private compensation distorted those advocates' incentives and attitudes. Private defense lawyers sought to win at all costs, and prosecutors responded by adopting the same stance, violating their purported obligation to seek justice. The profit motive on one side of the criminal courtroom corrupted both sides and eliminating it would improve both sides.

This critique proceeded, in turn, from a bedrock assumption that criminal trials could and should be organized around the discovery of objective truths, rather than serving as morality plays, entertaining spectacles, or gladiatorial "battles of wits."[94] Progressive reformers regarded the more theatrical dimensions of criminal trials as distractions. In their view, a trial's only legitimate purpose was to determine facts through empirical inquiry "conducted in the spirit of the scientific investigator."[95] The idea that public defenders should cooperate with prosecutors comported with this conception of the trial. If "the one, single, sole, admissible purpose of the trial is to get at the truth," then cooperation would serve that purpose better than "a fight."[96] Instead of prizefighting, the scientific laboratory offered the reformers' preferred metaphor for what criminal courts should aspire to be. "Suppose that scientists were paid to determine the laws of medicine, chemistry or mathematics . . . according to the interests of the men who paid them," one reformer asked. "How far would the human race have traveled along the path of progress on which science has led it?"[97] This comparison fit within a larger cult of science, defined in terms of methods and processes, pervasive among urban professionals in the early twentieth century: get the procedures and the inputs right, isolate the important variables and eliminate the irrelevancies, and the truth would follow.[98]

This strand of Progressive Era proposals for public defense—the suggestion that defenders should join with prosecutors in a collaborative inquiry into the truth—infuriated lawyers who were more fully steeped in America's adversarial legal culture. They echoed the standard defense of adversarialism—which posited that the "clash" of competing perspectives revealed rather than obscured the truth—but also emphasized that the state alone carried the burden of proof in criminal cases.[99] The celebrity Chicago defense attorney William Scott Stewart decried public defense as "a fraud upon the defendant" and a "violation of the constitution." All of the flashy courtroom tactics that reformers disdained as unethical tricks, Stewart celebrated as crucial checks and balances. "The public defender makes a virtue of giving up to the prosecution without a struggle," Stewart claimed. The "lowliest 'shyster', as he is now called by the gentlemen who write upon the subject," would never "brazenly throw away all of the rights of a defendant."[100] Of course, criminal lawyers' opposition to the public defender served their own economic interests, but the private criminal bar also had philosophical differences with the public defender's proponents. They were more skeptical of state power and more confident that client-driven advocacy in individual cases provided, in the aggregate, a bulwark against government overreach. In their view, if the state wanted to punish someone, then no one else had any duty to aid the state in that task. It was perfectly legitimate for individuals to fight criminal charges even if they were, in fact, guilty. Their model of criminal advocacy offered a vernacular, legalized variant of the classical economic theory that individuals acting in their own self-interest collectively promote the good of society. Legal scholars who rediscovered the Progressive Era public defender proposals in the 1980s reacted similarly to Stewart; they interpreted them as proof of a political alliance between elite lawyers and reformers to assist the state in convicting, punishing, and thereby controlling the immigrant poor.[101]

It is important to contextualize what Goldman and other reformers meant when they called for defenders and prosecutors to cooperate. Stewart interpreted these calls as invitations to one-sided acquiescence. But Goldman and his interlocutors did not call for defenders to submit meekly to prosecutors. They posited that redefining the criminal process as collaborative would yield cooperation from both sides, leading district attorneys to moderate their positions as well. In a less combative milieu, prosecutors might become more amenable to defenders' reasoned arguments for why a defendant was innocent without forcing the issue to trial. To latter-day observers who equate prosecutors with the immensely powerful district attorneys of the later twentieth century, such hopes can sound impossibly naïve at best. But in the hothouse reform moment of the 1910s and '20s, everything about the criminal courts appeared in total flux and the roles (and powers) of the participants less fixed. The aim of Goldman's envisioned cooperation was to ensure that the right defendants were punished, but also that no one was unjustly punished. Indeed, Goldman assumed that the public defender would not only elevate the tone of trials but also reduce the number of innocent defendants who pled guilty solely because their attorneys did not want to be burdened with their cases.[102]

It is also important not to assume that progressive reformers' prescriptive writings dictated later public defenders' actual practices. How practicing public defenders have defined their roles has varied over time and has been shaped by the local culture of particular offices. For example, the first generation of Los Angeles public defenders settled into a more traditionally adversarial professional identity by the 1930s and touted their skill as trial lawyers.[103] In 1934, the legal aid leader John Bradway circulated a draft report on indigent defense to Los Angeles public defender Frederic Vercoe. Bradway's initial draft described trials as a last resort for the public defender. Vercoe objected strongly to this language and requested revisions that made clear that he had not adopted Goldman's conception of the public defender's role. "We represent the defendant," Vercoe wrote, "the same as an attorney in private practice would represent a defendant in [the same] court."[104]

Still, it is undeniable that the vision of a future in which prosecutors and defenders collaborated to uncover objective truth displayed a remarkable degree of faith in the state as a benevolent social force. This optimism could have a tragic dimension, as poignantly illustrated by Goldman's use of the Leo Frank case as an argument for public defense. Frank, a Jewish factory manager outside of Atlanta, was tried and convicted for the 1913 murder of a 13-year-old girl who worked at the factory, and eventually lynched.[105] Following his pattern of attributing to public defense the power to right all evils, Goldman wondered whether Frank might have had a fair trial had a public defender been in place, "with the prestige of the State behind him, insisting upon production at the trial of all evidence favorable to the prisoner" and challenging the "unjust public prejudice" that pervaded the prosecution.[106] Frank was represented at trial by prominent Georgia attorneys, and later lynched by prominent Georgia citizens in an atmosphere of public hysteria. Goldman's supposition that introducing another Georgia public official, even if assigned to the defense side, would have changed "the atmosphere of the trial" did not fully grapple with the deep roots of anti-Semitism and racism.[107] And yet, it is understandable why Goldman, the grandson of German-Jewish immigrants to Louisiana, identified with Frank and grasped for ways to imagine that his fate might have been avoided.

Legal scholars expressed interest in public defender proposals, although they gave Goldman's writings mixed reviews. George Kirchwey, the dean of Columbia Law School and former warden of New York's Sing Sing prison, praised Goldman's book, as did reviewers in the *Yale Law Journal* and the *University of Pennsylvania Law Review*. At a time of renewed interest in "the foundations of liberty and justice in a democracy," one reviewer wrote, Goldman offered "timely" suggestions for modernizing criminal procedure.[108] Other scholarly readers, even if they agreed with Goldman's diagnosis of the problems plaguing the criminal courts, were put off by his strident tone. Some academic reviewers grumbled about his lack of specifics and complained that he oversold public defense as a panacea. In the *Michigan Law Review*, one professor dismissed Goldman's book as persuasive upon "a casual reading" but "wholly unconvincing" upon further examination. Perhaps the criminal courts were unfair, but Goldman presented little hard evidence to support his preferred fix and had no way of knowing that his imagined corps of public defenders would, in fact, prove as public-spirited as he assumed.[109]

Even when framed as criticism, such reviews identified an important theme in the Progressive Era public defender debate. The public defender was not—in the eyes of its proponents—merely a minor or technical reform, but a fix for nearly every judicial wrong. Goldman lamented that "the general public has gotten the somewhat indelible impression, that the poor man accused of crime is not on an equal footing with the rich defendant." But with the public defender in place, the average person would come to the "wholesome realization . . . that our much vaunted theory of 'equality before the law' has become a reality—instead of a mere high-sounding phrase."[110] Just as public prosecution decoupled criminal trials from private vengeance, so public defense would eliminate bitter reprisals against the state from defendants convinced they had been "unjustly punished." "There is as much danger of the destruction of public order from the use by the state of its resources to prosecute only, as there would be in its use of its resources only to defend those charged with crime," one lawyer proposed. "Thus, public order can, in the long run, rest only upon an even handed system of justice which defends, theoretically and practically, as efficiently as it prosecutes, those charged with crime."[111] Another attorney predicted that "a public defender's office would bring about splendid results, humanitarian and financial," and "breed a higher respect for law": "the innocent would regain their liberty sooner and the guilty would be convicted sooner. Both would get a fair trial, and the thousand and one complaints now heard would vanish into thin air." Public defenders, he insisted, would "go far, very far, toward strangling many evils that now afflict us."[112]

PUBLIC DEFENSE, promised its Progressive Era advocates, would also "purify the legal profession."[113] Negative stereotypes had long attached to lawyers generically, but as the modern bar splintered into specialties, lawyers at the bottom of the ladder—those who took criminal and personal injury cases—absorbed a disproportionate share of the reputational fallout. Such characters, as reformers described them, devoted most of their zeal not toward vindicating clients' interests but toward extorting whatever fees they could squeeze out of clients' families.[114] When lawyers and legal scholars praised the Los Angeles County Public Defender in its early years, it was typically because of its reported success in eliminating "jailhouse lawyers" from the Los Angeles courts.[115] Once defendants had upstanding public officials to represent them, there was no longer much demand for "so-called 'shyster lawyers.'"[116]

Yet if reformers and elites agreed about the existence of "disreputable lawyers," what precisely they meant by "purifying" the bar differed. For elites the impurities to be eliminated were certain types of people whom they deemed ill-suited to the profession, insufficiently steeped in "the historical background of our institutions."[117] Given the demographic profile of practice specialties defined as lower-status, this language of pollution blended racist and nativist prejudice with elite aspirations to heighten the educational requirements for joining the profession.[118] When invoked by public defender advocates, however, many of whom were not themselves especially elite (and often themselves of Jewish or Southern European descent), such nativist undertones acquired a more complicated valence. The public defender's proponents were generally not pedigreed corporate lawyers, who typically preferred private charity to public defense. Perhaps these writers were playing to the elite lawyers they imagined as their audience. Perhaps they also hoped that, for lawyers shut out of corporate work because of prejudice rather than a lack of skill, public defender offices could offer the career path that the exclusive corporate bar did not, and the esteem of public office would inspire a higher-minded approach to advocacy than the grubby market in "Tombs running" required. Public defender offices might offer future generations of lawyers like them an alternative route to legal respectability.[119]

For some reformers too, purifying the profession aimed more at lawyers for the rich than at lawyers for the poor. It was in this vein that some called for compulsory public defense: the mandatory assignment of public defenders for all defendants. Public defenders should eventually be legally defined as "the only recognized counsel for the defense," one lawyer proposed, thereby precluding criminal defendants from hiring their own attorneys.[120] Rich and poor alike would be "bound to accept a Public Defender, just as now the rich and poor alike have to accept prosecution by the same officer."[121] This advocate then made what must have struck many lawyers as an alarming prediction: "The time will come when, just as there has been an evolution from the private warfare of the past to the semi-civilized administration of justice of the present, the private Bar will be abolished."[122] In a fully civilized polity (just as in Bellamy's utopia), the state would provide a lawyer (and a doctor, and so on) for any situation where one was needed. The public defender idea, in its Progressive Era iteration, thus hinted at a long-term vision for restructuring the legal profession that could not be reduced to, nor in some variants even squared with, a defense of individual interests—whether the interests of lawyers or of defendants. If anything survived of Bellamy's version of public defense, it was this collectivist streak. The legal profession would "not be injured" by the abolition of the private bar, one advocate assured his readers, but rather, "elevated." But then he added that "even if [the profession] would be injured, the community interests are primary."[123]

If they displayed little concern for lawyers' interests (at least as the organized bar defined them), public defender advocates wrote more ambiguously about the individual rights of criminal defendants. They spoke the American vernacular of "rights talk"; Goldman, for instance, described public defense as a "right—not a privilege."[124] But often they invoked rights more for rhetorical emphasis than because they were making technical legal or constitutional arguments. Many assigned little value to individual rights as a structural check upon the state. Rather, they hoped to create an overall machinery that worked well enough on its own to reach just outcomes, obviating the need for elaborate procedural protections for each individual. Parmelee, the sociologist, traveled especially far in this direction, endorsing public defense as one component in his new "system of criminal procedure" modeled on continental European bureaucracy, with simplified, less legalistic procedures and a more active role for judges to guide juries through the facts. Assuming that his new "system" would reach accurate results and thereby adequately protect defendants' interests, Parmelee even called for abolishing the presumption of innocence, although he would not replace it with a presumption of guilt. Rather, he argued, judicial proceedings should begin without "any presumption whatever." Fact-finders should assess the evidence from a stance of total openness, alert to find the truth wherever it lay.[125] Instead of the undifferentiated legal education that American law schools offered, Parmelee proposed specialized training for the new public corps of criminal lawyers, who would alternate between the prosecutorial and defense roles "to avoid acquiring any bias." Judges could then be promoted from this open-minded cadre of criminal experts.[126]

Lawyers who endorsed public defense tended not to go as far as Parmelee toward endorsing Continental-style bureaucracy, but they shared his dismissive attitude toward the existing roster of constitutional protections for defendants. For the most part, the federal Bill of Rights, the majority of which concerns criminal procedure, had not yet been applied to the states, but the states had similar provisions in their own constitutions that typically guaranteed some form of access to counsel, trial by jury, and protections against self-incrimination. Advocates of public defense occasionally connected their proposals with the constitutional right to counsel, and other defendants' rights, though typically they cited constitutional provisions as supplemental support rather than as independent or primary justifications for the reform.[127] Generally they did not venerate the constitutional right to counsel, which was interpreted to protect the right to appear in court with one's own privately retained counsel—or in some cases the right to have court-appointed counsel—but not to require institutionalized public defenders. Those who endorsed compulsory public defense were especially indifferent toward the constitutional right to counsel—necessarily so, since compulsory public defense for the rich would violate the right if understood as an entitlement to hire one's own counsel of choice. If compulsory public defense could not be adopted "for constitutional reasons," one advocate wrote, then "so much the worse for these constitutional reasons." To the extent that it could be implemented, the public defender would "sweep away some of the obvious evils" of the status quo in the criminal courts.[128]

Alternatively, advocates of public defense referred to constitutional rights as vestigial relics: they might have once served a purpose, but now exemplified the kinds of archaic traditions that modernizing reforms like public defense would render obsolete. Because public defense would equalize both sides of the criminal trial, reformers claimed, it would render superfluous constitutional protections like the right against self-incrimination. One lawyer made the following argument: under historical conditions, defendants demanded special procedural rights to compensate for the fact that the state enjoyed superior power. But once public defenders were in place, the prosecution and defense would be equal in resources and talent, and "the state and individual" would face one another in court "on the same plane."

Only then would it be reasonable to abolish the presumption of innocence, requirements of jury unanimity, the privilege against self-incrimination, arcane rules of evidence, and the "rudimentary organ" of the grand jury.[129] Constitutional safeguards for defendants had been enshrined at a time when "the individual" existed "at the mercy of a strong State," he explained. It was true that such safeguards should be reconsidered in light of modern conditions. "But we cannot do it," he insisted, "till we have a Public Defender," to ensure an equal division of "advantages and disadvantages . . . between the individual and the State."[130]

THE MOST CAPACIOUS VERSIONS of the public defender idea, especially those versions that called for compulsory public defense, had little hope of adoption. They clashed too openly with the contemporaneous priorities of the self-appointed leaders of the legal profession. The Progressive Era public defender debate coincided with a moment when elite lawyers, often affiliated with corporate law firms, were organizing the profession into bar associations and consolidating their own control over the profession's standards of education and licensure.[131] Professional elites insisted upon maintaining a "unitary" bar—with identical educational and licensure requirements for all lawyers, regardless of specialty—rejecting proposals to acknowledge and formalize the profession's increasing degree of functional specialization.[132] This decision foreclosed the adoption of plans like Parmelee's to institutionalize specialized training and career tracks for criminal lawyers. Instead, all aspiring lawyers would undergo the increasingly standardized and ever-lengthening gauntlet of undergraduate and legal education, and master the whole of the common law, much of which concerned contracts and business transactions. Framed as an effort to maintain academic standards, this set of policymaking choices within the profession reinforced its exclusivity. Heightened standards made the path to a legal career lengthier and more expensive, maintaining barriers to entry for members of immigrant and minority groups and frustrating hopes to develop more focused training for lawyers who sought primarily to serve the poor or to practice in routine settings like the low-level criminal courts.[133]

In 1915, a committee of the leading professional organization for New York lawyers—the Association of the Bar of the City of New York—denounced Goldman's proposed public defender as "neither necessary nor advisable."[134] The committee's report offered two sets of reasons for rejecting the public defender. First, the report argued that there was no evidence that the injustices cited by Goldman and other advocates actually existed on a widespread scale in New York. Although unconvincing, this part of the report was telling as to whose perspective elite lawyers considered to qualify as evidence. The committee, for instance, reported that there was no proof that innocent defendants were routinely disadvantaged in court because of their poverty—based on a survey of judges and district attorneys, who self-reported that they did not know of any cases in which this had happened.[135] As a critic responded at the time, "judges and district attorneys, being human, could not, in the mass, be expected to admit their labors had been conducive to failures of justice."[136]

However, in a second and more interesting set of arguments, the committee report argued that the public defender would be inadvisable in New York even if the "wrongs" decried by Goldman "[did] exist."[137] This more principled rejection of public defense merits further discussion, because it cannot be explained by rote conservatism. The committee included a mix of types, ranging from former prosecutors to scions of the Wall Street bar such as Elihu Root, Jr., and Allen Wardwell.[138] Though patrician, this latter cohort eagerly supported reform efforts in New York in other policy realms, such as education. In many cases they endorsed standard, Progressive Era initiatives to introduce expertise to public administration and professionalize the civil service.[139] It is illuminating, then, to consider why the public defender did not interest them.

The crux of elite lawyers' aversion to the public defender was not specific to the criminal law; rather, it was their basic presumption that a lawyer's role within the American liberal order was to serve as an independent agent of his client's interests. By the 1910s, the most prestigious New York law firms had reoriented their practice away from courtroom advocacy in discrete legal disputes toward ongoing counseling and advisory services for large business corporations.[140] Yet they maintained an investment in their identity as independent professionals: they remained organized in private law firms rather than working in-house for their corporate clients, and they equally sought to maintain independence from the state.[141] Although bar leaders issued jeremiads about the merger between elite legal practice and big business, most corporate lawyers essentially came to accept it. In legal historian Robert Gordon's summary, they chose to "retreat into the role of apolitical technician with no ideology save that of craftsmanlike client service."[142] Though updated for the new mode of corporate practice, this role had deep roots in American legal culture, perpetuating the image of the lawyer, in one historian's words, as a "professional mouthpiece." Such a lawyer "discharged his duty to society by pleading his client's cause to the best of his ability" and "assumed no responsibility for the results."[143]

Viewed through this lens of the lawyer as independent advocate for the client's private interests, Goldman's proposal to reinvent defense lawyers as public officials appeared inscrutable. The bar committee did not only disagree with Goldman about whether their conception of the lawyer's role should be reconsidered; they disagreed with Goldman that it was workable to conceive of the lawyer's role in any other way. If public defenders behaved like the public-spirited, quasi-judicial officers that Goldman envisioned and refused to pursue dishonest defenses, then defendants would quickly learn to find other lawyers (or to "misrepresent the facts" to their public defenders), and the reform would collapse on itself. They assumed, in other words, that defendants too were rational actors, out to protect their private interests: "Most of those accused of crime have but one desire, that is, to escape."[144] If, instead, public defenders behaved in the same way as private defense attorneys, zealously pursuing every possible avenue toward acquittal, then the situation would become intolerably "anomalous," with the state paying to defeat itself.[145]

The bar committee could see no way to accommodate the defense lawyer's role as an adversary of the state while also making that lawyer a part of the state. "The aim of the State is, and must be, to do exact justice to all," the report explained. "The goal of the accused, on the other hand, is not justice, but impunity." This "divergence" of goals between prosecution and defense was perfectly natural, indeed necessary, but as a result of this divergence, it was a "fallacy" to suppose that the state could "conduct the defense, as well as the prosecution."[146] The committee also disagreed with Goldman's supposition that public office would convert lawyers into noble truth-seekers, immune to public hysteria in high-profile cases. To the contrary, without the motive of client loyalty, public defenders might feel pressure to defend the innocent less vigorously than private lawyers would. "Private counsel can and do conduct the defense" of their clients "fearlessly and effectively," the report explained, even when their clients are unpopular, because their sole interest is "the performance of their full duty to their client" and they "have no political considerations in mind."[147] If the poor did require legal assistance, then, it should be provided not by public officials, but by private entities, independent of the state. Only this arrangement could maintain the proper division between the state, seeking to enforce the law, and the individual, seeking to defend his own self-interest in avoiding punishment. The committee report spoke highly of the Legal Aid Society, which had been established in New York in the 1870s to provide civil legal assistance to the immigrant poor and relied upon private donations.[148]

In 1917, the New York bar introduced just such a private alternative to the public defender. Charles Evans Hughes, the once and future Supreme Court justice, who was serving a term as the president of the Legal Aid Society, announced an experimental "Voluntary Defenders Committee" to provide legal representation for selected defendants in the Manhattan criminal courts. The city provided office space, but otherwise the initiative was underwritten by private donors. The oil and finance magnate John D. Rockefeller, Jr., was among the benefactors who provided early support, earning the voluntary defenders the moniker of "Rockefeller lawyers."[149] As the Rockefeller appellation made comically clear, this experiment in private charitable aid for indigent defendants was not a grassroots effort, but nor was it merely an alternative spin on Goldman-style public defense. The voluntary defender experiment neither depended upon nor aspired to the "new system of criminal procedure" imagined by advocates of the public defender. Rather, it furnished privately donated counsel for the poor within the existing procedures.

To elite lawyers, the voluntary defender experiment quickly proved itself. In 1921, the Legal Aid Society absorbed the voluntary defenders as a permanent division (renamed, in 1939, the Criminal Courts Branch). As it expanded, the Criminal Courts Branch took over a significant portion of the indigent caseload within Manhattan, leaving the outer boroughs to continue using assigned counsel. This arrangement seemed to many lawyers and judges to provide an effective enough response to the problems that Goldman had highlighted, and to do so without resort to public funding. The institutionalization of the "Rockefeller lawyers" foreclosed further serious discussion of Goldman's public defender plan.[150] As a prominent example of privately funded indigent defense, New York's voluntary defenders also stalled the momentum of the public defender movement nationally. Elite lawyers in Philadelphia and Boston established privately supported voluntary defenders in the early 1930s, and in both Cincinnati and Pittsburgh, the local Legal Aid Society had added a criminal division by 1930.[151]

Goldman remained unconvinced. He maintained that an "indigent accused (and presumed to be innocent) should not be dependent upon any charity." Legal aid societies did "splendid work" under the circumstances, Goldman allowed, but in the long run, they were no substitute for the public defender.[152] He called for "justice—not charity" and made clear that he did not consider the two interchangeable.[153] Goldman's pamphleteering style meant that he did not engage in elaborate rumination about the requirements of justice or the difference between justice and charity, which of course have long been philosophical (and theological) subjects of inquiry. He used these terms in a more mundane, concrete way. "Justice" signified public administration and required that the defender be a public official; it was an "abstract" entitlement guaranteed to independent rights-holders. "Charity" had feminized connotations; it was an unpredictable gift, the hope of which rendered its would-be recipients "dependent" upon the whims of the donor class. Similar tropes pervaded twentieth-century legal thought, which associated "charity" with feminine caregiving, the province of settlement houses and social workers, and valorized "law," by contrast, as a masculine realm, the province of rights and entitlements, dictated not by emotional responses to suffering but by contractual relations between formally equal citizens.[154] Ironically, Goldman denigrated legal aid societies as "charity" even as male leaders in the legal aid movement were striving equally mightily to differentiate their work from "charity."[155] But where legal aid lawyers contrasted charity with law (implying the model of the private law firm), Goldman instead counterposed justice (which he defined narrowly to connote public office).

Goldman's critique of the private charity approach to indigent defense had two components. First, private organizations had no duty to serve everyone. They could (and, to some extent, did) choose which defendants merited their assistance—violating Goldman's definition of legal defense as "a right—not a privilege."[156] That objection alone might not have doomed the voluntary defender in Goldman's analysis, since legal aid organizations could theoretically meet this objection by agreeing to serve everyone (leaving aside whether they actually had the resources to do this). Goldman's second objection was more intractable: legal aid lawyers were simply not public officials, a distinction that Goldman regarded as crucial. Whether or not they sought to provide universal service, private organizations could never truly rival the district attorney's office, which enjoyed not only public funding, but also the public esteem that came along with government office. Every defendant, in Goldman's view, was "entitled as a matter of abstract right" not merely to legal representation, but to legal representation by a "public official."[157] "Philanthropy—though well intentioned—is not a substitute for a fundamental right."[158]

Tellingly, the most prominent endorsement of the public defender produced in the Progressive Era by an avatar of the legal establishment—the report *Justice and the Poor*, published in 1919 by the Boston lawyer Reginald

Heber Smith—came to its endorsement only by way of rejecting Goldman's definition of public defense. Smith was Goldman's opposite, in almost every biographical and professional detail.[159] A lifelong son of Massachusetts, he was born in Fall River in 1889, attended Harvard for both college and law school, and died in Boston in 1966. Unlike Goldman, Smith became one of the American legal establishment's most celebrated figures: inventor of the "billable hour," self-anointed founder of the legal aid movement, managing partner of the white-shoe law firm Hale and Dorr, and a moving force within the American Bar Association. Upon his death, Smith was eulogized fondly for hosting "light-hearted" parties where the "top brass" of the legal profession mingled with "distinguished guests." According to the *ABA Journal* itself: "No man ever lived who was more closely identified with the American Bar Association than Reg Smith."[160]

Smith galvanized the organized legal aid movement that gained ground beginning in the 1910s among elite lawyers, who sought to expand, standardize, and institutionalize legal aid nationwide. As legal historian Felice Batlan has uncovered, the men at the helm of this movement portrayed themselves as the first generation of legal aid lawyers in the United States, inventing a narrative that erased the earlier history of women's efforts to provide legal assistance through charitable organizations and settlement houses. They did so in order to distinguish legal aid from "social work," hoping to secure elite support for their efforts by establishing a professional identity for legal aid as masculine and respectable.[161] Early in his career, Smith had spent two years as the head attorney of Boston's Legal Aid Society, and came to believe that law not only failed to help the poor but actively made life worse for them. His views on the relationship between law and poverty were, in some ways, radical for a lawyer of his standing, but he muted his criticisms in his published works; his goal was to make legal aid palatable to his peers.[162] In his pathbreaking 1919 study, and in his subsequent advocacy, he touted legal aid as a path to assimilating immigrants into American institutions. He emphasized the need for procedural tinkering with existing legal processes—speedier case processing, reduced fees, and so on—rather than substantive changes to the law.[163] *Justice and the Poor* met initially with mixed reviews among the elite bar—some of whom rejected any suggestion, however muted, that the poor had valid complaints—but succeeded at making a name for Smith and reshaping the legal profession's discourse about poverty. The study was widely distributed in its own time and accepted for decades as the authoritative account of the early legal aid movement.[164]

Smith located the primary responsibility for legal assistance to the poor within the organized legal profession, not within society as a whole or its representatives in government. Working with the ABA, he urged local bar associations to take charge of legal aid in their communities. They might fulfill this responsibility by coordinating pro bono service on a case-by-case basis or, in cities, establishing organized legal aid societies. Either way, the goal was to ensure that legal aid remained "part of the monopoly that bar associations sought to exert over the practice of law."[165] This model, as Batlan observes, did not contemplate grassroots, community-based approaches to legal assistance. It also potentially conflicted with public defender proposals insofar as they insisted upon public defense as a substitute for (rather than a complement to) private legal assistance. Smith's associate John Bradway, the long-time chief attorney of the National Association of Legal Aid Organizations, was more open to government support for legal aid, but shared Smith's view that realistically, the delivery of legal aid would depend upon the participation of bar associations.[166] In correspondence about indigent defense, Bradway expressed the view "that legal aid work can be performed most economically if the civil and criminal aspects of it are handled by one organization." This formulation implied that he was not necessarily opposed to public defense, but if a private legal aid society already existed in a community, he might prefer to add criminal work to its purview rather than create a separate public defender.[167]

The chapter on criminal defense in *Justice and the Poor* papered over the details of proposals like Goldman's, obscuring the importance of public funding and administration to Goldman's version of the public defender idea. Although primarily about civil legal aid, *Justice and the Poor* included a chapter on "Defenders in Criminal Cases"—an organizational choice that, in itself, expressed Smith's understanding of indigent defense as a specialized subtopic within the organized bar's legal aid movement. Smith, accordingly, defined "the public defender" as merely "another name for legal aid in criminal cases."[168] The problem to which public defenders offered a solution, in Smith's view, was not that criminal procedure required an overhaul, but that poor defendants, like poor civil litigants, needed access to higher caliber lawyers to navigate existing procedures. Smith agreed with the public defender movement's low estimation of the criminal bar, echoing the stock caricatures of "'jail lawyers,' 'shysters,' and 'tombs runners'" and writing with horror of how a "devious" lawyer might cajole a defendant's wife "to sell herself on the streets" in order to pay her husband's legal bills.[169] Such lawyers should be replaced, but in Smith's view, they could equally be replaced by public defenders or by private legal aid groups. Framed this way, the problem could be resolved by lawyers in the way that Smith preferred—independently, through their professional organizations and civic outreach.

Even at the level of terminology, Smith rejected Goldman's insistence that there was anything essential about the public nature of public defenders. *Justice and the Poor* characterized the debate over public defense within academic journals as "confused," the product of unsophisticated thinkers who misunderstood the "essential issues" and fixated on "subordinate" minutiae. "Articles that condemn the public defender as unnecessary and then praise the voluntary defender have bewildered most readers and . . . side-tracked the discussion," Smith announced; from his functional perspective, both types of defenders fulfilled the same role.[170] That some defenders happened to be public was, for Smith, an incidental detail, perhaps an artifact of regional variations in the structure of local government. To avoid confusion, Smith explained, he had "eliminated" "the words 'public' and 'private'" from his discussion and would simply use the term "defender."[171] According to *Justice and the Poor*, the essential quality of such offices was not the source of funding but rather their structure: they centralized indigent defense for a jurisdiction into one entity, rather than distributing the responsibility across "a shifting group of attorneys" appointed case-by-case. Centralization would enable defenders to develop specialized expertise in indigent defense, "just as we have experts in patent, or mining, or corporation law."[172] But Smith did not think it mattered whether these salaried, expert defenders worked for private associations funded by philanthropic donations, for government offices supported by public funds, or some combination. "The defender in criminal cases," Smith concluded, "whether publicly or privately supported"—it did not matter which—offered "the best immediate method for securing freedom and equality of justice to poor persons accused of serious crimes."[173]

In collapsing voluntary and public defense into a single "method," *Justice and the Poor* elided differences that Goldman did not consider subordinate details at all, but central distinctions. Through the 1930s, Goldman persisted in calling for public defense and singled out the legal aid movement for criticism. "To compel poor people to seek charity to protect their rights," he wrote, "is not only tragic but degrading."[174] "Defense is a right, not a favor," he insisted, and "legal aid and other voluntary agencies lack the funds" to provide adequate defense for the accused. If the Wall Street bar considered the "Rockefeller lawyers" a successful experiment, Goldman reached the opposite conclusion: voluntary defenders, in his view, only proved "the imperative need for better defense," and should "point the way inevitably toward *public* defense. That alone means the democracy of justice."[175]

IN 1935, MAYER GOLDMAN gave a speech at the American Bar Association's annual meeting, which was held that year in Los Angeles, the birthplace of municipal public defense. As he had done twenty years before in the pages of the *New York Times*, Goldman extolled the public defender as the cure-all for the nation's woes, which now included widespread panic about "public enemies" like Al Capone.[176] "Substitute honest State defenders" for private defense attorneys, Goldman promised, "and the 'crime wave,' will diminish." "No 'over-lord' of organized crime," he continued, "plies his sinister trade today, unless his lawyer is nearby, ready to check-mate the law." For twenty years, Goldman had been a full-throated booster of the public defender for the indigent. Now he made clear that he equally endorsed "compulsory State defense for *all*—rich or poor." The time had arrived to "outlaw criminal lawyers" and redefine defense counsel as publicly accountable "Ministers of Justice." This change would bring wealthy defendants down to "parity with the poor," and guarantee every defendant what they were entitled to: "a fair trial—and only that," not "perjured defenses" or "delays and trickery."[177]

By the end of his life four years later, Goldman had given up on convincing the American Bar Association; in his final writings, he derided the "orthodox bar groups" as "timid" and "extremely selfish."[178] By implication, he had reached the same verdict about lawyers like Reginald Heber Smith who affiliated proudly with the ABA. Lawyers who sought to help the poor through philanthropy refused to confront the essential problem as Goldman defined it: the privatized nature of the defense bar. When the National Lawyers Guild was founded in 1936 as a leftist alternative to the ABA, Goldman quickly joined. The NLG forthrightly endorsed government-funded legal services for the poor in a wide range of contexts and, to Goldman's satisfaction, "unanimously adopted" his resolution in favor of the public defender at its first national convention.[179]

Years later, the consummate Wall Street lawyer, Harrison Tweed, would return the insult. In the 1950s, Tweed recalled the gadfly Mayer Goldman as a "zealot" who, "like so many other zealots, carried his zeal too far," and thereby doomed his own cause. "Not content with demanding that the poor must be taken care of by a Public Defender," Tweed recalled, Goldman "went further and insisted that every defendant in the criminal courts must be so represented and thus denied the right to select his own counsel." This extreme stance, Tweed supposed, helped to explain why Goldman's proposals were "perennially defeated."[180] Goldman might have agreed with Tweed's assessment of him as uncompromising. "If the public defender plan is 'socialized justice,'" he wrote, in one of his final articles, then "by all means let us have more of it."[181]

CHAPTER TWO

From Charity to Right

On a Sunday morning in December 1954, Richard LaPlante smelled smoke in the crowded apartment building where he lived with his parents in the down-luck mill town of Haverhill, Massachusetts. Richard was sixteen, and a junior at the Haverhill Trade School; he talked about maybe joining the Navy. Running down the stairs of the apartment building, he caught a glimpse of his downstairs neighbor Bacigalupo through a window, naked and holding a pan, muttering about a cigarette butt that had missed the can. He kept running out the door and all the way to the nearby fire station. By the time he ran back, the building was aflame. Looking up he saw his parents for the last time, trapped on an upstairs porch, screaming for help. The rest of that Sunday was a blur of interviews: news reporters, state fire marshals, the local police. He told the reporters about the neighbor, and the cigarette butt. But in his "state of shock," he neglected to mention those same details when he spoke to the police.[1]

At some point the fire marshal got it into his head that LaPlante was lying, that he was the one who set the fire, and also that he did it on purpose. An interrogation ensued. The boy denied it; the officials insisted. After several hours of this, the child gave up. He wrote in a statement that he had set fire to the building with a match, because he had never liked living in that building. He was taken to jail and booked on arson and five counts of manslaughter—two for his parents, three for the other residents of the building who had died. And then, almost as soon as he signed it, he recanted the statement. He told a probation officer who came to see him. He told the juvenile court chaplain. He told his parish priest. He told them all the same thing, "the police would not take no for an answer."[2]

LaPlante's fortune changed when Wilbur Hollingsworth agreed to represent him. For nineteen years, longer than LaPlante had been alive, Hollingsworth had served as the chief counsel of Boston's Voluntary Defenders Committee. He was, by virtue of this position, among the most experienced criminal defense lawyers in Massachusetts—described by Harvard Law School's dean, Erwin Griswold, as "a genius" in the courtroom—and he didn't charge for his services.[3] Hollingsworth discovered that the state had made no investigation of the fire, had not even inspected the remains of the building.

Nor had the police made any effort to track down the other surviving tenants to ask what they had seen. Fact by fact, witness by witness, Hollingsworth assembled the picture he would present to the jury. "No one set that fire," one of the victims had said in the hospital, shortly before he died. "It started in [Bacigalupo's] room from a cigarette." A relative of Bacigalupo explained that he was "nearly blind" and confirmed that he kept a bucket in his room for butts. Hollingsworth located the missing survivors, who told him they had seen smoke coming from Bacigalupo's room. They hadn't seen any fire in the hallway, where LaPlante's coerced statement placed it. Some of this evidence came in at trial, some of it was inadmissible for one reason or another, but Hollingsworth got the jury to see the case from the defendant's point of view. After five days of trial and five hours of deliberation, the jury announced its verdict: "Not guilty."[4]

Hollingsworth regarded *Commonwealth v. LaPlante* as among his most "satisfying victories." Later that year, he selected LaPlante's story to narrate as the central anecdote in his organization's annual fundraising pamphlet—the singular case, out of the 1,185 cases and 116 trials that the Voluntary Defenders Committee had handled in 1954, that best illustrated the importance of the committee's work. The pamphlet introduced the case as "a story that could not happen here because this is America."[5] With this phrase, Hollingsworth wryly invoked the midcentury conception of America as "a normative concept," trading upon the tendency in postwar discourse to extol the United States as the paragon of democracy.[6] Of course, it was not literally true that miscarriages of justice could not happen in America. In the 1950s, anyone who read crime novelist Erle Stanley Gardner's bestselling Perry Mason series might also know about Gardner's magazine column "The Court of Last Resort," which exposed real-world wrongful convictions.[7] But it was true that such things were not, according to the national mythology, supposed to happen. In the hot years of the Cold War, a false confession browbeaten out of a child smacked of tactics that Americans associated with their country's authoritarian enemies.[8] The story of *Commonwealth v. LaPlante* starkly connected Hollingsworth's daily toils in nondescript courtrooms with the global struggle to defend American values.

Yet the LaPlante case could have been narrated as a cautionary tale, one that exposed the weaknesses of the Voluntary Defenders Committee: its reliance on private donations, its necessarily selective assistance. When Hollingsworth received the phone call from Haverhill requesting help in LaPlante's case, he initially turned down the request. The committee's resources were extremely limited, he explained; ordinarily, he represented defendants in Boston and the immediate vicinity. If this was a Haverhill case, it would be tried in Essex County, and the Voluntary Defenders Committee didn't operate in Essex County. Given the tragic circumstances, Hollingsworth agreed to drive up and meet with the boy, but he made no promises. After he did some poking around, and realized what a hash the police had made—"I think it was the worst possible job of investigating," he told the *Boston Globe*—he agreed to make an exception and take the case.[9] Otherwise there was no telling what would have happened to LaPlante. Whatever happened every day to the typical defendant in Essex County—maybe the court appointed a lawyer who happened to be available but lacked Hollingsworth's knowhow; maybe friends attempted to hire a lawyer, with money they didn't have.

By the year of LaPlante's trial, Hollingsworth had doubts. Maybe his own organization was obsolete. Since its founding in 1935, the Voluntary Defenders Committee had assured donors that it provided counsel for "deserving men and women."[10] The committee was small and its funding tenuous; Hollingsworth had to make choices. Meanwhile, in a series of cases interpreting the constitutional requirement of due process, the Supreme Court had moved closer toward defining defense counsel not only as an aid to the defendant, but as essential to a fair trial. In their formal holdings, the justices did not yet require counsel in all cases. But in their asides, they intimated that modern law was too complicated to face without a lawyer. Deserving did not enter into it. Every defendant required expert assistance, not only to investigate the facts but also to identify potentially obscure legal challenges to the state's case. Like Hollingsworth, the Court related defense counsel to American democracy—describing counsel as a means of fulfilling those "immutable principles of justice which inhere in the very idea of free government."[11] Even as constitutional doctrine confirmed the significance of the Voluntary Defenders Committee's mission, it also posed an existential challenge. If legal representation was so important to American democracy, then perhaps it should be the government's obligation to provide.

BY 1940, VOLUNTARY DEFENDERS had been established in the three Eastern cities that together housed a large portion of the national legal elite: New York, Philadelphia, and Boston. Lawyers pointed in particular to New York's voluntary defender, now ensconced as the Criminal Courts Branch of the Legal Aid Society, as a model of "what can be done through voluntary, as distinguished from public, defenders."[12] In Manhattan, Legal Aid lawyers were routinely appointed to represent indigent defendants and appeared, in some courtrooms, in the majority of cases.[13] They had become, in one attorney's description, "an integral part of the legal machinery."[14] Following the New York example, Philadelphia's Defender Association opened in 1934, and Boston's Voluntary Defenders Committee the following year.[15] Both organizations enjoyed support from prominent local attorneys. The Philadelphia luminaries who had endorsed early plans for the Defender Association, in 1930, included the former U.S. attorney Francis Fisher Kane and the railroad lawyer, and soon-to-be Supreme Court justice, Owen Roberts.[16]

The case for the voluntary defender revolved around a single keyword: independence. Like their public counterparts, voluntary defenders defended individual rights, but they did so more effectively—the argument went—because they were unaffiliated with the state. This argument comported with a larger aversion among lawyers to government entanglement with the profession. In the late 1940s, American lawyers bristled at reports of an English program of public compensation for some forms of legal assistance. This was "socialization," and America might be next. Reginald Heber Smith responded with a detailed article that sought to reassure his peers that the English program, understood within context, was modest and did not amount in his view to socialism. But he agreed with the general proposition that public funding for lawyers presented serious risks. "To subsidize the medical profession may or may not be a wise thing," he wrote, "but to subsidize the legal profession involves something entirely different. The enemy of the doctor's patient is the disease; but the enemy of the lawyer's client may be the government itself." For the state to pay lawyers was akin to a situation where "the doctor's subsidies came from the microbes." In circumstances where public subsidy was unavoidable, it should be filtered through "the interposition of a strong, independent agency between the Government and the lawyer."[17]

In the realm of criminal defense, many lawyers believed that the safest approach was to avoid public subsidies altogether—and certainly to avoid public administration. A public defender, whether elected or appointed, might become enmeshed in local politics—the realm of ward bosses, spoils networks, and graft. LaRue Brown, the longtime board chair of Boston's Voluntary Defenders Committee, disparaged the public defender as prone to corruption and "subject to political pressure" in hiring decisions, "because politicians control the finances."[18] Brown was a self-described New Deal Democrat, but also a Protestant lawyer who had lived in Boston across the decades when Irish Catholics gained increasing political clout over local issues. Like many New England "Yankees," he viewed Boston's municipal offices, including the district attorney, as swamps of Irish patronage, and assumed that a public defender would become likewise bogged down.[19]

Independence, the argument went, would not only protect lawyers from improper hiring and firing; it would liberate those lawyers to zealously defend their clients, even in politically salient or high-profile cases. Herman Pollock, chief counsel of Philadelphia's Defender Association, cataloged the many ways in which his organization studiously maintained its independence—and, equally important, its appearance of independence. It was supported by private donations, "housed in a private office building" rather than the courthouse, formally constituted as a nonprofit corporation, and governed by a board "composed of leaders of the Philadelphia Bar," most of whom worked at private law firms. Together, all of these choices served "to make it plain that the Voluntary Defender is not a public official." No matter the case, Pollock wrote, and no matter how much "public resentment" against the defendant, his organization took no "'short cuts' which brush aside the defendant's legal rights. This a public defender might find more difficult to do."[20]

This rationale for the voluntary defender continued the debate begun during the Progressive Era, although it depended upon an increasingly outdated conception of the public defender. In the early twentieth century, some reformers had argued that public defenders should be legally defined as distinct from private defense attorneys. Instead of pursuing solely the interests of individual clients, they should be assigned the same general duty to pursue justice that bound public prosecutors. But the bar never embraced that idea, nor did practicing public defenders. In jurisdictions that actually established public defenders, they remained bound by the same legal and ethical duties to their clients as private attorneys. One longtime Los Angeles public defender explained, in 1948, that public defenders were "regularly admitted members of the bar," and therefore "subject to the same duties and obligations to the court and to their clients as an attorney in private practice."[21] Courts, too, generally rejected the argument that public employment did or should alter defenders' duty of loyalty to their clients. The California Supreme Court held that "when the public defender is appointed," he becomes the defendant's agent "to the same extent" as a hired lawyer. He remains "free from any restraint or domination by the district attorney," and "as free to act in behalf of his client as if he had been regularly employed and retained by the defendant he represents."[22]

Nevertheless, critics worried that regardless of how their duties were officially defined, public defenders would face pressure to soften their advocacy. They might encounter explicit political interference, or they might grow too friendly with judges and prosecutors. Owing their salaries to the state, they might feel some residual loyalty to the government. As they had done in earlier decades, some criminal defense lawyers continued to argue that the public defender violated due process, because "the public defender's master is the court rather than the client."[23] On this point, Herman Pollock dissented from the public defender's most strident critics, who wrote off the entire idea of public defense as "unsound in principle." Pollock emphasized that every lawyer had an obligation to defend his client's rights, and posited that there was no reason in theory why public defenders were categorically incapable of satisfying that obligation. But Pollock acknowledged that the public defender was more likely in practice to encounter "political pressures." The voluntary defender could "stand his ground" more confidently against a hostile judge or "an overzealous prosecutor." In this way, Pollock concluded, the voluntary defender came closest to providing "the indigent defendant" with the "independent representation traditionally enjoyed by those financially able to engage private counsel."[24]

The trope of cowering public defenders and fearless voluntary defenders overlooked countervailing facts on both sides of the ledger. As to public defenders, the evidence from jurisdictions that had adopted the reform implied a more nuanced picture. In the late 1940s, a federal prison official assessed public defenders in California, Connecticut, Illinois, Minnesota, and Nebraska, and reported that despite occasional complaints, all had assembled "generally good records."[25] The California experience furnished the occasional example of a public defender becoming mired in scandal. But it also furnished examples of public defenders providing diligent advocacy for extremely unpopular defendants, even in high-profile murder trials surrounded by public hysteria.[26] Conversely, the assumption that the voluntary defender was impervious to outside influence depended upon a narrow definition of political pressure. Voluntary defenders were potentially subject to pressure from benefactors and board members—a concern that was rarely discussed forthrightly by elite lawyers.

Over time, the voluntary defender also acquired a second justification: cost savings. This rationale was different from the familiar efficiency claim offered in the Progressive Era on behalf of both public and voluntary defenders, which posited that they would reduce court costs by avoiding unnecessary trials. Now, assuming some organized method of indigent defense, the voluntary defender was promoted as less costly relative to the public defender, because charitable organizations required less overhead. That was true for two reasons. First, voluntary defenders relied partly on unpaid or low-paid labor, including volunteer stints from lawyers in private practice and short-term employment of recent law school graduates. Second, even for permanent employees, voluntary defender organizations paid relatively low salaries—unlike public defenders who might be bound to civil service salary schedules.[27]

Voluntary defender salary scales instantiated the premise that indigent defense was not ordinary professional legal work, but either a training opportunity or, for the unusually altruistic lawyer, a noble endeavor whose rewards were not primarily material. Wilbur Hollingsworth earned a decent, if modest salary, around the median pay for a Massachusetts lawyer. But he was consistently paid less than his counterparts at urban public defender's offices in other states.[28] The pay gap was wider at the lower ranks. Hollingsworth was assisted by recent law graduates, who typically stayed for a year or two in order to gain trial experience before joining a private firm. This dynamic contrasted with public defender offices, where line defenders were long-term, civil-service employees.[29] Hollingsworth's assistants were unpaid in the organization's early years, and in later years, earned nominal salaries far below the norm for private practice.[30] Through the 1950s, Hollingsworth's assistants and secretaries earned "considerably" less than their counterparts in law firms, district attorney's offices, and even the Boston Legal Aid Society.[31] This arrangement was only partly dictated by budget constraints. LaRue Brown explained that the committee enjoyed "devoted service from underpaid staff members" because their "primary interest is the work they do [and] not what they get for it."[32] In a grant application, the committee disclosed that "hiring young lawyers" had "worked out so well over the years that it would probably be continued regardless of budgetary requirements."[33]

THE VOLUNTARY DEFENDER'S signal feature—private funding—was also its major shortcoming. Even proponents of the voluntary defender recognized this issue. Soliciting donations required continuous effort by staff and supporters and yielded volatile budgets. The New York voluntary defender, as part of the Legal Aid Society, received funding directly from individual benefactors and law firms, but neither the Philadelphia nor the Boston voluntary defenders developed a steady base of individual contributors. Instead, they came to receive most of their financial support through distributions from the local "community chest."[34] Such community funds, also known as "red feather" agencies, were established in many cities in the early twentieth century in order to consolidate charitable giving for the region into one umbrella organization. The community chest solicited donations from the general public each year and then distributed the proceeds to individual charitable groups.[35] For recipient organizations, participating in the community chest required annual negotiations over their share of the funds. To be sure, public appropriations might also require annual lobbying, but against the backstop of some legislative mandate to provide service, which voluntary defender organizations lacked. A public defender began by assessing who it had to serve and then petitioned for the requisite resources. Voluntary defenders began by assessing what resources they might be able to secure and then determined who they could serve.

Working within resource constraints, voluntary defenders allocated their assistance in various ways, ranging from simple geography to fuzzy conceptions of "worthiness." The New York Legal Aid Society's Criminal Courts Branch remained primarily limited to Manhattan; funds precluded consistent service for defendants in the outer boroughs, a constant source of frustration to the organization's supporters.[36] Boston's Voluntary Defenders Committee sought to "provide counsel for deserving men and women."[37] This formulation echoed a long-standing distinction in Anglo-American law and philanthropy between the "deserving" and the "undeserving" poor.[38] As a general approach, it was borrowed from civil legal aid societies, which developed detailed criteria to determine whether potential clients were "worthy" of assistance.[39] Voluntary defenders could not borrow exactly the same criteria, however; by definition, criminal defendants might not meet traditional standards of respectability for one reason or another. But, for instance, the committee might refuse to represent defendants who admitted their guilt yet refused to plead guilty, or who were "habitual criminals."[40]

The rhetoric contained in fundraising appeals, although likely unrepresentative of voluntary defenders' actual caseloads, provided insight into their assumptions about what types of defendants appeared most "worthy" to donors. The optimal clients were young men with no prior criminal history. They had found "themselves in jail" through no fault of their own, but rather "through some unfortunate set of circumstances" that left them falsely accused of "a crime they did not commit." They were "helpless to defend themselves," and ideally, "penniless." Bearing no responsibility for their situation, but also lacking the wherewithal to get themselves out of it, they were prime candidates for benevolence.[41] Richard LaPlante's case made an appealing fundraising story because, by all of these criteria, he was quintessentially "deserving." The *Boston Globe* coverage of the LaPlante trial revolved around a telling turn of phrase. Formally speaking, American juries decide only whether or not the government has proven the defendant "guilty." But the *Globe* reported that LaPlante "was found innocent."⁴²

At the other extreme were "professional criminals," whom the committee assured its donors that it did not represent. Such characters, the committee explained, had their own lawyers on retainer and did not seek out charitable help.⁴³ This disclaimer carried particular connotations. By the 1930s, the "gangster" had become a stock character in American popular culture, reinforced through fictional portrayals and sensationalistic news coverage of organized crime.⁴⁴ So, too, had the "lawyer criminal" who not only represented "gangsters" in court, but abetted them in concealing evidence and intimidating witnesses.⁴⁵ Any group asking for money to represent criminal defendants thus had to distinguish its work from these cultural associations. At the same time, the emphasis on the "penniless" quality of the voluntary defenders' clientele was also intended to reassure the legitimate private bar that they were not poaching business. Fundraising materials emphasized that the Voluntary Defenders Committee would not represent "anyone who can pay a lawyer."⁴⁶

Voluntary defenders' rhetorical emphasis on their clients' blamelessness also carried racial connotations, given the tendency of the legal category of innocence to become conflated with pernicious stereotypes. *Commonwealth v. LaPlante* offered an effective vehicle for presenting criminal defense as a generically American cause in part because it involved a white teenager (likely of French-Canadian descent, given his name, but ethnically unmarked in the Voluntary Defenders Committee's recounting of the case). American popular culture depicted white children as icons of purity and vulnerability, while withholding from black children any presumption of innocence and even denying their capacity to feel pain.⁴⁷ Layered atop those enduring cultural tropes were pseudoscientific rationalizations provided by the developing social sciences. Since the turn of the twentieth century, white social scientists had often described African Americans as uniquely prone to criminality.⁴⁸ How exactly such stereotypes shaped voluntary defenders' interactions with clients is difficult to glean from the annual reports. Hollingsworth's case summaries occasionally identified clients as "colored," but only in passing.⁴⁹ Still, racial ideology likely factored into the Voluntary Defenders Committee's worthiness determinations, at least implicitly, and certainly shaped how they presented their work to the public.

The extent to which voluntary defenders actually rejected would-be clients varied, both across organizations and over time. Some organizations presented their criteria in blunt terms. The Legal Aid Society of Pittsburgh, for instance, explained that its criminal division had the following policy: "If the client is guilty, he must plead guilty, or the voluntary defender refuses to handle the case."[50] As they gained experience, some defenders seem to have adopted a more flexible attitude. One New York voluntary defender recalled a client who insisted upon his innocence, though he had a long criminal history and an eyewitness had identified him as the culprit. The defender duly investigated; confirmed that the client did, in fact, have an alibi; and eventually convinced the district attorney to drop all charges. This case, the defender wrote, had taught him about the danger of "jumping too quickly to conclusions." It was not the attorney's job to serve as jury, and "if the defendant asserts his innocence," no matter how skeptical the lawyer remained, "the duty of the lawyer is to defend the prisoner according to the law, and invoke every defense which the law of the land permits."[51]

Worthiness seems to have functioned in some settings less as a fixed criterion than as a proxy for limited resources. In cities with the best-funded voluntary defenders—New York and Philadelphia—the worthiness formulation played a less prominent role even as rhetoric. New York supporters of the Legal Aid Society used the concept of worthiness to refer to financial need, not a character assessment.[52] In 1938, Wilbur Hollingsworth traveled from Boston to Philadelphia to meet his counterparts at the Defender Association and came away impressed by the differences. He reported that the Philadelphia defenders were more open to representing anyone who requested assistance and "more inclined to accept a defendant's story at its face value."[53] In Boston, by contrast, the Voluntary Defenders Committee remained persistently underfunded and unable to represent every would-be client. But even there, in years when the committee's budget expanded, it also became less likely to reject clients.[54] Still, the worthiness construct perpetuated a distinctive logic. It attributed to donors and lawyers the authority to decide whether or why the poor should receive legal assistance. That logic distinguished private charity from both the public defender model, which defined legal assistance as a universal service, and the ideal of the free market, in which private actors decided for themselves whether or why to hire a lawyer.

BY FRAMING INDIGENT DEFENSE as closer to volunteer service than professional legal work, the voluntary defender also tended to reinforce hierarchies within the legal profession. Notwithstanding this framing, some lawyers built distinguished careers as voluntary defenders. Hollingsworth remained at the Voluntary Defenders Committee for decades, and his counterpart in

Philadelphia, Herman Pollock, worked at the Defender Association from the 1940s through the late 1960s. In New York, Florence Kelley served for many years as head of the Criminal Courts Branch of the Legal Aid Society.[55] Overall, though, elite lawyers tended to regard such figures as exceptional and to define indigent defense as training fodder more than a career path.

In 1949, a group of Harvard law students formed a club to aid Hollingsworth and his staff. The next year, the law school recognized their group as an official student organization, awarding them office space and an annual subsidy. The Harvard Voluntary Defenders, as they became known, conducted legal research, interviewed clients in jail, tracked down witnesses, and appeared at arraignments.[56] Perhaps aggrandizing their involvement, they soon boasted that they had relieved Hollingsworth's "overworked staff from most of their jail, investigatory, and district (lower) court work."[57] Harvard's dean, Erwin Griswold, praised the program as a "considerable bargain," enabling "one lawyer operating out of the Boston office," in Suffolk County, to also serve clients in Cambridge, in neighboring Middlesex County, for "a very small expenditure of money." To Griswold, the legal problems of the poor could be "effective[ly]" handled by "young Law students . . . in their spare time."[58]

Griswold's view of indigent defense as a law student community service project, rather than a professional specialty, mattered not because Harvard was representative of American law schools—in resources and prestige, it was not—but because Griswold was enormously influential. During his tenure as Harvard's dean, from 1946 to 1967, Griswold became perhaps the single most "dominant figure in American legal education."[59] Law schools around the country had emulated Harvard since the late nineteenth century, when Harvard pioneered the "case method," in which courses focused on the parsing of appellate opinions. In the twentieth century, Harvard continued to serve as a model, both formally and informally. The American Bar Association and the American Association of Law Schools, which set accreditation requirements, often embraced standards introduced at Harvard; and nationwide, Harvard was the alma mater of a disproportionate number of law professors.[60] This influence channeled national discourse about legal education in pedagogically conservative directions. Griswold oversaw some significant reforms (such as opening Harvard Law to women, in 1950) but remained a staunch traditionalist in his views about the curriculum, emphasizing rigorous study of the law's internal logic and opposing efforts to incorporate social science perspectives.[61] He also urged law schools to tighten admissions requirements. America had "too many lawyers," Griswold opined, and legal education was not suitable for "those who are not endowed by nature with a reasonably high quantum of intellectual ability."[62]

As implied by Griswold's description of the Harvard Voluntary Defenders as a "spare time" activity, he neither expected nor encouraged students to pursue careers in criminal defense, and certainly not indigent defense. Harvard faculty, under Griswold's leadership, exalted corporate practice in a Wall Street law firm as the "ideal career type," adhering to the status ladder established in the early twentieth century.[63] As late as 1964, Anthony Lewis explained to his readers that "the typical American lawyer"—Lewis's term for the typical elite lawyer—"tends to look down on the 'criminal bar' as a collection of grubby characters who cannot make a go of it in the more remunerative corporate practice."[64] The curriculum at elite law schools reinforced the message. At Harvard, students took advanced courses in corporations, taxation, and financial accounting, but only one introductory course in criminal law.[65] The school made little effort to facilitate job placements in noncorporate positions, such as legal aid or even government.[66] Accordingly, among the twenty-eight students in the class of 1958 who participated in the Harvard Voluntary Defenders, none was working as a public or voluntary defender ten years after graduation, and only one was in government service, at the federal Department of Justice.[67]

The Voluntary Defenders Committee replicated, in microcosm, this professional hierarchy. Wilbur Hollingsworth, who handled the day-to-day work of managing the office and trying cases, had earned his law degree through night classes at the working-class Suffolk Law School.[68] He was overseen by a board of directors, composed primarily of lawyers in private practice.[69] Throughout Hollingsworth's tenure as chief counsel, the board was chaired by LaRue Brown, a graduate of Phillips Exeter, Harvard College, and Harvard Law School, a college classmate of Franklin Roosevelt, and a prominent lawyer who had served in the Wilson and Harding administrations.[70] Hollingsworth scuffled with the board about management decisions large and small. Board members, and other elite supporters, respected his skill as a criminal lawyer but regarded him as an idiosyncratic purist, stubborn and uncompromising in situations that required flexibility and moderation.[71] Still, they admired Hollingsworth's commitment to the work and thought he was excessively humble about his trial achievements. "Wilbur," one board member wrote, "is a bright star of a purity far beyond most of us."[72]

TRIAL LAWYERS LIKE Wilbur Hollingsworth moved quickly, on the surface of the law. They visited local courthouses each day and proved facts and made objections to lines of questioning. Each case had its peculiarities, but across hundreds of cases their work developed certain rhythms. For months or even years, the rules of the game did not change much. Deep beneath their feet the tectonic plates of constitutional law moved slowly, often imperceptibly. Sometimes they sent tremors up to the surface. Every once in a while, an earthquake. Over the course of Hollingsworth's career, the tremors became more frequent. What was moving the plates was litigation over a single, enormously consequential snippet of constitutional text: Section One of the Fourteenth Amendment, which provides that "no state" may "deprive any person of life, liberty, or property, without due process of law."[73]

The Fourteenth Amendment—ratified in 1868 as the price of the Southern states' readmission into the Union—combined something medieval with something new. Jurists traced the idea of due process back to Runnymede in 1215, when King John gave in to the rebel barons' demands and promised, in Magna Carta, never to harm a freeman except "by the law of the land."[74] In the early United States, due process found expression in the Fifth Amendment to the federal constitution and in comparable provisions in the state constitutions. The specific procedures "due" depended on the context, but due process signified, fundamentally, a protection against capricious rule.[75] What was new about the Fourteenth Amendment was to take due process out of the Anglo-American cultural ether and pin it down into a uniform federal standard. Before the Civil War, federal and state interpretations of due process could proceed on separate tracks. Even within a given state, judicial practices might vary from place to place.[76] The Fourteenth Amendment bound all states to a common national benchmark of procedural fairness. And whatever that benchmark entailed, it would be enforceable not only in the state courts—which might hesitate to criticize themselves—but potentially in the federal courts too.[77]

In a series of challenges to mob-dominated trials in the Jim Crow South, civil rights lawyers pressed the Supreme Court to specify the requirements of constitutional due process in the context of criminal proceedings. After the fall of Reconstruction, white Southerners had sought to reassert their social, political, and economic dominance through means both legal and extralegal. The "Redeemer" governments that recaptured control of the Southern states in the 1880s and 1890s had rewritten criminal codes to specify harsher punishments for black convicts, and through any number of both formal and informal decisions, police and prosecutors had channeled their authority toward the maintenance of white control over black people (and black labor).[78] By the twentieth century, Southern criminal law had settled into patterns that would long endure, with black defendants accused, convicted, and sentenced to prison at disproportionate rates.[79] Lynching, if narrowly defined as a mob ritual of extralegal violence, declined in frequency in the twentieth century, but activists accused Southern courts of taking over the job, arguing that the underlying phenomenon of racial terror had merely mutated into legalistic forms. White elites had learned to channel mob outrage into hasty, perfunctory trials, often with a lynch mob lying in wait to complete the job if the jury did not. Defendants convicted under such conditions argued that due process required a meaningful trial, not an empty ritual with a foregone conclusion.[80]

The Supreme Court's response to Jim Crow injustice yielded two doctrinal developments that would eventually have ramifications for lawyers and legal institutions around the country—including Wilbur Hollingsworth. First, the Supreme Court confirmed that the Fourteenth Amendment could be used as a vehicle for federal review of state-level criminal trials. *Moore v. Dempsey*, decided in 1923, held that a mob-dominated trial in state court would violate the Fourteenth Amendment's due process guarantee.[81] *Moore* stemmed from the Elaine, Arkansas, race riots of 1919. After hundreds of white men massacred over a hundred African Americans, a group of black men was rushed to conviction on trumped-up capital murder charges. They argued that they had received a trial "in form," but "only [in] form." Writing for the Supreme Court, Justice Oliver Wendell Holmes, Jr., reasoned that a trial fell short of due process if "the whole proceeding [was] a mask," with the verdict overdetermined "by an irresistible wave of public passion." The Court remanded the case to the lower federal court, in Arkansas, with instructions to conduct a factual inquiry into whether mob justice had, indeed, so infected the trial as to render it invalid.[82] *Moore* established that due process required something more than superficial courtroom formalities, and also confirmed that state prisoners could file habeas petitions in the federal courts to seek outside review of their state court convictions.[83]

Second, the Supreme Court highlighted defense counsel as an important ingredient, if not yet an absolute requirement, of due process. Holmes's opinion in *Moore* introduced what would prove an enduring puzzle for American jurists: how to tell that a legal process was infused with some genuine juridical spirit? For radical leftists, this question was easy to answer. Under capitalism, all criminal trials were shams. Even if an individual defendant seemed to receive some measure of justice, it was a show to lull the masses. This view derived from Marx and Engels themselves, who described law as a façade for "bourgeois interests," a tool that the ruling classes molded as needed in order to justify and entrench their rule.[84] For Southern reactionaries, the question was equally straightforward. All criminal trials were real. Lynching meant extralegal violence, detached from any judicial process. By definition, providing a trial within a courthouse, overseen by a judge, was not a lynching (even if the same individual was sentenced to die by the same people who otherwise would have constituted the lynch mob).[85] Illustrating that position, *Moore* occasioned a revealing dissent from the infamously disagreeable and racist Justice James Clark McReynolds, who dismissed the Elaine habeas proceedings as an instance of "five negroes" contriving "to escape electrocution" despite having been convicted in what he considered a perfectly adequate trial.[86] For everyone in between, the question proved vexing. Liberal jurists, unlike radical leftists, regarded the courts as basically legitimate; but unlike McReynolds, they recognized that courtroom rituals could be mimicked in the service of illegitimate ends. Although a venerable phrase in the Anglo-American legal tradition, the practical meaning of due process remained surprisingly elusive—"as elastic as rubber," in the words of then-senator, and future Supreme Court justice, Hugo Black.[87]

As jurists fumbled for metrics of a meaningful trial, defense counsel emerged as a useful indicator: whether the defendant had been represented by counsel at all, and if so, how actively counsel had participated in the trial. Like due process, the association between a zealous lawyer and a fair trial had both deep and green roots in Anglo-American legal culture. Lawyers for the accused first began to appear in seventeenth-century England, in treason trials, as wealthy aristocrats accused of intrigue against the Crown hired attorneys to defend them. Over the centuries, the lawyering rituals developed in these high-level affairs of state migrated across the ocean and downwards—first to murder trials, where the American courts had a long tradition of appointing counsel, and sometimes even into ordinary felony trials. Departing from informal traditions in which the parties spoke directly to the judge, lawyers seized control of courtrooms, honing expert tactics for examining witnesses and adhering to arcane rules of evidence.[88] Each generation of lawyers made legal proceedings more complex, heightening the next generation's need for lawyers. In the twentieth century this long-term process gained velocity. In the early United States, local court proceedings had remained relatively informal; in villages where everyone knew one another—for better or often for worse—legal disputes intertwined with everyday life and trials doubled as social occasions. Even serious criminal accusations were often settled between the parties outside of court, and when cases did proceed to trial, what determined the outcome was less the letter of the law than the adversaries' relative reputations in the community.[89] In the twentieth century, criminal proceedings became more formalized. Courtrooms became nodes in an expanding bureaucracy of police, social workers, and other agents of the state who sought to impose order upon urban life. Prosecutors became salaried state officials rather than part-time functionaries and redefined their mandate not in terms of resolving neighborly disputes, but in terms of strictly enforcing the law.[90]

As the courts became professionalized, counsel began to play the role that Anglo-American legal culture had once assigned to the jury: the procedural device that served to protect all the defendant's other rights. In the eighteenth century, the American revolutionaries had rallied around the banner of "trial by jury" as the guarantor of fair procedure and as a symbol of the limitations on government essential to republican governance. Along with legislative representation, trial by jury was given pride of place as a foundational protection that, if "left to operate in full force . . . would shelter nearly all the other rights and liberties of the people."[91] In twentieth-century doctrine and commentary, jurists assigned to the right to counsel a similarly overarching quality as "the 'most pervasive right' of an accused," "the master key to all the rules and procedures designed to achieve . . . due process."[92] Juries had not disappeared, even if their significance had diminished in practice with the rise of plea bargaining.[93] But even if a criminal case proceeded to a jury trial, it was lawyers who walked the jury through the evidence. By the end of the twentieth century, the Supreme Court could observe that it was virtually impossible for "an unaided layman" to prevail in court; every criminal defendant required "a guide through complex legal technicalities." Under modern conditions, "the assistance of counsel" was nearly "a requisite to the very existence of a fair trial."[94]

The Supreme Court's doctrinal elevation of counsel would take decades fully to work itself out, but it began in the 1930s, in the context of another Jim Crow "legal lynching" case. *Powell v. Alabama*, decided in 1932, emerged from the notorious Scottsboro prosecutions, in which nine black teenagers were tried and sentenced to death within a matter of days after false allegations that they had raped two white women on a train.[95] The case became a worldwide scandal, and the Communist Party's legal arm, the International Labor Defense, hired the prominent civil liberties attorney Walter Pollak to brief and argue the defendants' appeal before the Supreme Court.[96] Pollak argued that the defendants were denied due process because, among many reasons, they received cursory legal representation. The trial judge appointed a local lawyer for the defendants, but he met them an hour before the trial and took no steps to investigate or prepare. During the trial, the defense made some attempts at cross-examining the state's witnesses, but offered no opening or closing statements and proposed no jury instructions.[97] If "anything was to be done for the boys" in Scottsboro, Pollak argued, "it was only counsel that could do it." Instead, the defendants had been so weakly defended that there had been "in the constitutional sense no representation by counsel."[98]

The Supreme Court agreed, reversing the Scottsboro convictions in a nearly unanimous decision. Given the importance of counsel to a fair and reliable trial, *Powell* held that the Scottsboro court should have afforded the defendants more time to arrange for legal representation, and also that if the defendants had proven unable to secure counsel on their own, the trial judge had a duty to appoint "effective," and not merely "pro forma," counsel. This holding, the Court continued, with a pointed instruction to the once rebellious South, followed from "immutable principles of justice which inhere in the very idea of free government which no member of the Union may disregard." Without addressing what due process required in more routine prosecutions, *Powell* held that, at minimum, effective defense counsel was necessary to a fair trial under the circumstances present in Scottsboro: "a capital case, where the defendant is unable to employ counsel, and is incapable adequately of making his own defense because of ignorance, feeble-mindedness, illiteracy, or the like."[99]

Powell had limited practical significance in the short term. Doctrinally, it broke little new ground, because every state already made some provision for appointed counsel in capital trials.[100] For the Scottsboro defendants themselves, *Powell* was only one turning point in a decades-long ordeal of retrials and appeals, as Alabama prosecutors continued to double down on their theory of the case. Nor did *Powell* generate immediate change for black defendants in the South generally, most of whom continued to be represented, if at all, by less-than-zealous court-appointed lawyers.[101] Yet for all of its limitations, *Powell* appeared "spectacular" to legal scholars at the time, whose point of comparison was the Supreme Court's prior history of near-total reticence on local injustice. Before cases like *Moore* and *Powell*, the Court had almost never interfered with the results of a state criminal trial. Now, the Court had signaled a new intention to use "vigorous and orthodox application of the due process clause" as a vehicle "to insure a fair trial in the state courts."[102]

Powell's rhetoric would ultimately prove as consequential as its specific intervention into the Scottsboro case. The Court's opinion contained what remains the classic, and often quoted, disquisition on the role of defense counsel in American criminal procedure. Writing for the Court, Justice George Sutherland spelled out how the "right to be heard" implicit in due process depended, in turn, upon "the right to be heard by counsel":

> Even the intelligent and educated layman has small and sometimes no skill in the science of law. If charged with crime, he is incapable, generally, of determining for himself whether the indictment is good or bad. He is unfamiliar with the rules of evidence. Left without the aid of counsel he may be put on trial without a proper charge, and convicted upon incompetent evidence, or evidence irrelevant to the issue or otherwise inadmissible. He lacks both the skill and knowledge adequately to prepare his defense, even though he have a perfect one. He requires the guiding hand of counsel at every step in the proceedings against him. Without it, though he be not guilty, he faces the danger of conviction because he does not know how to establish his innocence. If that be true of men of intelligence, how much more true is it of the ignorant and illiterate, or those of feeble intellect.[103]

Technically this passage amounted to what lawyers call *obiter dicta*, incidental observations not strictly necessary to deciding the case at hand, and therefore not binding precedent. Such observations often reveal more about the justices' background assumptions than their painstakingly delimited holdings. The passage expressed doubt that anyone without formal training in criminal law and the rules of evidence, no matter how "educated" he might otherwise be, could defend himself in a modern courtroom. If accepted, that premise would seemingly apply to most, if not all criminal cases, and certainly could not be readily limited to circumstances as extreme as Scottsboro.

In a separate line of doctrine concerning federal criminal procedure, the justices soon confirmed what *Powell* had hinted: that they considered counsel essential to a fair trial even in the most humdrum of prosecutions. If it might require a Scottsboro-scale outrage for the Depression-era Supreme Court to intervene in a state criminal case, the justices had few qualms about prescribing requirements for federal criminal trials, for both doctrinal and institutional reasons. Doctrinally, whether the Bill of Rights applied to the states remained a subject of complicated jurisprudential debate through the early twentieth century. But everyone agreed that the federal courts were bound not only by the Constitution's general guarantee of due process, but also by the more specific requirements for criminal prosecutions spelled out in the Bill of Rights. Institutionally, the norm of federalism counseled a cautious approach to Supreme Court intervention in state matters. But the Court had direct authority over the lower federal courts.

In the 1938 case of *Johnson v. Zerbst,* the Court announced a blanket requirement of defense counsel in federal criminal trials. John Johnson and a fellow Marine were on shore leave in Charleston, South Carolina, when they were arrested on federal charges for possessing $500 in counterfeit twenty-dollar bills. At trial, Johnson represented himself, assuring the jury, unavailingly, that he could not be a "hoodlum . . . because they didn't keep [hoodlums] in the Marine Corps." Justice Hugo Black, then in his first term on the Court, wrote that Johnson's conviction violated the Sixth Amendment, which guarantees "the assistance of counsel" in "all criminal prosecutions." If Johnson could not secure counsel on his own, the federal district court should have offered to appoint counsel before allowing the trial to proceed.[104] With little fanfare, this holding upended the traditional interpretation of the Sixth Amendment. Traditionally, English courts forbade defense counsel from appearing in felony trials on the theory that the facts could be more readily ascertained if the accused responded in his own voice to the allegations against him. The Sixth Amendment expressed the American framers' rejection of the English rule (a rule that was fast eroding even within England by the eighteenth century). It assured defendants in federal criminal prosecutions the right to have a lawyer speak for them in court, if they chose.[105] *Johnson* went further, reading the assistance-of-counsel clause not merely to permit but also to require defense counsel. The only exception to this requirement was if the defendant himself willfully chose to forgo counsel. Otherwise, any defendant accused of a federal crime must have a lawyer, appointed by the court if needed, or the court would lack jurisdiction to try the case.[106]

Johnson did not apply to the states, but only because it relied upon the Sixth Amendment, which had not yet been incorporated against the states. Otherwise, Justice Black's explanation of the importance of counsel was not based on qualities specific to the federal courts. Describing defense counsel as a safeguard for the "fundamental human rights of life and liberty," Black opined that the framers had allowed for counsel because they recognized "the obvious truth that the average defendant does not have the professional legal skill to protect himself." That was especially true, Black continued, when "the prosecution is presented by experienced and learned counsel. That which is simple, orderly, and necessary to the lawyer—to the untrained layman—may appear intricate, complex, and mysterious."[107] The state courts equally threatened life and liberty, and state law was presumably equally "mysterious" to the layman. If and when the Court chose, this reasoning could readily be extended to require counsel in the state courts.[108]

Johnson, like *Powell*, was significant less for its immediate practical consequences than for the portent that it represented. Congress defined many new federal crimes in the twentieth century, but ultimately the scope of federal criminal law remained limited to conduct bearing some connection with federal interests or interstate commerce; the states wielded much broader authority to regulate day-to-day life. Therefore, the vast majority of criminal trials continued to take place in the state courts and were not bound by *Johnson*'s requirement of counsel.[109] But *Johnson*'s reception hinted at what might happen if the Court did extend a similar requirement to the states. *Johnson* mandated counsel in all federal criminal prosecutions but left uncertain how the lower federal courts should respond institutionally. Each federal district worked out its own methods of complying, either appointing private counsel case-by-case or making arrangements with local public or voluntary defenders in regions where they existed.[110] Proposed legislation to establish federal public defenders languished, and into the late 1950s, Congress had made no provision to compensate counsel for indigent federal defendants.[111] Notably, however, federal public defender legislation was endorsed by the American Bar Association as early as 1939, at a time when many lawyers still preferred privately funded or ad hoc counsel in their local communities.[112] *Johnson* and its professional reception offered a preview of a future dynamic. Once counsel was defined as a right, then it became associated even among the relatively conservative legal establishment with public provision.

THE TREMORS RIPPLED northward. In the spring of 1942, as total war raged around the globe, the justices of the United States Supreme Court hunkered down to deliberate about the fate of a Maryland farmhand. Smith Betts was serving an eight-year sentence for robbery. At the time of his trial in state court, Betts was "out of a job and on relief," and "too poor to hire a lawyer."[113] He asked the trial judge to appoint a lawyer, but the judge refused: the local rule was to appoint counsel for the indigent only in murder and rape cases. Betts, therefore, had no choice but to represent himself. He waived his right to a jury and instead requested a bench trial, in which the judge alone hears the evidence and then issues a verdict. Betts did his best to cross-examine the prosecution's witnesses. The judge, nevertheless, found him guilty. Betts filed for habeas in federal court, asserting that the denial of counsel rendered his conviction constitutionally invalid.

Betts v. Brady squarely placed before the Court the question of whether due process required defense counsel in all criminal prosecutions. In *Powell*, the Court could rely upon the defendants' youth and other unique vulnerabilities, as well as the life-and-death stakes of a capital trial, to portray the Scottsboro case as exceptional. The routine facts of *Betts* meant that ruling in the defendant's favor would necessarily create broadly applicable precedent. Betts was forty-three years old at the time of the trial, and robbery was a run-of-the-mill charge. In one out of three states, there was no uniform policy or practice of providing counsel in such cases.[114] Even in states that purported to guarantee counsel under state law, practices remained highly localized. Outside of cities, there were few public or voluntary defender organizations; it was doubtful whether most states were providing effective counsel in every single case, as the federal courts might demand on habeas review. Thus, when Betts asked the Court to hold "that, in every case, whatever the circumstances, one charged with crime, who is unable to obtain counsel, must be furnished counsel by the state," he was asking for a rule that would have required significant legal and practical change across the country.[115]

Given the choice between aligning the federal and state standards and avoiding widespread disruption for the state courts, the Supreme Court balked. In a 6-3 decision, the Court held that the Constitution permitted Maryland's denial of Betts's request for a lawyer. *Johnson* had established that, in the abstract, a majority of justices considered legal representation an essential ingredient of a fair and reliable trial. In settings that they directly supervised, like the lower federal courts, they were willing to enforce counsel as a jurisdictional requirement. *Betts* confirmed that a majority of justices nevertheless remained reluctant to impose the same requirement upon the state courts. That federalism overrode personal sympathies was indicated by the fact that the *Betts* majority opinion was written by Justice Owen Roberts, who, while still in private practice, had endorsed Philadelphia's Defender Association. Along with other bar leaders, he had signed his name to a pamphlet lamenting the "large number" of Philadelphians tried each year without counsel, and proposing a voluntary defender to reduce "the exploitation of helpless and ignorant defendants."[116] *Betts* asked, essentially, whether such appeals to professional charity also rose to the level of constitutional requirements, and to that question, Roberts answered no. Expanding the availability of indigent defense might promote justice in a general sense, but individual defendants did not necessarily have an enforceable right to legal representation in their particular cases.

However, *Betts* left the door wide open to revisiting the question. Justice Roberts's opinion declined to articulate any clear rule for when counsel had to be appointed. Due process, he explained, could not be reduced to "hard and fast rules"; it was "fluid." Determining whether a trial comported with due process required a holistic appraisal of "the totality of facts." "That which may, in one setting," appear "shocking to the universal sense of justice," could, "in other circumstances," appear reasonably fair. Denying a poor defendant's request for a lawyer might violate due process under some circumstances, but not others. It depended upon all the nuances: the severity of the crime alleged, the complexity of the facts and the law involved, the defendant's level of education.[117] In contrast to the straightforward *Johnson* rule that governed the federal courts, the due process precedents that governed the state courts now provided bipolar guidance. If the case was akin to Scottsboro, counsel must be appointed; if the defendant resembled Smith Betts, counsel need not be provided. How trial judges should handle all of the factual permutations in between, the Court pointedly left open for future, case-by-case elaboration.[118]

Writing in dissent, Justice Black questioned whether Betts had received a reliable trial. If Black alone had been deciding the case, it would have been straightforward: Black endorsed the constitutional theory of "total incorporation"—the view that the Fourteenth Amendment was intended to apply to the states the same limitations on government power that are enumerated in the Bill of Rights.[119] Under this theory, the Sixth Amendment right to counsel, as interpreted in *Johnson*, extended to the state courts and there was no need to engage in a separate, holistic due process analysis. Black also cited basic equality concerns. In Black's view, if a lawyer could reduce the risk of conviction, then not having a lawyer logically increased that risk, and it was unequal to operate a legal process that "subjects innocent men to increased dangers of conviction merely because of their poverty." But finally—and illustrating the malleability of the majority's "fluid" approach to due process—Black also disagreed with the *Betts* majority on its own terms, arguing that even applying the majority's flexible standard, Betts should prevail. In Black's reading of the record, the trial transcripts made clear that Betts had "little education," and it was not credible to maintain that he had managed his own trial as ably as a trained lawyer would have. As a result, there was no way of knowing whether Betts was in fact guilty; his case had never been "adequately presented."[120]

Betts v. Brady also sparked the ire of two lawyers then working in the Roosevelt administration, Benjamin Cohen and, notably, Erwin Griswold—the future Harvard dean, and not always an especially critical voice. Together, they published a blistering letter in the *New York Times* decrying Betts's trial as offensive to "basic ideas of civilized procedure" and identifying "the right to counsel, for the poor as well as the rich," as an "indispensable safeguard of freedom."[121] They accused the Supreme Court of denigrating this essential right "at a singularly inopportune time," in a moment when soldiers around the world were "fighting to be free from the fear of political trials and concentration camps." In the Court's reluctance to stiffen up the meaning of due process, Cohen and Griswold saw flickers of the illiberal regimes that the United States was battling. "[I]n a free world," they insisted, "no man should be condemned to penal servitude for years without having the right to counsel to defend him."[122]

Cohen and Griswold's criticism of *Betts* relied upon a dynamic conception of due process, which they agreed with the Court was "fluid," but in the sense that it could change over time, not that it should be permitted to vary from place to place. "History in the making is fluid," they wrote, and conceptions of due process could not remain "static": "a hundred and sixty years of experience justifies an expanding rather than a contracting recognition of what the right to counsel means in a democracy in the twentieth century."[123] Cohen and Griswold also disputed the Court's definition of what counted as evidence of collective intuitions about due process. Justice Roberts, in his *Betts* opinion, had relied on "law on the books," providing an exhaustive survey of relevant laws in all forty-eight states, filling entire pages nearly black with footnotes of small print. This research demonstrated that states had historically varied, both from one another and over time, as to whether or when courts were formally required to appoint counsel in felony cases; policymakers deemed the matter an issue of "legislative policy" rather than of fundamental rights.[124] Cohen and Griswold instead referenced the experiential insights of "law in action," what lawyers and officials actually did. In a revealingly tangled sentence, they wrote: "if a due regard for due process requires a modern community to provide legal aid or a public defender for its indigent members, there is no compelling reason for the courts to relieve the community of its responsibilities."[125] As this syntax papered over, whether indigent defense was required by due process was precisely the question. If Justice Roberts apparently regarded local defender initiatives as gratuitous aid beyond the constitutional minimum, or perhaps as simply tangential to the jurisprudential concept of due process, Cohen and Griswold interpreted new experiments as instantiations of the most up-to-date intuitions about fairness. The Court should constitutionalize those intuitions, they argued; instead, *Betts v. Brady* had sent the message that they were optional.

Cohen and Griswold's views could not yet command a majority of the Supreme Court, but *Betts* would not prove the backward step that they feared. Six years later, the Court restated the *Betts* rule in more expansive terms, holding that due process "requires counsel for all persons charged with serious crimes, when necessary for their adequate defense."[126] While still not a categorical rule in form, this formulation took the Court several steps closer toward a blanket requirement of counsel: the only remaining puzzle-piece was to eliminate the "when necessary" clause, or achieve the same result by specifying that counsel was always "necessary for [an] adequate defense." Case-by-case, the Court edged closer to such a result. No one knew it yet, but a little-remembered case called *Quicksall v. Michigan*, decided in 1950, would prove the last time that a majority of the Supreme Court voted to affirm a serious criminal conviction in a case where the defendant was prosecuted without a lawyer. Quicksall had pled guilty to first-degree murder—and a life sentence—without legal representation; but because he had not specifically requested counsel, the Court did not find a due process violation.[127]

After 1950, both the Supreme Court and the lower federal courts overturned a growing number of state convictions owing to the defendant's lack of counsel. Technically, the governing doctrine remained the rule of *Betts*: counsel was required only in cases involving "special circumstances."[128] Eventually, though, the Supreme Court began finding the requisite "special circumstances" in every right-to-counsel case that it decided. Notwithstanding any personal characteristics of the defendant, the simple fact that criminal statutes were complicated might constitute a circumstance requiring defense counsel: "the labyrinth of the law" had become "too intricate for the layman to master."[129] It was happening more gradually than Justice Black might have preferred, and too late to help Smith Betts, but the Court appeared bound toward the requirement of counsel that Betts had asked for back in 1942.

BACK IN BOSTON, the ground was quaking. Wary observers pronounced the post-*Betts* line of cases "a grave problem for Massachusetts."[130] In an annual report, the Voluntary Defenders Committee summarized the case law: "the Court has not yet announced a rule that every defendant must be represented," but it was only a matter of when. "The time is fast arriving when the conviction of the defendant in a criminal case who is not represented by counsel will be reversed as a matter of course."[131] Meanwhile, a survey revealed that half of Massachusetts defendants lacked legal representation; into the 1950s, Massachusetts remained one of the few states (along with a handful of Southern states) where state law continued to guarantee appointed counsel only in first-degree murder cases.[132] That translated into thousands of convictions each year that were vulnerable to reversal, in which case the state would either have to retry the defendant, which was not always feasible, or release them.

Another omen was the appointment as chief justice, in 1954, of Earl Warren, former governor of California and a one-time district attorney. Early in his tenure, the Warren Court foreshadowed its special concern for criminal defendants, and especially for indigent criminal defendants. The 1956 case of *Griffin v. Illinois* concerned an eminently mundane matter: the Illinois practice of charging a fee for stenographic trial transcripts. The problem was that the state courts would not hear a criminal appeal unless provided with copies of the transcripts. *Griffin* invalidated the fee as unfair to the indigent: states could not charge for a service while also making the use of that service a condition for accessing the courts. Contained within the *Griffin* opinion was a bold pronouncement about the relationship between due process, equal protection, and economic inequality: "There can be no equal justice where the kind of trial a man gets depends on the amount of money he has."[133] No one yet knew how literally the Warren Court planned to enforce this sentiment. The kind of trial a man got did depend, in many ways, upon the amount of money he had. The rich man who ran afoul of the law could buy advantages—high-priced lawyers, but also investigators, psychiatric evaluations, expert witnesses, bail, a fancy suit—that the masses of poor people charged with crime every day could not. Which of this panoply of imbalances the Court would attempt to equalize, and how, remained to be seen. But with *Betts* already wearing thin, counsel seemed like an obvious next step. In 1960, the attorney general of Massachusetts predicted that it was "just a question of time" before the Supreme Court overruled *Betts* and announced a constitutional requirement of counsel in every criminal case.[134]

At the Voluntary Defenders Committee, board members felt the tremors and hatched a plan: it was time to expand the voluntary defender statewide. Traditionally, the committee's work had been centered in Boston. But perhaps, with an infusion of donations, the organization could serve all of Massachusetts. If the courts defined counsel as a constitutional right, board members predicted, then the state would have to develop some organized method for providing counsel; it could no longer rely upon the "haphazard system of appointing members of the Bar." The question was whether the new organized method would resemble a public defender, with all of the downsides that elite lawyers associated with that model, or the "Voluntary Defender System," which they believed superior. "Many of our Board are dubious about seeking or accepting 'public funds,'" LaRue Brown explained, which would undermine "one of the chief merits" of the voluntary defender: its "wholly independent character." By getting ahead of the developing jurisprudence and preemptively expanding the Voluntary Defenders Committee, board members proposed to provide a "service to the entire nation": an experimental test of whether a private organization could "operate effectively on a statewide basis," on a scale "comparable with . . . a Public Defender."[135]

Funding for the expansion initiative came from the Fund for the Republic, a short-lived spinoff of the Ford Foundation established in 1952 to combat both communism and McCarthyism. The Voluntary Defenders' aspiration—to create a statewide infrastructure for defending individual rights against state overreach, but without expanding the state itself—fit snugly within that dual mission. "I would like to see the Boston group make a really good try to expand the voluntary system throughout the state," a Fund staffer wrote. "We all agree that almost every state in the union could use good counsel for criminal defendants," but as a method of meeting that need, he was inclined to prefer "a voluntary defender system as against a public defender system." But there was a nagging uncertainty. Existing voluntary defender organizations suffered from fundraising shortfalls. It remained unproven whether criminal defense could be made "sufficiently attractive to community chests" so that the work could "become self-sustaining," without need of public support. Only by placing "more emphasis" on its fundraising efforts—perhaps by retaining professional consultants who specialized in charitable campaigns—could the Voluntary Defenders Committee generate "a really good experiment" to test this question.[136]

Compared with the board members, Wilbur Hollingsworth responded quite differently to the emerging constitutional jurisprudence. The Fund for the Republic's representative was surprised, upon meeting with Hollingsworth, to learn that he was not especially interested in the board's proposed experiment. He wanted instead to conduct a nationwide study of the public defender model, because he doubted that private philanthropy would ever provide "substantial support" for indigent defense.[137] Hollingsworth had already sketched out draft plans for a "Public Defender for the Commonwealth," who would receive an annual salary of $13,000 and oversee a staff of deputy defenders and investigators throughout the state. At the time, his salary from the Voluntary Defenders Committee was only $8,000.[138] LaRue Brown concluded that Hollingsworth's motives for this proposal were self-serving, because Hollingsworth assumed that he would be named the statewide public defender himself.[139]

The Voluntary Defenders Committee did expand its reach with the Fund for the Republic grant, but never realized the board's ambition of statewide, privately funded coverage. In 1954, the committee opened its first branch office in Springfield, in Western Massachusetts. A survey had determined that two-thirds of defendants in that region were unrepresented—the worst ratio in the state. (In one of those long-range echoes of historical sonar, Springfield was not far from Edward Bellamy's old headquarters in Chicopee Falls.)[140] But soon, disaster struck. A new fundraising obstacle called into question not only the committee's expansion, but its future viability even within Boston.

It turned out that Hollingsworth was correct. Donors did not share elite lawyers' vision for combining a constitutional right with private funding. Boston's local community chest, United Community Services, threatened to withdraw all support from the Voluntary Defenders Committee in 1955, taking the position that "a job of this magnitude should be undertaken by the State rather than by a private charitable organization."[141] The threat was forestalled for a time, but the trajectory was apparent. The more that indigent defense became associated with a right, implying a state duty, the less eager were charitable funders to provide support. The ax fell in 1958, when the Massachusetts judiciary adopted a rule requiring trial judges to appoint counsel in all felony cases—in part because of the widespread assumption that the Supreme Court would soon overturn *Betts*. United Community Services announced that after 1960 it would no longer provide any allocation for the Voluntary Defenders Committee. If the state required defense counsel, then "let the state pay for it."[142]

THAT DEVELOPMENTS IN due process jurisprudence catalyzed initially by conditions in the Depression-era rural South would eventually spell fundraising doom for a private charity in Cold War-era Boston was unintended. This sequence of ripple effects resulted from changes in how Americans conceived of constitutional rights that were often incompletely theorized. On the surface, the Supreme Court's right-to-counsel cases did not speak to the legal profession's internal debate about the relative benefits of the public defender as against private charity. The cases only spelled out when trial courts were obligated to appoint counsel. Courts could meet that obligation

From Charity to Right   83

in a variety of ways. They could appoint a private attorney, or a public defender if one was available, or a lawyer furnished by a charitable group. Judges and lawyers expected that local courts would continue to rely upon the cooperation of private groups and professional associations to fulfill the expanding requirements of due process. Consider Erwin Griswold, who at different moments in his career both urged the Supreme Court to recognize counsel as a requisite of due process and celebrated the Voluntary Defenders Committee and its Harvard student volunteers. From this vantage point, the developing jurisprudence might have been regarded as a great boon to voluntary defenders. By associating defense counsel with due process, the Court validated the significance of their work, and by threatening federal oversight, the doctrine provided organizations with a new fundraising impetus. Legal representation could now be promoted not only as an altruistic gift but also as a way to support law and order, by insulating criminal convictions against appellate reversal.

Instead, as it happened, the Supreme Court's case-by-case expansion of the right to counsel proved eminently unhelpful to Boston's Voluntary Defenders Committee in its Sisyphean fundraising efforts. In ways both practical and conceptual, defining counsel as a right undermined the rationale for providing it through private charity. As the committee itself recognized, a right to counsel would morph the nature of the problem being solved, transforming "the provision of adequate defense to the impoverished defendant" from "a social need" into "a legal and, indeed, a constitutional need."[143] No longer could aid be limited to the deserving, and donors might bristle at underwriting state compliance with a legal obligation. From the state's perspective, too, the nature of the problem would change. To policymakers, it might seem intolerably risky to rely on private efforts if the consequence for gaps in service was not merely individual misfortune, but overturned criminal convictions.

Beneath pragmatic considerations lurked a latent theoretical incompatibility. The jurists who shifted over time toward describing defense counsel as a right made their doctrinal moves within the post–New Deal political order, a context in which "rights" to assistance for the needy, whether provided by the Constitution or (more typically, in the United States) by statute, were understood by both administrators and recipients as the opposite of "charity": as entitlements to be funded by the public and administered by the state.[144] In his 1950 study of American lawyers, the legal historian James Willard Hurst observed that "to support legal aid with public money was to put it on the basis of right, and not simply of friendly help or charity." As shown by the trajectory of the Voluntary Defenders Committee, the reverse implication also held true: to put legal assistance "on the basis of right" might require "public money."[145]

By the 1950s, local arrangements for indigent defense in the United States divided into three groups. At one end of the spectrum were parts of California, Illinois, and a few other scattered jurisdictions, where the public defender was well-established. These public defenders even inspired a short-lived television program, *The Public Defender*, starring Reed Hadley, which aired on CBS from 1954 to 1955.[146] At the other end of the spectrum, encompassing most of the South as well as rural areas throughout the country, were jurisdictions with little organized legal aid or indigent defense of any kind, public or private. Judges continued following the traditional practice of appointing counsel on a case-by-case, ad hoc basis. In 1955, the Georgia Supreme Court lavishly praised the state's lawyers for "giving their best, spending their own funds, and . . . with rare exception furnish[ing] the indigent accused adequate representation."[147] Public defenders were unimpressed. They expressed dismay at the persistence of the assigned counsel approach, which relied upon the goodwill of individual lawyers, typically without much oversight, and did not foster the kind of specialized expertise that public defenders could develop. "Justice for the indigent cannot be casual," wrote Ellery Cuff, the Los Angeles public defender.[148]

In between those two extremes fell the Eastern cities with voluntary defenders. The voluntary defender may have fit within a long American tradition of public–private governance, but here too, Cuff had doubts. Echoing the earlier writings of Mayer Goldman, he questioned whether private charities provided "a sufficient substitute" for the public defender. Private legal aid groups "may have one or two highly capable and experienced men at the top," Cuff acknowledged, but the lawyers who "carry the brunt of the workload are young attorneys who are starting out and who will be affiliated with the organization for only a short period of time." In addition, "most legal aid organizations suffer from a chronic lack of funds."[149] Although offered generically, this description painted an accurate picture of Boston's Voluntary Defenders Committee, and Wilbur Hollingsworth agreed with the critique. In the same year that Hollingsworth celebrated his victory in Richard LaPlante's arson trial, he gave a dispiriting speech to a local bar association. When it came to indigent defense, he said, Massachusetts was "one of the most backward states" in the country.[150]

CHAPTER THREE

Democratic Justice

> It has been suggested that . . . perhaps the entire Cold War, will be resolved in our favor by reason of the superiority of our administration of justice.
>
> —NATIONAL LEGAL AID AND DEFENDER ASSOCIATION, 1961

The French aristocrat Alexis de Tocqueville famously recognized lawyers as "the American aristocracy." He meant the comparison in a structural sense: American lawyers, like Old World nobles, functioned as stabilizers. In the absence of a hereditary titled class, and in a culture where "the people distrust the rich," it was lawyers—with their "instinctive penchant for order"— who injected into American political life the conservative streak necessary to check majority whims. At the time when Tocqueville wrote, it made sense to speak of lawyers and the rich as different groups. In the 1830s, a white man with an aptitude for self-study could become a lawyer simply by "reading law"—the familiar path out of the log cabin trod by lawyer-statesmen such as Abraham Lincoln. "The lawyer belongs to the people . . . by his birth," Tocqueville observed, "and to the aristocracy by his habits."[1]

By the twentieth century, a certain type of lawyer had come to resemble aristocracy in a more literal sense. Becoming a lawyer increasingly required formal education, whether as a professional norm or, eventually, as a matter of state law. "The bar" and "the rich," while never entirely interchangeable, became harder to box away into independent nouns. Elite lawyers, concentrated in the big-city law firms that represented investment banks and business corporations, were often the beneficiaries of inherited wealth and social status. What had not changed since Tocqueville's time was the degree of influence that lawyers exercised, whether formally involved in politics or not, over government at all levels. Lawyers believed themselves uniquely positioned "by temperament, training, and experience" to solve the nation's problems. The public-spirited among them spent a lot of their time serving on committees and commissions. Their qualifications, as they defined them, lay not in any particular subject-matter expertise but in their broad education and their analytical habits of mind. "It is obvious," Harrison Tweed opined in 1959, in a speech at the University of Chicago, "that a nation such as ours could neither have been created nor continue to exist without lawyers."[2]

Tweed exemplified this modern American aristocracy. His grandfather, William Maxwell Evarts, had represented Andrew Johnson in his impeachment proceedings and served a single but significant term in the Senate, where he sponsored the legislation that created the federal courts of appeals; later, he became the first president of the American Bar Association.[3] Tweed's father was in turn a successful railroad lawyer. As for Tweed himself, he had a desultory undergraduate career at Harvard, but once at the Harvard Law School, he discovered a talent for the skill that was taught and prized there: the careful parsing of judicial opinions.[4] He spent most of his legal career as a partner in the trusts and estates division at Milbank, Tweed—the Wall Street law firm that served as outside legal counsel to the Chase Manhattan Bank and to several generations of the Rockefeller family—having been brought into the firm by his law school classmate Winthrop Aldrich, brother-in-law and trusted adviser of John D. Rockefeller Jr.[5] In 1952, the professional organization of the elite bar conferred upon Tweed its highest honor—the American Bar Association Medal—with a joking citation that encapsulated how lawyers blended pedigree and acumen into their elaborate gradations of prestige. "Launched from St. Mark's, Harvard College, and the Harvard Law School, accomplished and handsome, an enthusiastic yachtsman, an intrepid polo player, a versatile sportsman—in spite of this," the prize citation read, Tweed had grown into "a lawyer worthy of [his] grandsire."[6]

Also like landed nobles of old, these lawyers maintained, or thought of themselves as maintaining, a respectable distance from the grubby world of commerce. The reason that Tweed's generation of white-shoe law firm partners could, if they wanted to, serve as a self-appointed leadership class, filling a fair amount of their working hours with volunteer service, was that elite firms, although they existed in the service of big business, did not themselves operate wholly as businesses. The top-tier firms counted on steady revenue from standing arrangements with long-term clients, to whom they could essentially dictate their prices. They did not poach clients or personnel from rivals; they did not engage in marketing, which was viewed as crass; and they did not face much pressure when it came to costs or profits. Corporate capitalism, which created this iteration of the Wall Street law firm, would later destroy it. Corporations would take notice of legal fees as a cost to reduce, and begin parceling out their legal work on a competitive basis; to survive, law firms would have to become the businesses they had pretended not to be, and begin insisting on profitable work from their employees and specializing and selling themselves. By the 1980s, Tweed's old firm would appear "stodgy" to legal up-and-comers.[7] But Harrison Tweed died in 1969. A man of his generation could still describe the life of a Wall Street lawyer as almost leisurely—a suitable niche for the well-born man who was reasonably "intellectual" but lacking in "literary flair." A good lawyer, in Tweed's estimation, was "a man" who "has no great acquisitiveness but wants to live comfortably," and "wants to be free to take a position on public questions."[8]

Among the public questions that came to occupy Tweed was the plight of the indigent. By his telling, he was selected to serve as president of New York's Legal Aid Society in 1936 despite having no previous ties to the organization, but surely his name was not selected out of the blue; his law firm's most prominent clients, the Rockefellers, were also the society's leading benefactors.[9] He proceeded to become a national leader for the cause, serving from 1949 to 1955 as president of the National Legal Aid Association. In 1963, Tweed also became a public face of the legal profession's response to the civil rights movement, when President John F. Kennedy named him the founding cochair of the Lawyers' Committee for Civil Rights under Law.[10] A liberal Republican, Tweed exemplified the particular midcentury liberalism of Northern elites, combining sanguine support for plutocratic capitalism with apparently genuine revulsion toward the apartheid order of the Jim Crow South—and especially toward the complicity of Southern law and lawyers in defending that order.

Tweed's public positions offered an index of elite lawyers' new interest, in the 1950s, in the public defender. In 1959, Tweed penned the foreword to a slim but influential volume, *Equal Justice for the Accused*, which signaled a growing acceptance, among the highest echelon of the corporate bar, of public funding for criminal defense. For decades, the public defender, though accepted in the West, had stalled on the East Coast because Wall Street lawyers thought it smacked of communism and would lead to the socialization of the legal profession. Now, in his 1959 foreword, Tweed chastised lawyers for claiming that the public defender "smacks of communism and leads to the socialization of the legal profession." This view, Tweed assured his readers, was a "hobgoblin"—a figment of the narrow imaginations of an earlier, more hidebound generation. "Happily," he continued, the legal profession's opposition to the public defender was now "diminishing" in the face of "recent decisions of the courts" and "the mounting pressure to demonstrate the soundness and workability of our American way of life."[11]

What had changed? The developing jurisprudence of due process had already encouraged the shift, but the Cold War definitively reshaped the terms of debate. It was not inevitable that the Cold War would render the public defender more palatable. Anticommunist hysteria might have had the opposite effect; into the 1950s, the ABA continued to associate government funding for civil legal aid with the specter of communism.[12] In the context of criminal law, Cold War culture channeled lawyers' thinking in a different way. Fixating on show trials as the paradigmatic evil of Soviet communism, lawyers and politicians contrasted "totalitarian justice" with America's elaborate protections for the accused, which they labeled "democratic justice." At the level of rhetoric and culture, a commitment to fair criminal trials became defined as a core feature of liberal democracy and intertwined with American national identity.[13] In turn, the criminal defense attorney—the figure in the courtroom most closely associated with protecting the accused—became a popular icon, embodied in fictional characters from Perry Mason to Atticus Finch. Television shows, complained one district attorney, aligned prosecutors like him "with the forces of oppression, corruption, and brutality." The defendant was typically a "downtrodden," "innocent victim of society," and the defense lawyer "the hero of the hour."[14]

Within this context, elite lawyers developed a new version of the public defender that, unlike its Progressive Era predecessor, they did not consider a threat to the political independence and economic structure of the legal profession. No longer was public defense envisioned as a way to infuse the traditional, adversarial trial with modern, scientific collaboration. Instead, the public defender was touted as a mechanism for extending to everyone the benefits of all-American adversarial justice. Within this framework, state-provided criminal defense could be justified not as the first step toward socializing other goods and services, but as a procedural requirement limited to the distinctive setting of the criminal courts. Thus, in a decade when anticommunism was at its height as a constraint upon American politics, could Harrison Tweed celebrate an idea once derided as socialist as an exemplar of "the American way." If the public defender would no longer lead to a socialized legal profession, as Tweed assured his readers, that was because the profession's leaders had reframed the arguments in favor of the public defender to ensure that they no longer contemplated socializing the profession. In 1963, it was this understanding that the Supreme Court would write into constitutional law, in the landmark case of *Gideon v. Wainwright*.[15]

IN THE POLITICAL VISION of postwar American intellectuals, the Cold War was not only an old-fashioned geopolitical rivalry for land and influence. It was also something larger than that, an existential battle between "two antagonistic patterns of social roles and norms, two profoundly different ways of organizing political power and authority, two competing understandings of the long march of history."[16] So understood, the fight against communism had implications for every detail of ordinary Americans' day-to-day lives and even for their psyches. Whether debating foreign policy or the fifth-grade curriculum, academics, psychologists, scientists, educators, politicians, and diplomats all invoked the same binary pairs to distinguish democratic life from totalitarian oppression: open vs. closed, creative vs. rigid, individual vs. conformist, tolerant vs. ideological, flexible vs. certain.[17] In this worldview, in which every sub-unit within a society was a microcosm of the whole, openness constituted a shared ideal for individuals, groups, processes, and institutions alike. In contrast to "open-minded" democratic citizens stood the prejudiced denizens of totalitarian states—and their domestic counterparts, including McCarthyites and Mississippians—whose very minds, the theory went, had been damaged by the pressure to conform. When midcentury Northern liberals tried to explain what made Jim Crow Mississippi seem un-American to them, outside the mainstream of "the American way of life," they described the Magnolia State as a "closed society."[18]

The symbol of democracy was one man, standing apart from the crowd and up against the state; behind the Iron Curtain, all was fuzz, the masses, a blur. Anxieties about individualism appeared again and again, across literature, film, journalism, and social science. American observers were offended not only by what dictators did, but also by how their victims seemed (at least to Americans) to meekly accept their fates. Totalitarian rule was so terrifying because it seemed somehow capable of overbearing the will to resist—the very thing that made humans human. Analyzing midcentury news coverage, the historian Susan Carruthers shows how uniformly the American media depicted Soviets as "joyless automatons," "shuffling through a drab landscape of identikit buildings, absorbing a sterile communist ideology that dulled resistance to the state."[19] Americans, in contrast, decided for themselves, and they fought back. The public intellectual Arthur Schlesinger Jr., celebrated postwar liberalism for reviving faith in the "integrity of the individual." Schlesinger's 1949 book, *The Vital Center*, urged readers to "reclaim their democratic values" and "make freedom a faith worth fighting for." Totalitarianism, in either its communist or fascist variety, was a "hoax," explained the book's dustjacket: "Its model subject is the submissive prisoner."[20]

These tropes combined two intellectual developments: the invention of "totalitarianism," but also the redefinition of "democracy." Coined in the 1920s to describe fascist Italy, the construct of the "totalitarian state" later became a pejorative label for any regime that aspired to expand state power into every corner of society.²¹ Under this umbrella term, analysts first combined Mussolini with Hitler, Franco, and other European dictators, under the rubric of fascism, and then combined fascism in turn with bolshevism. This latter conceptual move gained appeal after the fall of the Iron Curtain, when the United States no longer had to maintain a military alliance with the Soviet Union.²² The German émigré Hannah Arendt's book *The Origins of Totalitarianism*, published in 1951, consolidated and publicized the concept for intellectuals in the United States. The paradigm equated political extremes, whether on the far right or the far left, as offensive to liberal democracy because they sought to repress dissent and control individual behavior.²³

Totalitarianism was counterposed against democracy, a term that had also acquired new connotations. Early in the twentieth century, even before the interwar crisis in Europe, internal developments in the United States had triggered doubts about the prevailing theories of democracy—doubts that preoccupied American legal scholars, political scientists, and social critics. Rates of voter participation plummeted in the twentieth century, although this development was not necessarily mourned; scholars harbored mounting uncertainty about whether ordinary citizens were capable of managing the complex problems of modern society. If voting could no longer be venerated as the keystone of democracy, empirically or normatively, then democracy must be redefined. The educational philosopher John Dewey, for example, now measured democracy by how much autonomy society reserved for the individual and "the free mind." Dewey and other theorists distilled democracy to a cultural essence rather than a political order: a commitment to pluralism, pragmatism, and compromise.²⁴

The leading twentieth-century conceptions of democracy therefore did not connote solely, or even primarily, widespread access to the franchise, which had been the measure of nineteenth-century democracy. Voting rights, to be sure, remained a site of political struggle in the Cold War United States. African Americans battled for meaningful enforcement of constitutional protections for the franchise, and the Supreme Court, under the banner of "one person, one vote," struck down state-level apportionment schemes that gave disproportionate weight to rural votes. But the intellectual fetish for democracy as a contrast-type with totalitarianism was not primarily concerned with popular participation in elections.²⁵ Nor, as the Cold War progressed, did democratic theorists celebrate working-class identification with the government as material provider, which had been the achievement of Franklin Roosevelt's Democratic Party. Citizens enamored with the state, as such, might now raise concern. Social critics assumed that individuals in a democracy, or a free society as it was interchangeably called, should maintain a healthy separation from, and even a degree of opposition to, the state, which might otherwise seek to imprison or stunt them. After World War II, American elites conceived of democracy as "a state of mind" that encompassed both the consciousness of being an individual with rights and responsibilities and the courage to face the complexities of modern life without seeking comfort in an authoritarian protector.[26]

The equation of democracy with individual autonomy made its way into legal culture through several pathways. Legal scholars adopted this definition and conveyed it to their students. Published in 1952, the first textbook on civil rights law measured American democracy by the scope of individual freedom "to live and work and play" and the extent to which ordinary people remained "tolerant" and "ready to experiment." "The crucial question before us now," its authors predicted, "is whether, under the new conditions of the modern world which press upon us, we can continue to maintain the practices of democratic freedom or whether we shall abandon them for a stagnant and servile existence."[27] Jurists too deployed the concept. "The fair administration of justice," Supreme Court justice Felix Frankfurter wrote, also in 1952, furnished "a major test" of whether a nation was a "true democracy."[28] In reaction to Nazi and Soviet abuses, American jurists sought to reengineer constitutional doctrine across a range of issues to foreclose the possibility of totalitarian rule. As legal scholar Richard Primus has cataloged, the postwar Supreme Court invoked the Nazi and Soviet regimes—"both separately and together, sometimes in accord and sometimes in conflict"— to justify rulings on issues as diverse as religious dissent, racial discrimination, executive power, and sexual privacy.[29]

Because of their social and professional milieu, lawyers were all, to varying degrees and with varying levels of buy-in, exposed to antitotalitarian binaries. Though unable to write their own views into Supreme Court opinions, lawyers in the provinces likely encountered Schlesinger through the Book-of-the-Month Club, along with George Orwell, Winston Churchill, and other staples of the midcentury nightstand.[30] Countless lawyers and future lawyers, of course, had fought or otherwise participated in the war effort. Wherever they found the global contest with tyranny, lawyers brought it back into the way that they understood and talked about their own profession. In 1948, the Los Angeles County public defender celebrated his office as "Democracy at Work," the modern embodiment of the American aversion to "tyranny and injustice." These descriptions might seem like clichés, but they were new clichés. Earlier public defenders had tended to speak instead in the Progressive Era idiom of efficiency and good government, promising a "square deal" in the criminal courts. The ceaseless struggle against tyranny, the enduring lessons of "the formative years of our Republic," "the problems of government in the post-war world": these were new additions to the bureaucratic genre of the public defender's annual report.[31]

The antitotalitarian paradigm had special influence in the realm of criminal procedure. Every criminal prosecution is an argument by agents of the state that it is necessary to constrain some individual's liberty. If democracy meant respect for individual freedom, then the criminal courts became an obvious site for measuring democracy's strength. American lawyers now celebrated the adversarial criminal trial, which reformers had once questioned as archaic, for instantiating democracy's key qualities, including open-mindedness and solicitude for the individual. In the ideal American courtroom, judges and jurors patiently listened to the facts and followed the evidence wherever it led, with no preconceived outcome in mind. In their efforts to determine whether the evidence established guilt "beyond a reasonable doubt," they embodied the tolerance for ambiguity thought to separate democratic citizens from their totalitarian cousins.[32] The iconic American jurors were the 12 *Angry Men* of Sidney Lumet's 1957 film, who, through a process of deliberation, gradually overcame their prejudices and disagreements.[33]

Meanwhile both literature and the nightly news contrasted American due process with the totalitarian practice of "show trials." Such proceedings superficially resembled judicial trials, but their verdicts were predetermined, and they were not intended to discover some previously unknown truth. Rather, they were rituals for inculcating the state's ideological teachings and punishing those who failed to conform.[34] For highbrow readers, Arthur Koestler's *Darkness at Noon*, a fictionalized account of the 1930s Moscow purge trials, provided a cultural template of totalitarian justice. For most Americans, though, it was Orwell's dystopian best-seller, *Nineteen Eighty-Four*, that fixed their mental picture of "totalitarianism as liberalism's Other." Orwell depicted a "nightmarish world . . . in which the state pursues power for its own sake and all individual freedom, including even private freedom of thought, is systematically eradicated."[35] News stories further highlighted the contrast and revealed its real-world import for nonfictional Americans. In 1949, Robert Vogeler, an American executive based in Vienna, was arrested during a trip to Hungary on espionage charges. Vogeler's trial, which took place in Budapest, received extensive media coverage and high-level diplomatic attention. The American public reacted with outrage, decrying Hungarian justice as a farce and lambasting the State Department for failing to rescue Vogeler.[36]

The specter of totalitarian justice layered a Cold War update atop a long discursive tradition in which Anglo-American lawyers criticized foreign courts as despotic and secretive. For centuries, English jurists had disdained Continental European legal systems based on Roman canon law—in which the court itself, rather than the dueling parties, investigates the facts—both because of the Continent's history of judicial torture and because of the general English rivalry with Catholic empires. Even after modernizing reforms that abolished judicial torture and made European criminal procedure an arguably instructive model, English observers dismissed the notion that they had any legal lessons to learn from Continental Europe.[37] American jurists imbibed this same skepticism, using inquisitorial process as a favorite "contrast-model" against which to define American procedure.[38] In 1949, for example, Justice Frankfurter celebrated "Anglo-American criminal justice" for having "freed itself from practices borrowed . . . from the Continent whereby an accused was interrogated in secret for hours on end."[39] Generalized comparisons to a vaguely imagined Continental past remained in the American jurisprudential repertoire, but now they were complemented with references to a more specific, easterly, and contemporary contrast-model— the Soviet Union and its satellites.[40]

Within this discourse exalting the democratic quality of American criminal procedure, the defense lawyer played a central role. If what defined a fair trial was the genuine possibility that the state might lose, then there needed to be some party in the courtroom who was unbeholden to the state, someone who could write his own script, cross-examine the state's witnesses, and question the state's presentation of the evidence. Defendants themselves were unlikely to carry out these tasks effectively; if they were not literally brainwashed as they might (purportedly) be in Moscow, they lacked the forensic skills and legal knowledge that modern criminal trials required. Thus, American lawyers talked about the right to counsel not as an individual entitlement, but as a safeguard that vicariously protected everyone in society by ensuring that trials did not degenerate into show trials and, in the process, ensuring that democracy did not degenerate into tyranny. "To defend the individual defendant is to protect society," explained the Los Angeles public defender, "for if the rights and liberties of the individual are ignored a free society is endangered."[41]

Lawyers (and legal doctrine) had long acknowledged that defense counsel could be an important ingredient of a fair trial, particularly if the charges were serious. Now defense counsel became elevated into an essential element of what made trials not only fair, but also democratic. It was after Hungary denied Robert Vogeler's defense attorney an entry visa that Secretary of State Dean Acheson accused the Soviet satellite of "outdo[ing] even Nazi 'justice' in denying rights."[42] President Dwight D. Eisenhower's attorney general, Herbert Brownell, endorsed the long-languishing federal public defender bill as a way "to demonstrate the contrast between the 'humaneness' and 'fairness' of the American system and the 'cruelties' of the Communist system."[43] Supreme Court Justice William Douglas remarked in 1961, at a symposium about the right to counsel, that "a person has to go to a communist country . . . fully to appreciate the role that counsel can perform."[44] The right to counsel, defense attorneys, fair trials, America, and democracy blended together into a mélange of related ideas, symbols, and practices in which lawyers and jurists placed their faith. During the war, Cohen and Griswold had relied on the contrast with totalitarianism to criticize *Betts v. Brady*. While in 1942, that framing could not convince a majority of the Supreme Court, by 1960 it would be conventional wisdom.

IT WAS IN this milieu that Tweed wrote his 1959 foreword to *Equal Justice for the Accused*, which both reflected and encouraged the legal profession's new consensus in favor of the public defender. After surveying the existing arrangements for indigent defense around the country, the report concluded by recommending that every city establish some type of organized defender, whether a public defender or a public–private hybrid, which might be supported by government funding even if nominally independent. This recommendation indicated a subtle but significant shift in the legal elite's thinking. Although elite lawyers continued to imagine a role for private organizations in indigent defense, *Equal Justice for the Accused* signaled a new openness toward intertwining criminal defense with government, whether directly or through the acceptance of public subsidies. The report dismissed out of hand the old charge that the public defender was socialist, "unless socialism is understood to encompass every device through which . . . the community discharges a community responsibility." How "ironic," the report concluded, "that a charge which is sometimes intended to imply the exalting of the state at the expense of the individual should be levied against systems which grew up because of the recognition of the need for the individual to be protected against the state."[45]

A few years later came *Poverty and the Administration of Federal Criminal Justice*, produced by a blue-ribbon committee appointed in 1961 by Attorney General Robert Kennedy and chaired by Francis Allen, a professor at the University of Michigan. The Allen report was intended only to provide recommendations for the relatively small number of criminal prosecutions carried out in the federal courts, where defense counsel had been required since *Johnson v. Zerbst* in 1938. It did not expressly discuss indigent defense in the state courts, where the vast majority of criminal cases were tried, and where the Supreme Court had not yet established a requirement of counsel in all prosecutions (although it soon would). Nevertheless, the Allen report reflected its contributors' views about the issue of indigent defense more generally. The final report was submitted in February 1963, just one month before the Supreme Court's landmark right-to-counsel decision in *Gideon v. Wainwright*.[46]

Together, these two policy reports map the contours of elite legal thought about the public defender at the turn of the 1960s.[47] *Equal Justice for the Accused* divided its discussion of the right to counsel into two parts: first, the individual's need for counsel, and second, society's interest in providing public assistance for meeting that need. As to the first issue, there was nothing remarkable or novel in the report's summary of why an individual accused of a crime might personally benefit from legal representation. Few would dispute, by midcentury, that law was a technical field and court proceedings best navigated with expert help. Occasionally, a heterodox legal scholar, such as the Yale law professor Fred Rodell, suggested that lawyers themselves were the problem, and that instead of trying to provide lawyers to more people, lawyers should work to demystify the courts so people would not need lawyers. But that line of thinking typically met with disdainful reviews from the profession. Within academia, efforts to deflate the law's self-seriousness had enjoyed some cachet during the 1930s heyday of the "legal realist" school of thought, which described law as an ordinary human endeavor rather than a rarefied science.[48] But legal realism had fallen out of favor during World War II. Confronting the global rise of dictatorship, lawyers and legal scholars returned to transcendent principles like the "rule of law" and renewed their faith in "sound jurisprudence," administered by experts, as essential "to the preservation of civilization."[49]

But the observation that lawyers were beneficial to individual defendants could not by itself, within the parameters of liberalism, justify providing lawyers at public expense. There were many services that might be advantageous to individuals, yet midcentury American liberals did not necessarily conclude that the state must therefore provide those services—quite the opposite. Health care could be necessary to survival, but socialized medicine was derided by American politicians in the 1950s as "the Moscow party line."[50] To endorse the public defender, then, lawyers needed some explanation for why, in this particular arena, inequality between rich and poor implicated some governmental interest and thus should be remedied by the state.

Equal Justice for the Accused modeled just such an argument. It spelled out how "the representation of the criminally accused" might be understood to implicate not only the personal interests of the accused, but also the preservation of American democracy. The key sentence went as follows: "Our democratic society needs to have representation provided to all accused so that the scales of justice can be equally balanced and the goal of equal justice under law achieved."[51] On the surface, this sentence might read like an empty platitude, a string of stock phrases. But in fact, the equation of universal legal representation with the unimpeachable goal of "equal justice"— as if that equation were an uncontestable mathematical identity, rather than a debatable legal question—was historically new. Without this formula, the problem of the indigent accused would be just that—the indigent's problem. This formula transformed it into everyone's problem, which made it a policy problem suitable for state intervention. The individual defendant's plight was no longer in itself the target of that intervention, but an incident to the larger problem being solved: the preservation of "our democratic society."

The Allen report pursued this same theme, reasoning that all citizens had an interest in the "rule of law." American criminal law was adversarial, and thus, it could not function reliably unless both sides of the equation were represented by a competent adversary. Adversarial procedure, the report explained, "is the product of long historical experience," and "makes essential and invaluable contributions to the maintenance of the free society." But well-functioning adversarial courts depended upon "a constant, searching, and creative questioning of official decisions and assertions of authority at all stages of the process." Thus, providing defendants with lawyers protected "the health of the system" overall. It ensured that "official decisions" would undergo the requisite adversarial testing. When any particular defendant lacked counsel, it was not only his individual fate that was endangered, but also "the proper functioning of the system of justice" and, thereby, "the basic interests of a free community."[52]

The Allen report also added an alternative argument for the public defender, based on the fact that unlike civil litigation, criminal prosecutions—at least in the modern era—were necessarily initiated by the government. This argument too proceeded not from a premise of general concern for the poor, but by borrowing from private personal-injury law, in which it was accepted that parties who initiated a potentially harmful course of action might incur a duty of care they would otherwise not owe. "When a course of conduct, however legitimate, entails the possibility of serious injury to persons," the report stated, echoing a hornbook principle from every law student's first-year torts class, "a duty on the actor to avoid the reasonably voidable injuries is ordinarily recognized." So too, if "government chooses to exert its powers in the criminal area, its obligation is surely no less than that of taking reasonable measures to eliminate those factors that are irrelevant to just administration of the law but which, nevertheless, may occasionally affect determinations of the accused's liability or penalty."[53] This point showed that lawyers at midcentury found it advantageous to analogize to private law when rationalizing a proposal for public assistance. Such analogies separated the public defender from class-based concern for the poor and instead linked it to well-accepted, generally applicable legal principles.

In this way, Cold War advocates of the public defender carved the criminal courtroom apart from the rest of society, defining criminal law as a unique realm in which the state should assist the poor—not because there was anything generically salutary about state assistance for the poor, but because of qualities unique to the criminal trial that necessitated state assistance in order for the process to function. For some Progressive Era advocates, the public defender had formed part of a larger vision of socializing a wide range of services; they analogized the public defender to socialized medicine, because they assumed that the medical profession, too, would eventually be subsumed under public control. At midcentury, lawyers took pains to separate the public defender from any broader vision of social provision. They distinguished the public defender from "fire protection and hospitals and sanitation"—public goods that some communities might decide to offer, but which government had no enforceable duty to provide.[54] The Allen report emphasized that public defender proposals need not "depend upon some hypothetical obligation of government to indulge in acts of public charity": "The obligation of government in the criminal cases rests on wholly different considerations and reflects principles of much more limited application."[55] Perhaps, had the report been issued just a year or two later—after President Lyndon Johnson had declared war on poverty—its authors would have found this kind of argumentative gymnastics less necessary. In his own scholarly writing, Allen criticized the American tendency to respond to social problems with criminal punishment and called for robust investment in social services.[56] But in 1963, it remained necessary to reassure a federal audience that "government may not be required to relieve the accused of his poverty," even if "it may properly be required to minimize the influence of poverty on its administration of justice."[57]

Thanks to the circulation and repetition of such arguments, the public defender as a concept was no longer controversial by the early 1960s, at least on the surface. In 1956, federal judge Edward Dimock had condemned the public defender as the first step toward a "police state."[58] By 1961, that position sounded hysterical to many lawyers. One private defense attorney admitted to lingering questions about how the public defender would work in practice. But he dared not object to the idea in principle. As he put it: "One can't take a position against the public defender any more than one can take a position against motherhood or small children."[59]

GIVEN THIS CONTEXT, the events of March 1963 came as no surprise. In that month, the Supreme Court announced, in *Gideon v. Wainwright*, that every defendant accused of serious crime had a constitutional right to counsel provided by the state if necessary. The decision was unanimous. In his opinion for the Court, Justice Hugo Black presented the justices' conclusion as self-evident: "in our adversary system of criminal justice, any person haled into court, who is too poor to hire a lawyer, cannot be assured a fair trial unless counsel is provided for him. This seems to us to be an obvious truth." *Gideon* marked the moment that astute legal observers had been waiting for since the 1950s: the official rejection of the old *Betts v. Brady* rule, which required the states to appoint counsel only in cases presenting "special circumstances." Echoing so many midcentury celebrations of the "American way of life," Black connected the right to counsel to national identity: "The right of one charged with crime to counsel may not be deemed fundamental and essential to fair trials in some countries, but it is in ours."[60]

Although the justices had already decided to expand the right to counsel, they had waited to do so until the perfect case came along. In the early 1960s, several justices made it known to one another that they would vote to jettison *Betts*.[61] But they preferred to announce such a major decision in a case with nonthreatening facts. That preference excluded from consideration many of the criminal cases that yielded petitions for Supreme Court review (by definition, those convicted of extremely serious crimes have a greater incentive to pursue all available appeals). To overturn *Betts*, the justices also needed a case with a relatively ordinary defendant facing a relatively straightforward criminal charge. If the defendant had any distinctive personal vulnerabilities, such as youth or illiteracy, or the relevant criminal statutes were complicated in any way, then the case would present "special circumstances" and require counsel even under the *Betts* rule. Only the most run-of-the-mill criminal prosecution would force the Court to confront squarely the question of whether to overrule *Betts*.[62]

The winning case had arrived in the Supreme Court mailroom in January 1962, in the form of a petition that was handwritten in pencil, on prison-issued stationery, and sent from the state penitentiary in Raiford, Florida. The petition's author was Clarence Earl Gideon, "a fifty-one-year-old white man who had been in and out of prisons much of his life," serving time for a string of gambling and petty theft convictions. The petition reported that Gideon had most recently been convicted of breaking and entering, allegedly for breaking into a pool hall outside of the Panhandle town of Panama City and stealing wine and cigarettes. Gideon asked the Supreme Court to set aside his conviction as unconstitutional, because the trial judge had denied his request for an appointed lawyer. At the time of Gideon's trial, Florida was among the handful of remaining states that guaranteed appointed counsel only in capital cases. Gideon was placed in the very same situation as Smith Betts, twenty years before. Too poor to hire his own lawyer, he was forced to represent himself.[63]

Almost always, the justices denied petitions like Gideon's: handwritten pleas submitted by prisoners themselves, without the benefit of legal counsel. As the nation's highest tribunal, the Supreme Court has primarily discretionary jurisdiction; it picks and chooses which cases to hear, typically selecting cases that squarely present a difficult issue that has divided the lower courts. In the early 1960s, it received 2,500 petitions for review each year, from which it selected only about 150 cases for full briefing and argument. Self-drafted petitions like Gideon's were often too cryptic to pass muster. But Gideon's facts presented the ideal vehicle for addressing whether to overrule *Betts*. The Court granted Gideon's petition for review and notified the State of Florida to submit briefing arguing the position that *Betts* should be left in place. To argue that *Betts* should go, and present Gideon's side of the case, Chief Justice Earl Warren appointed the well-connected Washington, DC lawyer Abe Fortas, of the small but prominent law firm Arnold,

Fortas, and Porter. Founded by ex-New Dealers, the firm specialized in legislative, regulatory, and corporate work, with "a liberal and Democratic flavor"; Fortas was a close advisor both to Lyndon Johnson and to a bevy of corporate executives. Gideon, the pauper challenging his lack of trial counsel, would now enjoy representation at the Supreme Court by a flashy, shrewd, Rolls Royce-driving member of the Washington power elite.[64]

The briefs and oral argument in *Gideon* reassured the justices that the time had indeed come to entomb *Betts*. The lawyers at Arnold, Fortas, and Porter drew upon cutting-edge scholarly research, which amassed both legal sources and interviews with local officials to show that the states were already moving toward providing counsel for all defendants. Thirty-seven states now guaranteed counsel in felony cases, and many provided counsel in some misdemeanor cases. In thirteen states, appointed counsel was still required as a matter of law only in capital cases. But even in those states, judges often appointed counsel more widely in practice, particularly in cities.[65] There had never been much doubt that Fortas would prevail in *Gideon*; the justices were already largely settled on their plan to eliminate the "special circumstances" rule. One of the justices later remarked that "no lawyer could have lost that case." Still, the justices were impressed with Fortas's argument, which reassured them that a broad ruling would not prove intolerably disruptive to the states. Of course, there was something circular about the observation that the states were already taking steps to provide counsel; state-level officials had begun taking such steps precisely because they anticipated that a case like *Gideon* was on its way. To the justices, this development showed that the open-ended, fact-specific *Betts* rule had done its job—pushing states in the direction of a right to counsel without imposing a blanket rule all at once—and could now be replaced with a more straightforward requirement.[66]

Justice Black, to his great delight, was assigned the task of drafting the Court's opinion. *Gideon* combined two of his favorite subjects—whether to incorporate the Bill of Rights against the states, and the importance of defense counsel to the adversarial process—and it allowed him to write his *Betts* dissent into constitutional law.[67] Justice Frankfurter, the chief opponent of Black's incorporation theory, had recently retired, giving Black free rein. Although the Court never officially adopted the total incorporation theory, it did apply to the states, one by one, those pieces of the Bill of Rights that it deemed "implicit in the concept of ordered liberty"—which, it eventually turned out, was almost all of the Bill of Rights, except for a few minor clauses.[68] In *Gideon*, Black explained that the Sixth Amendment right to counsel was among those protections so significant to "ordered liberty" that it must be incorporated against the states as a requisite of due process. Reprising themes from his opinion in *Johnson v. Zerbst*, which had established the federal requirement of appointed counsel, Black described criminal defense lawyers as "necessities, not luxuries," essential to the orderly functioning of the "adversary system."[69]

Gideon formed part of a series of cases in which the Warren Court remade the Bill of Rights and the related case law into a detailed "code of criminal procedure" that the states must obey.[70] These decisions marked the culmination of developments begun decades before, when criminal defendants first used the Fourteenth Amendment due process clause to challenge unfair trials in state court. By the end of the 1960s, the Supreme Court had held that due process required states to comply not only with the right to counsel, but also with Fourth Amendment protections against unreasonable searches, the Fifth Amendment right against self-incrimination, and the Sixth Amendment right to a jury trial in criminal prosecutions. Some of those decisions, particularly the Court's rulings governing police searches and interrogations, were and remained extremely controversial. The talking point that the courts were placing too many restrictions upon the police, and thereby abetting criminals, became a centerpiece of Richard Nixon's 1968 presidential campaign. *Gideon*, in contrast, was warmly received, in part because it ratified a consensus already reached within the legal profession itself.[71]

The Supreme Court's opinion in *Gideon* did not expressly refer to the public defender, nor did it provide details about how exactly states were supposed to organize their efforts to provide counsel. But a penumbral *Gideon* quickly developed among journalists, lawyers, and academics, who interpreted the decision as a mandate to establish public defender offices and to solicit public funds for existing defender organizations. States ranging from Florida to Colorado to Oregon responded to *Gideon* with new public defender legislation.[72] Within a year of *Gideon*, an expert consensus had converged around the proposition that "there is no decent alternative in populous urban areas to an office that has a regularly employed staff of lawyers representing indigents," and that "some governmental participation is essential," whether in the form of public administration or public subsidies.[73] In their public speeches if not in their legal opinions, Supreme Court justices endorsed this consensus. At a national conference in 1969, Chief Justice Warren fondly recalled his days as a young district attorney sparring with the Alameda County public defender, and his recently appointed successor,

Chief Justice Warren Burger, predicted that "the organized defender approach" would soon "be the prevailing mode of representation."[74]

Throughout the 1960s and into the 1970s, this reading of *Gideon* was reinforced through professional handbooks and quasi-official guidance documents. A handbook published by the National Legal Aid and Defender Association in 1965 instructed local officials "in urban areas" to "consider the institution of a public defender."[75] In 1973, the federal government's National Advisory Commission on Criminal Justice Standards and Goals recommended that every jurisdiction maintain both "a full-time public defender organization, and a coordinated assigned counsel system involving substantial participation of the private bar."[76] Although contemplating that private counsel would still receive occasional appointments to indigent cases (for instance, if the public defender had a conflict of interest in a particular case), these standards envisioned public defenders as the nation's primary providers of indigent defense. The standards further specified that a city's head public defender should be paid as highly as "the presiding judge," while line defenders should receive salaries comparable to "associates in private law firms." Joint standards issued by NLADA and the ABA similarly proposed "experienced, competent, and zealous" public defenders paid comparably to prosecutors.[77]

Gideon also catalyzed an end to the long-standing inertia over public defenders for the federal courts. Although counsel had been constitutionally required in federal cases since 1938, Congress had never enacted any of the bills proposed over the years to provide compensation or an organizational structure for federal indigent defense. This left local federal judges to work out arrangements on their own. Even though it did not directly affect the federal courts, *Gideon* reaffirmed the nation's commitment to the right to counsel and contributed momentum in favor of a more institutionalized approach. In 1964, Congress passed the Criminal Justice Act, which authorized federal appropriations to compensate lawyers who accepted appointed cases in federal court. Six years later, Congress amended the Act to authorize federal judicial districts to establish public defenders as the defense-side counterparts to the national network of federally appointed prosecutors, known as United States attorneys. Districts were given the choice to establish a fully public defender, staffed by federal appointees, or to designate a nonprofit organization as the "community defender," which would receive ongoing federal appropriations. Federal defenders were eventually established or designated in ninety-one out of ninety-four districts nationwide.[78]

Gideon thus provided a new context for the public defender. After 1963, proposals to establish public defender offices could never again be ordinary policy prescriptions for local government; they were now mechanisms for implementing a constitutional guarantee. In the Progressive Era conception, the public defender was only distantly connected with the Constitution. Rather than valorize the Bill of Rights, Progressive Era reformers more often decried eighteenth-century protections as anachronistic hindrances to developing scientific courts: by equalizing the material resources on both sides of a criminal case, the public defender would obviate the need for convoluted procedural safeguards for defendants and might even enable the abolition of the Bill of Rights and its state analogs. In stark opposition, the Cold War public defender was extolled as an institutional mechanism for enforcing the Bill of Rights. Not only did the public defender fulfill the defendant's Sixth Amendment right to counsel, but the defender in turn could also make the technical arguments necessary to vindicate all the rights guaranteed by the Warren Court's other rulings.

By cloaking the public defender in constitutional rights, the Supreme Court made it difficult to sustain the old argument that any public obligation to provide counsel was a slippery slope to bolshevism. The state of Alabama, in an amicus brief filed in *Gideon* in support of Florida, had tried to revive that old battle cry. "The people of our United States have long favored a free enterprise system under which they take care of themselves," Alabama reminded the Court, and "have sought to avoid socialism which, as we understand it, is a state of affairs in which the government takes care of the people." Given that states were not constitutionally required to provide any other necessities — such as health care — it made no sense to "single out a state's failure to furnish counsel."[79] But by 1963, Alabama was not really arguing with anyone. Advocates of the Cold War public defender agreed with Alabama about the virtues of "free enterprise" and concurred in the view that states had no general obligations to the poor.

GIDEON'S VENERATION OF the Sixth Amendment took part in a larger midcentury revival of the Bill of Rights as central to American national identity. Before the twentieth century, politicians and lawyers paid surprisingly little attention to the first ten amendments to the Constitution, and infrequently used the appellation "Bill of Rights." The 1791 amendments had little practical significance for ordinary Americans, both because the Supreme Court decided few cases interpreting them and because they were understood to bind only the federal government.[80] In the twentieth century, the amendments' significance, both cultural and legal, expanded dramatically. President Franklin Roosevelt popularized the term "Bill of Rights," using the phrase not only as a term of art signifying the 1791 amendments as a unit, but also to symbolize, more generally, the American commitment to individual liberties.[81] During the war, that symbol offered a powerful rhetorical device for contrasting the United States with Nazi Germany; after the fall of the Iron Curtain, subsequent presidents picked up the motif as a tool for denouncing communism. This revival formed the cultural background for the Supreme Court's expanding use of the Bill of Rights as a legal basis for invalidating legislation or overturning criminal verdicts.[82]

The fact that *Gideon* did not mention public defenders, even though it was widely understood to require them, can also be explained by the paradigm of anti-totalitarianism. *Gideon* rhetorically scrubbed out the *public* side of the public defender equation and emphasized the *defender* side, comporting with the postwar political turn away from openly endorsing positive rights to government assistance. Roosevelt had often juxtaposed the original Bill of Rights, which limited government power, with his imagined "Second Bill of Rights," which would empower the government to guarantee employment, food, housing, health care, and education.[83] By the 1950s, the Second Bill of Rights was forgotten. As legal scholar Gerard Magliocca explains, a list of economic entitlements sounded too much like socialism to furnish a sharp contrast with the Soviet Union. But the first Bill of Rights safeguarded liberties that communist regimes did not, including religious freedoms. For distinguishing the United States from its Cold War rivals, the first Bill of Rights gained ascendance.[84]

By the time the Court decided *Gideon*, it did so against the harmonious backdrop of years' worth of presidential speeches that wrapped defendants' rights in the American flag. In 1950, President Harry S. Truman had credited the Bill of Rights as "the reason that our Government is strong, and the greatest democracy in the world." It might "be easier to catch and jail criminals if we did not have a Bill of Rights," but Truman "thank[ed] God every day that it is there," because a Bill of Rights "is what distinguishes us from the totalitarian powers."[85] Two years later Truman vetoed a bill to strengthen immigration restrictions on foreigners with criminal records, because it made no exceptions for people "convicted by 'courts' in communist countries." He continued, "I do not approve of substituting totalitarian vengeance for democratic justice."[86] Congress overrode the veto, but Truman's rhetoric encapsulated the widespread view that fair criminal courts were one of the core features that distinguished democratic from totalitarian states.[87]

Flickering with neon hypocrisy, the elite legal establishment joined in glorifying the Bill of Rights, even though the organized bar's commitment to the political freedoms of its own members was shaky. The ABA had historically been quite conservative, and some of its leaders had railed against the New Deal as a sign of impending dictatorial rule in the United States—leading to the formation, in 1936, of the rival National Lawyers Guild, an uneasy alliance of left-liberal elite lawyers and more radical lawyers at the grassroots.[88] In the climate of 1950s anticommunism, ABA leaders and powerful figures including Eisenhower's attorney general, Herbert Brownell, revived denunciations of the NLG as a communist front, nearly destroying both the organization and the careers of several members.[89] Bar leaders floated the idea of requiring members of state and local bar associations to swear loyalty oaths. Although such proposals were never implemented, they did not need to be. They formed part of what Jerold Auerbach, an acerbic historian of the legal profession, describes as "a sustained, invidious, and more successful effort to intimidate lawyers for unpopular defendants and to discipline those whose beliefs or associations were adjudged subversive."[90]

Throughout the country, lawyers who represented clients accused of violating the Smith Act—which criminalized Communist Party membership—found themselves charged with criminal contempt, jailed, harassed, and, in a few cases, disbarred. As a result, defendants charged with political offenses had trouble finding lawyers who would take their cases, even when they had the means to pay.[91] Corporate firms refused to touch political cases—apart from the rare exception like Arnold, Fortas and Porter, the same firm that would argue *Gideon* pro bono. These cases thus became the province of outsider lawyers: "the children of politically radical parents," labor activists, committed leftists, and the occasional idealist liberal, such as the Yale law professor Thomas Emerson, who found himself vilified as "Tommy the Commie."[92]

Sacher v. United States, decided by the Supreme Court in 1952, exemplified the legal establishment's ambivalence about the right to a zealous defense when invoked by political dissidents. *Sacher* arose out of a famous and raucous nine-month trial, held in the federal courthouse in Foley Square, Manhattan, in which eleven Communist Party leaders were convicted of conspiracy to overthrow the government, in violation of the Smith Act.[93] After the jury returned its verdict as to the defendants, the trial judge made an additional announcement: on his own initiative, he proceeded to summarily convict the defendants' *lawyers* of criminal contempt for their conduct during the trial. As "the courtroom gasped," he sentenced the lawyers to jail terms of up to six months.[94] The defense lawyers, he alleged, had "badgered and insulted him throughout the long months of trial" with "insolent, sarcastic" remarks, as part of a calculated "conspiracy to destroy his health."[95]

Perhaps the trial had not been a model of courtroom decorum, but the lawyers were given no opportunity to defend themselves against the allegations of criminal contempt. Reviewing the record, several justices of the Supreme Court concluded that the trial judge was equally at fault; he had taunted the lawyers throughout the trial and allowed himself to be baited into constant squabbling back and forth. The entire proceeding had degenerated into "an unseemly demonstration . . . of ill will and hot tempers."[96] A legal scholar who reviewed the transcripts agreed that the lawyers' conduct might appear "indefensible" if viewed in a vacuum, but within context, it may have been "an inevitable response to judicial goading." Subsequent high-profile Communist Party trials did not generate the same fireworks and showed that it was possible for judges to manage political trials in an "orderly" and "quiet" manner.[97]

In *Sacher*, the Supreme Court upheld the lawyers' contempt convictions, rejecting their argument that they should have been permitted a trial of their own in front of an impartial judge. Justices Frankfurter, Black, and Douglas issued withering dissents. Invoking the Cold War trope of democratic justice, Frankfurter emphasized that even if the lawyers deserved punishment, they were entitled to an impartial arbiter: "Due regard for such procedural questions, too often misconceived as narrow and technical, alone justifies the truth of one of the great boasts of our democracy, the essential fairness of our judicial system."[98] Justice Black, foreshadowing his celebration of adversarial advocacy in *Gideon*, objected to the trial judge's evident "disrespect" and "bitter hostility" toward the lawyers. Black scolded the judge for allowing his opinion of defense counsel to be "colored, however unconsciously, by his natural abhorrence" for their "unpatriotic and treasonable" clients. Before they were sentenced to jail, Black argued, the lawyers should have been given a trial, just as their clients had received. For judges to engage in the "summary blasting of legal careers," Black wrote, posed "an overhanging menace to the security of every courtroom advocate in America," and especially to "defenders of unpopular persons or unorthodox causes."[99]

Fred Rodell, the iconoclastic professor at Yale Law School who delighted in puncturing the legal profession's self-regard and also acquired a left-baiting nickname ("Fred the Red"), decried the legal establishment's "sorry" acquiescence to McCarthyite tactics.[100] The ABA nominally revised its position in 1953, reaffirming that the "unpopular" had the right to a legal defense, but it remained professionally risky for lawyers to represent dissidents.[101] It is illuminating to juxtapose this sorry record with the legal profession's simultaneous embrace of the public defender in indigent criminal cases, which started in the 1950s with local bar reports written by corporate luminaries and finally culminated in *Gideon*. The bar's ostensible concern for criminal defendants did not necessarily extend to labor activists and alleged communists, whose lawyers, far from being celebrated as defenders of due process and democracy, instead met with ostracism and even professional disbarment.

Some icons of the legal establishment proved consistent in their due process principles across indigent and political cases. Others stayed out of the fray and were never squarely tested. But regardless of their record in political cases, almost all lawyers would later join in the warm reception of *Gideon* as a hallmark of the profession's regard for the vulnerable. At a time when elite lawyers were simultaneously reviving a patriotic cult of the Bill of Rights and displaying a decided hostility toward certain of those rights—such as free speech and association, when invoked by the wrong groups—a newfound commitment to publicly funded indigent defense offered a way to thread the needle. Unlike defending far-left radicals, it may have been harder to imagine that providing legal counsel to petty thieves like Clarence Earl Gideon would destabilize the capitalist order. *Gideon* celebrated adversarial trials for ordinary criminal cases as an American hallmark, papering over what happened to lawyers who took adversarial testing of government power seriously enough to represent those accused of seeking to overthrow the government.

BY 1964, *Gideon* had been elevated almost single-handedly into a cultural icon by Anthony Lewis, the Supreme Court beat reporter at the *New York Times*. The day after *Gideon* was handed down, some newspapers covered it in roundups as one of several notable decisions issued on the same day.[102] Lewis and the *Times* singled out *Gideon* for front-page canonization as "one of the most important [rulings] ever made by the Supreme Court."[103] As a member of elite, legal-liberal social circles, Lewis played a more direct role than he disclosed to readers in shaping the events that he covered. For example, while *Gideon* was pending before the Court, Lewis socialized on Martha's Vineyard with Gerald Berlin, a friend in the Massachusetts attorney general's office, and encouraged Berlin to follow up on a request he had received from Walter Mondale, then the Minnesota attorney general, to file an amicus brief on Gideon's behalf.[104] The resulting brief, written by Berlin and signed by twenty-two states, was quoted in the *Gideon* opinion and taken by the justices as an important signal that federalism concerns need not trouble them; the states would eagerly comply with any new requirement to provide counsel. In his book about the case, Lewis describes Berlin discussing the possibility of an amicus brief with "some friends over cocktails," but does not identify himself as one of the friends.[105]

Lewis solidified *Gideon*'s place in the pantheon of widely revered Supreme Court decisions with his book-length account of the case, *Gideon's Trumpet*, published in 1964. The book was marketed as the inspiring tale of an underdog: the lonely Florida prisoner who sent a handwritten petition all the way to Washington—and won![106] But woven throughout the book was a second story: an unabashed tribute to legal elites, ranging from corporate lawyers to the justices of the Supreme Court.[107] Lewis praised the "bright young men" at the law firm of Arnold, Fortas and Porter, and devoted several pages alone to minutely chronicling the work of John Hart Ely, a Yale law student and summer associate at the firm, as he helped to research and prepare the *Gideon* briefs.[108] Ely went on to clerk for Chief Justice Warren, and later became a renowned law professor, whose tome *Democracy and Distrust*—dedicated to Warren—offered a comprehensive theory of constitutional law as a mechanism for perfecting the American political process.[109] *Gideon's Trumpet* conveyed the message that lawyers and judges were essentially noble and well-meaning, and in their offices all around the country, they were working diligently, if incrementally, to realize the nation's commitment to equal justice.[110] Not surprisingly, lawyers and judges warmly received this message; they celebrated *Gideon's Trumpet* as a redemptive narrative illustrating the best ideals of the American legal profession.[111]

Lewis was too urbane a writer to traffic in crude propaganda, but *Gideon's Trumpet* subtly reprises a number of Cold War themes. The book's only explicit Soviet reference appears within a shorthand retelling of back-and-forth memos between the young corporate lawyers who worked pro bono on Gideon's Supreme Court briefs: "What is the right to counsel under Russian law? Answer: very little."[112] In the book's final pages, Lewis also mentions "the experiences of totalitarian brutality" as one of the motivating forces for the Supreme Court's efforts to restrain government and protect individual rights.[113] Elsewhere, the contrast between American and totalitarian justice is left implicit but glimmers between the lines throughout Lewis's celebratory chronicle. Writing in his trademark detached but sympathetic style, he describes to his comfortable readers the isolation of the criminal defendant, lying in a cold jail cell, wracked by a "sense of loneliness" and "the feeling that [he] is caught up in a machinery he does not understand."[114] If this formulation acknowledges the negative side of the individualism that characterizes life in a democracy, it also foreshadows the possibility that this lonely individual will find his voice. Being "caught" in the machine means that, presumably, he can extricate himself. Unlike the paradigmatic Soviet subject, he is not himself a cog that is part of the machine.

Gideon's Trumpet portrays Clarence Earl Gideon as a loner who instinctively fights back when the state tries to deny him his rights, mailing his scrawled plea to the nation's highest court as if doing so were a reflex. Lewis opens the book by describing Gideon as "a perfectly harmless human being, rather likeable, but one tossed aside by life. . . . And yet," Lewis continues, "a flame still burned in Clarence Earl Gideon," an innate "sense of injustice." Later, Lewis quotes at length from a letter that Gideon wrote to Abe Fortas, in which he described himself as "individualist" and "a person who will not conform."[115] The fact that Gideon is not a particularly remarkable person, accused in a not particularly remarkable place of committing a not particularly remarkable crime, only helps to lend the narrative its quotidian, everyman quality. Democracy, rights, the rule of law—these principles, in the book's telling, are so thoroughly entrenched in American culture that even a picayune Panhandle drifter knows and believes in them.[116] Legal scholars often portray *Gideon* as a sequel to the Supreme Court's first famous right-to-counsel decision, *Powell v. Alabama* (1932), which emerged from the Scottsboro rape cases. But Gideon little resembled the Scottsboro defendants, whose plight laid bare American apartheid and furnished propaganda fodder for activists around the globe. Gideon, an ordinary alcoholic gambler languishing in a Florida prison, was unlikely to inspire mass rallies.

As Lewis presents the story, Gideon's nondescript quality is precisely what makes *Gideon v. Wainwright* so remarkable. The Supreme Court that is a character in *Gideon's Trumpet* holds within its regard every sparrow, even a petty criminal with no family or friends. If the hallmark of totalitarian law is to crush individuals, then the hallmark of American law is to lend their names to bedrock legal principles destined to redound for decades to come. "His triumph," Lewis writes in the book's conclusion, "shows that the poorest and least powerful of men" holds the power, in the United States, to remake constitutional law.[117] In telling the story this way, Lewis elided other lessons that Clarence Earl Gideon's experience might have revealed. As cultural historian Norman Rosenberg observes, in a rare critical reading of the widely admired book, "Gideon's desperate life on the margins of postwar society said a good deal about the continuing existence of poverty and the powerlessness of the poor." But "Lewis ultimately narrowed Gideon's story to the frame offered by the Supreme Court," exalting judges and judicial reasoning as independent from "pervasive patterns of socioeconomic injustice."[118]

The post-*Gideon* investment in the public defender as anti-totalitarian hero was not merely symbolic. The earlier Fund for the Republic grant to Boston's Voluntary Defenders Committee prefigured a later and much larger program of philanthropic support for indigent defense. Already two years before *Gideon*, the National Legal Aid and Defender Association had requested funding from the Ford Foundation for an ambitious, nationwide public defender initiative. NLADA was the most recent iteration of the National Association of Legal Aid Offices, a genteel organization founded in 1923, and sponsored by the ABA, that sought to encourage local bar groups to establish legal aid societies. Originally focused on civil legal aid, the organization added the "D" to its acronym, for "defender," in 1959.[119] In consultation with Ford Foundation program officers, NLADA developed plans for a national campaign to establish a public defender in every urban county; to improve indigent defense arrangements in rural counties; and to bring existing public defenders up to ABA standards. "It has been suggested," the proposal noted, vaguely but ominously, "that the contest in the lining up of the new and uncommitted nations, and perhaps the entire Cold War, will be resolved in our favor by reason of the superiority of our administration of justice."[120]

From the Ford Foundation's perspective, the proposed national defender initiative comported with several of the foundation's priorities: urban poverty, criminal justice, the legal profession, and the promotion of democracy. The Ford Foundation was the largest of the large philanthropic foundations that gained power in the twentieth century thanks to favorable legal changes to the regulation and tax treatment of private charitable giving. Instead of making one-time gifts to specific institutions, the relevant laws now permitted industrial magnates to create their own foundations to steward, in perpetuity, ongoing investment in favored causes. Under the umbrella of a general mission—such as the Rockefeller Foundation's commitment to "the well-being of mankind"—future generations of trustees and staffers would direct funds toward new programs and adjust priorities to changing conditions. Foundations became significant funders of schools and universities, academic research, public health initiatives, agricultural reform, and cultural outreach, both in the United States and abroad.[121] An overlapping leadership cadre, educated at East Coast prep schools and connected though military and national security service during World War II, shuttled between high-level positions in the federal executive branch and in private foundations, bringing ideas back and forth between them and using local, foundation-funded initiatives as prototypes for new federal programs.[122]

By the early 1960s, no foundation was more influential than the Ford Foundation, which had grown into what Senator Daniel Patrick Moynihan once called "a new level of American government." When first established in the 1930s, the foundation had been modest, mainly existing to administer the Ford family's charitable donations within Detroit. In the 1940s, Henry Ford and his son Edsel both died and bequeathed to the foundation most of their Ford Motor Company stock, rendering it, overnight, the largest foundation in the United States, with an endowment that dwarfed the resources of even the richest private universities.[123] Under the stewardship of Ford's grandson Henry Ford II, the newly engorged foundation embarked upon the global agenda for which it became famous: a wide-ranging grant-making program, imbued with Cold War liberalism and faith in American technocrats, oriented around the vague but appealing objectives of peace, democracy, education, and prosperity.[124] In its heyday, the foundation, described by one scholar as the "private advisory board for America's Cold War state," had ongoing initiatives around the world, ranging from cultural diplomacy (or "psychological warfare") in postwar Europe and technical assistance for rice farmers in India to juvenile delinquency outreach on the Lower East Side of Manhattan.[125]

Under the rubric of promoting democracy and the rule of law, the Ford Foundation displayed a special interest in funding legal institutions and reform efforts. In the 1950s, the foundation underwrote a massive project at the American Bar Foundation, the research arm of the ABA, to collect empirical data on all aspects of "the administration of criminal justice" nationwide.[126] The foundation's interest in underwriting public defender reforms comported with this prior effort, while also prefiguring a later development. After 1966, when erstwhile national security adviser (and Vietnam War architect) McGeorge Bundy took over as president of the foundation, the Ford Foundation would become the dominant funder and catalyst behind an expanding network of liberal public-interest law firms. The foundation provided start-up funding, hiring recommendations, and ongoing advisory assistance—but also close supervision—for a daunting list of entities, including, to name just a few, the Natural Resources Defense Council, the Mexican American Legal Defense and Educational Fund, and the American Civil Liberties Union Women's Rights Project.[127] Such investments in legal reform were encouraged by front-line staffers at the foundation, who often had an activist bent, but given an establishment veneer through the participation of elite lawyers, including several former ABA presidents, on grant recipients' oversight committees.[128]

Shortly after *Gideon*, the plans for a "National Defender Project" came to fruition. The Ford Foundation publicly announced a $2.3 million grant to NLADA—later increased to $4.3 million—to establish, expand, and assist public defenders nationwide.[129] While the project was already under discussion before *Gideon*, the Supreme Court's imprimatur infused the initiative with new urgency and inspired the Ford Foundation to recruit "a Project Director of national stature." In a fitting symbol of the project's Cold War dimensions, the foundation convinced Major General Charles "Ted" Decker, the Judge Advocate General of the United States Army, to retire from his military position so that he could fill the role.[130]

UNDERSTANDING *GIDEON* AS a product of the early Cold War, shaped by the politics of anticommunism and the intellectual paradigm of antitotalitarianism, helps to contextualize the later, and much lamented, limits of *Gideon*'s practical impact. It also helps to explain the persistent failure of arguments for a right to state-provided legal assistance in noncriminal proceedings. The fact that lawyers came to agree among themselves about the merits of the public defender in the 1950s, not in the 1910s (and not in the late 1960s), meant that the version of the public defender idea that they adopted was not the collaborative expert envisioned during the Progressive Era (nor the left-wing cause lawyer archetype that would later animate many law students). The Cold War public defender was combative, standing up for the lonely against the state. Rather than a step toward eliminating private markets in professional services, the public defender was now presented as a substitute for the privately retained lawyer. The criminal courtroom was set apart from the rest of American life as an exceptional realm in which rich and poor should stand on equal footing, with the implication that socialized provision was neither necessary nor desirable in any other realm.[131]

Gideon, then, is best understood as a belated product of the 1950s. But it is often remembered as a harbinger of the later 1960s: as a precursor to the War on Poverty; as part of a group with the Warren Court's more controversial policing cases; and as an essentially left-liberal legal artifact, notwithstanding its mainstream acceptance. There is something to all of these interpretations, but more because they capture how *Gideon* would later be understood on the ground than because they reflect the intellectual milieu from which it developed. Into the early 1960s, lawyers did not necessarily view the public defender as part of any larger agenda of state assistance to the poor. To the contrary, when elite members of the bar advocated for the public defender, they insisted that a right to state-provided counsel in criminal cases rested on premises other than a general concern for poor people's welfare and did not imply any other rights to government assistance. In the late 1960s, a younger generation of "poverty lawyers" would include criminal defense and prisoners' rights in their purview, but their vision for enlisting public defenders into campaigns for economic justice should not be read back onto the earlier part of the decade.[132] Finally, *Gideon* instantiated liberal values only under the broadest definition of liberalism, encompassing the entire mainstream American political spectrum. *Gideon* restated premises that, by 1963, were shared by leaders of the American legal profession. Lawyers could agree with those premises in their professional capacity as lawyers, regardless of their personal political commitments.

Gideon's Cold War trappings also help to explain why *Gideon* remained universally admired by lawyers across the political spectrum through the end of the twentieth century, even after the rise to power of a conservative legal movement that otherwise rejected many tenets of midcentury liberalism. Although elite lawyers and jurists lamented public defenders' actual working conditions, none seriously questioned *Gideon* as an ideal. That was true even within the heart of backlash to the Warren Court: the Reagan Administration's Department of Justice. In the 1980s, DOJ lawyers pursued an ambitious agenda to legitimate originalism as an approach to constitutional interpretation. Led by Attorney General Edwin Meese, these efforts laid the groundwork for limiting or rolling back many leading Warren Court decisions. The department's internal handbook sketched out plans for challenging *Mapp v. Ohio*, the 1961 case that required state courts to exclude unlawfully seized evidence, and *Miranda v. Arizona*, the 1966 case that required police to remind suspects of their right to remain silent. But the handbook did not mention *Gideon*; in fact, albeit in a different context, it offered a robust defense of "adversarial competition" as "the best way ultimately to reach the truth."[133]

Indeed, *Gideon* never became a target of the conservative legal movement. Looking back upon the Reagan years, Abe Krash, who had worked on *Gideon* as a young lawyer at Fortas's law firm, could think of "no responsible voices . . . saying that the Gideon case should be overturned. None of these critics of . . . the other [Warren Court] decisions say you should overturn the rule that a man is entitled to a lawyer."[134] On *Gideon*'s twenty-fifth anniversary, Anthony Lewis phoned Edwin Meese and asked how he felt about it. To Lewis's surprise, Meese assured him that he had "no quarrel with the

Gideon decision." Sounding more like a midcentury consensus liberal than a Reagan revolutionary, Meese explained that "representation by counsel in all criminal cases is essential to the fair and effective administration of justice."[135] In Lewis's words, *Gideon* made it through the Reagan Administration unscathed as the Warren Court's "one surviving landmark."[136]

BETWEEN 1960 AND 1964, two stories about the requirements—and limitations—of a fair criminal trial were stamped upon the American mind: not only *Gideon v. Wainwright*, as narrated to the general public by Anthony Lewis in *Gideon's Trumpet*, but also *To Kill a Mockingbird*, the bestselling novel and Hollywood film in which the small-town Alabama lawyer Atticus Finch defends a black man accused of raping a white woman. Both narratives celebrate the defense attorney, the noble presence at the core of *Mockingbird* and the missing piece in *Gideon* whose absence renders Clarence Earl Gideon's original trial unjust. But of course, *To Kill a Mockingbird* is a highly stylized work of fiction and can be readily recognized as a didactic reflection upon the meaning of justice, not an accurate depiction of the nation's criminal courts. The book and especially the movie present the Deep South as a place out of time, the story as a free-floating parable.[137] Like so many artifacts of American culture, *To Kill a Mockingbird* uses a criminal trial as a screen on which to project large questions about the individual and the community, truth and prejudice, mercy and vengeance. At times, the novel skewers the American penchant for self-congratulation. "Say it all together, class," a grade-school teacher in Jim Crow Alabama instructs her white charges: "We are a democracy." Unlike the Nazis, "we don't believe in persecuting anybody."[138] Overall, though, the novel's message is optimistic; Atticus Finch symbolizes the midcentury faith, written off by later generations as quaint, in principled moderation as a solvent for myopic bromides. As a lawyer-of-all-trades who occasionally takes a criminal case out of civic duty, Atticus resembles the nineteenth-century ideal of a lawyer more than a typical lawyer of the 1960s or even the 1930s, when the novel is set. As told by Lee and especially as adapted on film, *To Kill a Mockingbird* holds out hope that civic-minded white moderates might salve the Deep South's woes—even though, at the time of the novel's publication, public opinion among white Southerners was increasingly polarized.[139]

The Supreme Court's opinion in *Gideon* and Lewis's retelling in *Gideon's Trumpet* express the same gauzy midcentury optimism. Justice Black's lofty prose in *Gideon* paints an idealized image of the criminal trial with skilled, hardworking professionals on both sides, engaged in a clash of proofs destined to yield the truth. *Gideon's Trumpet* is a work of nonfiction, but as stylized as a novel, written to explain and justify the Warren Court to the average American. It is still today the most readable explanation an American can buy of the arcane rules of Supreme Court procedure. But its perspective is that of a journalist intimately familiar with the justices and the lawyers who argued before them, lawyers like the friends with whom Anthony Lewis socialized in Cape Cod, and not the perspective of, for instance, an ordinary defendant in the Boston Municipal Court. In the book's epilogue, the Supreme Court having voided his original conviction, Clarence Earl Gideon is retried in Panama City. This time he has a respected local defense attorney representing him—and he is acquitted by a unanimous jury. It was the "perfect ending," a Harvard law professor wrote in his admiring review of *Gideon's Trumpet*.[140] Actually, Anthony Lewis's gauzy optimism exceeded Harper Lee's, for the fictional trial at the heart of *To Kill a Mockingbird* has a more realistic ending. Tom Robinson has the noblest attorney in all the land, and at the end of the trial, the jury votes to convict. Not long after, he is shot and killed by prison guards, who say he was trying to climb the prison fence. The novel's narrator, Atticus's young daughter Scout, recalls how her father came into the house one afternoon to tell the news, hat in hand and face "white." "Seventeen bullet holes in him," Atticus says. "They didn't have to shoot him that much." "Atticus had used every tool available to free men to save Tom Robinson," Scout later comes to realize, "but in the secret courts of men's hearts Atticus had no case."[141]

CHAPTER FOUR

A Permanent Crisis

On 1 November 1963, a hundred judges, legislators, journalists, and lawyers gathered in Boston, in the Rooftop Ballroom of the Parker House Hotel, for the closing banquet of a two-day conference on "The Defense of Indigent Persons Accused of Crime." It was not unusual for Boston lawyers to have a meeting or dinner to attend at the Parker House, renowned for its buttery dinner rolls and colorful past. John Wilkes Booth had reportedly stayed there once, as had Mark Twain, and John F. Kennedy's bachelor party was held there. Tourists might visit for those reasons, and brides might book the Rooftop Ballroom for its panoramic views, but for the kinds of men who served on committees, it was a place to meet, a block from Boston Common and in between the State House and City Hall. Among the many purposes it served in the life of Boston, the Parker House offered a convenient setting where professional men could gather in comfort and talk about their civic preoccupations, which included the perennial question of what to do about poor people. It was not every Parker House banquet, however, that featured an actual Kennedy in person. The highlight of the November 1963 dinner was the keynote speech, delivered by the president's brother, the attorney general.[1]

Some of Robert F. Kennedy's remarks to the group were anodyne banquet fare, but for those who listened closely, there were darker notes laced through his speech on the topic of the "indigent accused." He touted the Supreme Court's recent *Gideon* decision for illustrating "our judicial system at its best . . . and the basic sense of human justice on which it is founded." Presenting in condensed form the canonical narrative soon to be published in Anthony Lewis's book, he described *Gideon* as a case in which "an obscure Florida convict" had altered "the whole course of American legal history." He concluded his address with the requisite Cold War non sequitur: "The vitality of our adversary system—the very survival of our belief in democratic justice—will depend to a greater and greater extent on the infusion of skilled advocacy in our criminal trials." Yet at other moments, Kennedy seemed less to celebrate *Gideon* than to puzzle over why it had taken the Supreme Court so long. Historically, he lamented, the legal profession had "failed frequently" to provide equal justice for rich and poor, and "it wasn't until March of this year" that the Court fully recognized "the poor man's right to appointed legal counsel." Now, Kennedy continued, the time had come for action. Lawyers throughout the United States must mobilize to translate "the principles laid down by the *Gideon* decision" into "a meaningful standard in our courts." Would they meet the challenge? Kennedy hinted at some doubts. Among lawyers and judges, he observed, *Gideon* had "aroused an atmosphere of crisis."[2]

These ominous undertones comported with a theme in Kennedy's tenure as attorney general, during which he became a vocal critic of his own profession. He was especially dismayed by the spectacle of Southern resistance to *Brown v. Board of Education*, the Supreme Court's 1954 ruling invalidating racial segregation—not because he was unusually enlightened on racial questions, but because he was horrified by what looked, from the outside, like lawlessness. As the African American military veteran James Meredith battled for entry into the University of Mississippi, Kennedy pestered his colleagues at the Department of Justice with a repeated question: "Where are all the lawyers?"[3] In the climactic confrontations of the civil rights movement, the South's (white) lawyers were not actually missing. They were the ones standing on the steps and crying "Segregation forever" (Governor George Wallace, Alabama Law '42) or inciting white students to riot over Meredith's admission (Governor Ross Barnett, Ole Miss Law '26). The American Bar Association, as late as 1963, had demonstrated little interest in civil rights issues; its president during the 1962–63 term was John Satterfield of Mississippi, who took to the pages of the *ABA Journal* to accuse the Supreme Court of undermining states' rights.[4] Kennedy and many other lawyers outside the Deep South were repulsed by their perception that fellow members of the legal profession, purported leaders of the Southern bench and bar, would openly advocate defiance of federal court orders. In 1962, Kennedy went so far as to compare (white) Southern lawyers with Nazi sympathizers—"maybe now we can understand how Hitler took over Germany"—a remarkable rebuke, coming from the highest-ranked lawyer in the federal government.[5] This context perhaps helped to explain why Kennedy could manage only tepid optimism that lawyers around the country would rally around the spirit of *Gideon*.

Three weeks later all those judges and lawyers must have thought back to that banquet, when they turned on their televisions and saw Bobby Kennedy again, walking down Pennsylvania Avenue behind his brother's casket. RFK had been onto something when he described an "atmosphere of crisis." In Massachusetts, lawyers fretted that *Gideon* had launched the state courts into "serious crisis."[6] A thousand miles to the south, Atlanta lawyers warned that convictions might be reversed, and "law enforcement severely hampered," "unless adequate procedures are adopted" to ensure the Georgia courts' compliance with the Warren Court's thickening thicket of precedents. *Gideon* and related decisions had made it "crystal clear that the old procedures do not have the approval" of the Supreme Court.[7] In Los Angeles, *Gideon* itself occasioned less worry, given the presence of a long-established public defender's office. But the nation's oldest public defender was not immune to the larger changes that *Gideon* augured. After 1965, state-level legislative changes in California guaranteed a public defender in misdemeanor cases, prefiguring the Supreme Court's extension of *Gideon* to serious misdemeanors in 1972. Along with rising criminal caseloads generally, the expansion threatened to overwhelm the Los Angeles public defender with "an ever increasing demand for services."[8]

What is notable about these quotations is that Massachusetts, California, and Georgia were all states that, according to law on the books, already made some provision for appointed counsel prior to *Gideon*. For example, the Georgia Supreme Court had interpreted the state constitution to require appointed counsel for indigent defendants as early as 1874.[9] As these reactions demonstrate, *Gideon* occasioned worry among lawyers on the ground, in states all around the nation, regardless of what steps their states had taken prior to *Gideon*. That was true for at least three reasons. First, even though Supreme Court observers had been expecting a case like *Gideon*, the stakes became higher once it had actually been decided. Defendants denied their right to counsel were no longer limited to state remedies but could cite federal constitutional law or file a federal habeas petition. Second, national organizations promoted *Gideon* not only as a case about appointed counsel, but also as an impetus to establish or expand public defender agencies. Following that guidance would require an overhaul of local court procedures in states like Georgia that provided counsel through the traditional method of trial judges appointing private lawyers case by case. Finally, *Gideon* in these discussions symbolized something larger—the Warren Court's ongoing campaign to transform the Bill of Rights into a national "code of criminal procedure"—and no one yet knew where that campaign would ultimately end. In Atlanta, lawyers located *Gideon*'s "significance . . . not in the facts of the case but in the implications of the opinion," and predicted that *Gideon* was unlikely to "be the last word from the Supreme Court on the subject."[10]

Nationwide, local bar leaders received *Gideon* as a mandate for change, even as they debated what exactly that mandate required. Legal scholars often describe *Gideon*, and the Warren Court's criminal procedure cases more generally, as concerned primarily with imposing national standards upon recalcitrant Southern states.[11] The historical evidence makes clear that this interpretation is oversimplified. Certainly, the South occupied a place of special concern for the Court, and many Warren Court decisions required, or should have required, significant change in that region. But *Gideon*'s ramifications spread far more widely. It was sometimes stated, both at the time of *Gideon* and in later scholarship, that *Gideon* only affected five states: Florida, Alabama, Mississippi, North Carolina, and South Carolina. But that tally derived from a 1962 study, which, in its original presentation, was more nuanced. The study arranged the states along a spectrum. The five Southern states were at the far end, because they provided no right to counsel in state law (outside of capital cases) and also made weak (if any) efforts to provide counsel in practice. Eight other states, not all in the South, also provided no legal guarantee of counsel; they were placed in the middle of the spectrum, however, because they appeared to provide counsel in practice, at least in cities.[12] *Gideon* affected states throughout the country both because law in action was more variable than law on the books, and also because lawyers did not read *Gideon* narrowly. They focused not on "the facts of the case" but on the larger "implications of the opinion."

Understanding *Gideon* as only the first step in a long-term expansion of criminal defendants' rights, many lawyers feared that guaranteeing the right to counsel on paper would no longer satisfy the Supreme Court's rising standards. Many concluded that their states needed to build stable, well-funded defender organizations to ensure that their criminal courts could withstand federal judicial scrutiny. Yet in subsequent years, the Supreme Court provided little follow-up guidance about these questions of implementation. Instead, to divine what *Gideon* and related decisions meant for their own local institutions, lawyers blended guidance from national professional groups like the American Bar Association and the National Legal Aid and Defender Association, official directives from the Department of Justice and the lower federal courts, and their own local traditions and norms. In November 1963, lawyers might assume that the "atmosphere of crisis" identified by Kennedy amounted merely to a short-lived set of doubts about what to do next, soon to dissipate once lawyers took up his call to action. But months turned into years and the crisis never seemed to melt away. By the turn of the 1970s, crisis had become a permanent state of affairs for the criminal courts.

IN *GIDEON'S TRUMPET*, Anthony Lewis distinguished between "the dream of *Gideon*" and the "social task" of "bring[ing] to life the dream." The "dream of *Gideon*," as Lewis summarized it, was "the dream of a vast, diverse country in which every man charged with crime will be capably defended, no matter what his economic circumstances, and in which the lawyer representing him will do so proudly, without resentment at an unfair burden, sure of the support needed to make an adequate defense."[13] Tucked into a subordinate clause, "the support needed to make an adequate defense"—which is to say, money—would presumably come from somewhere; it was not in the nature of dreams to say where. Lewis's diction captured one understanding of the institutional role of the Warren Court. The judicial task was to dream up an ideal country, and everyone else's "social task" was to bring that dream to life. This was a conception of the judiciary in which the Supreme Court was not itself engaged in anything so pedestrian as a task. Lewis and other admirers celebrated the political and even moral leadership of the Warren Court. They praised the justices for providing blueprints for democracy through their rulings on racial segregation, civil rights, voting, free speech, and criminal procedure.[14]

This conception of the Supreme Court's role caused difficulties for local lawyers and institutions—and also for the criminal defendants whose rights the Court sought to define. As legal scholars recognized, *Gideon* and similar decisions, filled with "ringing pronouncements," existed on a different plane from the "Dickensian netherworld of mass criminal adjudication" that they ostensibly sought to govern.[15] That disconnect helps to explain the crisis atmosphere engendered by *Gideon*, whose long-term implications for the "netherworld" lawyers could only speculate about. In *Gideon* and other criminal procedure rulings, the justices had set in motion "the most ambitious attempt" in United States history to bring "the celebrated ideals of the federal Constitution to bear on the day-to-day realities of urban administration of criminal justice." Yet in some ways, they failed subsequently to follow through on that attempt. When it came to nuts-and-bolts enforcement, the otherwise formidable Warren Court displayed "uncharacteristic remedial timidity." *Gideon* was paired "with no remedial instrument whatsoever acting directly, coercively or prospectively upon the persons whose behavior was purportedly controlled." The states were simply trusted to comply; in *Gideon*'s immediate aftermath, the Supreme Court set up no procedure or doctrinal framework for ongoing adjudication of whether each state was maintaining "an adequate system of providing counsel."[16]

In truth, Lewis's image of the Warren Court as lofty dreamer did not universally apply; in the context of education, for example, the Court did descend into the muck of implementation. *Brown v. Board* had sidestepped questions of enforcement, but was augmented a year later with *Brown II*, a follow-up ruling that spelled out how local school districts should proceed. *Brown II* required districts to desegregate "with all deliberate speed," and directed the lower federal courts to monitor "implementation of the governing constitutional principles" by fashioning decrees tailored to local conditions and holding further court hearings, if necessary.[17] *Brown II* gave rise to decades of action both by the Supreme Court and the lower federal courts to coerce local schools into compliance, using judicial injunctions, consent decrees, and the threat of contempt proceedings for officials who resisted. This phenomenon required substantial procedural innovation on the part of the Warren Court, which reimagined the injunction, long a feature of labor and business litigation, as a device for federal oversight of units of local and state government.[18]

This is not to valorize *Brown II*, whose formula of "all deliberate speed"—rather than immediate compliance—was regarded by many critics as a capitulation to foot-dragging local officials.[19] It is only to note that, for all of the shortcomings of *Brown II* and subsequent enforcement litigation, *Gideon*'s implementation received even less judicial oversight and benefited from even less procedural creativity. Instead of structural reform litigation, the Warren Court's rulings regarding criminal trial rights would be enforced primarily in the same way that they had come about: through the accumulation of individual appeals and habeas petitions, filed by individual prisoners often long after their initial convictions.[20] In the late 1970s, living under the more conservative Burger Court, and worrying that the "ringing pronouncements" might begin to lose their force if not backed up with action, the Yale law professor Robert Cover and his student Alexander Aleinikoff puzzled over this discrepancy. At best, they wrote, habeas litigation offered a "roundabout way" of coercing state institutions to change, and one that "sacrificed some of the momentum for reform of state criminal justice" that *Gideon* had initially promised.[21]

Cover and Aleinikoff proposed several explanations for the Warren Court's reluctance to engage in large-scale coercive oversight of the states in the realm of criminal trial rights. In the American constitutional tradition, criminal law had historically been defined as a matter for local control, and doctrinal norms of comity limited the federal judicial appetite for intervening in state-level courts. A similar tradition of local control had not kept the federal courts out of schools, but perhaps that was the point: perhaps, Cover and Aleinikoff suggested, the experience of massive resistance to *Brown v. Board* had spooked the Court. Avoiding coercive injunctions spared the

Court, in the criminal procedure context, from another "Russian Winter of direct enforcement of an unpopular constitutional innovation."[22] *Gideon* was not itself unpopular—certainly not compared to the Warren Court's more controversial policing decisions—but perhaps it would have become unpopular had the Court used it to justify active intervention into ongoing criminal proceedings in the state courts.

Cover and Aleinikoff's final explanation was most intriguing and also most troubling. Ultimately, they concluded, Americans were "ambivalent and contradictory social selves." They believed strongly in constitutional values in the abstract but remained wary of the practical implications of living out those values. By leaving enforcement indirect, the Court permitted Americans to continue having it both ways: "to act as if we were not committed to these uncertain constitutional values and to cherish them as indispensable." The Warren Court chopped up the responsibility for enforcing defendants' rights into roundabout mechanisms that left those rights incompletely enforced at the local level. By doing so, Cover and Aleinikoff posited, the Court had created a convoluted legal process that allowed "society to enact, ritualize, project its own ambivalence in jurisdictional terms."[23]

After *Gideon*, the right-to-counsel case law continued to proliferate, and in that sense, the requirements on the states became ever more complex, but throughout, the Supreme Court remained aloof about the related institutional questions of implementation. *Gideon* technically established only the right to counsel at trial; the Court subsequently decided a string of cases explaining when the right attached at other stages of the criminal process, both before and after trial. The lower courts continued to respond to habeas petitioners' frequent complaints that counsel had offered "ineffective assistance" in their individual cases, establishing some (relatively minimal) standards of quality for defense representation.[24] Questions about how the requisite counsel should be provided or paid for remained up to localities, states, and the legal profession to work out on their own. The Court apparently trusted that individual criminal defendants, by filing appeals or habeas petitions if their trials were unfair, would bring to judicial attention any egregious failures to comply. The odd result was to diffuse among the nation's criminal defendants the collective burden of enforcing their own rights—rights guaranteed by a body of jurisprudence animated by the foundational premise that defendants were incapable, without expert assistance, of understanding their own rights. Cover and Aleinikoff introduced the label of "dialectical federalism" to describe the two-track scheme in which the states handled "the pragmatic end" of managing "our system of mass criminal justice" and the federal courts occasionally stepped in to "exert a utopian tug"—but only a "tug."[25]

The resultant divide between utopian constitutional principles and ground-level mass processing corresponded in a rough way to Anthony Lewis's distinction between the dream of *Gideon* and the social task of implementing it. Writing in 1964, however, Lewis either did not foresee or did not admit to foreseeing that the social task would be handled in such a desultory way. He acknowledged the difficulties ahead. The project, he allowed, was an "enormous" one. The "new responsibilities" that *Gideon* imposed upon lawyers and local courts were "heavy." But there was "no sign," in Lewis's view, "that the American legal community" considered *Gideon*'s burdens "unjustified." To support this point, he furnished some boilerplate quotes from leaders of groups like the American Bar Association. "There is a long road to travel," Lewis allowed, "before every criminal court in the United States reaches the goal that appears on the façade of the Supreme Court building: *Equal Justice Under Law*." But within the discursive loop of *Gideon's Trumpet*, the assumption was that the country was at least *on* the right road.[26]

The optimism of *Gideon's Trumpet* about law and legal institutions made for a striking juxtaposition with a collection of essays that Lewis published in the same year, which castigated law and legal institutions as thoroughly "corrupt"—at least, as they operated in the Deep South. "Again and again today," Lewis wrote in *Portrait of a Decade*, "Negroes in certain parts of the South find themselves caught up in the machinery of the criminal law because of entirely innocent acts—that is, acts that would be innocent anywhere else." Lewis described how Southern governors, legislators, judges, police officers, district attorneys, and (white) jurors together engaged in the "wholesale perversion of justice," using courts not for the neutral enforcement of the law but rather for the maintenance of white supremacy—so that black defendants were overcharged and railroaded, while white defendants accused of murdering civil rights leaders escaped with impunity. Law in Mississippi, Lewis went so far as to conclude, operated according to "the Marxist idea of law." It was nothing more than the "instrument of the ruling class in a caste system."[27]

It was remarkable that Lewis could develop such scathing impressions of the Southern legal profession yet express such faith in *Gideon's Trumpet* that the legal profession as a whole was devoted to "equal justice." Like many midcentury liberals, he presented Mississippi as aberrational, its courts and lawyers as deviants from an otherwise sound legal culture.[28] Here Lewis's account of what happened to the typical Southern black defendant was telling: "he is charged with a crime, arrested, convicted on no evidence of anything that constitutionally can be a crime, held on bail that is difficult or impossible for him to raise, forced to go through a long and frustrating and expensive legal process before someone—probably the Supreme Court— ends the lawless course of law."[29] Thus even though Lewis was cynical about the Southern courts, he positioned the Supreme Court as a dependable backstop, even if the path to get there might be "long and frustrating." But the crisis, real or discursive, that *Gideon* inaugurated would not remain bounded by the Mason-Dixon line.

WHEN *GIDEON* WAS HANDED DOWN, Boston's Voluntary Defenders Committee was already in the throes of a rocky conversion from private charity into state agency. After the withdrawal of community chest funding, the board of directors had belatedly taken its erstwhile funders' advice and lobbied for statewide public defender legislation. In response, in 1960, the state legislature had enacted a barebones bill establishing the "Massachusetts Defenders Committee," whose members would be appointed by the Judicial Council, the administrative arm of the state judiciary.[30] Initially, the agency was essentially just the Voluntary Defenders Committee under an altered name. The legislation provided few specifics about how the agency would be organized or funded; it stated only that the MDC would henceforth provide counsel for indigent defendants in all cases where counsel was legally required, and authorized the agency to "adopt such rules and regulations," and "appoint such professional, clerical and other assistants as may be necessary" to carry out that task.[31] The Judicial Council appointed a few new board members, but LaRue Brown remained the chair, Wilbur Hollingsworth stayed on as chief counsel, and for a time, the agency even continued using its charitable predecessor's leftover stationery.[32] Although the legislature had been convinced to establish the agency, the legislators who managed the Commonwealth's finances remained reluctant to fund it. In 1961, Brown complained that "we have never seemed to have any friends" in the relevant committees. "Criminals don't seem to have any vote appeal."[33]

Even after *Gideon*, the legislature remained stingy. One board member complained in 1964 of the MDC's "extreme difficulty" in securing the funds needed "to perform its duties . . . [as] required under the Constitution."[34] Despite Brown's quip about criminals lacking "vote appeal," he later concluded that the legislature's intransigence stemmed less from antipathy toward defendants than from protectionist concern for lawyers, a sizeable caucus in the Massachusetts legislature. Brown observed that—like some of the public defender idea's early opponents—legislators believed that "spending the state's money to defend criminals . . . takes away fees from some deserving lawyers."³⁵ The agency tried to make clear to the political branches how *Gideon* had raised the stakes of fulfilling defendants' right to counsel. In funding requests, the agency explained that its "volume of cases" would multiply as a result of recent Supreme Court decisions, and warned "that convictions [would] be overturned" by the federal courts if defendants were not provided adequate counsel.³⁶ These entreaties moved neither the legislature nor the governor, John Volpe, who slashed the agency's requested budget for 1965 by two-thirds before sending it to the legislature.³⁷

Meanwhile, the demand for the Massachusetts Defenders' services continued to grow. About a year after *Gideon*, Wilbur Hollingsworth argued in a test case that *Gideon* required counsel in cases prosecuted in the district courts—the lowest-level Massachusetts courts, where lawyers had traditionally been sparse on all sides. The state's highest court rejected Hollingsworth's constitutional argument but agreed that it was "prudent" for district courts to appoint counsel in all but "the most trifling" cases. Soon thereafter, state judicial rules were revised to require district courts to appoint counsel in all cases with a possible prison term.³⁸ Complying with that rule presented enormous logistical challenges. One statewide study estimated that 60 percent of defendants facing "serious charge[s]" in the district courts lacked counsel. That translated, by one estimate, into 32,250 cases per year in which counsel was required but not yet provided.³⁹ To expand its caseload by that order of magnitude, the Massachusetts Defenders Committee would need perhaps twenty-six times its current number of lawyers. In light of these calculations, Brown described *Gideon*'s "burden" on defenders as "almost appalling." Board member Raynor Gardiner grumbled that trying "to take care of all the more serious cases in the district courts is a little like trying to bail out the ocean."⁴⁰

Hollingsworth and the more patrician board of directors divided over how aggressively to lobby for funds, in part because they disagreed about what type of salary public defenders should expect. After *Gideon*, the ABA's professional standards recommended that defenders earn salaries commensurate with law firm associates or prosecutors. In Massachusetts, implementing that recommendation would have required large raises for line defenders.⁴¹ In 1964, public defenders earned "the lowest salary" of any full-time attorneys employed by the state of Massachusetts.⁴² Hollingsworth seethed over this pay gap.⁴³ Whether out of genuine belief in *Gideon*, self-serving reasons (as the board suspected), or a combination of both, he maintained that public defenders should be paid exactly the same as prosecutors. Accordingly, when the board asked him to prepare a post-*Gideon* budget estimate, he replied by simply sending them a copy of the district attorney salary scale.[44] Hollingsworth's insistence on comparing defender and prosecutor salaries exasperated the board. "We need figures of [the number of] cases" to calculate the budget, LaRue Brown wrote, "not . . . salaries of politically appointed assistant district attorneys," which Brown thought were higher than the MDC could realistically seek.[45]

Brown worried that requesting too large a budget would provoke a backlash: angry legislators might eliminate the agency altogether and revert to an appointed counsel system. But his lack of urgency on the salary issue also derived from his long history with the pre-*Gideon* voluntary defender model. For years, he had endorsed that model's low-pay, high-turnover salary scale. Even after *Gideon*, Brown described indigent defense not as a career track but as a waystation for "young attorneys," providing "valuable training and experience, which they later made use of when they went with a law firm."[46] Hollingsworth thought *Gideon* rendered this model obsolete, and criticized the board for continuing to view the agency as "a training ground for young lawyers."[47] Hollingsworth had quickly grown frustrated with what he considered the board's sluggish response to *Gideon*. Three months after the decision was handed down, he complained that "for three and one-half months, with all of the experience and knowledge at our command, we have done nothing but talk." *Gideon*, he wrote, "is now the law of this Commonwealth and makes it mandatory to provide counsel in every court of the Commonwealth to every defendant charged with a serious crime . . . The Massachusetts Defenders Committee is not presently providing such representation."[48]

Partly because of the deepening rift over the import of *Gideon*, the board fired Hollingsworth in June 1964. Hollingsworth retaliated by giving a scandalous quote to the press: "I think that at the present time the public defender project in Massachusetts is a complete failure."[49] More than a parochial personnel conflict, Hollingsworth's termination prefigured dynamics that would trouble *Gideon*'s implementation nationwide. At the level of elite discourse, lawyers had settled on a shared vision of what *Gideon* required, especially in cities: well-funded public defender offices, staffed by career lawyers earning professional salaries. But it was no simple matter to realize that vision, which required lobbying state legislators and local policymakers for the requisite changes and then navigating the complex politics of state and local budgets. The Supreme Court never fully spelled out whether the ultimate responsibility for implementing *Gideon* lay with the states, with local courts, or some other place. NLADA handbooks and DOJ guides provided more specific standards, but still not much political guidance about how to meet them. In a complex federal polity with thousands of differently organized and partially overlapping court systems, each with its own procedures, terminology, and funding sources, even widely shared principles required extensive translation to map onto local institutional realities. Predictably, that translation process often became contentious. Rather than an exceptional instance in which *Gideon* was undermined by local politics and personality conflicts, then, the Massachusetts story exemplified how *Gideon*'s implementation nationwide was structurally vulnerable to such conflicts.

WHEN THE STATE balked at its budget requests, the Massachusetts Defenders Committee revived the venerable tradition of public–private governance and looked elsewhere. In 1965, the state defender agency partnered with Action for Boston Community Development, a public-private hybrid established to coordinate Ford Foundation urban renewal grants for metropolitan Boston. The MDC, together with ABCD (the 1960s were an age of acronyms), secured one of the first, and largest, grants from the Ford-funded National Defender Project, which it used to hire dozens of new defenders for the Suffolk County district courts.[50] The next year, the MDC secured an even larger grant from the federal Office of Economic Opportunity, the lead agency in President Lyndon Johnson's War on Poverty, which enabled the hiring of defenders for all of the district courts statewide.[51] In securing an OEO grant, the MDC took advantage of a brief window before Congress clarified that War on Poverty funds were not intended for criminal defense.[52] With the outside funding, the MDC nearly doubled its legal staff, bringing the total to fifty-eight attorneys, and opened regional offices throughout the state. This was not the twenty-six-fold increase once forecasted, but it was deemed a success. Toward the end of 1966, Hollingsworth's replacement as chief counsel—one of his former assistants, Edgar Rimbold—reported that the Ford and OEO grants had enabled the agency to provide "complete representation" in all seventy-two district courts statewide, "a striking increase" from the previous year. Rimbold continued: "This is 'volume representation' of the type that appears to be mandatory for any state to furnish, if it is to conform with the *Gideon* requirements."[53]

Outside funding worked where reasoned argument had failed and convinced the legislature to expand the MDC's budget. With grant monies, the agency could hire staffers on short-term contracts and then ask the legislature to fund their salaries on a permanent basis, replacing abstract budget requests with actual people who would lose their jobs absent legislative action. In 1967, with the OEO grant scheduled to terminate at the end of the year, MDC staffers personally contacted every member of the state Senate. Their lobbying succeeded; the state assumed the salaries of the OEO-hired lawyers.[54] The next year, the agency again warned of looming layoffs. The legislature responded with an appropriation that fell short of the agency's request but was, nevertheless, enough to "absorb all of the [Ford Foundation] Model Defender Program" and "all of the work . . . under the OEO program."[55]

Still, defenders' salaries remained relatively low. Rimbold explained that he had to hire a revolving cast of recent law school graduates "because we can not pay a high salary." One public defender who worked in Boston told a magazine reporter, "The pay's bad . . . but I live with my parents, so I manage. A married man couldn't really afford this job."[56] In a withering 1972 report, independent evaluators from NLADA lambasted MDC's "inexcusably low salaries" and—as Hollingsworth had done nearly ten years before—recommended a pay scale "roughly competitive" with law firms and "at least equivalent to . . . the district attorney's office."[57] Apparently unaware that Hollingsworth and the board had battled over this very issue just a few years before, the evaluators interpreted the agency's pay scale as straightforward evidence of a stingy state commitment to *Gideon*. They failed to recognize that state funding levels derived from the board's own post-*Gideon* decisions to start its budget requests from a low baseline, over the objections of the ousted Hollingsworth, who had urged a more aggressive lobbying strategy.

In the district courts, local judges bristled at the new public defenders, whom they regarded as unwelcome meddlers with their traditional prerogatives. The notorious chief justice of the Boston Municipal Court, Elijah Adlow, proved to be public defenders' most obstinate foe, often simply refusing to appoint them to cases. Adlow felt that the higher courts, in interpreting *Gideon*, had "gone too far," and complained that MDC attorneys "worr[ied] too much about constitutional rights and things like that in petty cases." In Adlow's view, public defenders "should only handle serious cases" and "'petty stuff' should be . . . handled by the judge in his own way." As an example of Adlow's "own way," he claimed "that in his court the Negro people were treated less harshly because they were not as responsible for their conduct as white people."[58] Perhaps Adlow meant this statement as a reassuring illustration of his leniency, or, more likely, as a provocation implying that he might stop being so lenient if lawyers kept challenging him. Board members at the MDC heard instead a distressing admission that

Adlow decided cases according to paternalism, racism, and personal whim—all the more reason why defendants in his courtroom needed lawyers. Adlow's notoriety reached the point that the radical activist and historian Howard Zinn, while teaching at Boston University, sent a group of students to observe his courtroom. On another occasion, a Harvard undergraduate who happened into Adlow's courtroom described the experience as "a frightening confrontation with irrational authority."[59]

As Judge Adlow's obstinacy demonstrated, *Gideon*'s welcome reception among both legal elites and the general public was not always replicated in the nation's front-line criminal courts. Nor was the resistance to *Gideon* limited to the South, where it could be fit within a pattern of opposition to the Warren Court since *Brown v. Board*. If Adlow was especially "flamboyant," he was not, in one lawyer's words, "atypical." From Roxbury to Lowell, New Bedford to Dorchester, the MDC encountered district court judges who either refused to appoint public defenders—sometimes appointing personal friends to indigent cases instead—or appointed public defenders but then sentenced their clients more harshly.[60] Nor were Massachusetts judges unique: public defenders nationwide complained of judicial pressure and abuse. Particularly in low-level cases, local judges did not always agree with the Warren Court that every step of the criminal process should be governed by the Constitution. A reporter for the *New Yorker* observed in 1973, ten years after *Gideon* and four years after Chief Justice Warren's retirement, that many judges "apparently share Judge Adlow's resentment toward lawyers who get in the way."[61]

Nevertheless, Massachusetts garnered praise as a national leader in implementing *Gideon*. Speaking at the 1967 NLADA convention, General Ted Decker of the National Defender Project "singled out" the Massachusetts Defenders Committee as "the best project in the country."[62] Viewed from a distance, it is possible to understand why the Massachusetts response to *Gideon* could have appeared exemplary. Lawyers long involved with indigent defense in the state had quickly mobilized, assessed what *Gideon* required, anticipated where the Court was likely to move next, and lobbied for expanded state appropriations for the public defender agency—just the sorts of social tasks that Anthony Lewis had predicted. When the legislature and governor initially balked, these lawyers then resourcefully secured outside funding from foundations and the federal government to expand the agency's reach, all the while continuing to lobby the state to take over funding, which it eventually did. Underlying all foundation and federal grants was the expectation that they would spur local innovations that politicians would then recognize as valuable and arrange to support on a permanent basis. But rarely did that expectation play out so seamlessly as it seemed to have done in Massachusetts. Defenders continued to struggle with low salaries and stubborn judges, but, by the late 1960s, Massachusetts had set in place a foundation on which to build. That, at any rate, was the official story.

Viewed up close, the foundation appeared riven with fissures. Bought with threats of layoffs, the legislature's fiscal commitment to the MDC remained uncertain, and the resistance of local figures like Judge Adlow portended that defenders would spend much of their time fighting for appointments to cases rather than fighting on behalf of their clients. But the largest problem was one that did not initially occur to the MDC board: the organization continued to make decisions without input from the communities that public defenders served. Though now a state agency, MDC continued to operate under the oversight of a board of directors made up primarily of lawyers. This remained largely true even during the brief period when the agency received federal OEO funds, which required recipient organizations to make space for the "maximum feasible participation" of poor people themselves.[63] As a result of this requirement, many OEO projects around the country invited genuine grassroots leadership—to an extent that fueled conservative backlash against the program and discomfited even many liberals within the D.C. establishment.[64] But the MDC met the "maximum feasible participation" requirement in a more hollow fashion: by reviving the corporate entity of the defunct Voluntary Defenders Committee as the official recipient of the grant and adding six slots for community members to the Voluntary Defenders board. If such members did regularly participate in meetings—which is unclear—they would have been meetings of the rump Voluntary Defenders Committee, which was now an accounting vessel.[65] If Massachusetts represented a best-case scenario for *Gideon*'s implementation, then perhaps the right to counsel held less promise to remake the courts into paragons of democratic justice than Anthony Lewis, Robert Kennedy, and the Supreme Court itself had hoped.

IN PHILADELPHIA, the Defender Association followed an initially similar but ultimately divergent trajectory. At first, similar to its Massachusetts counterpart, the Association cobbled together a mix of foundation and federal grants to respond to *Gideon*'s mandate. For years the Defender Association had been supported primarily by the city's community chest, but after *Gideon*, it augmented its budget with short-term grants from the OEO, the Ford Foundation, and other sources, and expanded its staff through a

National Defender Project partnership with the University of Pennsylvania. Before *Gideon*, the Defender Association remained a small charity employing six attorneys. By 1967, its offices buzzed with forty lawyers, ten investigators, fifteen secretaries, and one social worker.[66] As in Massachusetts, the Defender Association looked to public sources to maintain the expanded operations once the private grants expired—though in their case they turned to the city of Philadelphia rather than to the state government.[67]

Unlike its Boston counterpart, however, Philadelphia's voluntary defender never fully converted into a public agency, remaining incorporated as a private nonprofit. Even as the Defender Association began to depend on municipal subsidies for the first time, it fought tooth and nail to remain institutionally separate from the city. Through a series of conflicts with the city over this question, the Defender Association maintained that effective criminal defense required political independence from local government, and that only institutional separation could maintain this independence. In this way, the Defender Association's leadership sought to blend the public and voluntary defender models into a new, hybrid approach to indigent defense. They accepted the necessity of public funding in order to expand on the scale required by *Gideon* and related legal changes, but otherwise sought to maintain the organization's long-standing autonomy. They grappled for a way to accept the new reality of fiscal dependence on the state without otherwise compromising their organization's independent character.

The trouble began in 1969, in the aftermath of an ill-fated municipal takeover attempt of the Defender Association during the administration of Mayor James Tate. The City Council had balked at funding the organization's budget, now nearing $1 million annually, and instead proposed "the creation of a wholly new public defender program" whose head "would be appointed by the Mayor." The Defender Association rallied community support to ward off this change, citing the organization's long history of providing "independent legal defense services of the highest quality." Subsequent negotiations produced a compromise: the Defender Association would remain nominally private, but would enter into a contract with the city of Philadelphia—signed in January 1969—to provide indigent defense services, funded by annual appropriations from the City Council. In turn, the city would receive an expanded presence on the reconstituted board of directors. Rather than a diffuse board of fifty members, the board would now consist of thirty members: ten selected by the Defender Association, ten selected by the mayor, and then ten selected jointly. Thus, the city would directly control one-third of the Board's membership and have some say in selecting another one-third.

Depending on how the city wielded this influence, the mayor might effectively control a majority of the board.[68]

A narrow majority of the Defender Association's board of directors approved the compromise, but a group of dissenters resigned in protest and filed suit. They challenged the arrangement as a violation of Pennsylvania law governing nonprofit organizations. A standard provision of Pennsylvania corporations law required that all amendments to nonprofit charters must be "beneficial and not injurious to the community." The objecting board members argued that the compromise arrangement with the city—particularly the city's outsized presence on the board of directors—undermined the Defender Association's requisite political independence and was therefore "injurious" to the community welfare.[69] The concern that the city would seek to control the organization was not frivolous, given that the city provided 92 percent of the Defender Association's operating budget by 1969. Moreover, Mayor Tate had already demanded the resignation of the organization's acting chief defender, Martin Vinikoor, who had previously run for City Council on an opposing ticket. A former city councilor testified that municipal control of the Defender Association risked depriving defendants of their right to "a lawyer who is completely fearless . . . and dedicated within the limits of legal ethics to a zealous, outspoken, forward defense of his client."[70]

While the litigation was pending, the stakes rose with the election in 1971 of Frank Rizzo, the first police chief in the United States to ascend to mayoral office and—in the words of his critics—"the cop who would be king." As police commissioner under Mayor Tate, Rizzo had gained enormous popularity among Philadelphia's blue-collar white voters because of his aggressive policing tactics, violent crackdowns on African American protestors, and "law and order" rhetoric.[71] Rizzo expressed open disdain for lawyers who represented the poor. In 1967, while still police commissioner, he threatened to terminate a program allowing police officers to donate via payroll deductions to the United Fund, the local community chest, because the United Fund supported the Legal Aid Society. Organizations that "fight the Police Department . . . won't get a penny" from police, he threatened. Also while commissioner, he set up a meeting with several criminal judges and demanded that they "change their 'lenient' sentencing practices." As a justice of the Pennsylvania Supreme Court noted drily: "The above events can hardly be viewed by the Community and indigent defendants as an assurance that the City will in no way attempt to influence the criminal defense of those unable to retain private counsel."[72]

The Defender Association lawsuit opened up into a wide-ranging debate about how independent public defenders should be from politics. Philadelphia's district attorney, Arlen Specter, testified against the compromise, arguing that defenders "should be totally non-political" to ensure they could provide their clients with "independent representation." Specter worried that subjecting public defenders to city oversight would introduce "political factors" into hiring and other decisions, factors that "have no place in either the prosecution or defense of criminal cases." This phrasing was somewhat odd since Specter was himself an elected official, but his testimony revealed the extent of support for insulating defenders from the city's elected leadership. Another prosecutor, who had previously practiced criminal defense, warned that the city might seek to subordinate the Defender Association to the Rizzo Administration's "war on crime" agenda. If "the Police" were given "a say," however indirect, "over . . . those defending people we're warring on," he worried that defenders might "back off" and "not take as forthright a stand as they otherwise would."[73]

In the end, the Pennsylvania Supreme Court dismissed these concerns and upheld the Defender Association's compromise with the city. The court did not disagree that public defenders must be independent advocates. Pennsylvania's highest court proceeded from the assumption that public defenders were no different from privately retained lawyers: "Like any lawyer, a person chosen to represent an accused indigent person may serve but one master—the client." But the Pennsylvania court rejected the assertion that city oversight would necessarily generate a conflict of interest or undermine defenders' appropriately adversarial role. Even if the mayor nominated some number of board members, he would not participate in the board's deliberations and decision-making. The court declared that it was "sheer speculation" to assume that the board would function "as a rubber stamp for the Mayor." The court also declined to assume that Rizzo's "attitude of antagonism to criminal defendants" would inevitably be transmitted first to the board, from there to the chief defender, and downward to line defenders. Instead, the court presumed that "the standards of professional conduct" governing all lawyers should suffice to ensure that public defenders acted in "the best interests of their clients."[74]

In a blistering dissent, two justices on the Pennsylvania Supreme Court disputed this optimistic account. The dissenting justices predicted that the compromise arrangement would "destroy [the Defender Association's] necessary independence and non-political character." The dissenters emphasized not only the mayor's power to appoint half of the board (either directly or indirectly), but also the City Council's control over the Defender Association's budget and its power to terminate the contract at any time. In their view, these conditions amounted to an intolerable conflict of interest. The arrangement "raise[d] serious questions" about whether the Defender Association would be permitted to "give undivided loyalty to those it represents." It also raised the equally troubling concern that members of the community would perceive a conflict of interest, no matter what defenders actually did. In closing, the dissenters asked: "Can the community which the Defender Association serves and the indigents it defends have confidence and trust in an Association significantly controllable by the Mayor, who also appoints the Police Commissioner . . . whose interests are obviously those of the prosecution and antithetical to the defense?"[75]

This account of the need for independent defense reprised earlier arguments in favor of the voluntary defender, but now with a changed valence. It was no longer realistic for indigent defense organizations to reject public resources entirely. *Gideon* and subsequent cases required the states to provide counsel in a growing number of situations, and efforts to provide universal legal representation with purely private funding had failed. But lawyers continued to value independence and sought ways to protect that value even within taxpayer-funded organizations. The entire debate revealed how thoroughly the Progressive Era public defender idea had faded from legal consciousness. No member of the Pennsylvania court deemed it necessary to address progressive reformers' vision that defenders and prosecutors, by virtue of shared public office, could be trusted to work together in the mutual interest of defendants and the public alike. At the turn of the 1970s, that vision would have seemed both impossibly naïve and incompatible with the defense lawyer's proper role as a staunch adversary of the state, a role that the bar had, by then, extended to public defenders. Everyone assumed that prosecutors and defenders served opposing interests; the only question was whether the city's proposed governance structure permitted defenders to pursue those interests zealously.

The Progressive Era dream of a collaborative judicial bureaucracy was out of step with the Cold War fetish for adversarial courtroom advocacy. It was equally anathema to Vietnam-era critics of the Cold War consensus, who adopted an oppositional stance toward the state both within the courtroom and without. The issues raised by the Philadelphia dispute would recur throughout the nation as the public defender model spread. How could lawyers paid by the government, and working for organizations that depended upon the government for their budgets, also defy the government?

As mayor, Frank Rizzo did not engage in the kinds of overt attempts to manipulate defenders that they had feared, perhaps because the lawsuit put city leaders on notice that the Defender Association would jealously guard its independence if pushed.[76] But there were other ways to mute advocacy. In Philadelphia and around the country, it would turn out that the real threat to public defenders' freedom of action was not direct interference, but an overwhelming amount of work.

IN 1967, TWO LAW STUDENTS at the University of Pennsylvania signed up for an unusual summer job: conducting an observational study of the Defender Association of Philadelphia. All summer, the two students spent their days shadowing Philadelphia defenders both in court and in the office. Their task was not to assist the defenders with their work, or to try to learn from them, as in a typical law school internship. Rather, their task was to evaluate them. On standard worksheets, they recorded what the defenders did throughout the day, tallied how many minutes they spent on each activity, and sought to assess the quality of the legal representation provided. The students worked under the supervision of Professor Louis Schwartz, one of the objecting board members who would later file suit over the Defender Association's political independence. Funded by the Ford Foundation's National Defender Project, their study constituted one of the first efforts, post-*Gideon*, to collect data about basic empirical questions such as what exactly public defenders did all day, and to evaluate the changes that *Gideon* and the National Defender Project were introducing into the nation's criminal courts.[77]

What the students found did not impress them. It turned out that defenders spent nearly half of their time in the courtroom "simply waiting" for their cases to be called. Conversely, in the students' view, defenders seemed to spend shockingly little time on legal work. In many cases, the students wrote, the time spent on "an indigent's entire defense could be calculated in terms of minutes." Even defendants facing relatively serious charges, such as larceny, typically received fewer than four hours of legal work on their behalf.[78] The Philadelphia courts did not rely on plea bargaining to the same extent as other jurisdictions, but only because local practice allowed for defendants to waive their jury rights and proceed to a quick bench trial in which the parties stipulated to most of the facts. These trials typically required "45 minutes to 1 hour" in the courtroom.[79] While some defenders appeared "client-oriented," others, the students worried, seemed to care less about their clients' interests than about moving quickly through their list of cases each day and keeping the judges happy. The students also worried that each defender's list of cases was far too long. Even though the Defender Association had added dozens of lawyers with Ford Foundation funds, their caseloads continued to spiral upwards as the organization expanded the number and types of cases eligible for its services. The students pondered whether the post-*Gideon* expansion, both in the organization's numbers and in the services it offered, amounted to meaningful progress. "Impressive as statistics in an annual report may be," they observed, "if the individuals behind the numbers are handled as assembly line products, receiving little individualized, creative attention, then expansion could only be described as retrograde."[80]

This version of the students' study remained unpublished. When General Decker, at the National Defender Project, reviewed their first draft, he wondered whether they might give their findings a more positive spin. Perhaps the students were "too critical" of the Philadelphia office; the Defender Association was among the country's oldest indigent defense organizations and, in Decker's view, it was "doing a better job than most."[81] Within the National Defender Project, the students' quantitative findings were less surprising than they were to the students themselves. Even before the students had completed their work, project staffers had hypothesized that any empirical study would find "that very little time is spent on preparation by defenders and prosecutors in most cases."[82] When Decker reviewed the students' report, he was less alarmed by their data, which confirmed that hypothesis, than by their pessimistic interpretation of the data. Perhaps the lesson of the students' findings, he wrote, was "that it doesn't take as much time as we had thought to handle successfully many of the less complicated cases."[83]

In 1968 the study appeared in the *University of Pennsylvania Law Review*, but the published version was stripped of the first draft's dour tone. Decker had made clear that he did not want "to hinder scholarly publication or any other freedom of speech," and he provided the students with his "full permission to publish as they see fit." But he urged them to consider how their critical remarks might be taken out of context and misused to justify defunding the Defender Association—something that the students surely would not want if they had "a sincere interest in the welfare of the poverty-stricken poor defendant."[84] Project staffers had also made specific editorial suggestions, such as deleting a reference to defenders "staring blankly into space." In context, this reference was not especially damning: the students' draft, by way of acknowledging a methodological challenge, observed that a defender "sitting in the courtroom staring blankly into space" might be doing nothing, but "might well be thinking how he should handle his next case"; there was no way to know.[85] The suggestion to remove this remark altogether indicated the degree of concern that any hint of negativity might be twisted to malign the Defender Association.

Professor Schwartz assured General Decker that the students could excise their editorial commentary, focusing instead on the data collected and the methodology used. Schwartz agreed that it was essential "to avoid injuring our Defender Association" which was doing an "outstanding job . . . with utterly inadequate funds."[86] Instead of a critique of "assembly-line" defense, the published article framed the students' findings as a first and tentative foray into a novel field of empirical study. "Mass representation in the United States is a recent development," the published study explained, without clear standards "to judge the adequacy of representation." Indigent defense organizations worked within "overwhelming" funding constraints. Continued investigation was needed to determine how "to provide maximum return on an invariably inadequate investment."[87]

The discrepancy between the law students' initial gloom and the professionals' more hopeful interpretation of their findings was telling, not because either version was objectively correct, but because it revealed the range of possible interpretations, even within the legal profession, of what *Gideon* was supposed to provide. The students who conducted the study had completed a year of law school, but neither had any prior work experience in criminal law.[88] They were steeped in the dream of *Gideon*. After a year of reading carefully selected, well-reasoned appellate opinions in which esteemed jurists parsed minute questions of doctrine, it was understandable why they might have assumed that every criminal case would be handled with a similar degree of sensitivity to nuance, particularly once every criminal case had a skilled lawyer on both sides—after all, "individualized, creative attention" was what lawyers were supposed to provide. But almost anyone who spent significant time observing local criminal courts in operation quickly witnessed that the day-to-day reality was different. In fact, in those jurisdictions that responded most aggressively to *Gideon*, taking it as a mandate to expand access to public defender services at every stage of the criminal process, the most immediate and visible result was exponential growth in defenders' caseloads, typically without concomitant increases in their budgets. Before *Gideon*, the typical defender organization, whether public or private, might handle several hundred or at most, a few thousand cases per year. By the late 1960s, large urban defender offices' caseloads had spiraled into the tens of thousands.[89]

One way to spin the numbers was to interpret the growing number of defenders, and those defenders' growing caseloads, as signs that *Gideon* was working. Public defenders were reaching more defendants than ever before, in more communities, and providing the expert legal assistance that every defendant needed. The more sanguine among the nation's growing corps of public defenders shared this sunny perspective. Edgar Rimbold, chief counsel of the Massachusetts Defenders Committee, described the agency's soaring caseloads as evidence that it was providing the "volume representation" required "to conform with *Gideon*," and assured the organization's funders at NLADA that the "quality" of representation "did not decrease with the increase in volume."[90] But this view was not uniform. Many people with a close-up view, whether law students, public defenders, or defendants themselves, tended toward bleaker interpretations. Frequently they described the criminal courts by resorting to dehumanizing metaphors like the assembly line. At a time of mounting skepticism about government, they described public defenders as yet another bureaucracy providing subpar and impersonal service—not "volume representation," as Rimbold put it, but in the Penn law students' words, even in the more muted published version of their article, "mass representation."

Legal scholars often recognized this disconnect, as did sociologists, who were trained to look through ideals and observe how institutions actually operated. These included Malcolm Feeley, a researcher in the "law and society" tradition, which examined how law and legal institutions functioned within their social contexts, beneath the hood of abstract principles and formal categories. Feeley published a study entitled *The Process Is the Punishment*, based on extensive observation of the lower criminal courts in New Haven, Connecticut, in the 1970s. Feeley's study joined a long line of sociological examinations, before and since, of the front-line criminal courts. As Feeley observed, these courts played a central role, second only to the police, "in forming citizen impressions" of criminal law. Yet they tended to operate in a "chaotic and confusing" manner that resembled neither the televised drama of fictional trials nor the actual operations of higher-level courts.[91] Feeley's central argument, captured in his title, was that low-level courts should not be understood as carrying out an adjudicative process for determining whether someone will be punished. Rather, "the process itself" functioned as "the punishment." The defendant lost "time, effort, money, and opportunities" simply by having to interact with the courts; by the time a sentence was pronounced, he had likely already served the requisite time in jail, or lost wages equivalent to the legally prescribed fine.[92]

By the time of Feeley's study, *Gideon* had been extended to require counsel in misdemeanor and other low-level cases, if the state sought imprisonment as a penalty. The Supreme Court's 1972 decision in *Argersinger v. Hamlin* concerned a Florida defendant who did not have a lawyer when he was sentenced to ninety days in county jail for carrying a concealed weapon. The Court held that even for this misdemeanor offense, the defendant was entitled to appointed counsel. It was true, Justice William Douglas explained, that the Court's earlier right-to-counsel cases, *Powell v. Alabama* and *Gideon v. Wainwright*, both "involved felonies. But their rationale has relevance to any criminal trial, where an accused is deprived of his liberty." The "legal and constitutional questions" posed by a misdemeanor charge were not necessarily "any less complex" than in a more serious case. *Argersinger* did not expressly require counsel in all petty prosecutions but held the state could not imprison someone for any length of time unless they had been provided with counsel.[93]

Argersinger completed the long-term development in which counsel became elevated over the jury as the all-purpose procedural guarantor of fair criminal proceedings. Notably, the Supreme Court had recently held that the Constitution did not require a jury trial in a case like *Argersinger*; the jury right did not attach to charges with a maximum penalty of less than six months' imprisonment.[94] Nevertheless, the Court in *Argersinger* held that counsel might be constitutionally required even if a jury was not. And Justice Lewis Powell Jr., in his separate concurrence, explained how the jury right itself depended, for its efficacy, upon the right to counsel: "An unskilled layman may be able to defend himself in a nonjury trial before a judge experienced in piecing together unassembled facts, but before a jury the guiding hand of counsel is needed to marshal the evidence into a coherent whole."[95]

Argersinger imposed additional requirements upon the states at a time when they were still perceived to be struggling to comply with *Gideon*. For this reason, several of President Richard Nixon's recently appointed, conservative justices did not sign onto the blanket rule announced by Justice Douglas's opinion, although they concurred in the judgment that counsel should have been provided in *Argersinger* itself. For lower-level offenses, Justice Powell proposed reviving the flexible, *Betts v. Brady* approach (presumably to the posthumous chagrin of Hugo Black, whom Powell had replaced on the Court). He posited that judges could decide whether counsel was needed on a case-by-case basis, appointing a lawyer when there was some special reason why the case was especially complex or the defendant especially vulnerable.[96] Powell noted that misdemeanor proceedings in many states remained extremely informal, with lay judges and without lawyers on the prosecution side; in such cases, it was less clear that the typical rationales for defense counsel applied.[97] Powell also questioned whether there were physically enough lawyers in the country to provide defense counsel in the immense number of low-level prosecutions each year. Most lawyers, Powell observed, "work for governments, corporate legal departments, or the Armed Services and are unavailable for criminal representation. . . . In few communities are there full-time public defenders available for, or private lawyers specializing in, petty cases." Across the country, "the ability of various States and localities to furnish counsel varies widely."[98]

Academic observers like Feeley, traveling into the nation's local courts with their notebooks, developed rich portraits of the local variations that Powell identified. Even in those localities that did have public defenders available for petty cases, Feeley highlighted lawyers' divergent interpretations of the changes wrought by *Gideon* and *Argersinger*. Most critics, in Feeley's estimation, lacked "historical perspective." They accused public defenders of undermining the courts' supposedly timeless adversarial nature, instead of comparing contemporary practice with a true picture of the past, in which misdemeanor defendants rarely had counsel at all. Feeley noticed the same gap in expectations revealed by the Penn students' study: "Some expected *Gideon v. Wainwright* and later *Argersinger v. Hamlin* to cause a radical restructuring of the criminal process, replacing perfunctory 'processing' with well-reasoned and vigorous adversarial proceedings," while "others may have felt that the expansion of public representation would serve primarily as a screening function to discover and treat occasional 'problem' cases who wanted full-blown adversarial proceedings."[99]

Feeley predicted that this divergence was likely to persist. The Supreme Court had effectively required the states to establish public defenders "without waiting for agreement on answers" to these deeper questions about what exactly all the new public defenders were for.[100] Feeley also questioned whether there was really any crisis of overwhelming caseloads. Instead, he posited that there was a socially constructed crisis produced by the Supreme Court, which by extending the right to counsel and other procedural requirements, had established "a much higher set of standards" for evaluating the criminal courts and also exposed those courts to new forms of public scrutiny. The new disconnect between ideals and practices that emerged in the 1970s was caused, in Feeley's account, not by novel degradations in the conditions of practice, but rather by a steady "upgrading of the *ideal*" against which practices were compared.[101] Lawyers remained hesitant to absorb or concur with such lessons. Many continued to indict the speedy adjudication of low-level cases as a departure from what *Gideon* and *Argersinger* had envisioned.

BY 1973, *Gideon* and the changes it launched had remade the criminal courts in many parts of the United States. Just prior to *Gideon*, only a quarter of Americans lived in an area with an organized defender. Ten years later, nearly two-thirds did, and almost every large city had some type of public defender. Even nominally private defenders usually now depended upon public funds. The public defender model made much less progress in the South and Southwest than in other regions, and all states continued to rely on assigned counsel for some types of cases. But for the typical defendant in much of the country who could not afford private counsel, and especially in cities, the most likely scenario by the mid-1970s was representation by a public defender.[102]

The transformation was especially stark in the low-level courts. Though the specifics of jurisdiction varied by state, lower courts typically tried misdemeanors, handled preliminary hearings for felony cases, and managed various other types of non-trial criminal proceedings. Historically, in many places, these courts had been relatively free of lawyers on all sides; before *Gideon*, only five states attempted to provide counsel in "less serious criminal cases." By 1970, that number had mounted to thirty-one. As two law students observed, "If the intent of the Supreme Court in *Gideon* was to urge, without expressly commanding, the states to expand the Sixth Amendment guarantee of counsel to defendants other than accused felons, the results have been very satisfactory."[103] Two years later, *Argersinger* confirmed that misdemeanor defendants had a right to appointed counsel, at least if their case threatened jail time, and further accelerated the lawyerization of low-level proceedings.[104]

As a result of these changes, within ten years of *Gideon* the process of being prosecuted in criminal court often entailed encountering a public defender. Though curiously invisible in pop-culture representations of criminal law (as compared with private attorneys, or police officers), public defenders became fixtures in the experiences of actual defendants.[105] Conversely, from defenders' perspectives, they were representing exponentially more clients than ever before. Massachusetts exemplified the trend. In 1958, the old Voluntary Defenders Committee handled 1,120 cases, total. Ten years later, the MDC handled over 18,000 cases. By 1972, it was handling 42,000 cases a year.[106] Charitable defenders had complained about heavy caseloads, but their fundraising materials had also highlighted trial victories and the plight of individual clients. Now, defenders spoke constantly about heavy caseloads as a defining feature of their work. The MDC no longer published annual reports filled with suspenseful narratives of individual cases. It made grant reports in which clients merged into faceless sums. Nationwide, too, numbers replaced dramatic true-crime accounts as the currency for measuring indigent defense. In the early 1970s, public defenders reported processing 400 cases a month in Chicago; 922 cases at a time in New York City; "merely" 300 cases in Oakland; and in Philadelphia, up to 50 cases a day.[107]

The combination of ballooning caseloads and budget plateaus caused post-*Gideon* public defenders to reconceptualize their role: since they could not contain their dockets by rejecting clients, they redefined their duties as triage. They would select a few cases to investigate thoroughly and facilitate guilty pleas in the rest. In 1970, the Boston Lawyers' Committee for Civil Rights observed that the MDC used "plea bargaining" as "a necessary technique to deal with an overwhelming caseload."[108] This description revealed how far defenders had moved from the rhetorical emphasis upon factual investigation and vindicated innocence typical of their predecessors in both public and voluntary defender offices. During his tenure as voluntary defender, Hollingsworth had measured his successes by tallying acquittals. The MDC measured success in terms of sentencing outcomes. In the low-level district courts, they counted guilty pleas as "favorable result[s]" if clients avoided jail time.[109]

When describing their day-to-day work, defenders now spoke in the vocabulary of deal-making, rather than emphasizing factual investigation or courtroom advocacy. In 1973, Edgar Rimbold explained, "Our men know the system. They know the judges, the prosecutors, and the best way to get a good deal for their clients. That's what attorneys from this office do—get the best possible deal for their clients." For Rimbold, defenders' deal-making prowess merited praise; he argued that the quality of representation had improved with rising caseloads, because through repeated interactions with district attorneys, public defenders "could secure more favorable bargains" than private counsel. "We have been dealing with the prosecutors for a long time," Rimbold explained, and "we have a reputation for being able to evaluate a case. They trust us."[110] Line defenders also described their work as high-volume deal-making but, unlike Rimbold, betrayed grave doubts about the practice. "I try to get back to the office at the end of each afternoon and interview some of the people I'm going to have to represent here," one Massachusetts public defender said, but usually "I can't manage it. So I meet the client here [in court] for the first time and devote all of five or ten minutes to him when he may face several years in prison. It's just not right."[111]

By the early 1970s, the MDC's plea-bargaining practices were widely criticized; courtroom observers disputed Rimbold's contention that deal-making benefited defendants. Evaluators from NLADA concluded that the agency's "caseload is so high as to preclude meaningful representation." The *Boston Globe* spotlighted a "case crush" overwhelming public defenders.[112] A magazine reporter who visited Boston allowed that "the public defender who has any intelligence quickly learns the ropes and learns how to help a client," but immediately added the caveat that defenders were "crippled by huge case loads that often compel them to rush through cases." A judge granted that the MDC did "as good [a job] as one can expect, I suppose, under the circumstances," but decried the circumstances: "no attorney can handle twenty cases a day."[113] The Boston chapter of the Lawyers' Committee for Civil Rights similarly questioned the virtues of "volume representation." Under this system, the Lawyers' Committee reported, "defendants are depersonalized. They become cases, charges, numbers, instead of clients."[114]

Massachusetts offered a microcosm of the national discourse. Complaints about "assembly-line justice" had appeared, and attained an authoritative imprimatur, in both of the major criminal justice documents produced by the Johnson Administration. In 1967, the President's Commission on Law Enforcement published *The Challenge of Crime in a Free Society*, a sweeping report on all dimensions of crime and punishment. "The Commission found overwhelming evidence of institutional shortcomings in almost every part of the United States," the report sadly observed, but especially in the lower courts, which were characterized by "cramped and noisy courtrooms, undignified and perfunctory procedures, badly trained personnel overwhelmed by enormous caseloads."[115] The next year, the Kerner Commission, convened in response to the 1967 riots in Newark, Detroit, and other cities, cited "structural deficiencies in criminal court systems" as a factor both in generating rioters' grievances and in weakening cities' capacity to respond to large-scale disorder.[116]

The charge that public defenders preferred plea deals to trials had now become a stock trope—regardless of whether the defender agency under discussion was fully public or nominally private, long-standing or recently established. In Roxbury, defendants complained that the Massachusetts Defenders were "government lawyers" who could not be trusted.[117] San Francisco defendants groused that their city's public defenders were "reluctant to go to trial." In 1970, New York City inmates petitioned the mayor with their grievance that Legal Aid lawyers opened every client meeting by proposing a plea deal.[118] Public defenders fared little better in academic studies. Criminologists published their findings that indigent defendants felt pressured to plead guilty.[119] In interviews with a political scientist, Connecticut prisoners described their lawyers not as advocates but as middlemen who simply relayed plea offers. "A public defender," one prisoner explained, "is just like the prosecutor's assistant."[120]

Defenders' new identity as dealmakers, whether embraced or maligned, likely reflected changes in defenders' (and observers') conception of defenders' role more than it reflected overall changes in plea rates or case outcomes. Even if plea rates climbed higher after *Gideon*, the increase started from a high baseline. Most criminal cases have always been resolved through guilty pleas or, at most, through quick trials such as Philadelphia used, and widespread plea bargaining predated the public defender in many jurisdictions, including Massachusetts.[121] As a matter of historical causation, then, plea bargaining did not originate with public defenders. Nor was it a practice exclusive to public defenders; under many circumstances, private attorneys also negotiated pleas for their clients. But public defenders themselves now talked about plea bargaining as if it were a practice distinctive to public defenders. Sometimes, like Rimbold, they implied that public defenders were uniquely skilled at it. More frequently, like his deputies, they implied that public defenders were uniquely forced into doing it, against their better judgment, by resource constraints. Such commentary cemented a cultural association between plea bargaining and public defenders while also appearing to detach the practice both from thorough investigation of the facts and from principled consideration of the client's best interests. Plea bargaining became defined as the default for public defender clients, rather than one option to weigh against other options.

Superficially, such accounts of the public defender's role might seem like the fulfillment of Progressive Era proposals to make defenders and prosecutors more cooperative—but that interpretation would be mistaken. True, Progressive Era reformers had predicted that the public defender would reduce the frequency of trials—but they had envisioned that trials would become unnecessary for a different reason. They had imagined defenders and prosecutors of equal pay, resources, and esteem, collaborating scientifically to uncover the facts and thereby divine the truth. Trials would become unnecessary not because the facts were irrelevant but because the facts could be efficiently discovered without trials. One might find that vision appealing, or one might find it naïve, but either way, it bore little resemblance to the courts of the early 1970s. In post-*Gideon* courts, the public defender was widespread but did not have resources, esteem, or political clout equal to the prosecutor. Prosecutors and defenders negotiated guilty pleas not out of a shared commitment to scientific rigor but against the understanding that prosecutors wielded most of the power and that, at best, defenders might be able to manipulate prosecutors into making concessions. In 1970, a Los Angeles public defender explained how he exploited the prosecutor's desire for impressive "statistics." He recounted how he negotiated a guilty plea to a charge that looked serious on paper (which made the prosecutor look tough), but carried a lesser sentence than the alternative (which aided his client): "this way, the prosecutor thinks I'm giving him a break. So maybe later he'll give me a break."[122]

Rather than reviving the Progressive Era debate, the 1970s discourse around the public defender as dealmaker, and public disillusionment with that role, derived precisely from the long-term consequences of elite lawyers having largely shut down the Progressive Era debate about whether to redefine the lawyer's relationship with individuals, society, and the state. The public defender continued to be measured against the imagined yardstick of the privately retained lawyer as single-minded agent of the individual client, providing maximally adversarial defense of the client's individual interests. Whenever public defenders were overwhelmed or underfunded, the comparison to private lawyers meant that the proposed solutions were the same: reduce caseloads and augment funding, motivated by the hope that doing so would yield more aggressive advocacy, more in-depth investigation, and more frequent jury trials.

Calls for more funding were certainly merited as far as they went, but failed to grapple with a deeper issue: the public defender would need to find, or revive, some source of institutional legitimacy that was not an analogy to the marketplace, whether the metaphorical marketplace in plea deals or the literal marketplace in private lawyers. Even under conditions of maximal funding, neither public defenders nor their clients would have the same unfettered autonomy to decide how much time and money to spend on a defense as the hypothetical private attorney whose client chose the amount of time he wanted to pay for. Someone else would make the final decision about how to allocate public defender resources—whether the administrator of the agency, rules of state law or local policy, or the individual defender herself. Thus, the comparison to privately retained lawyers yielded perennial disappointment, because the two types of lawyers operated according to different logics. But there was now little room within American legal culture for addressing that disappointment forthrightly. Instead of a more creative, expansive discussion of what the public defender's role should be and how to combine independent advocacy with the necessarily different context of public office, observers (and defendants themselves) defaulted to the model of the privately retained lawyer.

Similarly, although the assembly line played a part in both Progressive Era and 1970s reform discourse, it would be ahistorical to assume that the trope meant the same thing in both time periods. Of course, the most obvious change was that it had morphed from an aspiration into an epithet. Fifty years earlier, lawyers had dreamed of Taylorizing the courts. The assembly line in the Progressive Era was an innovation. Off the assembly line came Model-T Fords and refrigerators for the masses, infusing luxury into ordinary people's daily lives. By the turn of the 1970s, reformers complained that the courts operated like mass production factories. They did not commemorate this development as the long-awaited fulfillment of progressive goals. Instead they longed to revive that most archaic form of dispute resolution, the trial by combative rivals. In part, this rhetorical shift signified that Vietnam-era critics had a more cynical view overall of the merits of industrial efficiency than did Progressive Era reformers. But there was more to the rhetorical shift than a flip-flop of the assembly line's connotations. The trajectory was not a story of Progressive Era dreams being fulfilled and only then belatedly recognized as misguided. For the courts of the 1970s did not fulfill Progressive Era dreams. They were not assembly lines in the way that earlier reformers had wanted them to be.

In fact, both Progressive Era and Vietnam-era reformers had a similar underlying critique of the criminal courts, beneath their seemingly opposite invocations of the assembly line. What Progressive Era reformers had wanted the courts to do more efficiently was not to process cases for the sake of processing, but rather, to uncover the truth. After *Gideon*, the work of the criminal courts still seemed, to many observers, to have little connection to uncovering the truth. That was fundamentally what all the complaints about the disappearance of the trial were really about: the perceived lack, in most cases, of any in-depth, public adjudication of the facts. But now, lawyers no longer sought to fix this problem by reimagining their own role. They doubled down on traditional adversarialism and the competitive pursuit of individual interests as the best way to find the truth. No longer did reformers imagine a new "system of criminal procedure," as Maurice Parmelee once had. They got a new system anyway, because introducing public defenders into the majority of cases necessarily changed courtroom dynamics and defendants' perceptions. But it was not the one they might have devised through full and open debate. And because the change happened without frank discussion of what it should mean—because it was smuggled in under the fiction that the states were merely providing substitute private counsel for all defendants, which they were not doing and could not do—the criminal courts now seemed illegitimate to many observers.

IN 1972, the MDC board responded to the mounting complaints about "assembly-line" representation by replacing chief counsel Edgar Rimbold with a young and idealistic Harvard Law graduate, Gerard Schaefer. NLADA, in its 1972 evaluation of the agency, had castigated Rimbold's leadership. Like Hollingsworth before him, Rimbold had attended Suffolk Law School, and he tended to hire fellow Suffolk alumni; the evaluators wondered why the MDC did not hire more attorneys from what they referred to as the "excellent law schools" in Boston.[123] Just as the NLADA report did not fully capture the longer-term causes for the agency's low salary scale, it also overlooked the deep roots beneath the office's personnel patterns. The evaluators personalized their assessment of the office's hiring practices into an attack on Rimbold for lacking vision, while also casting elitist aspersions on a law school that served a broad range of students. Of course, the so-called "excellent law schools" had, for decades, discouraged their students from considering indigent defense as a career. Rimbold's replacement, like the evaluators, viewed the MDC staff lawyers as insufficiently zealous. Rather than hiring recent graduates who wanted only "to get experience," Schaefer aimed to hire "young lawyers who . . . really want to be public defenders."[124] By then, LaRue Brown had died, and William Homans Jr., a Boston-area civil liberties luminary, had joined the board. All of these changes presaged elite lawyers' newfound interest in indigent defense, which was gaining liberal cachet as part of the burgeoning field of poverty law. But beneath the specific personalities and developments involved, the constant administrative turmoil again expressed something deeper—the basic instability of *Gideon*'s implementation.

It had taken several years of legislative wrangling and grant writing for Rimbold to get the MDC into the district courts. Then, in 1972, Rimbold's replacement pulled the agency back out of most Boston-area district courts, in order to pare down defenders' caseloads. Limiting caseloads, Schaefer explained, would allow "our lawyers, interviewers, and investigators . . . to do the job right. Of course," he added, "the reshuffling was bad for the defendants who now get no representation . . . except by private lawyers appointed by the court, who are often worse than no lawyer at all."[125] Again, defenders stumbled over the ambiguity of *Gideon*'s ultimate meaning: was the goal providing a public defender to as many defendants as possible, or providing public defenders in fewer cases but allowing them to "do the job right"? If the latter, was that much different from the old voluntary defender model, which selected "worthy" defendants for representation? Within ten years of *Gideon*, the MDC had undergone the full cycle of *Gideon*'s implementation, which has repeated ever since, with local variations, throughout the country: administrative reorganization, rising caseloads, fights for legislative funding and judicial recognition, internal debates over the ethics of indigent defense, ending with another administrative reorganization.

Social scientists debated whether complaints about the quality of public defenders were well founded. Empirical studies tended to find that public defenders performed no worse than private lawyers, and in some settings, they performed much better.[126] It was soon clear, however, that elite lawyers had been overly optimistic to assume that simply expanding the ranks of public defenders—without some broader discussion about what their role should be—would make defendants believe the courts were fair. Of course, prisoners complained about the courts before *Gideon*. But now, public defenders, far from alleviating defendants' concerns, often became the focus of their complaints. This outcome would have dispirited both the Progressive Era philanthropists and their Cold War successors who touted legal aid's potential to insulate the urban poor from radical politics and shore up America's commitment to liberal democracy. Black Panther Party leader Eldridge Cleaver, in a 1968 interview, derided public defenders as "penitentiary deliverers." He explained the party's appeal by describing a typical black defendant who, "in a stupor of confusion," takes his public defender's advice to plead guilty in exchange for a lesser charge. Then he "wakes up in the penitentiary, starts exchanging experiences with other guys who have been through the same mill; and if he wasn't a rebel when he went in, he'll be a revolutionary by the time he gets out."[127]

Initially, some legal scholars interpreted cynicism about public defenders as a dissonant note in the larger story of *Gideon*'s implementation. In 1967, Abraham Blumberg, a lawyer-turned-sociologist and acerbic critic of the legal profession, observed the tension between *Gideon*'s emphasis on "*adversary, combative*" lawyering and the reality that courts operated like bureaucracies. This disconnect, Blumberg predicted, would yield "ironic" consequences. Doctrine aimed at protecting individual rights would end up "enriching court organizations with more personnel and elaborate structure, which will in turn maximize organizational goals of 'efficiency' and production. Thus, many defendants will find that courts will possess an even more sophisticated apparatus for processing them toward a guilty plea!"[128] More than a decade later, Malcolm Feeley placed a more positive but still ironic spin on *Gideon*'s effects, reprising some of his arguments from *The Process Is the Punishment*. By professionalizing the local courts, Feeley wrote, the expanding right to counsel had also "raise[d] expectations" and "expose[d] practices to greater scrutiny . . . Thus, an irony: as things get better they appear to get worse."[129]

But *Gideon*'s role in bureaucratizing (or professionalizing) the criminal courts soon faded from memory. As *Gideon* receded into the past, scholars and advocates reinterpreted public defenders' high caseloads, volatile funding, and avoidance of trials not as "'volume representation' of the type that appears to be mandatory under *Gideon*," but as signs that *Gideon*'s mandates had been neglected. In 1983, the American Bar Association identified a "crisis in indigent defense funding" and worried that *Gideon* was at risk of becoming "undone."[130] From that report on, advocates would describe indigent defense in an unchanging language of crisis. In policy reports, law review articles, and op-eds, invocations of crisis took on a ritualistic quality, serving as a recurring apology for the legal profession's failure to solve the problem of the indigent accused. In the 1960s, it was Robert Spangenberg, as a young Boston University law professor, who had alerted the Massachusetts Defenders Committee to defendants' concerns about impersonal advocacy. In the 1990s, Spangenberg—now an expert consultant on indigent defense policy—expressed the same concerns on a national scale, lamenting that "overburdened public defenders are often forced to pick and choose which cases to focus on." That observation appeared in an ABA report that was published in 1994 but could have been published in any year. It was entitled, *The Indigent Defense Crisis Is Chronic*.[131]

CHAPTER FIVE
Local Injustice

The young lawyer could hardly believe what he was seeing. It was February 1968, and he was observing a criminal trial in the Dorchester section of Boston. Even for February, and even for Boston, it was cold outside. Inside, what the lawyer saw reminded him—he would type, the next week, in a memo—of judicial proceedings he had once witnessed while traveling "in the very back country of Africa." The charges: assault and possession of a deadly weapon. The defendant: a veteran, just out of the Army, "no prior record." There had been some sort of a fight between the defendant's mother and her boyfriend. No one was hurt, but someone had called the police and the defendant was who they arrested. The mother and the boyfriend had not shown up to court; they preferred to put the whole thing behind them. A police officer got on the stand and "testified as to what the mother and her boyfriend might have said had they been present." On the basis of this conjecture, the judge found the defendant guilty and offered a sentence of three years' probation. The defendant inquired about filing an appeal. This was a district court, the lowest level of the Massachusetts judiciary, and state law guaranteed to any defendant convicted in district court the right to request an entirely new trial one level up—in the superior court. Okay, the judge responded. If you appeal, the sentence is two years' prison, and bond will be set at $5,000. The defendant "change[d] his mind about appealing" and accepted the probation.[1]

The young lawyer who described this example of day-to-day "due process" belonged to the corps of staff attorneys at the National Defender Project, who traveled around the country to observe at work all of the public defenders being paid from the Ford Foundation's largesse. Later that same year, another staffer traveled due south from the project's Chicago headquarters to the Gulf of Mexico and found himself in the shipbuilding outpost of Pascagoula, Mississippi. The grant recipient he had been sent to visit was, ostensibly, a pilot public defender's office for Mississippi's Nineteenth Judicial Circuit. The staffer was in his twenties and fresh out of Northwestern Law School. Pascagoula's then-incumbent public defender was also a recent law graduate—from the University of Mississippi, or Ole Miss—and brought his Chicago counterpart to visit the Pascagoula city jail. There, they saw "a 14 year old

Negro boy" lying in a "maximum security" cell. The child appeared "to have suffered a severe head injury." No one had called a doctor. Purportedly the child was awaiting trial on charges of "attempted rape of a white girl." No court date was scheduled. The defender passed along the police explanation for the injury. Their story was that "the boy had broken into a local school and in so doing knocked over a large case which landed on his head." The Chicago visitor duly recorded this information in his memo for the files of the National Defender Project. "When asked why he did not take action in the case," the memo also noted, Pascagoula's then-incumbent public defender "reported that he had not been asked to do so and was not willing otherwise to get involved."[2]

In truth, what the National Defender Project was funding in Pascagoula bore little resemblance to established public defender offices or legal aid organizations in large cities. The grant had been awarded on the basis of an application proposing to pay for a full-time administrator to better coordinate the county's existing procedures for appointing counsel to indigent cases. No such administrator had been hired. Instead, local private law firms had arranged for their junior associates to take over the jurisdiction's indigent caseload, rotating through the "public defender" role for six months at a time. During each lawyer's term as public defender, he would handle all of the court-appointed cases in exchange for a salary paid out of the Ford Foundation grant funds, while also continuing to represent his paying clients. Twice a year, these temporary defenders hosted a clambake for the local police and prosecutors.[3] When project staffers came down from Chicago, the Pascagoula lawyers told them candidly about all of the cases in which they thought the state had taken "illegal or unconstitutional action." Had they filed any motions or appeals, in any of those cases? No, not one. Project staffers concluded that the Ford Foundation was wasting its money in Pascagoula. The services being provided were not "lawyer-like" and the defenders were being "grossly overpaid for the amount of work they do."[4] In contrast, staffers spoke highly about the Massachusetts defenders. They were knowledgeable about the law; they carried themselves well in court. Against "the onslaught of district court justice" they nevertheless appeared "as impotent . . . [as] a small boy trying to stop an oncoming locomotive."[5]

Whether in Massachusetts or Mississippi, *Gideon* and other Warren Court decisions seeped like rivulets of cave water into the hard rock of local power structures — political, institutional, and racial. Each community's justice was unhappy in its own way, belying the nationwide uniformity that constitutional criminal procedure was supposed to guarantee. It was not as though nothing had changed, or the Court's landmark rulings had proven merely a "hollow hope."[6] Public defender offices were being established or expanded all around the country and there were new sources of funding coming in. In the sliver of criminal convictions that turned into appeals or habeas petitions, state appellate courts and the lower federal courts were duly enforcing *Gideon* and other new precedents. In Florida alone, nearly a thousand men who had been tried without counsel were back home now, and not in prison, thanks to *Gideon*.[7] But the appellate and federal courts, much less the Supreme Court, only ever saw a fraction of the many thousands of criminal prosecutions going on all around the country at any given time. New personnel and new doctrinal protections for defendants could not so easily dislodge entrenched ways of doing things in local communities, and day to day it was those entrenched ways of doing things, and not the abstract ideals invoked by the Supreme Court, that provided the script for police, prosecutors, and judges, and in many places, for defense lawyers too. The observations recorded by the National Defender Project's corps of project staffers in the memos they typed up as they traveled around the country echoed descriptions in policy reports, reform proposals, and newspaper exposés in the late 1960s and early 1970s. In much of the country, lawyers, reformers, and journalists who visited local criminal courts, jails, and public defender offices expressed surprise or even shock at what they found. Here were entire judicial institutions and even states that did not bear much resemblance to the visions of a free society that animated the Warren Court's celebrated rulings.

The disconnect was not so simple as a straightforward refusal to adhere to the Supreme Court's dictates. It was as though the Supreme Court had been dictating rules for some other country. The Court's opinions celebrated elaborate requirements of due process and a supposedly timeless and deeply ingrained Anglo-American adversarial tradition. On the ground, lawyers encountered criminal courts better described as inquisitorial, with lawyers on both sides either absent or passive and judges interrogating witnesses and even arguing the cases.[8] They found judges eager to penalize defendants who dared invoke their rights, purportedly the jealously guarded inheritance of Anglo-American jurists dating back to Magna Carta. At best, they found public defenders who were zealous but "impotent"; at worst, they found public defenders baking clams for their adversaries. To describe the courts they saw, observers fell back upon stereotypical icons of backwardness, places that white professionals had been taught to consider uncivilized: "the very back country of Africa." When describing Mississippi, the comparison made itself since the Deep South had long occupied a position in liberal reform discourse as almost an internal colony, a ravaged and desperate "problem" region that required solving from the outside.[9] The ready resort to Third World analogies conveyed something about their authors' lenses on the world but also, in a fractured way, something significant about what they saw through those lenses. Race was the unspoken elephant in the stories told by outside observers back from the bowels of America's criminal punishment machinery. Everywhere, they saw the same people bearing the brunt of the "erratic course of justice" they described: people who were poor, certainly, but also more often than not, people who were black.

Precisely because there was some dimension of criminal courts that seemed not fully permeable by constitutional doctrine, witnessing what went on in those courts did not yield ready solutions or obvious policy proposals. Already by the late 1960s, something called the "indigent defense crisis" was well on its way to becoming a fixture in criminal justice discourse. Across legal scholarship and policy reports, crisis talk pervaded. But that talk was mostly about a crisis of resources: not enough funding, not enough lawyers, too many cases. On that logic, the theory of *Gideon* was sound, but needed material backup to put into practice. Conceived as a fiscal emergency, the "indigent defense crisis" had a straightforward solution, which was more funding. And it accordingly generated a flood of policy reports and scholarly articles calling for more funding. This solution may have been difficult politically and practically. There were details to debate: what level of government should provide the funding, what role should the private sector play, whether the courts should step in if legislatures failed. But conceptually, calling for funding was straightforward.

On the ground, other and more destabilizing crises also loomed—a crisis of power; a crisis of comprehension. Not enough funds for some things, but "gross overpayments" for others. Too much policing, perhaps, of the wrong kind. Too many lawyers of the wrong kind, white lawyers in Massachusetts who did not really know their place in the communities they served and white lawyers in Mississippi who knew it all too well. These other crises would prove continually flummoxing to legal liberals. They were difficult not only to solve but even to discuss. They never produced the same policy consensus, the same repetitive literature with its familiar reform proposals recycled through the decades; instead they produced a more fractured discourse. Horrific anecdotes appeared in odd isolation within otherwise workaday memos, as if someone just thought someone else should know. Complaints traveled a game of telephone from neighborhoods to lawyers to other lawyers back to committee meetings, where they generated months of discussion, but little agreement about what should be done. These problems needed more than funding; perhaps they also needed more than the received parameters of legal-liberal thought and the received structure of the American legal profession. The public defender idea presumed the lawyer as specialized expert, whose value was precisely that he understood different things than the defendant understood—he understood the law and how the courts worked; he alone could steer his client through the law's choppy straits. But defendants themselves wondered if public defenders really knew as much as they thought they knew, and whether it might be better if they could have lawyers who understood more of the same things they did. "Government lawyers" did not seem to understand, for example, what it meant to be a black teenage boy in Roxbury, Massachusetts, or the way that a criminal accusation defined as a single case in the eyes of the law could form part of a whole constellation of encounters with the neighborhood police.

The clash, in the late 1960s and early 1970s, between liberal ideals of a fair trial and local realities of race and power forced even the legal profession's mainstream elite to confront a genre of question they had spent most of the past century studiously sidestepping: whether it was possible for courts to guarantee "equal justice" within a larger society that was imbricated with interlocking forms of social, political, and economic inequality. For lawyers on the radical left, of course, this question was easy because the answer was obviously no. For lawyers more or less aligned with the liberal mainstream of the midcentury legal profession, this question could be destabilizing. In the discussions and debates that culminated in *Gideon*, legal liberals had walked an intellectual tightrope to explain how an affirmative right to government assistance in criminal cases could be differentiated from the affirmative rights characteristic of socialism (or FDR's rejected "Second Bill of Rights"). They did so by carving the criminal courtroom apart from the rest of society, defining it as a special realm where equality was guaranteed for reasons specific to the internal functioning of that realm, and also where equality could potentially be achieved—at least formal legal equality. It was never so easy or even really possible to carve actual criminal courtrooms into a realm apart. Society spilled in.

BY ITS OWN STANDARDS, the National Defender Project succeeded. The final grant report submitted to the Ford Foundation celebrated "phenomenal growth" in the number of public defenders and "giant strides on the path toward equal justice." "In 1961 organized defense services existed in only 3% of the counties" nationwide, according to the report. "By 1973 well over two-thirds of the nation's population was served by organized defender offices . . . in large part due to the examples set by the model demonstration projects designed by NDP." The National Defender Project also brought closure to the once-contentious debates within the legal profession about the public defender, making clear the elite preference for full-time, organized defender agencies over the nineteenth-century inheritance of case-by-case appointments of private counsel. The model projects funded by the Ford Foundation had proven "the viability of organized defense delivery systems." The report acknowledged the persistence of practical obstacles that must be overcome "before a truly complete defense can be assured to every indigent criminal defendant." On balance, though, the report assured the Ford Foundation that it had made a sound investment. The National Defender Project had "set a standard for the future of defender services, and its successes far out-weighed its failures."[10]

The National Defender Project exemplified both the promise and the limitations of the theory of institutional change advanced by large philanthropic foundations in midcentury America. The Ford Foundation's preference was to underwrite innovative pilot projects, rather than existing infrastructure. The theory was that philanthropic dollars could invest more nimbly in experiments than could government. If a program worked, then the government could adopt and expand it on a permanent basis.[11] In many states where the National Defender Project made grants, this approach played out as hoped. For example, the project provided temporary funding for new public defenders in two rural Missouri counties. Although those two offices soon closed, they served as proof of concept for the Missouri legislature, which enacted legislation in 1972 to establish a statewide defender agency. In total, the project funded forty-nine defender offices around the country on a pilot basis, and almost all were continued in some fashion by the state or local government. Only three withered on the vine after the Ford Foundation funds dried up.[12]

The Ford Foundation's emphasis on pilot projects developed in part out of internal concerns within the foundation, but it comported with broader tenets of midcentury liberalism, which cohered around an "Enlightenment meets Atomic Age" view of history as a process of one-directional progress toward more perfect understanding. At the time, some critics derided the foundation's motivating assumptions as facile. "It's hard to give away a lot of money without doing harm," an observer from another large foundation remarked about the Ford juggernaut.[13] One social scientist, in a study of an amorphous, Ford-funded antipoverty initiative in 1960s Boston, skewered the initiative's "rationalistic faith" in "local elites." The pilot project approach assumed that local leaders "could be educated to judge the demonstration projects by scientific criteria, temporarily suspending opposition to threatening programs in order to discover whether their objections were in fact empirically grounded," and that programs deemed "'successful'... would be irresistibly attractive to local decision-makers and would inevitably be implemented."[14] This description applied also to the National Defender Project, which officially proceeded from the premise that local officials needed only to see proof of the public defender idea (or in their words, "the viability of organized defense delivery systems"), and then funding and support would follow. Behind the scenes, however, project staffers and board members were often well aware that local dynamics were not so simple.

The National Defender Project's internal memos thus proved more insightful than its more official documents, which typically included a potted history of the right to counsel from thirteenth-century England through *Gideon*. There was little room for politics in this oft-recited chronicle, much less culture. There was an apparent "path toward equal justice" and the task for institutions, whether public or private, was to keep making "strides" down that path through time. The project's final report began with rote invocations of Magna Carta and the Sixth Amendment, which were quoted in order to demonstrate the long-standing "concern for the rights of the indigent defendant" within the Anglo-American legal tradition, at least in seed form. It then skipped ahead to the twentieth century, when that concern had flowered into "reality." Doctrinally, it was a story of judicial steps forward (*Powell* "began to lay the groundwork for *Gideon*"), temporary setbacks (with *Betts*, "the momentum" toward *Gideon* "was encumbered"), and finally apotheosis (with *Gideon* as the apex of a history that began on the fields of Runnymede). It was a story of decades of "almost uninterrupted, accelerating growth," culminating in the Supreme Court's stirring endorsement in *Gideon*. The 1960s represented "the most active and important" phase in this illustrious history: a decade of "explosive" growth in the number of defender offices, spurred both by *Gideon* and the Ford Foundation's grant funding.[15]

In his memorable 1955 portrait of the Ford Foundation, the New York intellectual Dwight Macdonald skewered the language used by "philanthropoids," which he labeled "foundationese." "This language is like Latin," Macdonald observed, "written rather than spoken, and designed for ceremony rather than utility. Its function is magical and incantatory." When writing in foundationese, it was essential "to accentuate the positive" and "not to go to undue lengths—or, in fact, to any lengths at all—to avoid the obvious."

(To make his claims seem as noncontroversial as possible, a fluent writer of the language might begin with the sorts of sweeping statements college freshmen are routinely downgraded for making: *Democracy is an important value*, or *It has often been observed that resources are helpful for achieving goals*.) The typical artifact of foundationese "abstracts from reality enough of its life, variety, and general sloppiness to allow it to be embalmed in a staff memorandum."[16] Anthropologist James Ferguson would later identify a similar distance from reality in the genre of reporting that so-called nongovernmental organizations produced when they visited Third World countries and assessed the level of "development" a country had achieved or, more often, failed to achieve. Development discourse functioned, Ferguson argued, as an "anti-politics machine," "everywhere whisking political realities out of sight, all the while performing, almost unnoticed, its preeminently political operation of expanding bureaucratic state power."[17]

In the catechistic histories of grant reports and bar association speeches, the engine of legal and institutional change over time was not politics or even really human agency, but a vaguely explained and gradual awakening by "the profession" and the courts and benevolent organizations like the Ford Foundation. Actions were taken on the basis of ideas once those ideas proved themselves. Ordinary people appeared in these accounts insofar as they happened to supply the names of cases. Whatever was happening to such people during those earlier periods when the seeds of justice were still just seeds was not dwelled upon. Even ordinary lawyers were a faceless mass: "the profession." The profession was getting it right, the profession was on the right track. "The dynamics of the profession," Chief Justice Burger wrote in his concurring opinion in *Argersinger*, as if trying to reassure himself, "have a way of rising to the burdens placed on it."[18] Burger, though a conservative jurist, shared the legal-liberal vocabulary on this particular question of criminal court reform. He spoke of inexorable "dynamics" and ineffable "ways of rising." Somewhere in America, some twenty-five-year-old just out of law school was now supposed to go into a courtroom and object strenuously to some act of brutality carried out by some police officer he probably knew from high school, on behalf of a client he met five minutes before and who resembled people he had been taught from his earliest childhood to define as beneath him. The profession would have a way of rising.

Self-evidently, this mode of discourse depended upon the capacity to pretend away or at least hold in mental abeyance the messy world of politics and conflict out in society. Less self-evidently but equally significantly, this mode of discourse also depended upon pretending away politics and conflict even within the narrow confines of the elite stratum of the legal profession. Decades of history in which legal elites were either uninterested in or ambivalent about the public defender faded away into an imagined trajectory of "uninterrupted, accelerating growth." Just as Reginald Heber Smith had done decades before in *Justice and the Poor*, the National Defender Project sidestepped the Progressive Era dichotomy between private charity and public defense, and instead conflated public and private defenders into one category of "organized defense delivery systems."[19]

The National Defender Project's final report concluded by acknowledging "the present funding crisis" in indigent defense and allowing that it would be premature to indulge in "self-congratulation." But, the report concluded, in a paragraph of dense foundationese: "The fact that more remains to be done need not blind us to the tremendous progress which has been made in the past ten years—progress which was supported, encouraged, and often initiated by NDP. By funding working demonstration models of high quality, cost-effective defense delivery systems and by initiating standards and constructive innovations in providing defense services, the Ford Foundation has enabled this country to make giant strides on the path toward equal justice."[20]

BY STANDARDS OTHER THAN the technocratic metrics of liberal philanthropy, it was less clear how to evaluate the changes introduced by *Gideon* and the National Defender Project. To legal elites, for instance, the Massachusetts response to *Gideon* was exemplary. Meanwhile, in the predominantly black and poor neighborhood of Roxbury—perhaps the section of Boston most frequently in need of "service" from "defense delivery systems," given its targeting by police—the Massachusetts Defenders Committee was not celebrated. According to students and staff in the Boston University Law School's clinic in Roxbury, many people in the community did not even "know what the Mass[achusetts] Defenders is." For the most part, people knew in the abstract "what a public defender is," but were "unaware of the services rendered by MDC."[21] Those residents of Roxbury who were aware did not necessarily have favorable views. Robert Spangenberg, who directed the clinic, reported "that some of the Roxbury defendants distrusted" the MDC attorneys and complained that they "were not socially sensitive."[22] Rumors circulated, never corroborated but frequently discussed at MDC board meetings, that Roxbury defendants preferred to hire their own counsel if possible, or even that community leaders were encouraging defendants to reject the service of public defenders. At a meeting in October 1968, the board discussed concerns that "some of the attorneys may not be sympathetic with the problems or the culture of the people in the neighborhoods, nor have the attorneys lived in those areas."[23]

Another question on the agenda for the October 1968 meeting raised a related issue: "Why are there no black attorneys on the staff of the MDC?"[24] Similar questions were being asked around the country. The ranks of public defenders certainly did not reflect the diversity of their clients, but they also did not reflect the growing diversity of the legal profession at a time when African Americans were moving into both the professions and public office in growing numbers, and the Civil Rights Act of 1964 had enshrined federal protections against racial discrimination in hiring. In 1967, an Atlanta civic group criticized a fledgling Fulton County public defender's office for employing not a single black lawyer. The city of Atlanta was majority black; by one estimate, 75 percent of the public defender's clients were likely to be African American. The group sent a telegram to Fulton County's chief judge, urging the office to hire "Negro lawyers."[25] The National Defender Project's final report had acknowledged similar concerns, although only obliquely, in a brief section about coordinating medical assistance for clients who needed it. "Defenders should be sensitive to the underlying psychological, social, or physical problems of those they represent," the report noted. "It would be a mistake to allow too narrow a definition of a lawyer's role to hinder the work of a defender's office."[26]

By expressing their grievances, both defendants themselves and other community members forced public defender agencies to reconsider their assumptions about legal assistance and, in a literal sense, what it meant to be represented by a lawyer. Organizations like NLADA and the ABA measured post-*Gideon* progress by tallying the percentage of jurisdictions "served by organized defender offices." As defendants' complaints revealed, expanding the ranks of public defenders into new areas did not necessarily make residents of those areas feel subjectively that they had been well-served.[27] The public defender might be experienced by the defendant as yet another state official with whom to have an alienating encounter. Public opinion polls reported that only 46 percent of Northern black respondents viewed their state government as "helpful," and only one-third said the same of local government.[28] Surely, a lawyer and her client did not need to share identical backgrounds in order to develop a positive relationship. But to many community members, there was something unseemly about large numbers of black defendants being appointed lawyers who seemed to have little understanding of their lives.

Within the MDC, staff and board members became convinced that diversifying the staff would help to resolve the agency's problems. One board member suggested that it might "prevent alienating some of the feelings of black defendants" to "have a negro attorney" and "a negro investigator."[29] Board members also discussed the possibility of opening a branch office in Roxbury. The agency's only office in Boston was located downtown, where it was not "easy for all people" to get to.[30] But hiring African American lawyers was easier said than done. Edgar Rimbold, the chief counsel, insisted "that he had informed the bar and others of his desire to engage the services of a negro attorney more than two years ago" but received "no response." The hiring effort was complicated by the fact that the bar itself had traditionally defined indigent defense as quasi-volunteer work. Because of new antidiscrimination norms and legal protections, black lawyers who graduated from school in the late 1960s enjoyed opportunities within the profession denied to past generations. In this landscape, many were not interested in taking a relatively low-paying, low-status job at a relatively new public agency. Rimbold reported that two black attorneys had worked at the agency briefly but left when they received higher-paying job offers.[31]

Calls for "Negro lawyers" in the late 1960s showed that elite lawyers' discourse about indigent defense was beginning to change. From the Progressive Era through the 1960s, the predominantly white male lawyers at the top of public and voluntary defender offices had often managed to discuss the issue under the pretense that it had nothing to do with race. The Ford Foundation's brochure inviting applications for the National Defender Project invoked Anglo-American traditions and Magna Carta, not present-day questions of civil rights or racial justice—which was not surprising, for explicit discussions of race were "verboten" within the foundation into the early 1960s.[32] Based on records of their meetings, both the MDC and its charitable predecessor had carried out their internal discussions for decades without much explicit attention to the racial dimensions of their work. As late as 1965, it was possible for the Atlanta Bar Association to produce a report on the effects of *Gideon* that did not mention race.[33]

FOR AN ENTITY committed to democracy, the Ford Foundation was not especially democratic in its own governance structures. The average person had no say in how the foundation spent its funds, yet those very funds might determine that very person's access to health care, education, or legal representation. From the beginning, the philanthropic foundations born of corporate wealth in the United States were bedeviled by questions about their unaccountable power. By midcentury, the Ford Foundation had amassed the clout to remake professions, cities, states, and even countries. Yet it had no obligation to hold elections or public hearings, or to maintain open records of its internal decision-making—a discrepancy that troubled even some staffers within the foundation. "What right had the Ford Foundation to decide how the social institutions of Boston or any other city should be arranged?" asked one social scientist.[34] The National Defender Project might have raised the same question, but with even more urgency. It amounted to a nationwide intervention into local criminal courts, in response to a new constitutional requirement, under the direction of a private foundation and private professional organizations. Lawyers had long arrogated to themselves a remarkable degree of policymaking authority. Philanthropic backing empowered them further and shrouded their activities in layers of opaque bureaucracy.[35]

Upon receiving the Ford grant, the first order of business for the National Defender Project was to assemble "a prestigious governing body."[36] There was no prestige in being a poor person, so poor people were not included. The project's National Advisory Council was chaired by the corporate law firm partner and NLADA leader Orison Marden, and comprised seven judges, including one retired Supreme Court justice; four law school professors; seven leaders of the American Bar Association; one district attorney; and one former public defender. Grants were approved by an executive committee that included partners at corporate law firms, including Orison Marden, Maynard Toll, and Harrison Tweed; William T. Gossett, past general counsel of the Ford Motor Company; Raynor Gardiner, of the Boston Legal Aid Society; and Florence Kelley, the longtime head of the Criminal Courts Branch at New York's Legal Aid Society.[37] This was an impressive roster, including conscientious and committed luminaries of the organized bar's legal aid movement. And it did include some lawyers with direct experience in indigent defense. They asked shrewd questions about the grant proposals they were asked to review. Still, they presumably asked different questions than the "indigent accused" themselves would have asked.

ON PAPER, the National Defender Project had truly national reach. The final report included a map of the United States with a small black dot representing the location of each grant recipient. Dots appeared in every region of the country. Between 1963, when the Ford Foundation awarded the first grant installment, and 1971, when the project closed its doors, the project made grants to seventy initiatives in thirty-three states; answered countless phone calls and requests for information from lawyers around the country; published and distributed the *Defender Newsletter* to 12,000 lawyers, judges, and libraries; and underwrote dozens of fellowship programs, research endeavors, and professional conferences.[38] Among its many initiatives, the project provided start-up funding and organizational impetus for local efforts in Boston and New Haven; statewide public defender agencies in Minnesota and Wisconsin; a federal defender in San Diego; and municipal defender offices in Salt Lake City and Las Vegas. It underwrote new or expanded organizations in Colorado and Hawaii, Michigan and Arizona, New Jersey and Florida.[39]

Counting the number of grants belied a more complicated story—and, in particular, exaggerated the project's depth of outreach into the Deep South. On the map, each grant was signified by a dot of equal size, but there were significant differences in the amount and duration of funding that local projects received. The first and most generously funded projects were almost all located in the Northeast. In line with the Ford Foundation's larger programmatic agenda, the National Defender Project gave initial priority to grant applications from localities that had previously been selected to receive urban renewal grants through the foundation's Gray Areas program: Boston, New Haven, Philadelphia, Washington, D.C., and the state of North Carolina.[40] The Gray Areas program targeted what Ford staffer Paul Ylvisaker described, borrowing the term from an economist, as "the 'growing range of deteriorating real estate between central business district and suburb.'"[41] Whatever the merits of the Gray Areas selection criteria for an economic development program, those criteria were not tailored to indigent defense. The National Defender Project did not give specific reasons for adopting the Ford Foundation's Gray Areas framework, stating that "the advantages of starting our activities in these communities are obvious."[42]

Only in the National Defender Project's second round of funding did it give equal attention to applications from throughout the country. At that point, the project aimed "to encompass as wide a geographical area as possible" and gave priority to applications from locations that had not yet received a grant. General Decker focused his personal outreach upon the Deep South states, which had little history of organized legal aid or indigent defense.[43] But the National Defender Project's initiatives in the South were smaller in scale and less successful than those in the Northeast. The project celebrated the fact that, out of the forty-nine pilot defender offices that it launched around the country, forty-six remained in place after the Ford Foundation funding was terminated. All three exceptions were Southern: Mobile, Alabama; Fayette, Mississippi; and a prisoner assistance project at the University of Arkansas.[44]

The National Defender Project's own map did not include dots to represent the places where no one ever applied for a grant, or where grants were pursued but ultimately denied for failing to meet the requirements. But behind the scenes, the nonexistent and failed grant proposals revealed the limitations of the Ford Foundation's approach. Especially consequential was the foundation's insistence that grant recipients could not rely entirely on outside funds but must also assemble "local matching funds." This requirement reinforced the philanthropic fiction that foundations did not directly make policy, but only aided policy experiments already underway—a fiction that helped to assuage foundation staffers' own hesitation about whether their efforts were democratic.[45] It also derived from the assumption that initiatives with preexisting local support would prove more sustainable in the long run. But the requirement of local matching funds tended, by definition, to direct resources to places that already had resources, which placed rural and poorer communities (whether Southern or otherwise) at some disadvantage. A community's ability to raise funds from local sources and to marshal support from local officials does not necessarily correlate with need, and it might inversely correlate with need in a context like indigent defense: the places where local officials are least willing to sign on to a public defender initiative are probably the places where defendants would most benefit from adversarial advocacy on their behalf.

Atlanta, where the National Defender Project came close to awarding a grant but ultimately never did, offered a case in point. In some ways, conditions in Atlanta appeared auspicious for a new defender initiative, because the city combined an extreme degree of need with some unique institutional and political advantages. As to the need, civil rights activists decried the Georgia courts as sites of "jim crow railroaded justice."[46] Like other Southern states after Reconstruction, Georgia had deputized the criminal law into the service of white supremacy, and well into the twentieth century, only a handful of black lawyers practiced in the entire state. Thus, while many criminal defendants were black, the lawyers appointed to represent them—along with the judges and jurors—were virtually all white.[47] In 1955, the Georgia Supreme Court celebrated the state's lawyers for "giving their best" in indigent cases, but this was almost certainly an exaggeration, not least because court-appointed lawyers received no compensation for their work.[48] In Atlanta, there was no organized office providing indigent criminal defense, whether public or private, prior to *Gideon*. Into the 1960s, the Fulton County courts continued to rely on case-by-case appointments, selecting counsel for indigent felony defendants from "a group of 10 to 12 lawyers who make themselves available."[49]

As to the advantages, Atlanta lawyers and civic leaders were always anxious for any opportunity to burnish the city's image. To entice business investment, boosters rhapsodized about Atlanta as an oasis of racial moderation and gradual progress: "the city too busy to hate." It was a sales pitch—a concerted effort to distinguish the New South metropolis from regional competitors like Birmingham, now tarnished by embarrassing civil rights conflagrations—but it was not entirely puffery. While other Southern officials were railing against Washington, Atlanta's mayor, Ivan Allen Jr., famously testified in favor of the federal Civil Rights Act.[50] The organized bar did not expressly relate *Gideon* to the ongoing civil rights movement, but Atlanta lawyers recognized that maintaining the city's New South bona fides required some response to the Supreme Court's directives. After *Gideon*, committees formed by the Atlanta Bar Association and the Georgia State Bar endorsed various proposals for public defender legislation and related reforms.[51] Atlanta was also the only Southern city with a long-standing civil legal aid office—the Atlanta Legal Aid Society, established in 1924 and the only organization of its kind in the South prior to the 1960s. Though small and underfunded, Atlanta Legal Aid provided more of an institutional base than most Southern cities had at the time.[52]

What scuttled Atlanta lawyers' efforts to secure a Ford Foundation grant was not lack of interest, but the requirement of local matching funds. In 1967, the Atlanta Legal Aid Society requested funds from the National Defender Project to hire seven full-time attorneys who, along with volunteers from the local bar, would represent felony defendants in the Fulton County criminal courts. Project staffers were eager to fund an initiative in Atlanta, given its regional prominence and lack of any existing defender organization. The NLADA executive committee reviewed the Atlanta Legal Aid proposal and voted to approve a two-year grant.[53] However, the grant was made conditional upon the Legal Aid Society's ability to secure equal matching funds from Fulton County. The county board of commissioners refused to appropriate the requisite funds, and so the grant was nullified before any funds were disbursed.[54]

Atlanta lawyers proposed several explanations for why the county declined to provide the requisite matching funds, but the decisive factor seems to have been the commissioners' general fiscal stinginess, rather than generic opposition to the idea of a public defender. One lawyer explained that the commissioners "[did] not want any 'fat' in the program" and preferred to establish a county public defender, whose finances they could oversee more directly, rather than partnering with the private Legal Aid Society.[55] The commissioners also believed that the federal government might provide funding on more generous terms than the Ford Foundation. While considering the National Defender Project offer, the commissioners were in simultaneous talks with the federal Department of Health, Education, and Welfare, which they believed would provide a grant that required a smaller county match. However, the county's ultimate efforts proved meager. In 1968, Fulton County did establish a public defender office, but its staff lawyers only represented misdemeanor defendants. Felony defendants continued to receive court-appointed private attorneys, who were compensated only $50 per case, and were not appointed until after the preliminary hearing—a crucial stage in a criminal case, at which the state previews its evidence.[56]

In 1968, the Atlanta Legal Aid Society made a final attempt at funding from the National Defender Project. The society had recently hired a young firebrand, Michael Padnos, as its head attorney and received an infusion of federal War on Poverty funds for its civil legal aid work. Thus emboldened, the organization hired dozens of new lawyers and pursued an aggressive course of litigation against Atlanta public housing authorities, private slumlords, and the Georgia welfare bureaucracy.[57] Still hoping to expand the society's bailiwick to encompass criminal defense, Padnos requested a small grant from the National Defender Project to represent felony defendants in preliminary hearings and fill the gap left by Fulton County's meager appointed counsel system. Within the project, one staffer strongly urged funding this proposal. He was overruled by General Decker, who pointed out that the National Defender Project was nearing the end of its life. In February 1969, Padnos's grant proposal was formally declined. The window for philanthropic investment in a public defender for the "city too busy to hate" was, at least for the moment, closed.[58]

THE NATIONAL DEFENDER PROJECT'S efforts in Mississippi exposed most starkly the limitations of elite philanthropy's apolitical approach to policy change. This approach proceeded as if local inequalities stemmed from local policymakers' insufficient expertise.[59] State courts that adhered to different rules of criminal procedure than constitutional law required, or seemingly to no rules at all, required technical assistance. This framework elided the possibility that local courts might appear to adhere to different rules because they were doing something other than adjudicating criminal accusations. In Mississippi, another and perhaps primary function of the criminal courts was maintaining white supremacy by, among other mechanisms, encouraging fear of the police, expressing the differential value that the state placed upon white and black lives, and distributing felony convictions that hindered access to the franchise.[60] It was no accident that Mississippi's state penitentiary, Parchman Farm, was an operational cotton plantation, where prisoners, almost all black, tended "miles of flat Delta land green with cotton plants," under the watch of "shotgun-toting overseers."[61] White leaders were unlikely to embrace reforms that might interfere with these arrangements, no matter how proven the "delivery system."

Mississippi's white leaders were also unlikely to welcome either the advice or the assistance of outside legal organizations. There were three black lawyers in Mississippi who took civil rights cases, but the state's white lawyers, nearly uniformly, refused such cases.[62] In 1964, the Lawyers' Committee for Civil Rights sent a group to Mississippi hoping to convince the local bar to "shoulder its responsibility and begin to represent civil rights workers." The Mississippi State Bar responded with a perfunctory statement in support (or, non-non-support) of this effort, but it quickly became apparent that this was an "empty gesture."[63] The Lawyers' Committee, one participant later recalled, "had seriously underestimated" both the hostility of white Mississippians to the civil rights movement and "the economic or physical reprisals" that local lawyers would face for getting involved.[64] Instead, Mississippi civil rights activists received legal assistance from outside organizations, including the NAACP Legal Defense Fund and the National Lawyers Guild. Under the auspices of the Lawyers' Committee for Civil Rights and other groups, dozens of volunteers from around the country visited Mississippi in 1964 and 1965 to coordinate criminal defense and other legal assistance for the civil rights movement.[65] In 1965, with funds from the Ford and Rockefeller foundations, the Lawyers' Committee opened a permanent office in Jackson, which continued providing criminal defense and also began to file plaintiff-side civil rights lawsuits. The Mississippi State Bar responded by withdrawing its earlier agreement to permit out-of-state lawyers to practice in the Mississippi courts.[66]

Lawyers and other observers from outside the state continued to have difficulty making sense of these dynamics except by categorizing Mississippi as un-American. One volunteer lawyer came away with the impression that "Mississippi is not a part of the United States, and if she is to join the other 49 states in the Union, she must be rehabilitated and democratized in the same fashion that Germany and Japan were democratized—through use of an army of occupation."[67] These observations echoed pervasive tropes in media and journalism, for the Magnolia State occupied a special place in the American liberal imagination of the 1960s. Mississippi was objectively distinctive in many ways: it was the poorest state in the nation and remained heavily rural; it had, proportionally, the largest African American population of any state; and the state's white leadership did engage in especially flagrant and violent defiance of federal mandates to desegregate.[68] But beyond these facts, Mississippi was often depicted in almost mythical terms, as "the singular site of political authoritarianism and racial extremism in 1960s America." As the historian Joseph Crespino observes, this framing enabled observers to keep their faith that democracy and moderation could be trusted to prevail elsewhere: "If Mississippi was a closed society, America was by implication an open one."[69]

Ideas about law—or its purported absence—were central to the myth of the closed Mississippi. In many descriptions of the era, the state's people were depicted as ungoverned, not by rational thought and certainly not by law. The journalist Theodore White, in his widely admired series that chronicled presidential campaigns, described Mississippi in 1964 as the habitat of "two kinds of human animals . . . black and white; the whites have the guns and the machinery of government, and in their semi-beast relationship the white man is the hunter animal, the Negro the prey." These two groups, White continued, lived "entirely separated, hating and fearing each other in a condition of total lawlessness and immorality . . . [F]or three centuries they have had only animal relations with each other, and all politics, all decision, is magnetized by the primordial fact of race hatred."[70] White's callously debased description reflected the kind of genteel "race hatred" that enabled him to completely ignore the organized efforts of black people in Mississippi to defy the state's reign of terror.[71] It also reflected the simplistic reduction of racism to "primordial" hatred that enabled him, in the same way that visiting lawyers did, to misdescribe the role of law in structuring the conditions of Mississippi life. White claimed that "there [was] no law to govern the relations between the races in Mississippi" and the state was therefore "an illegal society." Similarly, a visiting lawyer concluded: "There is no law in Mississippi."[72]

Outside observers misapprehended the mechanisms at work when they attributed Mississippi's reign of terror to lawlessness, or to some mystical, timeless rage. Black observers were much less likely to describe Mississippi racism itself as exceptional. Martin Luther King Jr., famously said that he "had never seen, even in Mississippi, mobs as hostile and as hate-filled as in Chicago."[73] What emboldened white supremacy in Mississippi was not that it was lawless, but the opposite. The mobs were the law, and that was one source of their capacity to terrorize. When outside observers described Mississippi as lawless, they typically meant that its officials refused to comply with federal court orders. But law, in the form of lawyers, judges, and state-backed violence, certainly did exist in Mississippi and wielded immense power. The Mississippi State Sovereignty Commission, essentially a secret police force that operated from 1956 to 1977, targeted dissidents and dissenters using subpoenas and state investigators. State courts convicted black defendants readily and just as readily, acquitted white defendants who had murdered or lynched. Meanwhile, state officials' rejection of federal supremacy was, itself, framed as a legal argument. The position of the Mississippi State Bar was that civil rights decrees constituted "unwarranted invasions of the reserved powers of the Several States."[74] By assigning primary significance to federal law, Northern liberals could write off state law as not really law at all, preserving the image of American law as unitary and enlightened.

Law did govern Mississippi, and governors learned how at the University of Mississippi's law school. Since its founding in 1854, the law school had functioned as an annex to the state government, operating as Mississippi's "prep school for political power."[75] There was no other law school in Mississippi, few of its aspiring lawyers and politicians traveled out of state for their studies, and most of the law school's graduates planned to remain in Mississippi. In addition to Governor Ross Barnett, the school could count as alumni the state's most recent four governors, eight of its nine state supreme court justices, all of its federal district judges, three-fourths of all lawyers in the state, and "enough" of the state senate "to control all legislation."[76] The law school's curriculum focused on Mississippi practice, cases, and statutes, in contrast to the relatively generalist curriculum at most American law schools. In a 1966 article, *Time* magazine assigned partial blame for the state's ongoing racial violence to the law school's insular focus, which enabled its future leaders "to ignore the winds of U.S. constitutional change" and to graduate "with their Deep South views untouched, after which they ran the state with an isolated narrow-mindedness that has mired Mississippi in racial tragedy."[77]

It was against this backdrop that, in August 1965, a law professor at the University of Mississippi made an inquiry to the National Defender Project about the possibility of grant funding. In response to *Gideon*, the law school had begun an "embryonic" public defender clinic involving students in the Oxford courts, and now sought outside funding to expand the clinic.[78] The professor also proposed a pilot defender project in Pascagoula because, in his estimate, the gulf city contained "the highest percentage of indigent criminal defendants of any area of comparable population in the United States." Lawyers in Mississippi were more forthright than lawyers outside the South tended to be when discussing the racial dimensions of indigent defense, and the Ole Miss grant applications spelled out the stakes quite frankly: in Mississippi, 80 percent of felony defendants were "Negro . . . and the vast majority of these are financially unable to employ counsel to represent them." Experimental defender efforts in Oxford and Pascagoula, then, might "serve as a pilot program" not only for Mississippi but also for other "rural Southern states with large indigent Negro populations."[79]

Because of Mississippi's notoriety, the grant application raised red flags among the NLADA executive committee. Before voting to approve the grant, the New York corporate lawyer and longtime legal aid supporter Orison Marden requested specific assurance that the attorneys receiving funding would not turn away "civil rights cases."[80] Harrison Tweed followed up to request express confirmation that the attorneys would engage in the "representation of Negroes. Perhaps such a statement is not needed," he added, "but I rather think that it is."[81] Tweed's concerns stemmed from his experience as cochair of the Lawyers' Committee for Civil Rights, which was simultaneously battling with the Mississippi State Bar. That context also helps to explain why Marden's inquiry received a noncommittal response. The grant applicants assured staffers over the phone that the Mississippi defenders would handle "all criminal cases[,] including civil rights cases," but cautioned that "it would be impractical to spell it out in the application."[82] Presumably, this was because openly identifying the project as a civil rights initiative might cause trouble with the Mississippi bar or the general public. Although the grant application was nominally cosigned by the university and the Mississippi State Bar, the bar refused to provide administrative assistance with processing the funding or managing the program.[83]

But there were also some reasons for optimism about funding a Mississippi initiative; by 1965, America's internal "closed society" seemed to be opening, at least somewhat. Even Theodore White had appended an asterisk to his hallucination about Mississippi's "human animals," noting "a faint glimmer of light at the end of tunnel": state leaders had begun grudgingly "to comply with Federal law" in certain contexts.[84] As demonstrated by the grant application itself, changes were underway at the Ole Miss law school. By 1966, the school would have nine black students enrolled—a higher number, *Time* magazine noted sharply, than "almost any non-Negro law school in the U.S."⁸⁵ Within the National Defender Project, General Decker was encouraged by his phone conversations with the law school's recently appointed dean, Joshua Morse. Though a Mississippi native, Morse had spent a year at Yale Law School as a visiting fellow and returned from New Haven eager to shake his pupils out of their "provincial outlook," even recruiting eight Yale graduates to join the faculty.⁸⁶ Since the 1930s, Yale had enjoyed a reputation within legal education as unusually innovative, a reputation that was somewhat exaggerated but nevertheless captured real distinctions between Yale and Ole Miss. (Like many Northern liberals, the Yale grads equated Mississippi with a Third World country and their work there with a development project. Teaching at Ole Miss was "like the Peace Corps," one said, "except we're given much more responsibility."⁸⁷)

The Mississippi grant was ultimately approved but yielded mixed results. Upon receiving the application, National Defender Project staffers made preliminary visits to Oxford and Pascagoula and reported back that the lawyers and judges seemed "well qualified" and relatively "enlightened." After these reports, the board, in February 1966, approved a three-year grant, and later that spring, both the Pascagoula and Oxford initiatives got underway.⁸⁸ The University of Mississippi component fulfilled some of the National Defender Project's hopes, generating lasting changes in the law school's criminal procedure curriculum. However, National Defender Project staffers became extremely frustrated with the Pascagoula initiative and debated terminating that stream of the grant early.⁸⁹ There were constant hassles over administrative details and the disbursement of funds. The Pascagoula defenders persistently neglected the paperwork requirements that came along with the grant, and never seemed to have fully assembled the required local matching funds.⁹⁰

Program staffers also developed concerns about the substance of the Pascagoula program. One source of frustration was the Pascagoula defenders' inadequate supervision of the law students assigned to help them. Even had the program been impeccably managed, effectively involving the students would have been challenging, since Oxford was a seven-hour drive away from Pascagoula. The program was not impeccably managed. Students complained that there was not enough work for them to do, because the defenders prioritized their paying clients and never knew anything about the indigent cases "until the last moment before trial."⁹¹ Project staffers who made site visits confirmed the students' account. The defenders exaggerated how much time they spent on their indigent cases. One of the Pascagoula lawyers claimed that his public defender cases left "very little if any time" for his private practice. The National Defender Project staffer who visited his office encountered several paying clients in his waiting room, awaiting appointments.[92]

Most troubling to project observers was the Pascagoula defenders' chummy rapport with local officials. Because of their close ties with prosecutors, the defenders avoided "activities which tend to rock the boat," a project staffer reported.[93] On one occasion, the police rearrested a public defender's clients while they were walking out of the courtroom and the defender never followed up or did anything about it. The Pascagoula defenders claimed that they almost never took cases to trial because the district attorney offered plea deals "too good to pass up."[94] Thanks to the clambakes, perhaps, it was easy to persuade the prosecutors to drop or reduce dozens of felony indictments at a time. The National Defender Project's young staffers, most of whom had recently graduated from law school, conceded that such deals might benefit individual defendants but denied that this type of behavior was "lawyer-like." Reading between the lines, such findings may have also hinted at local prosecutors' tendency to harass people by filing charges they knew they could not prove, and later reducing them.[95] When cases did proceed past the indictment stage, the Pascagoula defenders proved unwilling to file any motions, much less go to trial. They "had done no work in the area of sentencing alternatives" and made "no vigorous attempt to challenge inequities in the proceedings or in the method of prosecution."[96]

Nevertheless, the Ford Foundation's funds continued to flow south to Mississippi. Local lawyers repeatedly assured the National Defender Project staffers that public defender legislation was making its way through the state legislature, and that terminating the pilot project early could scuttle the bill's chances.[97] One Mississippi state senator submitted a letter of support, which praised the Pascagoula defender initiative for "demonstrating that such a program is not 'socialistic'" and "is feasible for [Mississippi]."[98] But, as the project staffers repeatedly witnessed, the Pascagoula office was never much of a model, and it failed to inspire statewide change. Between 1968 and 1970, several public defender bills were introduced in the Mississippi state legislature, but none passed.[99]

The belief in "Southern exceptionalism," the conviction that the Deep South was essentially aberrational in some profound way, had a number of deleterious effects for twentieth-century American political culture. One effect, which historians have documented, was to generate complacency among Northern liberals about their states' own forms of brutality, which the urban uprisings of the late 1960s and the Attica prison riot of 1971 would force into the forefront.[100] At the same time, the discourse of exceptionalism could also reinforce Southern brutality, by depicting racism as a regrettable but entrenched regional trait, almost beyond the capacity of rational intervention. According to project staffers, for example, Mississippi's backwardness was largely to blame for the weaknesses of the Pascagoula initiative; the Ford Foundation grants had achieved all that was "politically possible" in such a retrograde state.[101] General Decker assessed the Mississippi project as a "good" one overall, "given the area in which the program operates."[102] The fiction that foundations made no policy themselves, but only supported existing local initiatives, enabled foundations to claim credit for projects that succeeded while absolving outside funders of responsibility for investments not made and projects that failed.

In July 1969, the National Defender Project received a final and somewhat unusual request from Mississippi. The letter came from Martha Wood, the city attorney of Fayette, Mississippi, a tiny town in the state's southwest corner that was briefly the focus of national attention.[103] Fayette had just elected Mississippi's first black mayor since Reconstruction: Charles Evers, the older brother of Medgar Evers, the NAACP leader who had been assassinated six years earlier by a member of the Ku Klux Klan. "Hands that picked cotton," Evers sloganeered, "can now pick the mayor." Charles Evers was a divisive figure within Mississippi—unlike his more diplomatic brother, he was often resistant to collaboration and given to moralizing harangues—but he was "charismatic" and developed a favorable national image as a "responsible moderate."[104] Shortly after Evers was elected, Wood wrote the National Defender Project requesting $4,000 to start a public defender office for the town. Wood was white; her husband, Fayette's police chief, was black, a domestic arrangement that could still have been criminalized just two years before.[105] Originally, Wood and Evers proposed to hire Ruben Anderson as public defender—the first black law graduate of the University of Mississippi—although for reasons that are unclear, Evers later hired someone else instead. The Fayette grant request appeared to offer one last opportunity to fund an initiative in Mississippi—one that would send grant funds not to the white-dominated legal establishment, but to an unusual town in which decisions were made by "hands that picked cotton."

By rights, Wood's letter should have arrived too late. The National Defender Project was scheduled to sunset by the end of the year, and had ceased awarding new grants.[106] Ostensibly, that was why the most recent entreaty from Atlanta had been rejected. But it seems that Orison Marden personally intervened and urged considering the proposal.[107] General Decker asked one of his young staffers to travel to Fayette and see if he could help develop a workable grant application. The staffer, who observed a day of sessions at the Fayette police court, found the visit unsettling. Pursuant to state law, the mayor officiated personally over the police court, although he had "no legal background whatsoever." In one case, a white attorney carried out an "atrocious" defense of a black man charged with drunk driving; the attorney himself was drunk throughout the proceedings. At one point, Mayor Evers appointed the visiting National Defender Project observer himself to represent a defendant. Despite the chaotic scene, the staffer recommended funding the Fayette proposal. The amount of money requested was trivial relative to other grants the project had made, and the endeavor had what the staffer referred to as "obvious racial overtones."[108] Accordingly, as one of its final disbursements, the National Defender Project authorized a one-time "emergency grant" to Fayette, Mississippi. For one year, from 1970 to 1971, these funds underwrote a part-time public defender.[109]

But the local circuit court judge refused to accept the public defender in his courtroom. The reason, as Evers explained, was straightforward: "the Circuit Judge is, or was the senior trial lawyer for the Ku Klux Klan in the area."[110] After the "emergency grant" ran out, the Fayette public defender's office closed up shop. The National Defender Project's final report acknowledged that, because of resistance from "the local courts," the Fayette initiative "was not continued."[111] The KKK connection was not specified. The specific power of white supremacy, acknowledged in internal correspondence, became in the final report bleached out into generic local politics, a kind of free-floating irrationality common to "local courts" in "the rural south." Even though the Fayette initiative could not be uncritically adjudged a success, the final report tried to give it a positive spin: "the attempt to introduce the defender concept in the rural south does indicate the geographical reach of NDP. Grant funds were expended in almost every type of community . . . The very existence of NDP programs generated a new range of experience, demonstrating the effect of an organized defender office on those different types of communities."[112] Spending funds became its own achievement, a way of "demonstrating" what would happen if someone opened a public defender office in rural Mississippi, even if what would happen was that the office would close.

IN 1973, the *New Yorker* magazine published an investigation of "Our Criminal Courts," with a focus on Boston. The symbolic opposite of Mississippi, Massachusetts enjoyed a reputation as eminently enlightened. The magazine writer selected Boston to visit because he assumed that, as one of America's oldest and most liberal cities, its courts must be relatively "civilized." He was quickly disabused of this notion, in part by his encounters with the Massachusetts Defenders Committee; most of the *New Yorker* series was devoted to criticizing the MDC's overwhelming caseloads and cursory representation.[113] In Roxbury, by contrast, the *New Yorker* writer was immensely impressed by two African American lawyers he met. Roderick Ireland and Wally Sherwood, both twenty-seven years old, had recently launched the Roxbury Defenders Committee, a community-based alternative to the state public defender agency.[114]

Established in 1971, the Roxbury Defenders Committee had support from the MDC — the idea for a neighborhood branch office had been floated by MDC board members as a response to defendants' feelings of alienation — but differed from the MDC in several key ways. First, the Roxbury offshoot was supervised by its own "Community Board," which included black lawyers, members of black community organizations, and liaisons to social service providers.[115] Second, the Roxbury lawyers quickly adopted a more aggressive stance toward the state than traditional MDC attorneys. When they opened the office, Sherwood and Ireland were still, in Ireland's memory, "rookie lawyers, really more like 'kids.'" The first ten staff attorneys they hired were "all very young and equally inexperienced." What distinguished these young lawyers was their eagerness to file motions, take cases to trial, and challenge actions taken by police and prosecutors. Ireland jokingly recalled his time with the Roxbury Defenders as a "post-graduate education in subjects law schools do not teach, such as 'Fighting with the Judiciary 101.'"[116] Their efforts, the *New Yorker* writer concluded, had generated a paradox: "In Boston, the average criminal defendant who has the best chance of ending up with a capable lawyer is the poor black who lives in the worst slum — Roxbury."[117]

Sherwood and Ireland posited that defendants needed not simply lawyers, or better-funded lawyers, but a new kind of lawyer. They reimagined the public defender not merely as a substitute for retained counsel within the context of an individual criminal case, but as a friendly neighborhood resource. The MDC offices had long been located in downtown Boston; instead, Sherwood and Ireland set up their office in the heart of Roxbury, near their clients' homes. The Roxbury Defenders maintained a 24-hour telephone hotline so potential clients could speak to an attorney as soon as they were arrested, rather than having to wait until their first court appearance. The office also enforced strict caseload limits to ensure that lawyers had adequate time to meet with each client. In addition to criminal defense, the Roxbury Defenders hosted "know-your-rights" workshops for teenagers, published a community newsletter, and broadcast a weekly call-in radio show. "We even had a traveling basketball team," Ireland recalled years later, "and played games against patients of several drug treatment programs whom we also represented in court."[118]

By the 1980s, the Roxbury Defenders had further expanded their work to encompass prisoners' rights litigation, offering civil legal aid for incarcerated men and women with complaints about prison conditions. The office's attorneys argued that providing public defenders on the front end was not enough: "Legal assistance must also be provided to black people who do not escape the peril of prison," because it was the prison, "more than any other institution," that maintained "the tradition of racist oppression of black people." Prisoners' rights litigation, they argued, offered a way to demonstrate concern for black prisoners and to "symboliz[e] the commitment to end the use of prisons as instruments of racist oppression of black people."[119] Both inside and outside of court, the Roxbury Defenders advanced an insistently racial critique of American criminal justice. In interviews with the *Boston Globe*, they criticized the "white, middle-class orientation" of the judiciary, denounced the criminal law as a "repressive tool . . . against blacks and Puerto Ricans," and channeled Roxbury residents' anger about the twin scourges of "police abuse and police neglect."[120] These critiques brought into the public defender's office echoes of ideas long central to the black liberation movement.

AN IRONIC FACT about the Roxbury Defenders Committee suggested the constrained position of lawyers who opposed the state while also working within it. Despite its origins as a response to complaints about "government attorneys" and its lawyers' vocally anti-carceral, antiracist politics, this pioneering holistic defender owed its existence to a law-and-order federal agency: it was originally funded by grants from the federal Law Enforcement Assistance Administration, established by the Safe Streets Act of 1968. LEAA was established at a moment when political commitment to the War on Poverty had waned and the emphasis of federal social policy had begun to shift toward the War on Crime.[121] Most of LEAA's funds were distributed to states in the form of block grants, which state-level administrators could then disburse to local projects as they saw fit. As demonstrated by the Roxbury Defenders grant—awarded through the state planning agency that administered LEAA funds in Massachusetts—states used LEAA block grants in a wide variety of ways.[122] But the bulk of LEAA funds ended up in the coffers of local police departments, who used them to acquire new weapons and military-grade technology. In a dismal cycle, militarized police inflamed hostilities in inner-city neighborhoods, which reinforced the perception in the minds of policymakers that cities were akin to war zones and required a heavy police presence.[123]

At the same time, LEAA made unprecedented federal outlays for state and local indigent defense programs. Between 1969 and 1977, LEAA reported total appropriations of $23 million for criminal defense programs—nearly four times the $6.1 million ultimately spent by the Ford Foundation's National Defender Project, the next-largest underwriter of *Gideon*'s implementation.[124] LEAA also funded research studies on indigent defense, a national training program for public defenders, and a two-year project to develop a guidebook for "legal defense systems," published in 1976 and distributed at a conference that brought together 400 judges, prosecutors, and defenders from around the country. By one estimate, thanks to LEAA, the federal government was briefly the nation's "principal supporter of public defense."[125] Public defenders later remembered the LEAA years as the heyday for federal funding. The 1970s were a "very exciting time," recalled one Chicago public defender. There were "new programs all around the country" and "money available from Washington."[126]

LEAA's outlays generated excitement not because they were especially significant within the context of LEAA, but because they appeared generous in contrast to the dearth of local and state funding for public defenders. LEAA funds accounted for only 3 to 5 percent of a typical state's overall criminal justice spending, and within that slice, grants for indigent defense represented a minuscule sliver.[127] In 1973, the National Legal Aid and Defender Association published a report complaining that defenders had received less than 1 percent of all LEAA grants.[128] Partly, this imbalance stemmed from confusion at the state level about whether criminal defense was statutorily eligible for LEAA funding. In 1973, at NLADA's urging, Congress expressly defined "defender services" as within the ambit of "law enforcement and criminal justice" in order to make clear that defender programs were eligible for grants.[129] Even still, prosecutors' offices and police departments continued to capture the lion's share of federal infusions. In the period between 1969 and 1977, LEAA's $23 million in grants for defenders were dwarfed by outlays of $144 million to prosecutors.[130]

The significance of LEAA funding was not that it coopted local defender organizations or muted the politics of individual public defenders. Most

LEAA funds were distributed through state intermediaries with wide latitude to fund programs, so long as they had some plausible connection to criminal justice; federal oversight of how the funds were used was effectively nonexistent.[131] From the perspective of local organizations, LEAA funds were no more or less compromising than any other source of taxpayer dollars. But LEAA funding did place implicit constraints upon the now-national political debate about the public defender. At a time when local defenders faced constant fiscal instability, a law-and-order agency offered the most promising funding source. Thus, when NLADA published its report urging LEAA to devote more generous funds to indigent defense, it framed the request in law-and-order terms. The report acknowledged that the federal and state governments were pursuing a "War on Crime." With public funds flowing into law enforcement, there would be "more police" and in turn, "more arrests." Unless public defenders were also adequately funded, jails would "become crowded past the bursting point with persons awaiting trial."[132] A more straightforward response to the War on Crime might have been to call for reversing the trend toward "more arrests," but that would have required a longer-term political strategy, could have antagonized lawmakers in the short term, and would not, in the meantime, have helped to alleviate public defenders' immediate fiscal pressures. Thus did the public defender, once part of legal liberals' strategy for winning the Cold War, become redefined as materiel for the War on Crime.

WITHIN THE National Defender Project's final report, completed in the early 1970s, there was a single and ominous footnote that signaled the gathering storm clouds. The report observed that the burdens imposed by *Gideon* and especially by *Argersinger* would have been challenging for the legal profession even under stable conditions. But conditions were not stable, because the "demand for defender services" was growing: the number of arrests, according to the report, had increased 300 percent in the previous ten years. The footnote appended to that statistic observed that no one really knew why the number of arrests was increasing: whether the statistics reflected "better reporting methods, greater success in law enforcement, or [that] more crimes are in fact being committed."[133] Historians have only now begun to piece together the complex dynamics, at the intersection of law, politics, policymaking, and social change, that produced this new degree of police targeting beginning in the 1960s, especially in poor urban neighborhoods, and would ultimately generate the phenomenon of mass incarceration.[134] At the time, the National Defender Project's final report could only quote Lewis Carroll's *Through the Looking Glass*, in which Alice finds that in Wonderland, no matter how fast you run you never get anywhere. If the number of defenders increased but the number of criminal cases increased faster, then perhaps "the National Defender Project merely allowed the defender movement to run fast, like Alice, only to find itself in the same place."[135]

Ten years after *Gideon*, many lawyers considered "the problem of the indigent accused" to have been largely mapped out, at least as a question of doctrine and policy. The string of Supreme Court cases from *Gideon* in 1963 to *Argersinger* in 1972 had specified the constitutional requirements for the provision of counsel in criminal proceedings. Efforts by the National Defender Project, national and local bar associations, and the growing number of public defenders around the country had yielded a body of knowledge and guidelines. Particularly in rural and Southern jurisdictions, local courts continued to rely on the old method of case-by-case appointments to comply with *Gideon*, but professional norms now recommended phasing out that method as much as possible. What remained necessary, in the legal profession's internal accounts of this history, was funding and continued effort to render *Gideon* meaningful. Such accounts did not downplay the practical challenges that remained, but the challenges were now practical—not conceptual. Lawyers no longer debated among themselves whether the public defender was a step toward a "police state." Eighty years after Clara Foltz delivered her speech at the Chicago World's Fair, the public defender was no longer considered a utopian scheme or a "strange project."

Compared to that relatively tidy picture of shared understandings, conditions on the ground remained discouraging and confusing to many lawyers—and defendants. One set of dark uncertainties concerned the existing courts. Elite lawyers had come to embrace the public defender in theory, but post-*Gideon* efforts raised questions about whether local courts around the country were equally prepared to embrace the public defender in practice. *Gideon* assumed that defense counsel held the key to a fair trial and could, in some sense, compensate for the inequalities of society, but visitors to local courts quickly began to doubt this assumption. Defense counsel was only part of a complex picture, in which law and society were inseparably blended. A second set of dark uncertainties concerned the future courts. Lawyers had coalesced around the public defender as a nationwide court reform against the backdrop assumption that the courts themselves were a steady-state feature of American life. Assuming a rough equilibrium in the overall numbers involved in the criminal courts each year, then the legal establishment had time and space to measure what was happening and introduce gradual adjustments to render the courts more fair. But if politicians, police, and prosecutors were now planning to funnel into the courts ever-spiraling numbers of defendants each year, then the courthouse foundations would become unsteady beneath defenders' feet, denying the public defender the time and space needed to become ensconced.

Epilogue

Conventionally, the 1984 case of *Strickland v. Washington* is cited as the most significant right-to-counsel decision since *Gideon*. *Strickland* concerned a federal habeas petition filed by a Florida death row prisoner, David Leroy Washington, who had committed a string of violent attacks, including three murders. Washington did not dispute his guilt, only his death sentence. He argued that his court-appointed public defender had shirked his duties, and that he was entitled to a new sentencing hearing with an effective lawyer.[1] Washington's counsel had, indeed, neglected several basic tasks. He never requested a psychological evaluation or a full investigation into Washington's background; he failed to investigate and subpoena character witnesses; and he did not prepare a meaningful sentencing memorandum—the document in which defense lawyers make the case for mercy. "I had a hopeless feeling," the lawyer later said to explain his indifference. "I can honestly say that I don't know that I felt that there was anything which I could do which was going to save David Washington from his fate."[2]

The Supreme Court granted review in *Strickland* in order to resolve a question that had long confused the lower courts. By the 1980s, it was clearly established that defendants had the right to counsel if the state sought to deprive them of life or liberty, and that indigent defendants had the right to counsel at public expense. It was also established that the right to counsel meant, more specifically, the right to "*effective* assistance of counsel." What remained unclear was the definition of "effective." How much effort did the lawyer have to put into the case? Did the lawyer have to specialize in criminal law, or demonstrate any particular level of experience? What if she made a mistake during the trial? What if she fell asleep? Or what if she meant well, but was overwhelmed by her caseload and did not have time to prepare? The lower courts had divided on these questions. Some appellate courts recognized "ineffective assistance" only when the quality of legal representation fell so far beneath any minimum professional standard that it made a "mockery of justice." A few jurisdictions imposed more detailed and rigorous standards of professional performance. In practice, though, courts tended to presume that "as long as there was a lawyer seated at the defense table . . . the defense was adequate."[3]

In *Strickland*, the Supreme Court aimed to provide the lower courts with a uniform definition of "effective assistance." In a majority opinion authored by Justice Sandra Day O'Connor, *Strickland* created a two-part test for proving "ineffective assistance of counsel." First, the lawyer had to have made grievous mistakes. It was not enough to show that he had made a mistaken judgment call or a negligent oversight. His conduct had to fall beneath even the most rudimentary standards of professional competence. Second, the defendant had to prove that the lawyer's mistakes might have prejudiced the outcome of his case. Specifically, he had to show "a reasonable probability" that the verdict or sentence might have come out differently with a competent lawyer. Thus, the *Strickland* Court endorsed a relatively minimal constitutional baseline for effective assistance of counsel. There was no need to impose rigorous standards for defense counsel as a matter of constitutional law, the Court explained, because the legal profession could ordinarily be trusted to impose its own internal standards. "The Sixth Amendment refers simply to 'counsel,'" Justice O'Connor wrote, "not specifying particular requirements of effective assistance. It relies instead on the legal profession's maintenance of standards sufficient to justify the law's presumption that counsel will fulfill the role in the adversary process that the Amendment envisions."[4]

The second prong of the *Strickland* test implied that a defendant's obvious guilt could undermine his standing to complain about inadequate counsel. If the evidence against him appeared overwhelming, then a defendant would later find it difficult to prove that any lawyer might have changed the outcome. As Justice Thurgood Marshall observed in a challenging dissent, this component of *Strickland* implied "that the only purpose of the constitutional guarantee of effective assistance of counsel is to reduce the chance that innocent persons will be convicted." But due process, Marshall insisted, was not a privilege that belonged only to the innocent: "Every defendant is entitled to a trial in which his interests are vigorously and conscientiously advocated by an able lawyer." Marshall would have required a new trial any time a defendant received incompetent representation, regardless of whether the defendant could prove prejudice.[5] Marshall also echoed a point that Justice Hugo Black had made in 1942, in his *Betts v. Brady* dissent: there was often no way to tell whether a trial might have turned out differently if the defendant had received expert legal assistance. Appellate judges, reading a cold trial record long after the fact, could not know for sure "whether a defendant . . . would have fared better if his lawyer had been competent. Seemingly impregnable cases can sometimes be dismantled by good defense counsel."

That, after all, was the reason why defendants had the right to counsel in the first place.[6]

Strickland also held that David Leroy Washington had failed to show the requisite prejudice. Justice O'Connor opined that the evidence that Washington claimed his lawyer should have presented "would barely have altered the sentencing profile"; given the facts of his crimes, he would probably still have been sentenced to death.[7] Washington was executed later that year. Because of the minimal baseline that it established for constitutionally "effective assistance," many legal scholars decry *Strickland* as a betrayal of *Gideon*. By 1984, the Supreme Court—more than a decade into the leadership of Chief Justice Warren Burger—had begun to impose limits upon many Warren Court decisions, not necessarily overturning them, but curtailing their transformative potential.[8] It is true that the *Strickland* Court declined an opportunity to expand *Gideon*'s practical significance. Still, in its broad premises, *Strickland* comported with many of the lawyerly assumptions that *Gideon* had elevated into constitutional law. Like *Gideon*, *Strickland* assumed that the right to counsel was the primary guarantor of a fair and reliable trial. But also like *Gideon*, *Strickland* was highly deferential to the organized legal profession when it came to implementing that right. The Supreme Court's jurisprudence continued to rest upon a faith, never entirely justified by the available empirical evidence or past decades of experience, that lawyers could generally be trusted to develop and enforce their own internal standards and that these professional norms, rather than judicial oversight or government intervention, would typically suffice to ensure fair trials.

Strickland's strange legacy further illustrates the enduring centrality of the defense lawyer to the American conception of a fair trial. After *Strickland*, the "ineffective assistance of counsel" claim became the most common vehicle for challenging a death sentence. In the early 2000s, 81 percent of federal habeas petitions challenging state capital convictions raised a claim of ineffective assistance.[9] That figure reflected the continued prevalence of inadequate lawyering in capital cases, but it was also an artifact of the narrow terms in which the convoluted machinery of American law incentivized prisoners to frame their complaints. During the 1980s and 1990s, the courts and Congress together imposed a maze of new procedural hurdles for federal habeas claims and other forms of postconviction review. Doctrinal narrowing in other areas of the law led prisoners to repackage their claims into the type of claim that courts seemed willing to entertain: ineffective assistance of counsel. Rather than presenting mitigating evidence, argue that defense counsel failed to investigate mitigating evidence. Rather than arguing actual innocence, argue that defense counsel failed to investigate the possibility of actual innocence. As a legal handbook for jailhouse lawyers advised: "Ineffective assistance of counsel claims can be very useful because they can allow you to present claims that would otherwise be barred."[10]

The *Strickland* standard is nearly impossible to meet, and so few *Strickland* claims succeed. Nevertheless, *Strickland* and its progeny are often the only viable precedents of use to prisoners who want to challenge their convictions. Procedural limitations largely prevent appellate and federal courts from reopening the facts of a criminal case. Once a conviction has been finalized in the state courts through the ordinary appeals process, a prisoner generally cannot argue that he was actually innocent (unless some genuinely novel evidence has come to light that could not have been found before the initial trial) or that he was simply punished too harshly. He can almost always, however, try out the argument that his trial was procedurally invalid. The American judicial process for reviewing criminal convictions has become, to a surprising degree, an elaborate ritual in which defendants complain that their lawyers weren't good enough and then the courts respond that their lawyers indeed made mistakes but not serious enough mistakes to render the proceedings fundamentally unfair. The defense lawyer stands in as both scapegoat and absolution for all of the obvious problems with the criminal courts that are harder to frame in constitutionally or legally cognizable terms.

Because the appellate machinery grinds slowly, and federal habeas proceedings can take years or even decades to finalize, prisoners convicted in lower-level courts, and sentenced to prison terms measurable in months or single-digit years, typically do not have enough time to pursue ineffective assistance of counsel claims before they are released and the claims become moot. But for public defenders in the lower-level courts, the 1980s also brought new pressures. The escalation of the "War on Drugs" represented, in the words of one analyst, "the public defender's losing battle." By 1991, drug prosecutions had multiplied and, depending on the state, some 70 to 90 percent of defendants facing drug charges qualified for representation by a public defender. Even as state and federal governments invested in aggressive enforcement of drug laws, they did not augment defenders' budgets accordingly, eroding any "semblance of balance between police, prosecution, and indigent defense resources."[11] The Los Angeles County Public Defender, the nation's oldest, succumbed to the undertow. During the 1980s, the number of drug cases in Los Angeles doubled, while hiring and budget growth stalled. By 1990, the Los Angeles public defender was "refusing approximately

1,000 cases a month because the office [could not] provide proper representation due to the volume, primarily, of drug cases."[12] With present conditions appearing bleak, one lawyer described the public defender's courtroom advocacy as aimed instead at posterity. The defender's role, he explained, is to "stand there and articulate the defense" of whoever it is that "society at that moment deems to be the pariah of all time . . . and insist that they be treated decently and fairly."[13]

The Roxbury Defenders Committee had offered one local response to disappointment with *Gideon*'s implementation: a community-based public defender. In 1984, the Roxbury office became an outpost of the Committee for Public Counsel Services, the successor agency to the Massachusetts Defenders Committee. The model pioneered in Roxbury has now become the gold standard for indigent defense. New York now has multiple community defender alternatives to the Legal Aid Society—including the Bronx Defenders and the Neighborhood Defender Service of Harlem—whose leaders credit the Roxbury Defenders as pioneers of holistic advocacy.[14] In recent years, traditional public defender offices have also incorporated elements of the holistic model by hiring social workers, expanding their community outreach, and engaging in public advocacy on behalf of the communities they serve.[15] These efforts may represent an improvement over more limited conceptions of the public defender, but they also represent one more example of American institutions that happen to interact with large numbers of poor people—whether public defenders, police departments, or schools—being pressed into service beyond their missions and asked to solve problems that might better be addressed through more expansive public health and welfare programs.

The fact that the Roxbury Defenders Committee was initially funded by the federal Law Enforcement Assistance Administration presaged a second oft-proposed response to disappointment with *Gideon*'s implementation: relocating responsibility for indigent defense not downward to the community but upward, to the federal government. Though the two strategies might seem ideologically contradictory, they have sometimes overlapped in practice. But local public defenders have not yet succeeded in securing a stable commitment to federal support. After LEAA was phased out in 1982, some federal grants continued to trickle through various successor entities within the Department of Justice, but not on the same scale. In 1979 and 1980, Senator Ted Kennedy and Representative Peter Rodino introduced legislation, based on an American Bar Association proposal, to establish a dedicated, federal Center for Defense Services, which would fund and advise local public defenders. But the legislation made no headway.[16] In contrast, federal funding for police and prosecutors remained generous even after the demise of LEAA itself. In 1991, one analyst lamented the growing imbalance. States could "look to the federal government for grants and assistance for police, prosecutors, and some treatment programs," but federal aid for indigent defense was, "for all intents and purposes, unavailable." Federal policy assumed instead "that indigent defense is solely the responsibility of state and local governments."[17]

In recent years, advocates have continued to endorse both holistic approaches to indigent defense and dedicated federal funding. Public defenders involved with the Black Lives Matter movement continue the tradition, exemplified by the Roxbury Defenders Committee, of connecting indigent defense with a broader politics of racial justice.[18] The ABA has continued to propose federal support for local and state public defenders, and during the 2016 presidential campaign, the idea was discussed in prominent news outlets like *The Nation* and the *New York Times*.[19] Meanwhile, defender organizations have continued to cobble together funding from philanthropic sources, although—indicating how far rightward American politics have moved since the 1960s—today one of the most significant funders of indigent defense reform is Koch Industries.[20] Federal funding would likely help to fill a structural gap in *Gideon*—its lack of specificity as to who bears the responsibility for implementation. The prospects for philanthropic funding are less certain. The checkered results of the Ford Foundation's National Defender Project suggest that private investment in matters of state, regardless of the source, often generates the least change in those places where the need is greatest.

The shortcomings of *Gideon*'s implementation have left defendants with uneven access to expert, well-funded defense counsel—the opposite outcome of what the Warren Court intended by declaring the right to counsel a federal constitutional right, which should theoretically apply equally regardless of geography. In the South, the public defender idea continued to meet with resistance; major cities like Houston and New Orleans only established full-time public defender offices after the turn of the twenty-first century.[21] The South also remained regionally distinctive in its tenacious commitment to capital punishment. The convergence of Southern states' weak infrastructure for indigent defense with their persistent deployment of the death penalty produced a litany of horrific cases in which court-appointed lawyers were useless at best, drunk or even asleep at worst, during capital trials. In 1994, the renowned advocate Stephen Bright, of the Atlanta-based Southern Center for Human Rights, described in a now-classic article how defendants received the death penalty "not for the worst crime but for the worst lawyer."[22]

Meanwhile, in many ways, elite lawyers' rhetoric has hardly changed. In 2010, attorney general Eric Holder delivered a speech that differed little from Robert Kennedy's 1963 speech to the New England Defender Conference. Holder, echoing Kennedy, described a "crisis" in indigent defense, and just as Kennedy did, he promised backing from the Department of Justice for lawyers seeking to improve "the defense that poor people receive in state and local courts."[23] In 2013, on the occasion of Gideon's fiftieth anniversary, lawyers, legal scholars, and journalists produced tens of thousands of pages lamenting Gideon's "broken promise" but—with only a few contrarian exceptions—celebrating Gideon itself.[24] Newspapers, magazines, and online news outlets have continued to generate articles about public defenders reeling under the pressures of excessive caseloads, insufficient budgets, dubious funding structures, and resistance from hostile judges and politicians. The permanent crisis permanesces.[25]

Criminal defense lawyers are often heroes, both in life and in fiction, but they are also beleaguered bureaucrats, extolled as the best of American justice and blamed as the worst of American justice in countless court filings reciting the legalese of "ineffective assistance of counsel." During the twentieth century, the leaders of the American legal profession developed a vision of modern democracy in which lawyers stood at the center and in which every individual, no matter how poor or friendless, could count on the state to provide him with a lawyer to make his case against that same state. As the state grew, it would never grow too much, because lawyers distributed throughout its many courtrooms and jailhouses would poke holes in its claims to authority, invite the light into its darkest rooms, and hold up shields to protect its most vulnerable targets. The (mostly) men who developed this vision overestimated the power of lawyers and underestimated the power of the state, and in many ways, they also misapprehended the sources of the vulnerability of the state's targets. They were right to insist upon equality before the law, but what is also needed is a broader conversation, not about how to carve out pockets of equality in the criminal courts, but about law's role in structuring inequality to begin with.

FOR TRACING THE public defender's trajectory as a character in American legal culture, it is not Strickland—nor Gideon nor Argersinger—but rather the obscure 1981 Supreme Court case of Polk County v. Dodson that provides the most fitting ending. In that case, an Iowa prisoner filed a civil rights lawsuit against his erstwhile appellate public defender, arguing that she had failed to pursue his desired appeals and thus deprived him of due process. In some circumstances, federal law allows for damages lawsuits against government officials who deprive or cause someone to be deprived of a constitutional right. But the Constitution binds only "state action," and so the threshold question in such lawsuits is whether the person acted "under color of state law," meaning, vested of government authority.

The Supreme Court held in *Polk County* that public defenders were not "state actors" in the constitutional sense. Writing for the Court, Justice Lewis Powell Jr., explained that a public defender, once appointed, "owes a duty of undivided loyalty to his client"—and not, as Progressive Era reformers had once proposed, a dual obligation both to the individual client and to the general public. "Except for the source of payment," the public defender's relationship with her client is "identical to that existing between any other lawyer and client"—an ideal at odds both with the Progressive Era vision, and also with many defendants' perception that public defenders are not identical to hired lawyers. Indeed, Powell continued, the state had a "constitutional obligation . . . to respect the professional independence" of public defenders and allow them to represent their clients "free of state control"—a description contradicted by the reality that states controlled, if nothing else, the amount of resources that public defenders could use in investigating and defending cases, both through explicit budgetary allocations and implicitly through decisions that determined defenders' caseloads. "A public defender is not acting on behalf of the State" when he represents defendants, Justice Powell observed; "he is the State's adversary."[26]

Polk County enshrined in case law the version of the public defender that the legal profession had settled upon by the time of *Gideon*. American criminal trials operate from the premise, in Justice Powell's words, "that a defense lawyer best serves the public, not by acting on behalf of the State or in concert with it, but rather by advancing the undivided interests of his client. This is essentially a private function, traditionally filled by retained counsel, for which state office and authority are not needed."[27] Public defenders, then, were not really government officials at all, but a government-provided substitute for private defense lawyers. One reading of *Polk County* might hold that the Supreme Court had reverse-engineered this conclusion to limit the number of civil rights lawsuits, leaving defendants with only the difficult pathway of "ineffective assistance" claims if they wanted to challenge a public defender's performance as inadequate.[28] But the justices were presumably genuine in their inability to grasp how a defense lawyer opposing the state could also be part of the state. In all of the major right-to-counsel cases of the twentieth century, the counsel in question had been figured as the state's adversary.

A coterie of Progressive Era reformers had once imagined the public defender as a vehicle for transforming criminal defense into a state function, removing private interests and the profit motive from the public business of criminal adjudication. In one sense their idea succeeded wildly, just as they predicted, with characteristic progressive zeal, that it inevitably would. By the early 1970s, public defenders appeared in criminal courtrooms throughout the nation. In many jurisdictions the majority of criminal defendants experienced representation by a defender both employed by and provided by the state. In another sense their idea disappeared into oblivion, another of the dozens of forgotten reform endeavors of history's trash heap. Public defenders came to exist, but the legal profession pretended away the *public* part of the equation. Thus could the Supreme Court insist in 1981 that the public defender, although a government employee, performed a "private function."

Notes

Abbreviations Used In Notes

ABA	American Bar Association
ALAS	Atlanta Legal Aid Society Records
CLD	General Charles L. Decker Collection
DA	Defenders Association Records
FFA	Ford Foundation Archives
FFR	Fund for the Republic Records
FHV	Frederic H. Vercoe Papers
HLB	Papers of Herman LaRue Brown
ISOJ	"In Search of Justice: The Final Report of the National Defender Project," 25 April [1973?], grant #06400098, reels 2070-2071, FFA
JSB	John S. Bradway Papers
MDC	Massachusetts Defenders Committee
NLADA	National Legal Aid and Defender Association
OMR	Office of the Messrs. Rockefeller Archives
RFA	Rockefeller Foundation Archives
RS	Red Set Student Manuscript Collection
VDC	Voluntary Defenders Committee
WCR	United States Wickersham Commission Records

Introduction

1. Burt A. Folkart, "Ellery Cuff, 92; Joined Public Defender in '28," *Los Angeles Times*, 16 September 1988; Cuff, *Annual Report of Public Defender of Los Angeles County July 1, 1954 to June 30, 1955*; Cuff, "Public Defender System," 734.

2. Tweed, "Foreword," in Special Committee . . . , *Equal Justice for the Accused*, 5-6.

3. Meras, "Kay Tweed"; Keeffe, "Harrison Tweed—The 'Democratic Aristocrat," 1094-97; Pollock, *Turks and Brahmins*, 33-36; James B. Stewart, *The Partners*, 286-87, 291-92.

4. See Wall, *Inventing the "American Way*," 4-5, 11. Historians emphasize that the liberal consensus was a political myth, not an accurate description of American public opinion. The idea of an American consensus was promoted by "[mainline] churches and synagogues, in government bureaucracies, in universities and foundations, [and] in sections of the media," but establishment liberals constituted only "one of several vocal political groups" in the struggle to define post–World War II politics. Gerstle, "Race and the Myth of the Liberal Consensus," 580, 584; and on postwar consensus as also forged by the legacies of earlier contestation, see generally Wall,

Inventing the "American Way." While not hegemonic, consensus liberalism is a useful concept for understanding the story told in this book because it captures the politics of many elite lawyers, particularly those like Tweed (a quintessential Rockefeller Republican) who constituted the legal profession's national leadership.

5. Wall, *Inventing the American Way*, 5, observes that different actors "seized on the notion of a unifying and distinctive 'American way' and sought to define it in ways that furthered their own political and social agendas." Bliss, *Directory of Public Defenders 1957*, listed public defenders in many California, Connecticut, and Illinois counties; a statewide public defender in Rhode Island; and scattered public defenders in a few other states.

6. NLADA, *The Other Face of Justice*, 13; Goldberg, "Defender Systems of the Future," 723–24. The 1973 statistic includes both public agencies and nominally private but publicly funded organizations.

7. NLADA, *The Other Face of Justice*, 159.

8. "Publicly-financed counsel represented . . . 82 percent of felony defendants in the 75 most populous counties in 1996." Bureau of Justice Statistics, press release, 29 November 2000.

9. In 2007, there were 957 public defender offices in 49 states and the District of Columbia, employing more than 15,000 attorneys and handling more than 5.5 million cases. Bureau of Justice Statistics, *Census of Public Defender Offices*.

10. Each of these topics is the subject of a voluminous specialist literature in legal scholarship. An accessible point of entry into these debates is the 2013 symposium issue of the *Yale Law Journal*, vol. 122, no. 8, available at https://digitalcommons.law.yale.edu/ylj/vol122/iss8. For a recent policy report presenting evidence that public defenders receive inadequate funding, see Furst, *A Fair Fight*.

11. Tweed, "Foreword," in Special Committee . . . , *Equal Justice for the Accused*, 6. See also "The Reminiscences of Harrison Tweed," 96.

12. Tweed, "Foreword," 6. With respect to civil legal aid, public funding remained extremely controversial. On the elite bar's 1950s "counteroffensive" against socialization in that realm, see Davis, *Brutal Need*, 19.

13. Dimock, "The Public Defender," 220.

14. Dimock, 220, 219, 221. Dimock was grudgingly open to public reimbursement for court-appointed private counsel, though his ideal was fully privately funded legal aid. But he rejected the idea of defense counsel as full-time public employees.

15. "The Reminiscences of Harrison Tweed," 96.

16. As observed by a military intelligence report, in 1919, on the Socialist Party of the United States. Flood, "Bolshevism in the United States and Russia," letter VII, p7. For an example of elite lawyers quoting the Socialist Party plank with alarm (in the context of a discussion of civil legal aid), see *The Necessity and Advisability of Creating the Office of Public Defender*, 26.

17. In 1950, the great legal historian James Willard Hurst observed in passing that the public defender, "however desirable" as policy, "was still in advance of lay or professional opinion and interest." Hurst, *The Growth of American Law*, 153. This book seeks both to explain the divides within the profession that underlay Hurst's observation, and also how and why professional opinion changed.

18. Dolan, *In Search of American Catholicism*, 8. Scholars have similarly defined "legal culture" as encompassing "the cluster of norms, rituals, assumptions, traditions, jargons, and guildlike behavior of the American legal community." Johnson, *American Legal Culture*, 6.

19. Gideon v. Wainwright, 372 U.S. 335, 344–45 (1963). On *Gideon* and other mid-century cases as expressions of antitotalitarian sentiment, see Primus, "A Brooding Omnipresence."

20. Thus, the book does not cover the equally rich but distinct history of criminal defense provided by private organizations as part of "cause lawyering" on behalf of social or political movements (such as the ACLU, the NAACP, and the International Labor Defense); nor does it cover debates about government-funded legal aid for civil disputes.

21. On the English law and practice, see Langbein, *The Origins of Adversary Criminal Trial*; a comprehensive reference on the right to counsel as it developed through 1955 is Beaney, *The Right to Counsel in American Courts*.

22. Bliss, *Directory of Public Defenders 1957*, lists public defenders in nineteen of fifty-eight California counties. On specific episodes in the history of California public defenders, see Mayeux, "'An Honest but Fearless Fighter'"; Mayeux, "The Case of the Black-Gloved Rapist."

23. Rodgers, *Atlantic Crossings*, 6.

24. This formulation of the phases of American liberalism is informed most proximately by Brinkley, *The End of Reform*, 8–11; see also Gerstle, "The Protean Character of American Liberalism." On lawyers as both creators of and believers in liberal narratives about American development, an illuminating overview is Gordon, "Taming the Past." This book is concerned with liberalism—and a concomitant, reflexive antisocialism—as the crude politics of practicing lawyers. Thus, the book's focus is not philosophical debates about liberalism as an ideology embedded deep within legal doctrine and/or floating high over academic legal thought—debates that have given rise to many schools and sub-schools of legal scholarship. For an introduction to liberalism as promulgated and debated by law professors in the later twentieth century, see Kalman, *The Strange Career of Legal Liberalism*.

25. See Gordon, "'The Ideal and the Actual in the Law,'" 62–63. On nineteenth-century American legal culture's veneration of the market as the realm of private law, and how this distinction faced new challenges in the twentieth century, see Horwitz, "History of the Public/Private Distinction," 1425–26.

26. Wigmore, "Shall the Legal Profession Be Reorganized?," 641–43. Wigmore's question prefigured a debate within the profession several years later about educational and licensing standards, spurred by the 1921 Carnegie report on legal education. The report's author described the law as a "public profession" and its practitioners as, in effect, "part of the governing mechanism of the state." Quoted in Stevens, *Law School*, 113.

27. Rodgers, "In Search of Progressivism," 114, 123; Rodgers, *Atlantic Crossings*, 53–54, 115–17; Wiebe, *The Search for Order*. As used here, the term "progressivism" refers to a mode of political thought that emphasized expertise, efficiency, the application of scientific data to social problems, and a belief in forward-moving civilizational

development. From the 1870s through the 1920s, these values animated reformers, professionals, and politicos across ideological lines, even if their specific proposals and priorities differed. On progressivism as analytically useful for the history of criminal law, see Green, "Freedom and Criminal Responsibility in the Age of Pound," 1950 (identifying 1870s–1920s as the "founding era of modern criminal justice administration"); White, "From Sociological Jurisprudence to Realism" (noting that progressivism in the legal realm remained significant into the 1920s).

28. On progressivism as a "bureaucratic order," see Wiebe, *The Search for Order*, 222 & passim; on the progressive bureaucratization of courts, see Willrich, *City of Courts*.

29. Rodgers, *Atlantic Crossings*, 115–16.

30. On nineteenth-century legal culture as rooted in local communities, see Edwards, *The People and Their Peace*; on the shift toward more state-centered processes, see Steinberg, *The Transformation of Criminal Justice*; Parrillo, *Against the Profit Motive*.

31. Parrillo, *Against the Profit Motive*.

32. E.g., "Address by Mayer C. Goldman: 'Should Public Defenders Be Substituted for Defense Counsel in All Criminal Cases,'" 15 July 1935, box 4, FHV.

33. For a synthesis of this tradition as an influence on twentieth-century governance, see Balogh, *The Associational State*. The blending of public and private initiative is a central theme in the historiography of the modern United States. For overviews, see Gerstle, *Liberty and Coercion*; Novak, "Public-Private Governance"; Zunz, *Philanthropy in America*. Excellent samplings of recent work engaging this theme are collected in two edited volumes: Cebul, Geismer, and Williams, *Shaped by the State*; and Sparrow, Novak, and Sawyer, *Boundaries of the State in U.S. History*.

34. Wiebe, *The Search for Order*, 295, 222. Wiebe's 1967 synthesis of the Progressive Era must now be read alongside more recent studies, but it remains illuminating as an overview of the rise of a bureaucratic, professionalized ethos.

35. On the origins of the ABA, see Stevens, *Law School*, 26, 94–100 (statistic for 1920 is at page 97); see also Wiebe, *The Search for Order*, 117.

36. See Novak, "Public-Private Governance," 31; for example, the New York Society for the Prevention of Cruelty to Children prosecuted violations of child labor laws. Robertson, *Crimes Against Children*, 25–28.

37. "The Reminiscences of Harrison Tweed," 96.

38. On the lawyer-as-agent as an element of nineteenth- and early-twentieth-century legal culture, see for instance Bloomfield, *American Lawyers in a Changing Society*, 343; Gordon, "'The Ideal and the Actual,'" 53–54, 57.

39. This book's focus is how elite lawyers grappled with this difficulty at a cultural or conceptual level; for an illuminating sociological study of how practicing public defenders navigate their anomalous role as both employee and adversary of the state in their day-to-day work, see McIntyre, *The Public Defender*.

40. R. F., "An Argument for the Public Defender," 925.

41. See Auerbach, *Unequal Justice*, 4–10. Given the bar's exclusivity through the twentieth century, this book's focus on elite lawyers also leads to a focus on white male lawyers. Although not a major theme of analysis in this book, the interplay be-

tween masculinity, elite legal culture, and criminal defense merits further consideration. For a pathbreaking historical study of gender and civil legal aid, see Batlan, *Women and Justice for the Poor*; on law's construction "as a masculine profession," see Grossberg, "Institutionalizing Masculinity."

42. See Auerbach, *Unequal Justice*; Davis, *Brutal Need*, 19.

43. For an excellent recent discussion and historical overview of race and the right to counsel, see Ossei-Owusu, "The Sixth Amendment Façade." As Shaun Ossei-Owusu describes, "the politics of race *fundamentally shaped* indigent defense jurisprudence and policy," yet legal scholarship and pedagogy on the subject have often overlooked the significance of race (1163). To the extent that legal scholars have inherited the modes of discourse traced in this book, the history recounted here provides additional insight into the origins of the blind spot that Ossei-Owusu's article identifies and critiques.

44. In a way this mode of discourse also resembled the liberalism of white progressive intellectuals prior to World War II, who often regarded racial, religious, and ethnic divisions as expressions of irrational or emotional affinities, and thus beyond the reach of rational policymaking. Gerstle, "The Protean Character of American Liberalism," 1057.

45. See Borstelmann, *The Cold War and the Color Line*; Dudziak, *Cold War Civil Rights*.

46. The dean of Harvard Law School, for example, described one voluntary defender as "a remarkable fellow" but cautioned that "his talent is in the actual handling of these cases," not "organizing the work on a larger scale." Erwin Griswold to David Freeman, 23 February 1955, box 68, folder 1, FFR.

47. That the organized American legal profession defined itself as basically liberal (in the big-tent sense of the word), and was virulently anticommunist throughout the Cold War, are well-established facts within the scholarship on legal history; it was for this reason that dissenters frustrated with the conservative politics of the ABA formed the National Lawyers Guild. For a somewhat dated but still forceful account of how professional organizations, law schools, and corporate law firms became oriented around protecting elite interests and forestalling radical social change, see Auerbach, *Unequal Justice*.

48. This book joins a growing literature examining how Americans grappled with the requirements of liberal democracy in potentially authoritarian institutions and contexts (such as punishment and the military), with their thinking shaped by the contrast with totalitarianism. On mid- and late-twentieth-century thought regarding liberalism, democracy, and policing, see Agee, *The Streets of San Francisco*; Seo, "Democratic Policing"; Seo, *Policing the Open Road*; on liberal anxieties about state power generally, see Kornhauser, *Debating the American State*. As Sarah Seo observes, "as midcentury jurists were hashing out what due process required, they were also trying to define what it meant to be an American living in a free society." Seo, "Democratic Policing," 1258. This process of definition equally informed efforts to hash out what democracy required in other spaces that required discipline (and thus could easily slide into authoritarianism), including the Army, occupied zones, and public schools. On World War II–era efforts within the armed forces to square democracy

with military discipline, see Alpers, *Dictators, Democracy, and American Public Culture*, 157–72. For an examination of how the concept of democracy shaped the American occupation of postwar Japan, see Miller, *Cold War Democracy*; for an essay on how midcentury political culture shaped school curricula, see Phillips, "The New Math and Midcentury American Politics."

49. Davis, *Brutal Need*, 15–16; Auerbach, *Unequal Justice*, 53–62.

50. See Goldman, "Public Defenders in Criminal Cases," 19; McConville and Mirsky, "The Origins of the Indigent Defense System," 599–602.

51. This theme of the book reinforces historians' interpretation of the Cold War as both an impetus for and constraint on midcentury social and legal change. Dudziak, *Cold War Civil Rights*, traces how Cold War foreign policy imperatives motivated the federal government's support for domestic civil rights while also channeling that support in particular ways. The federal government aimed to prove that American democracy was superior to communism because it could accommodate gradual social change without dictatorship. Marable, *Race, Reform, and Rebellion*, maps how the virulent McCarthyism of the early 1950s dampened civil rights activism until later in the decade. Scholars have also demonstrated how anticommunism precluded open political discussion of economic inequality, channeling economic debate in terms of individual opportunity rather than equality across groups; see for instance Wall, *Inventing the "American Way,"* 11–12.

52. For instance, attorney general Herbert Brownell endorsed federal public defender legislation as a way "to demonstrate the contrast between the 'humaneness' and 'fairness' of the American system and the 'cruelties' of the Communist system." "County Bar Backs Public Defenders," *New York Times*, 26 February 1954.

53. Noting the significance of the Ford Foundation's defender project and related initiatives, see Teles, *The Rise of the Conservative Legal Movement*, 29–34; Lewis, *Gideon's Trumpet*, 211–12. On the Ford Foundation generally, see Zunz, *Philanthropy in America* (especially 146–47, on its anticommunist stance). By the 1950s, the foundation's cultural prominence made it "the kind of folklore symbol the Ford car once was." Macdonald, *The Ford Foundation*, 5.

54. This phrase is from Balogh, *The Associational State*.

55. Kornacki, *The Red and the Blue*, 306.

56. Lewis, *Gideon's Trumpet*; on the reception and influence of *Gideon's Trumpet*, an excellent essay is Rosenberg, "Gideon's Trumpet: Sounding the Retreat from Legal Realism." Rosenberg describes *Gideon's Trumpet* as a narrative of "evolutionary" progress (107–8).

57. See, for example, Fiss, "A Life Lived Twice," 1118. The Yale law professor Owen Fiss described America in the 1950s as a country of widespread oppression, where, among many evils, criminal trials "proceeded without counsel"—but celebrated America's subsequent transformation owing to the Warren Court's "almost revolutionary" vision.

58. For a prominent example, see Lewis's own twenty-fifth anniversary column, "A Muted Trumpet," *New York Times*, 17 March 1988. For a list of citations to the voluminous body of commentary in the "failed promise" vein, see Mayeux, "What *Gideon* Did," 86n352.

59. Rosenberg, *A Hollow Hope*; Klarman, *From Jim Crow to Civil Rights*; Seo, "Democratic Policing," and Seo, *Policing the Open Road*; see also Stuntz, *The Collapse of American Criminal Justice* (arguing that the Warren Court reinforced a fixation on procedure rather than substantive rights). For an overview of scholarly assessments of the Warren Court and an argument that the Court's jurisprudence was more conservative than is generally understood, see Driver, "The Constitutional Conservatism of the Warren Court."

60. Auerbach, *Unequal Justice*, 204.

61. See, for example, McConville and Mirsky, "The Origins of the Indigent Defense System"; see also the critical essay, McDonald, "In Defense of Inequality," which argues that the elite bar came to support public funding for indigent defense for self-interested reasons. For a summary and bibliography of the broader social science literature, a useful starting point is McIntyre, *The Public Defender*, 2–4. McIntyre, *The Public Defender*, is an illuminating book-length sociological study, drawing both on historical research and on interviews and observations of Cook County public defenders in the 1980s, and provides a more complex portrait of public defenders as part of the judicial bureaucracy than had prior sociological work. McIntyre argues that public defenders serve a legitimating function for the courts (beyond simply promoting order), which requires that they are seen as having some autonomy; and she finds that individual public defenders are motivated to provide meaningful advocacy both by client loyalty and their own professional reputations (171–73).

62. Gordon, "'The Ideal and the Actual,'" 53.

63. See, for example, ABA, "Public Defense Summit to Examine Racial Justice and Role of Public Defender"; Adachi, "10 Things Public Defenders Can Do"; Michelle Miller, "Atlanta Lawyer Rapping Wins MacArthur 'Genius' Grant," *Atlanta Journal-Constitution*, 17 September 2014 (describing public defenders as "doing this generation's civil rights work").

64. See, for example, MacArthur Foundation, "Criminal Justice" (describing, in inscrutable foundationese, efforts to improve "local justice systems" through a "long-term strategy of investment in local reform, research, experimentation, and communications intended to create national demand for local justice reform"); Koch Newsroom, "NACDL Selected to Receive Significant Grant from Koch Industries" (describing a major grant from Koch Industries for indigent defense initiatives).

Chapter One

1. Edward Marshall, "Office of Public Defender Proposed for New York," *New York Times*, 7 June 1914.

2. Marshall, "Office of Public Defender Proposed for New York."

3. On Foltz, see Babcock, "Inventing the Public Defender"; Babcock, *Woman Lawyer*. On nineteenth-century proposals to introduce an "advocate-general" for defendants, see Bloomfield, *American Lawyers*, 49.

4. Parmelee, "Public Defense in Criminal Trials" (1911); Gibbons, "Say, Whatever Became of Maurice Parmelee, Anyway?."

5. Goldman, "Public Defenders for the Poor in Criminal Cases," 275 (quote is from editors' biographical footnote).

6. "Mayer C. Goldman, Defender of Poor," *New York Times*, 25 November 1939.

7. Goldman, *The Public Defender*, x.

8. Goldman's obituary stated that he wrote 800 articles on the public defender. "Mayer C. Goldman, Defender of Poor." For a sampling, see Goldman, "The Necessity for a Public Defender"; Goldman, *The Public Defender*; Goldman, "Merit Discovered In Public Defense" (letter), *New York Times*, 23 December 1934; "Address by Mayer C. Goldman: 'Should Public Defenders Be Substituted for Defense Counsel in All Criminal Cases,'" 15 July 1935, box 4, FHV; Goldman, "Public Defenders in Criminal Cases"; Goldman, "Public Defenders for the Poor in Criminal Cases." His missive to the Wickersham Commission is noted in "Circular to Commissioners No. 48, Digest of Suggestions through the Mails," 15 October 1929, box 13, folder 1, WCR.

9. On the larger political history of debates about the profit motive in governance, see Parrillo, *Against the Profit Motive*. On elite opposition to Goldman and the defeat of his proposal in New York, see Tweed, *Legal Aid Society*, 25; McConville and Mirsky, "The Origins of the Indigent Defense System," 599–602; Babcock, "Inventing the Public Defender," 1278–79; Maguire, *The Lance of Justice*, 269–70.

10. Goldman, "Public Defenders in Criminal Cases," 19; McConville and Mirsky, "The Origins of the Indigent Defense System," 599–602. American lawyers' aversion to socialization of the profession is such a deeply embedded assumption that it is often implicit rather than explicitly discussed. Legal scholar John Rappaport argues that the prospect of socializing the criminal defense bar remains anathema to lawyers and jurists, and therefore serves as an unarticulated premise of constitutional doctrine. Rappaport, "Structural Function."

11. Parmelee, "Public Defense in Criminal Trials" (1911), 739.

12. On criminal courts and urban governance, see generally Willrich, *City of Courts*.

13. Babcock first made this connection in "Inventing the Public Defender," 1298–1301.

14. The depiction of Bellamy in this paragraph draws upon Morgan, *Edward Bellamy*, and Thomas, *Alternative America*.

15. Morgan, *Edward Bellamy*, 192–93 ("petroleum"). Works relied upon for analysis of *Looking Backward*'s appeal and historical context include Wiebe, *The Search for Order*; Thomas, *Alternative America*; and Lipow, *Authoritarian Socialism in America* (advancing a darker interpretation of Bellamy's vision as authoritarian).

16. See especially Lipow, *Authoritarian Socialism in America*, as well as Thomas, *Alternative America*, 249–50.

17. See Wiebe, *The Search for Order*, 69–70; for sales figures, Thomas, *Alternative America*, 262–65. On Bellamy's later appeal to Progressive Era and New Deal reformers who similarly regarded the book as a soft inspiration rather than "blueprint," see Thomas, 355–56.

18. Bellamy, *Looking Backward*, chap. 19; Willrich, *City of Courts*, 68–86. For examples of nineteenth-century legal standards, see People v. Haun, 44 Cal. 96, 97–98 (Cal. 1872) (murder defined as killing "with malice aforethought"); People v. Doyell,

48 Cal. 85, 95 (Cal. 1874) (intent required to prove murder may be inferred from facts showing "an abandoned and malignant heart").

19. Bellamy, *Looking Backward*, chap. 19.

20. Morgan, *Edward Bellamy*, 117–21 ("constitutional questions" quote is from 119, quoting an unpublished novel that was thinly veiled autobiography); Thomas, *Alternative America*, 30; Lipow, *Authoritarian Socialism in America*, 37–38. Bellamy's anti-lawyer sentiments had antecedents in occasional proposals to abolish the bar in Jacksonian America; on such proposals, see Bloomfield, *American Lawyers in a Changing Society*, chap. 2.

21. Quoted in Lipow, *Authoritarian Socialism in America*, 38.

22. Lipow, *Authoritarian Socialism in America*, 75.

23. Thomas, *Alternative America*, 340–42; Lipow, *Authoritarian Socialism in America*, xix–xx, 116, 279–88.

24. Quoted in Babcock, "Inventing the Public Defender," 1299n231; on Bellamy's public defender plan, see Babcock, 1299–1300.

25. Babcock, "Inventing the Public Defender," 1299.

26. Foltz, "Public Defenders" (1897); Babcock, *Woman Lawyer*; Babcock, "Inventing the Public Defender."

27. Foltz, "Public Defenders" (1897), 398.

28. Babcock, "Inventing the Public Defender," 1300–01, 1274–79.

29. Foltz, "Public Defenders" (1893), 431–32.

30. Babcock, "Women's Rights, Public Defense, and the Chicago World's Fair," 494–95. For context on gender and nineteenth-century lawyers' professional identity, see Grossberg, "Institutionalizing Masculinity," 145–49. Women made up less than 1 percent of the bar in 1910 (Grossberg, 149).

31. Newspaper coverage quoted in Babcock, "Inventing the Public Defender," 1273.

32. The office was chartered and conducted hiring examinations in 1913 but began operations on 7 January 1914. Kraus, "The Office of Public Defender in Los Angeles County," 12.

33. Cal. Stat. 245, sec. 5 (1921); Shea, "Recollections of Alameda County's First Public Defender."

34. Bliss, *Directory of Public Defenders 1957*. In addition to the Los Angeles office, one 1915 report also identified "unofficial" or volunteer (and apparently temporary) defenders in Portland, Oregon, and Houston, Texas, and an Oklahoma official called the "public defender." However, despite the similarity in name, the Oklahoma official did not focus on criminal defense, but primarily represented Indian children in guardianship proceedings against "unscrupulous white guardians," and also pursued reforms of jails and other public institutions. *The Necessity and Advisability of Creating the Office of Public Defender*, 4–7.

35. McIntyre, *The Public Defender*, chap. 2, provides a thorough account of the Cook County public defender.

36. Hobson, *The American Legal Profession and the Organizational Society*, 175.

37. There is a vast literature on juvenile courts; a useful starting point are the historiographical essays collected in Platt, *The Child Savers*, 40th anniv. ed. On Chicago's municipal court, see Willrich, *City of Courts*. California's practice of charging by in-

formation was upheld by the Supreme Court in Hurtado v. California, 110 U.S. 516 (1884).

38. This paragraph's biographical information was assembled from "Mayer C. Goldman, Defender of Poor"; "Mrs. Goldman, Mother of Band Leader, Dead," *New York Times*, 23 January 1932; Mike McCormick, "Historical Perspective: Achievements of Former Terre Hautean Mayer Goldman," *Terre Haute Tribune Star*, 6 July 2014; Dorothy Koltzman, "Goldman, Edwin Franko," *American National Biography*. Some sources list Goldman as a graduate of "New York Law School," but a newspaper notice lists Goldman among the 1895 graduates of the "Law School of the City of New York," the precursor to New York University (the item refers to "Chancellor MacCracken," presumably NYU chancellor Henry MacCracken). "Bachelors of the Laws: Degrees from the City University for Young Women and Men," *New York Times*, 11 January 1895.

39. Gilfoyle, "'America's Greatest Criminal Barracks,'" 532, 534.

40. Gilfoyle, "'America's Greatest Criminal Barracks,'" 538.

41. Gilfoyle, "'America's Greatest Criminal Barracks,'" 541–43.

42. Murphy, *Scoundrels in Law*, xix, 266–67.

43. See Friedman, *American Law in the 20th Century*, 39–41.

44. Murphy, *Scoundrels in Law*, xvi. Howe and Hummel were also the subject of an earlier account, the 1947 book by Rovere, *The Magnificent Shysters*.

45. Murphy, *Scoundrels in Law*, xix, 266–67.

46. Cummings, "The Lawyer Criminal."

47. Murphy, *Scoundrels in Law*, xix, 24–25, 104–5.

48. For a representative description of the criminal bar, see Delahunt, "The Gentlemen at the Bar," in Moley, *Our Criminal Courts*, 62–67.

49. Pound, *Criminal Justice in America*, 195.

50. Examples of such cases are discussed in Mayeux, "Ineffective Assistance of Counsel before *Powell v. Alabama*."

51. See Mack, *Representing the Race* (chronicling lives of several African American lawyers who took criminal cases early in their careers); Babcock, "Women Defenders in the West" (describing women who took criminal cases).

52. Gilfoyle, "'America's Greatest Criminal Barracks,'" 534–36.

53. E.g., Cummings, "The Lawyer Criminal."

54. Darrow described most crime as a function of poverty and decried the harsh penalties common in American courts. *The Story of My Life*, 74–80, 334–42.

55. Gordon, "The Legal Profession," 289; Auerbach, *Unequal Justice*, 4–6; Grossberg, "Institutionalizing Masculinity," 143; Friedman, *American Law in the 20th Century*, 29.

56. Quoted in Rogers, "'A Sacred Duty,'" 445.

57. Goldman, *The Public Defender*, 19–20; Smith, *Justice and the Poor*, 119; Delahunt, "The Gentlemen at the Bar," in Moley, *Our Criminal Courts*, 66.

58. Carle, "Race, Class, and Legal Ethics," 135nn135–36.

59. American Bar Association Canons of Professional Ethics, Canons 27–28 (1908).

60. See Murphy, *Scoundrels in Law*, 4; Gilfoyle, "'America's Greatest Criminal Barracks,'" 532.

61. There is an extensive literature on the history of the social sciences. This formulation is drawn from Kern, *A Cultural History of Causality*, 285.

62. Willrich, *City of Courts*, 97. Calls for "socialized law" were especially important in criminal law, but part of a broader shift toward "sociological jurisprudence" (which itself can be classified within the broader, modernist "revolt against formalism"). See Morton White, *Social Thought in America* (for the phrase "revolt against formalism"); G. Edward White, "From Sociological Jurisprudence to Realism"; Menand, *The Metaphysical Club*.

63. Willrich, *City of Courts*, 98; on leading sociological jurisprude Roscoe Pound's conception of judges, see also White, "From Sociological Jurisprudence to Realism," 1010–12; Simon, "Visions of Self-Control," 115.

64. Green, "Freedom and Criminal Responsibility," 1951, describes the "deluge of writings" produced by reformers concerned with criminal justice in the 1910s and '20s.

65. Willrich, *City of Courts*, chap. 3; Simon, "Visions of Self-Control," 115–23; Rothman, *Conscience and Convenience*.

66. Willrich, *City of Courts*, 114–15.

67. See Wiebe, *The Search for Order*, 164–66.

68. Willrich, *City of Courts*, 86; see also Simon, "Visions of Self-Control," 116–21; Green, "Freedom and Criminal Responsibility," 1922.

69. Between 1910 and 1919, the *Journal of Criminal Law and Criminology* ran twenty-one articles focused on the public defender, and ninety-four articles mentioning the subject—averaging an article in almost every other issue, and more than one mention per issue. In the 1920s, the *Journal* ran thirteen articles on the subject and fifty-six mentions—still averaging a mention per issue, and an article in every third issue. These figures are based on title and keyword searches of Jstor's database of the journal. The journal was originally called the *Journal of the American Institute of Criminal Law and Criminology*; its name was shortened in 1931. On the journal's importance, see Willrich, *City of Courts*, 106; Green, "Freedom and Criminal Responsibility," 1951–52.

70. Barrow, "Public Defender. A Bibliography." For later legal scholarship revisiting these Progressive Era writings, see Babcock, "Inventing the Public Defender"; Fisher, *Plea Bargaining's Triumph*, 194–200; McConville and Mirsky, "The Origins of the Indigent Defense System"; Barak, "In Defense of the Rich" (providing a Marxist analysis). Babcock's article compares Foltz's plan in detail with those of her successors, especially Goldman. The analysis in this book departs from these works primarily in its emphasis upon viewing public and voluntary defenders as distinct projects, rather than as variants within a single lineage eventually culminating in the modern public defender.

71. Adelman, "In Defense of the Public Defender," 496.

72. Ferrari, "The Public Defender," 711–12.

73. E.g., Goldman, "The Necessity for a Public Defender," 660 (goal of trial is "to ascertain the truth").

74. Parmelee, "Public Defense in Criminal Trials" (1911), 738–39.

75. Goldman, "The Necessity for a Public Defender," 665.

76. Adelman, "In Defense of the Public Defender," 495. For background on Taylor and management science, see Lears, *Rebirth of a Nation*, 258–65.

77. Ferrari, "The Public Defender."
78. R. F., "An Argument for the Public Defender," 928.
79. Ferrari, "Analysis of New York and County Bar Reports," 26–27.
80. R. F., "An Argument for the Public Defender," 927.
81. See Bloomfield, *American Lawyers in a Changing Society*, 343; Gordon, "'The Ideal and the Actual,'" 53–54.
82. Berger v. United States, 295 U.S. 78, 88 (1935).
83. Ferrari, "The Public Defender," 706-7.
84. Goldman, "The Necessity for a Public Defender," 663.
85. Goldman, "The Public Defender," 281–82.
86. Ferrari, "The Public Defender," 707–11, 714–15; see also R. F., "An Argument for the Public Defender," 926–27 (public defender would not suborn perjury or cause delay, and advise plea bargains where appropriate); Robert Ferrari et al., "On the Public Defender: A Symposium," 373 ("The Public Defender would not dicker").
87. Ferrari, "The Public Defender," 706-7.
88. Goldman, "The Necessity for a Public Defender," 663.
89. Forster in Ferrari et al., "On the Public Defender: A Symposium," 378.
90. Ferrari in Ferrari et al., 375; R. F., "An Argument for the Public Defender," 926.
91. Ferrari in Ferrari et al., "On the Public Defender: A Symposium," 375.
92. Ferrari, "Analysis of New York and County Bar Reports," 25; R. F., "An Argument for the Public Defender," 926.
93. For a leading critique of Anglo-American adversary criminal trial as theoretically unjustifiable, because it both impairs truth-seeking and disadvantages the poor, see Langbein, *The Origins of Adversary Criminal Trial*, 1–9.
94. Parmelee, "Public Defense in Criminal Trials" (1911), 742 (prosecutors and defense lawyers "stimulated" "an unhealthy public interest in crime"); Goldman, "The Public Defender," 280 (trials must "cease to be an unequal contest . . . A 'battle of wits' . . . is not the true conception of a criminal trial").
95. See Goldman, "The Public Defender," 280 ("primary" purpose of trial is "ascertainment of the truth"); Goldman, "The Necessity for a Public Defender," 660 (goal of trial "is [or ought to be] to ascertain the truth—and not a mere contest"); "scientific investigator" quote is from Adelman, "In Defense of the Public Defender," 496.
96. R. S. Gray, "The Public Defender," 653. See also Adelman, "In Defense of the Public Defender," 496–97 (with both sides represented by officer of the state, "both sides would be operating under a system tending to elucidate the truth, whichever side it hurt or benefited").
97. Adelman, "In Defense of the Public Defender," 496.
98. See Wiebe, *The Search for Order*, 147–51, 170.
99. For the "clash of proofs" rationale, Landsman, "Rise of the Contentious Spirit," 500. On the development of adversarial legal culture as related to American identity, see Kessler, *Inventing American Exceptionalism*.
100. Wm. Scott Stewart, *Stewart on Trial Strategy*, 1982, 1399; see also Stewart, "A Criticism of the Public Defender System"; Stewart, "The Public Defender System Is Unsound in Principle." For a more detailed discussion of Stewart's differences with the Cook County public defender, see McIntyre, *The Public Defender*, 41–43.

101. E.g., McConville and Mirsky, "The Origins of the Indigent Defense System," 592n40 (describing indigent defense as the product of "a political and economic alliance between defense providers, the state, and the private bar"). More recent legal scholarship gives the Progressive Era writings a more sympathetic reading. Babcock suggests that the differences between Progressive Era proposals and the more adversarial tenor of Foltz's writings may have been differences "of emphasis only" ("Inventing the Public Defender," 1279). Fisher interprets Progressive Era public defender advocates' promises of cost savings and plea bargains not as reflecting their genuine sentiments but as strategic efforts to reassure policymakers and win legislative support for the idea. *Plea Bargaining's Triumph*, 196–97.

102. Marshall, "Office of Public Defender Proposed for New York."

103. Mayeux, "'An Honest but Fearless Fighter.'"

104. Frederic Vercoe to John Bradway, 21 March 1935, box 24, JSB.

105. A comprehensive account of the Frank case is Oney, *And the Dead Shall Rise*.

106. Marshall, "Office of Public Defender Proposed for New York."

107. Quote is from Marshall, "Office of Public Defender Proposed for New York." Frank's defense counsel included Luther Rosser, a prominent corporate lawyer in Atlanta. Oney, *And the Dead Shall Rise*, 49.

108. Quote is from Lichtenberger, review of *The Public Defender*, 187; for *Yale Law Journal* review, see Howard, review of *The Public Defender*. Kirchwey's quote appeared as a blurb in the front matter of the 1919 printing of the book.

109. Waite, review of *The Public Defender*, 279–80.

110. Goldman, "The Necessity for a Public Defender," 661, 660.

111. Adelman, "In Defense of the Public Defender," 494.

112. Ferrari, "The Public Defender," 711, 714. As sociologist Lisa McIntyre observes, early advocates of public defense "had an almost utopian vision of the public defender's role." McIntyre, *The Public Defender*, 40–41.

113. Parmelee, "Public Defense in Criminal Trials" (1911), 739.

114. For representative criticisms, see Goldman, *The Public Defender*, 19–20; Miller, "Guilty or Not Guilty?," 363; Smith, *Justice and the Poor*, 119; Sienna Delahunt, "The Gentlemen at the Bar," in Moley, *Our Criminal Courts*, 66.

115. E.g., Miller, "Guilty or Not Guilty?," 361 (praising Los Angeles for having "freed the prisoner at the bar from ruthless exploitation by shysters so common elsewhere").

116. Parmelee, "Public Defense in Criminal Trials," 739.

117. Harvard luminary Roscoe Pound identified a "lower stratum" of the bar, "little educated or uneducated," and lacking knowledge of "the historical background of our institutions." Pound, *Criminal Justice in America*, 195.

118. Auerbach, *Unequal Justice*, 10; Stevens, *Law School*, 100–101.

119. Babcock makes a similar argument about Clara Foltz in "Inventing the Public Defender," 1282–83.

120. R. F., "An Argument for the Public Defender," 925.

121. Ferrari in Robert Ferrari et al., "On the Public Defender: A Symposium," 375.

122. R. F., "An Argument for the Public Defender," 925. He compared this prediction to his understanding that "the private physician is almost abolished in England today" due to public health provision.

123. R. F., 925.

124. Goldman, "The Public Defender," 282-83; see also Goldman, *The Public Defender*, 79 ("An accused person . . . should be entitled as a matter of abstract right to be defended by a sworn public official"). Rakove, *Original Meanings*, 288, defines "rights talk" as 'Americans' marked propensity to assert their claims in a language not merely of legitimate interest or net public good but of absolute entitlements.'

125. Parmelee, "A New System of Criminal Procedure," 360-61. Parmelee allowed that the presumption of innocence might have a place in "the theory of the law" but did not think that presumptions should "have any practical effect" upon courtroom procedure.

126. Parmelee, "A New System of Criminal Procedure," 365-66.

127. Federal and state constitutional provisions are mentioned in Ferrari, "The Public Defender," 704, 705-6.

128. Adelman, "In Defense of the Public Defender," 497.

129. R. F., "An Argument for the Public Defender," 928; Ferrari, "Analysis of New York and County Bar Reports," 27.

130. Ferrari in Ferrari et al., "On the Public Defender: A Symposium," 374.

131. Wiebe, *The Search for Order*, 116-17; Stevens, *Law School*, 25-26, 92-113.

132. Stevens, *Law School*, 112-16.

133. Stevens, *Law School*, 191-96.

134. *The Necessity and Advisability of Creating the Office of Public Defender* (hereafter *Necessity and Advisability*), 1. For additional discussions of this and other New York bar reports expressing opposition to the proposal, see McConville and Mirsky, "The Origins of the Indigent Defense System," 611-13; Babcock, "Inventing the Public Defender," 1277-79. The analysis here focuses on *Necessity and Advisability*, as additional reports produced by other bar groups were "almost identical." Ferrari, "Analysis of New York and County Bar Reports," 18.

135. *Necessity and Advisability*, 13.

136. Ferrari, "Analysis of New York and County Bar Reports," 18.

137. *Necessity and Advisability*, 2.

138. Committee members are listed in *Necessity and Advisability*, 27. The chair was George Gordon Battle, a graduate of Columbia Law School and former district attorney. Wilkinson, "George Gordon Battle." Wardwell was partner in the firm that became Davis, Polk, and Wardwell, which represented J. P. Morgan. Davis Polk, "Historical Timeline." Root Jr., son of the former secretary of state, was at the firm Root, Clark, & Bird, a predecessor to Dewey, Ballantine. "Elihu Root, Jr., Lawyer, Is Dead," *New York Times*, 28 August 1967. The committee also included Joseph M. Proskauer, later an adviser to presidential candidate Al Smith. "Joseph M. Proskauer, 94, Dies," *New York Times*, 11 September 1971.

139. Gordon, "'The Ideal and the Actual,'" 52-53.

140. Gordon, "'The Ideal and the Actual,'" 61.

141. Gordon, "'The Ideal and the Actual,'" 63. To be sure, many thinkers, including Louis Brandeis, sought in various ways to reconceptualize the lawyer's role away from apolitical client service, but that view did not win over the majority of the practicing corporate bar. For a discussion of how the rise of corporate practice unsettled the

manly idea of the lawyer as independent practitioner, see Grossberg, "Institutionalizing Masculinity," 143.

142. Gordon, "'The Ideal and the Actual,'" 66.
143. Bloomfield, *American Lawyers in a Changing Society*, 343.
144. *Necessity and Advisability*, 17–18, 20.
145. *Necessity and Advisability*, 21–22.
146. *Necessity and Advisability*, 16–17.
147. *Necessity and Advisability*, 18.
148. *Necessity and Advisability*, 25; see also McConville and Mirsky, "The Origins of the Indigent Defense System," 614–18.
149. McConville and Mirsky, "The Origins of the Indigent Defense System," 617–18. Voluminous correspondence regarding the Rockefellers' support for the Legal Aid Society is preserved in OMR, Welfare Interests-General, Record Group III-2-P. Because the Rockefellers requested detailed audits from organizations they supported, these files also include records of the Legal Aid Society's annual donations from New York law firms.
150. See McConville and Mirsky, 617–18 (describing the voluntary defender as breaking "the political stalemate" in New York over the public defender debate).
151. The Boston and Philadelphia voluntary defenders are discussed in more detail in chapter 2. For Cincinnati and Pittsburgh, see Fabricant, "Voluntary Defenders in Criminal Cases," 27.
152. Goldman, "The Necessity for a Public Defender," 664.
153. Goldman, "The Public Defender," 282–83.
154. Batlan, *Women and Justice for the Poor*; Tani, "Welfare and Rights Before the Movement," 360.
155. Batlan, *Women and Justice for the Poor*.
156. Goldman, "The Public Defender," 282–83.
157. Goldman, *The Public Defender*, 79.
158. Goldman, "The Need for a Public Defender," 275.
159. For essential background and analysis of Smith, see Batlan, *Women and Justice for the Poor*, 123–27, 135–53.
160. Wilmer Hale, "Slice of History"; Dimock, "Reginald Heber Smith," 1138.
161. Batlan, *Women and Justice for the Poor*, 123–27.
162. Batlan, *Women and Justice for the Poor*, 135–39.
163. Batlan, *Women and Justice for the Poor*, 139; Davis, *Brutal Need*, 15–16.
164. Batlan, *Women and Justice for the Poor*, 144–46.
165. Batlan, *Women and Justice for the Poor*, 144, 151.
166. Batlan, *Women and Justice for the Poor*, 147–51.
167. [Bradway to] Thomas E. Cogan [unsigned carbon copy], 5 June 1940, box 9, JSB.
168. Smith, *Justice and the Poor*, chap. 15.
169. Smith, *Justice and the Poor*, 114.
170. Smith, *Justice and the Poor*, 105–6.
171. Smith, *Justice and the Poor*, 106. Smith and Bradway reprised this framing in their work for the Department of Labor on a report, *The Growth of Legal Aid in the United States*, which stated that they would instead use the term "defender" rather than

"public defender" because "his compensation may come from the State or from some private organization." Drafts of the report are in box 24, JSB.

172. Smith, *Justice and the Poor*, 116, 119.

173. Smith, *Justice and the Poor*, 127.

174. Goldman, "Merit Discovered in Public Defense" (letter), *New York Times*, 23 December 1934.

175. Goldman, "Legal Aid to the Indigent" (letter), *New York Times*, 21 February 1939 (emphasis added).

176. Ruth, *Inventing the Public Enemy*.

177. "Address by Mayer C. Goldman: 'Should Public Defenders Be Substituted for Defense Counsel in All Criminal Cases,'" 15 July 1935, box 4, FHV. Goldman also responded to the position that compulsory public defense would violate the constitutional right to counsel, arguing that the relevant cases had not squarely decided this question and pointing out that poor defendants already had to accept the counsel appointed for them.

178. Goldman, "Public Defenders in Criminal Cases," 19.

179. Goldman, "Public Defenders in Criminal Cases," 19; on the NLG, see Auerbach, *Unequal Justice*, 198–200, 236–37.

180. Tweed, *The Legal Aid Society*, 27.

181. Goldman, "Public Defenders in Criminal Cases," 19.

Chapter Two

1. Case facts in this and following paragraphs are derived from VDC, "'I Confess' [Annual Report for 1954]," box 5, folder 2, HLB; Wilbur Hollingsworth to David Freeman, 4 February 1955, box 68, folder 1, FFR; "Jury Acquits LaPlante Boy of Setting Fire Fatal to Five," *Boston Globe*, 2 February 1955. See also transcript of LaRue Brown reminiscences on Voluntary Defenders, 1963, p12-13, box 16, folder 4, HLB.

2. VDC, "'I Confess' [Annual Report for 1954]."

3. Erwin Griswold to David Freeman, 23 February 1955, box 68, folder 1, FFR.

4. VDC, "'I Confess' [Annual Report for 1954]"; "Jury Acquits LaPlante Boy."

5. VDC, "'I Confess' [Annual Report for 1954]."

6. Purcell, *The Crisis of Democratic Theory*, 256–57, 271–72.

7. Norris, *Exonerated*, 16–17. Gardner's efforts built on a tradition dating to the 1930s, when Yale law professor Edwin Borchard published a book-length accounting of dozens of wrongful convictions. Borchard, *Convicting the Innocent*; Norris, *Exonerated*, 14–16.

8. Carruthers, *Cold War Captives*, describes in detail how American national identity was forged in opposition to totalitarian states, depicted for the American public through media stories of false confessions, punishment without fair process, and regimes overbearing the individual will.

9. "Jury Acquits LaPlante Boy of Setting Fire Fatal to Five."

10. "The Voluntary Defenders Committee: Its Story and Its Service," 1936, box 5, folder 3, HLB.

11. Powell v. Alabama, 287 U.S. 45, 71–72 (1932).

12. Tweed, *The Legal Aid Society*, 98.

13. Beaney, *The Right to Counsel in American Courts*, 207. By 1953, the Criminal Courts Branch represented 62 percent of defendants in New York's general sessions court and 76 percent of defendants in the court's specialized "youth term part." Tweed, *The Legal Aid Society*, 87.

14. Fabricant, "The Voluntary Defender in Criminal Cases," 77.

15. "Annual Report of the Directors of the Philadelphia Voluntary Defender Association," 26 April 1935, box 1, folder 11, DA.

16. "A Voluntary Defender in Philadelphia for Defendants in the Criminal Courts . . . ," 28 March 1930, box 16, folder 1, WCR; also in series 3, box 36, folder 502, RFA.

17. Smith, "The English Legal Assistance Plan," 455.

18. "Suggestions Re Voluntary Defenders Communication Re Budget," n.d., box 6, folder 10, HLB.

19. Brown identified himself as a lifelong Democrat and "convinced New Dealer." Typescript, ca. 1938, box 12, folder 8, HLB. He also identified himself as "a Protestant—locally 'Yankee'—Democrat" within the context of Massachusetts. Brown to Adlai Stevenson, 8 August 1956, box 18, folder 9, HLB. On Brown's involvement with New Deal programs, see also Trout, "Curley of Boston," 187. On the larger pattern in Boston of patrician skepticism toward Irish patronage politics, see Vale, *From the Puritans to the Projects*, 290–91.

20. Pollock, "Voluntary Defender as Counsel," 176.

21. Neeley, *Report of Public Defender*, 9. A graduate student who interviewed Los Angeles public defenders reported that their "work in theory differs not at all from that of private counsel." Kraus, "The Office of Public Defender in Los Angeles County," 50.

22. In re Hough, 24 Cal. 2d 522, 528–29 (Cal. 1944). For further background on *In re Hough*, see Mayeux, "The Case of the Black-Gloved Rapist."

23. Pollock, "Voluntary Defender as Counsel," 175.

24. Pollock, "Voluntary Defender as Counsel," 176–77.

25. Bennett, "To Secure the Right to Counsel," 179.

26. On a scandal involving the San Francisco public defender—the incumbent himself was tried for murder—see Shea, "Recollections of Alameda County's First Public Defender"; for examples of advocacy for unpopular defendants, see Mayeux, "'An Honest but Fearless Fighter.'"

27. On volunteers from law firms, see Fabricant, "Voluntary Defenders in Criminal Cases," 25; Pollock, "Voluntary Defender as Counsel," 176; Tweed, *The Legal Aid Society*, 88–90. From the law firms' perspective, loaning out lawyers allowed them to gain trial experience (without, a cynic might note, risking lawyers-in-training on paying clients).

28. In 1948, Hollingsworth's salary was $5,400—approximately the median net income for a salaried Massachusetts lawyer around that time. VDC budget submission to Greater Boston Community Fund, 18 November 1948, box 6, folder 9, HLB; Blaustein and Porter, *The American Lawyer*, 16. Noting that the Chicago public defender's reported salary was $8,500, see Wilbur Hollingsworth to Samuel Vaughan, 16 February 1939, box 6, folder 4, HLB. Around this time (although seemingly unbeknownst to

Hollingsworth) the Los Angeles public defender reported a salary of $7,200. Financial statement, 12 August 1937, box 8, FHV.

29. According to staff lists in the organization's annual reports, most assistants stayed for one or two years (with some exceptions). For a detailed list, see Mayeux, "What Gideon Did," 33-34. For a case study of a career Los Angeles public defender, see Mayeux, "'An Honest but Fearless Fighter.'"

30. In 1948, Hollingsworth's assistants earned, respectively, $1,500 and $2,000. VDC budget submission to Greater Boston Community Fund, 18 November 1948, box 6, folder 9, HLB.

31. "Notes for Budget Meeting," 1954, box 1, folder 6, HLB.

32. Handwritten notes, "Voluntary Defenders Committee," 11 October 1955, box 1, folder 8, HLB.

33. "Report for First Six Months of Expansion Program under Grant from the Fund for the Republic," 30 June 1954, box 1, folder 6, HLB.

34. In Philadelphia, the Defender Association was supported by the United Community Fund. "Sixth Annual Report of the Directors of the Philadelphia Voluntary Defender Association," 21 June 1940, box 1, folder 12 (archival photocopy), DA; Pollock, "Voluntary Defender as Counsel," 176. In Boston, the VDC received most of its funding from the Greater Boston Community Fund, which later became United Community Services. "Bay State Called Backward in Legal Aid For Needy," *Quincy Patriot Ledger*, 5 October 1955.

35. Zunz, *Philanthropy in America*, 51-52, 69, 177; Thernstrom, *Poverty, Planning, and Politics in the New Boston*, 9-10. Local community chests federated into the national organization United Way in 1970.

36. A branch did open in the Bronx in 1952. Tweed, *The Legal Aid Society*, 88.

37. "The Voluntary Defenders Committee: Its Story and Its Service," 1936, box 5, folder 3, HLB; Daniel Lyne, fundraising appeal, 18 December 1936, box 6, folder 1, HLB.

38. Katz, *The Undeserving Poor*; for examples of how this distinction translated into legal aid, see Batlan, *Women and Justice for the Poor*, 132; Grossberg, "Altruism and Professionalism," 15-16.

39. Grossberg, "Altruism and Professionalism," 15-16, describes the Boston Legal Aid Society's "elaborate screening process."

40. VDC Annual Report, 1 June 1936; VDC Annual Report, 1 September 1938, both in box 6, folder 11, HLB.

41. VDC Annual Report, 1 September 1938, box 6, folder 11, HLB ("the Committee is careful not to judge a man solely by his police record, 'first-offender cases' have a special claim on its services"); VDC Annual Report, 1941, box 6, folder 11, HLB; Raynor Gardiner to Samuel Vaughan, 8 June 1937, box 6, folder 2, HLB.

42. "Jury Acquits LaPlante Boy of Setting Fire Fatal to Five."

43. VDC Annual Report, 1 June 1936; VDC Annual Report, 1 September 1938; VDC Annual Report, 1937; all in box 6, folder 11, HLB.

44. Ruth, *Inventing the Public Enemy*.

45. Cummings, "The Lawyer Criminal." See also "Exterminate the Lawyer Criminal!."

46. VDC Annual Report, 1 September 1938, box 6, folder 11, HLB; see also McConville and Mirsky, "The Origins of the Indigent Defense System," 625n274 (on similar policy of New York voluntary defenders).

47. Bernstein, *Racial Innocence*; Agyepong, *The Criminalization of Black Children*, 3–6.

48. Muhammad, *The Condemnation of Blackness*.

49. E.g., VDC Annual Report, 1945 ("we were asked to represent four colored soldiers"); VDC Annual Report, 1952 (describing client as "extremely polite and naive little colored boy"), both in box 5, folder 2, HLB. It should be noted that Boston, the main focus of this chapter's case study, had a relatively small African American population prior to World War II (the city was 3 percent black in 1940, compared with 16 percent in 1970). More detailed case studies of voluntary defender organizations in cities like Cincinnati and Philadelphia, which reported high percentages of African American clients early in their histories, would likely enrich historical understandings of how race influenced voluntary defenders.

50. Legal Aid Society of Pittsburgh letter to John Bradway, 28 November 1934, box 24, JSB.

51. Fabricant, "The Voluntary Defender in Criminal Cases," 76–77, 79.

52. E.g., Tweed, *The Legal Aid Society*, 66–67 (listing financial qualifications for clients, for instance they cannot own a new car).

53. Wilbur Hollingsworth to Samuel Vaughan, 16 March 1938, box 6, folder 3, HLB. Another significant difference was support from judges. Hollingsworth thought that the Pennsylvania judges viewed voluntary defenders "as a necessary part of the administration of criminal law."

54. The committee declined to take one-third of potential cases in its early years. By the 1950s, it declined only about one-tenth. Mayeux, "What *Gideon* Did," 40–41, 47.

55. Pollock joined the Defender Association in 1942 and served as chief defender from 1946 until 1969. Defender Association Board of Directors, minutes, 24 October 1972, box 1, folder 6, DA. On Kelley, see Tweed, *The Legal Aid Society*, 58.

56. "Voluntary Defender Committee Hailed as Permanent Harvard Law Function," *Harvard Law Record*, 1 March 1950; "Harvard Law Underwrites HVD Group," *Harvard Law Record*, 8 November 1950; Woodey, "For the Indigents Voluntary Defenders Defend," *Harvard Law Record*, 20 September 1960.

57. Harvard Voluntary Defenders, "Third Annual Report 1951–1952," box 10, folder 3 #8636257, RS.

58. Erwin Griswold to Robert Prouty, 26 October 1955, box 1, folder 7, HLB.

59. Dennis Hevesi, "Erwin Griswold Is Dead at 90; Served as a Solicitor General," *New York Times*, 21 November 1994; see also Seligman, *The High Citadel*, vii.

60. Stevens, *Law School*, 36–63, 173–209; Friedman, *American Law in the 20th Century*, 33–37.

61. Kalman, *Legal Realism at Yale*, 208–15; Seligman, *The High Citadel*, 74, 80–84.

62. Quoted in Stevens, *Law School*, 208.

63. Seligman, *The High Citadel*, 91–92; on the hierarchy generally, see Gordon, "The Legal Profession," 287–90.

64. Lewis, *Gideon's Trumpet*, 207–8.

65. Sutherland, *The Law at Harvard*, 367, 337–39; on the history of criminal law pedagogy at elite law schools, see also Walker, "The Anti-Case Method." As early as the 1930s, Justin Miller, dean of Duke University's law school, had decried the inadequacies of the law school curriculum as it related to criminal law and the tendency of instructors to discourage students from criminal practice. Miller, "Lawyers and the Administration of Criminal Justice," 77–78.

66. Seligman, *The High Citadel*, 91–92. A minority of professors, including Felix Frankfurter, dissented from the curriculum's corporate emphasis, although they typically envisioned high-level federal government service as the preferable alternative. See Auerbach, *Unequal Justice*, 140, 168.

67. This statistic was derived by comparing names in the relevant Harvard Law School yearbooks and alumni directories, both available in the Harvard Law Library stacks. For the class of 1963, one graduate was listed as working at the Seattle public defender ten years later, out of twenty-six participants in the Harvard Voluntary Defenders. That statistic reflects the 1960s increase in elite interest in public interest careers, but also the limitations of that development.

68. On Hollingsworth, see Andrew Garber, "Average Students Stand Out in These College Scholarships: Wilbur Hollingsworth Has Given $70,000 to 140 Students While Living on Social Security," *Portland Press Herald*, 28 November 1998. On skepticism of Suffolk Law School among elites, including Harvard faculty, see Stevens, *Law School*, 80–81. Suffolk's dean envisioned the school as making the law accessible to the poor; the school admitted large numbers of students, and emphasized practical, lecture-based instruction rather than the Harvard case method.

69. As of 1953, the board included LaRue Brown and Daniel J. Lyne, of prominent law firms; Raynor M. Gardiner, chief counsel of Boston's Legal Aid Society; three lawyers in private practice who had worked briefly as assistants to Hollingsworth; and Frank W. Buxton, former editor of the *Boston Herald*. "Plan and Proposal for an Extension of the Work of The Voluntary Defenders Committee . . . ," August 1953, box 68, folder 1, FFR.

70. Brown summarized his life in an autobiographical statement preserved in box 18, folder 9, HLB. His wife was Dorothy Kirchwey, daughter of Columbia Law School dean George Kirchwey. See also "Obituaries: LaRue Brown Dies, 85," *Boston Globe*, 4 April 1969.

71. Griswold called Hollingsworth "a remarkable fellow" but cautioned that "his talent is in the actual handling of these cases," not "organizing the work on a larger scale." Erwin Griswold to David Freeman, 23 February 1955, box 68, folder 1, FFR. Outside funders worried about Hollingsworth's "natural conservatism" and "lack of imagination." David Freeman, file memo, "Voluntary Defenders—Boston," 16 September 1954, box 68, folder 1, FFR. On one occasion, LaRue Brown described Hollingsworth as a "problem child" and contemplated replacing him with someone more amenable to the board's direction. LaRue Brown to Raynor Gardiner, 8 February 1957, box 6, folder 12, HLB.

72. Henry Channing to LaRue Brown, 10 February 1954, box 1, folder 6, HLB. On "Hollingsworth's ingrained modesty," see David Freeman to Hutchins and Perry, 22 March 1955, box 68, folder 1, FFR.

73. Due process was the subject of significant debate in the twentieth century across a number of contexts, both as a precise legal term and as a more amorphous cultural concept. A helpful general overview is Dripps, "Due Process: A Unified Understanding." On congressional debates about due process and the administrative state, see Grisinger, *The Unwieldy American State*, chap. 2. On due process and policing in midcentury legal culture, see Seo, "Democratic Policing."

74. Howard, *The Road from Runnymede*, 299 (what Magna Carta "called 'law of the land' we would call 'due process of law'"). For an example of a subsequent statutory restatement demonstrating the changed terminology, see 28 Edw. III 3 (1354), which provided that "no man . . . shall be taken, nor disinherited, nor put to death, without he be brought to answer by due process of law."

75. Howard, *The Road from Runnymede*, 211–13 (on constitutional provisions); 302–7 (summarizing doctrinal lines stemming from due process and collecting quotes about arbitrary rule). Howard describes due process as "an attitude" in Anglo-American legal thought that disfavored "rule by magisterial discretion" (1). See also Holt, *Magna Carta*, 45–46 (discussing American reception of Magna Carta as a source of "individual rights enforceable against authority in all its forms").

76. A rich study providing an immersive sense of the localized nature of antebellum legal culture is Edwards, *The People and Their Peace*.

77. On the significance of the Fourteenth Amendment for remaking American legal and political culture, see Edwards, *A Legal History of the Civil War and Reconstruction*. Nelson, *The Fourteenth Amendment*, shows that the amendment was drafted as a broad statement of national principles, and only over time became a more concrete doctrinal tool, as litigants brought new claims into court seeking to enforce the constitutional text. Among the most significant procedural vehicles for federal review of state criminal procedure was the 1867 Habeas Corpus Act, 14 Stat. 385, authorizing the federal courts to hear petitions from state prisoners that they were unconstitutionally incarcerated; see Mayers, "The Habeas Corpus Act of 1867." Legal scholars debate whether federal habeas jurisdiction depends upon this statutory authorization or is implied constitutionally. See Halliday and White, "The Suspension Clause." In any event, the Habeas Corpus Act was little used before the twentieth century, but thereafter developed into a primary vehicle of federal oversight over state criminal courts. For a key precedent endorsing the use of federal habeas litigation to reopen issues decided in state court, see Brown v. Allen, 344 U.S. 443 (1953). Since 1948, federal habeas jurisdiction has been codified at 28 U.S.C. 2241-55.

78. Ayers, *Vengeance and Justice*, 150, 173–74, 186–92, 218; see also Litwack, *Been in the Storm So Long*, on Southern efforts to regain control over black labor. Studies of convict labor and convict-leasing include McLennan, *The Crisis of Imprisonment*; Mancini, *One Dies, Get Another*; Shapiro, *A New South Rebellion*.

79. Ayers, *Vengeance and Justice*, 169, 176, 179–80, 197. Studies of Jim Crow punishment include Oshinsky, *Worse than Slavery*; Blackmon, *Slavery by Another Name*; Haley, *No Mercy Here* (emphasizing the experience of black women). The 1890 census revealed for the first time that black men were statistically overrepresented in prisons; on subsequent national discourse about this data point, see Muhammad, *The Condemnation of Blackness*, 3–4.

80. Freedman, *Redefining Rape*, 252; Klarman, *From Jim Crow to Civil Rights*, 117-35; Klarman, "The Racial Origins of Modern Criminal Procedure." Whether an observer considered lynching to have genuinely declined, or merely to have mutated, depended in part upon their definition of the term lynching. For an illuminating examination of definitional debates, see Waldrep, "War of Words."

81. Moore v. Dempsey, 261 U.S. 86 (1923); for background on the case, see Cortner, *A Mob Intent on Death*; Klarman, *From Jim Crow to Civil Rights*, 117-23.

82. *Moore*, 261 U.S. at 87, 91.

83. The new hearing never took place; the defendants instead agreed to plead guilty to second-degree murder in exchange for a furlough from the governor.

84. Marx and Engels, *The Communist Manifesto*, 76, 87. An in-depth study of how this view informed the radical labor defense tradition in the United States is Hill, *Men, Mobs, and Law*.

85. Klarman, *From Jim Crow to Civil Rights*, 130.

86. Moore v. Dempsey, 261 U.S. 86, 92 (1923) (McReynolds, J., dissenting).

87. Quoted in Newman, *Hugo Black*, 213.

88. On the English trajectory, see Langbein, *The Origins of Adversary Criminal Trial*, 2-6. For a case study of the increasing presence of lawyers in Maryland, and effects on procedure from the 1680s through the 1830s, see Rice, "The Criminal Trial before and after the Lawyers"; an illuminating study of the development of nineteenth-century adversarial legal culture, though not focused on criminal courts, is Kessler, *Inventing American Exceptionalism*. Local studies suggest that by the nineteenth century, defense counsel was common, though not universal, in American felony trials. For example, in one Indiana county, 65 percent of felony defendants who went to trial were represented by counsel in the 1830s and '40s. Bodenhamer, *The Pursuit of Justice*, 197n63; see also Fisher, *Plea Bargaining's Triumph*, 97 (finding 51 to 60 percent of defendants represented in nineteenth-century Massachusetts). In misdemeanor and other lower-level proceedings, counsel remained rare into the early twentieth century. See Friedman, *Crime and Punishment in American History*, 245; Willrich, *City of Courts*, 13.

89. Edwards, *The People and Their Peace*, especially 68-68, 76-77, 114-15, 130; Steinberg, "From Private Prosecution to Plea Bargaining"; Parrillo, *Against the Profit Motive*, 259-60; Ayers, *Vengeance and Justice*, 109-11.

90. On the transition in the prosecutorial role, see Parrillo, *Against the Profit Motive*, 259-69; Steinberg, *The Transformation of American Criminal Justice*; Steinberg, "From Private Prosecution to Plea Bargaining." On earlier, part-time prosecutors, see Ellis, "The Origins of the Elected Prosecutor," 1539-40; Ayers, *Vengeance and Justice*, 112; Friedman and Percival, *The Roots of Justice*, 50. An excellent study of the bureaucratization of local courts is Willrich, *City of Courts*.

91. Rakove, *Original Meanings*, 293.

92. Kamisar, "The Right to Counsel," 1, 7.

93. An in-depth study of the rise of plea bargaining is Fisher, *Plea Bargaining's Triumph*; the Supreme Court observed the continuing significance of jury trials in Duncan v. Louisiana, 391 U.S. 145, 153-54 (1968).

94. United States v. Ash, 413 U.S. 300, 307 (1973); Argersinger v. Hamlin, 407 U.S. 25, 31 (1972). Notably, the Court incorporated the Sixth Amendment right to counsel

against the states several years before it incorporated the right to jury trial in Duncan v. Louisiana, 391 U.S. 145 (1968).

95. Powell v. Alabama, 287 U.S. 45 (1932). The comprehensive account of the case is Carter, *Scottsboro*; an overview of the legal dimensions and analysis of the Supreme Court ruling in *Powell* is Klarman, "Powell v. Alabama." For an overview contextualizing the case within NAACP and ILD efforts to defend Southern black men accused of rape, see Freedman, *Redefining Rape*, 246–69.

96. On the international campaign, see Miller, et al., "Mother Ada Wright." On Pollak's involvement, see Pollak, "Advocating Civil Liberties," 5–8. Pollak was familiar with the plight of indigent defendants generally, and African American defendants in the South specifically, from his work a year before on the federal Wickersham Commission. Along with his *Powell* co-counsel, Carl Stern, and the Harvard law professor Zechariah Chafee, Pollak researched police torture, aggressive prosecutors, and biased judges for the commission's most shocking publication: Report No. 11, *Lawlessness in Law Enforcement*. Describing their scope of research, see Zechariah Chafee Jr., Walter Pollak, and Carl Stern, "Circular to Commissioners No. 221," n.d., box 16, folder 4, WCR.

97. A second lawyer present, sent from Tennessee by family members of the defendants, was unfamiliar with Alabama practice and denied that he was officially serving as defendants' counsel, although he did attempt some steps on their behalf. For a description of the defendants' trial counsel, see Carter, *Scottsboro*, 17–18.

98. Gunther and Casper, eds., *Landmark Briefs*, vol. 27, 255, 264.

99. *Powell*, 287 U.S. at 71–72 (internal quotation marks omitted).

100. Klarman, *From Jim Crow to Civil Rights*, 123–25; Klarman, "Powell v. Alabama," 13–14, 29.

101. David M. Oshinsky, "Only the Accused Were Innocent," *New York Times*, 3 April 1994; Klarman, "Powell v. Alabama," 15–37; Klarman, *From Jim Crow to Civil Rights*, 153–57.

102. Orfield, *Criminal Appeals in America*, 243; see also Klarman, "Powell v. Alabama," 12.

103. Powell v. Alabama, 287 U.S. 45, 68–69 (1932). Israel, "Gideon v. Wainwright," 238n155, notes the passage's frequent quotation in later opinions. For an example, see United States v. Cronic, 455 U.S. 648, 654n8 (1984) (quoting the passage and asserting that "[t]ime has not eroded the force of Justice Sutherland's opinion").

104. Johnson v. Zerbst, 304 U.S. 458, 461, 467–68 (1938).

105. Langbein, *The Origins of Adversary Criminal Trial*, 2–3; Betts v. Brady, 316 U.S. 455, 466 (1942).

106. *Johnson*, 304 U.S. at 467–68.

107. *Johnson*, 304 U.S. at 462–63.

108. Confirming this point, Justice Black extensively quoted *Powell*'s passage about the importance of counsel, blending Sixth Amendment and Fourteenth Amendment due process precedents into one analysis. *Johnson*, 304 U.S. at 463.

109. On the traditionally limited purview of federal criminal law, see Henderson, *Congress, Courts, and Criminals*; Preyer, "Jurisdiction to Punish." On the modern expansion of federal criminal law, see Richman, et al., *Defining Federal Crimes*, 7–12;

Brickey, "The Commerce Clause and Federalized Crime"; Langum, *Crossing Over the Line* (for a case study of one federal morals statute). Despite the conceptual expansion of federal criminal law, enforcement remained selective; even today, federal prosecutions comprise only 5 percent of criminal prosecutions. Richman, et al., *Defining Federal Crimes*, 7.

110. See Charles Wyzanski Jr. to LaRue Brown, 21 October 1955, box 1, folder 7, HLB, for a discussion of one district court's difficulties in making the necessary arrangements to comply. In New York, the Legal Aid Society began furnishing counsel for indigent federal defendants in 1949 with funds from John D. Rockefeller Jr. Tweed, *The Legal Aid Society*, 87.

111. Mars, "The Problem of the Indigent Accused," 272-75.

112. Goldman, "Public Defenders in Criminal Cases," 19-20; Mars, "The Problem of the Indigent Accused," 274.

113. Betts v. Brady, 316 U.S. 455, 474 (1942) (Black, J., dissenting).

114. This fraction is based on Israel, "Gideon v. Wainwright," 267, who counts thirty-one states as having a policy or practice of providing counsel in serious but noncapital cases as of *Betts*, leaving seventeen out of forty-eight states without such a policy or practice. Israel notes that Justice Black's *Betts* dissent listed thirty-five states in this category, but subsequent scholarship revealed that four states were misclassified. It is possible that even the count of thirty-one states is overstated. Even for states with a formal policy of providing counsel, practices likely varied significantly at the local level.

115. Betts v. Brady, 316 U.S. 455, 462 (1942).

116. "A Voluntary Defender in Philadelphia for Defendants in the Criminal Courts . . . ," 28 March 1930, box 16, folder 1, WCR.

117. Betts v. Brady, 316 U.S. 455, 462 (1942).

118. *Betts* exemplified the jurisprudential tension between rules and standards. Rather than impose a bright-line requirement of counsel upon the states all at once, the *Betts* majority introduced a flexible standard whose details could be filled in incrementally. As a body of case law developed applying the standard to different facts, states could gradually adjust. But such a standard could prove confusing for state judges, who, at the outset of each trial, had to decide whether to appoint counsel. Critics argued that a bright-line rule would better serve the goals of federalism: give the state courts a straightforward directive one way or another, and then get out of the business of case-by-case review. See Israel, "Gideon v. Wainwright," 261-66.

119. Betts v. Brady, 316 U.S. 455, 474 (1942) (Black, J., dissenting); see also Adamson v. California, 332 U.S. 46, 71-72 (1942) (Black, J., dissenting). The development of Black's view on incorporation is traced in Newman, *Hugo Black*, 293-95, 349-60.

120. *Betts*, 316 U.S. at 474-77 (1942) (Black, J., dissenting).

121. Benjamin V. Cohen and Erwin N. Griswold, "Denial of Counsel to Indigent Defendant Questioned," *New York Times*, 2 August 1942; Lewis, *Gideon's Trumpet*, 118. Griswold's Harvard colleague Henry Hart later described him as an unimaginative defender of "conventional ideas," although it should be noted that he defended civil liberties during the Cold War. Hart quoted in Kalman, *Legal Realism at Yale*, 207-8; Seligman, *The High Citadel*, 73. Cohen had arrived in Washington in the 1930s as part

of the circle of lawyers encouraged to join the New Deal administration by then-law professor Felix Frankfurter. On Cohen, see Brinkley, *The End of Reform*, 50–55.

122. Cohen and Griswold, "Denial of Counsel to Indigent Defendant Questioned."

123. Cohen and Griswold, "Denial of Counsel to Indigent Defendant Questioned."

124. Betts v. Brady, 316 U.S. 455, 465–72 (1942). Justice Roberts defined state constitutional and statutory provisions as "the most authoritative sources" on the question (465). For the classic distinction, see Pound, "Law in Books and Law in Action."

125. Cohen and Griswold, "Denial of Counsel to Indigent Defendant Questioned."

126. Uveges v. Pennsylvania, 335 U.S. 437, 441 (1948).

127. Quicksall v. Michigan, 339 U.S. 660 (1950); Lewis, *Gideon's Trumpet*, 181, 200.

128. Bute v. Illinois, 333 U.S. 640, 677 (1948).

129. Israel, "Gideon v. Wainwright," 251–55; for "labyrinth" quote, Chewning v. Cunningham, 368 U.S. 443, 446 (1962).

130. "Defenders' Service Launched," *Springfield Union*, 23 August 1954.

131. VDC Annual Report, 1955, box 5, folder 2, HLB.

132. The survey, of cases from 1949 to 1952, found that 54 percent of all defendants lacked legal representation. VDC, "Survey of Criminal Prosecutions in Massachusetts for the Years 1949-1950-1951-1952," box 1, folder 3, HLB. For comparison with Southern states, see "Defenders' Service Launched," *Springfield Union*, 23 August 1954.

133. Griffin v. Illinois, 351 U.S. 12, 19 (1956); on *Griffin*'s import and how it did (and arguably did not) relate to *Betts*, see Israel, "Gideon v. Wainwright," 245–47.

134. Edward McCormack Jr. to Paul Feeney, 25 May 1960, box 1, folder 12, HLB.

135. "Plan and Proposal for an Extension of the Work of The Voluntary Defenders Committee, Inc., respectfully submitted to The Fund for The Republic for its consideration," August 1953, pp. 13–14, box 68, folder 1, FFR. See also Reginald Heber Smith to John Higgins, 4 February 1952, box 1, folder 4, HLB (proposing a dinner to discuss how VDC might expand "without resort to government subsidies").

136. David Freeman, file memo, "Voluntary Defenders—Boston," 16 September 1954, and Freeman to Case, 15 September 1953, both in box 68, folder 1, FFR. the Fund generally, see Zunz, *Philanthropy in America*, 187–88; Macdonald, *The Ford Foundation*, 70–80.

137. David Freeman to Case, 15 September 1953, box 68, folder 1, FFR.

138. "An Act providing an office of Public Defender for the Commonwealth" (typescript, with handwritten notation "As Drafted by Hollingsworth of Vol. Defender"), n.d. (but located between correspondence dated 1955), box 68, Folder 1, FFR. David Freeman to Case, 15 September 1953, box 68, folder 1, FFR.

139. LaRue Brown to Raynor Gardiner, 8 February 1957, box 6, folder 12, HLB.

140. "Ratio of Defendants Lacking Counsel Brings Free Legal Service to Area," *Springfield Union*, 24 August 1954.

141. R. Gardiner, "Memo in Regard to Voluntary Defender," 28 September 1955, box 1, folder 7, HLB.

142. United Community Services to Raynor Gardiner, 8 February 1960, box 1, folder 12, HLB; Brown, "Equal Justice Under the Law," 59. There may have been other factors behind the withdrawal of UCS funding. On one occasion, Hollingsworth

complained about press criticism about the use of "red feather" funds in a case involving a defendant who escaped from jail. "Bay State Called Backward in Legal Aid for Needy," *Quincy Patriot Ledger*, 5 October 1955. LaRue Brown also recalled disagreements with UCS over particular cases but described the transition toward a right to counsel as "the more important difficulty." See transcript of LaRue Brown reminiscences on Voluntary Defenders, 1963, p10, box 16, folder 4, HLB.

143. VDC Annual Report, 1955, box 5, folder 2, HLB.

144. "To speak in terms of rights . . . was a way of seeking government protection and intervention without assuming the posture of the supplicant." Tani, "Welfare and Rights before the Movement," 360; see also Tani, *States of Dependency*, on post–New Deal changes in poor relief.

145. Hurst, *The Growth of American Law*, 153.

146. Bliss, *Directory of Public Defenders 1957*; Boetticher, et al., *The Public Defender*.

147. Bibb County v. Hancock, 86 S.E.2d 511, 515 (Ga. 1955).

148. Cuff, "Public Defender System," 719.

149. Cuff, 725. Gerstle, *Liberty and Coercion*, provides an overview of U.S. history that highlights the theme of "public-private interpenetration as a mode of governance" (155).

150. "Bay State Called Backward in Legal Aid for Needy," *Quincy Patriot Ledger*, 5 October 1955; "Bay State Lag Seen in Legal Aid to Needy," *Christian Science Monitor*, 13 October 1955.

Chapter Three

1. Tocqueville, *Democracy in America*, 256, 252, 254. On the apprenticeship model that prevailed in the nineteenth century, see Stevens, *Law School*, 3–21. Given that the United States lacked legally formalized status distinctions, law functioned as "the most obvious vehicle both for claimed respectability and for upward mobility—at least for white males" (Stevens, 21). Lincoln did not formally apprentice but studied on his own using books borrowed from a law firm.

2. Tweed, "The Lawyer as a Public Servant," 14–15, 9.

3. Connell, *The Lawyers' Committee for Civil Rights Under Law*, 85, describes Tweed as "one of the corporate legal establishment's most aristocratic members"; see also Keeffe, "Harrison Tweed—The 'Democratic Aristocrat.'" Among other notable Evarts descendants was his great-grandson Archibald Cox, who had his own eventful career as a member of the legal aristocracy.

4. "The Reminiscences of Harrison Tweed," 1–11.

5. Stewart, *The Partners*, 286–87; Pollock, *Turks and Brahmins*, 35–37.

6. "American Bar Association Medal," 915.

7. Stevens, *Power of Attorney*, 1.

8. Tweed, "The Lawyer as a Public Servant," 9.

9. See "The Reminiscences of Harrison Tweed," 84–86.

10. Connell, *The Lawyers' Committee for Civil Rights Under Law*, 85.

11. Special Committee . . . , *Equal Justice for the Accused*, 5–6.

12. Auerbach, *Unequal Justice*, 236–37; Davis, *Brutal Need*, 19.

13. Through an examination of discourse around policing in midcentury legal culture, Sarah Seo similarly finds that "a fair trial with requisite procedures . . . symbolized the difference between democracy and totalitarianism." Seo, "Democratic Policing," 1257.

14. Worgan and Paulsen, "The Position of a Prosecutor in a Criminal Case," 55.

15. Gideon v. Wainwright, 372 U.S. 335 (1963). For a doctrinal analysis of how lawyers' aversion to socializing the bar functions as a continuing, if implicit, influence upon right-to-counsel jurisprudence, see Rappaport, "Structural Function of the Sixth Amendment."

16. Rodgers, *Age of Fracture*, 16.

17. Cohen-Cole, *The Open Mind*. On the trope of "flexibility," see also Phillips, "The New Math and Midcentury American Politics," 460–61. That anti-totalitarianism was itself a kind of totalizing concept, leaving no part of the human experience untouched by its analysis, is among the many ironies of the era.

18. Cohen-Cole, *The Open Mind*; Crespino, *In Search of Another Country*, 5–6.

19. Carruthers, *Cold War Captives*, 12. On the idea that totalitarianism was characterized by the complete submission of the individual to the state, see also Purcell, *The Crisis of Democratic Theory*, 136–38.

20. Schlesinger, *The Vital Center* (quotes from dustjacket); Alpers, *Dictators, Democracy, and American Public Culture*, 278–84.

21. On the migration of the term *stato totalitario* "from a local description of Italy to a more general theory of the modern state," see Chappel, "Catholic Origins of Totalitarian Theory," 563.

22. Though used as early as the 1930s in its modern sense, totalitarianism became a widely accepted concept during the Cold War. Purcell, *The Crisis of Democratic Theory*, 135–38; Alpers, *Dictators, Democracy, and American Public Culture*, 8–11, 250.

23. On Arendt's resonance with U.S. intellectuals, see Alpers, *Dictators, Democracy, and American Public Culture*, 295–97. Prior to the concept's enthusiastic reception in Cold War America, totalitarianism had an earlier career in the interwar crisis of European democracy. Although the standard genealogies of totalitarianism emphasize its origins in secular liberalism, James Chappel locates important early iterations in interwar European Catholic discourse. This lineage casts Americans' later adoption of the idea into ironic relief. Interwar Catholic thinkers regarded the totalitarian state not as the antithesis of liberal democracy but as the ultimate culmination of secular liberalism's tendency to exalt the nation-state at the expense of "natural communities," such as the family or the church. Chappel, "Catholic Origins of Totalitarianism Theory," 585. For Catholic anti-totalitarian thought, liberal individualism was another enemy, whereas Americans would uphold liberal individualism as the antithesis of totalitarianism.

24. Purcell, *The Crisis of Democratic Theory*, 137, 205–13. On Dewey and the broader intellectual history of pragmatism and pluralism, a valuable introduction is Menand, *The Metaphysical Club*.

25. On the nineteenth century, see Wilentz, *The Rise of American Democracy*; for a general overview of how voting rights have contracted and expanded over time, see Keyssar, *The Right to Vote*. The "one person, one vote" decision is Reynolds v. Sims,

377 U.S. 533 (1964). Twentieth-century theorists deemphasized voting and even defended nonvoters as valuable components of a pluralistic society because their lack of interest in politics meant that they were nondogmatic. Purcell, *The Crisis of Democratic Theory*, 216.

26. Miller, *Cold War Democracy*, ch. 1, especially 53–56. To be sure, the American state itself had not become any smaller. Quite the opposite: World War II ushered in a massive expansion of the state, arguably more significant even than the New Deal. James Sparrow argues that this expansion was legitimized through nationalism and militarism, symbolized by the soldier; government expansion could be most readily justified when it could be framed as aiding some war effort, national security, or materially supporting soldiers and veterans. Sparrow, *Warfare State*. In comparison, Roosevelt's Democratic Party, in the 1930s, gained working-class support when it "promote[d] a notion of government that protected the well-being of ordinary Americans." Cohen, *Making a New Deal*, 2.

27. Quoted in Pollak, "Thomas I. Emerson," 326.

28. Sacher v. United States, 343 U.S. 1, 23 (1952) (Frankfurter, J., dissenting).

29. Primus, "A Brooding Omnipresence," 437–50 (quote from 437).

30. *Nineteen-Eighty-Four* was a Book-of-the-Month Club selection in 1949; *The Vital Center* was not a Book-of-the-Month Club selection but, over the years, several of Schlesinger's other books were provided through the subscription service. See the historian Daniel Immerwahr's compilation of Book-of-the-Month Club selections at http://www.booksofthecentury.com.

31. Neeley, *Report of Public Defender of Los Angeles County July 1, 1946 to June 30, 1948*. For comparison to the progressive rhetoric of Neeley's predecessor, see Mayeux, "'An Honest but Fearless Fighter.'"

32. Cf. Cohen-Cole, *The Open Mind*, 41 (describing how psychologists used ability to tolerate ambiguity as a marker for "authoritarian personality"). Sarah Seo discusses how midcentury legal scholars who focused on policing also emphasized the importance of a fair trial, to ensure that the courts rather than the police made the final adjudication of guilt. Seo, "Democratic Policing," 1279.

33. For an interesting although brief discussion of the film's reception in the Soviet Union, where it was screened in 1961, see Thaman, "The Good, the Bad, or the Indifferent."

34. Of course, this view was the mirror image of the communist critique of American trials as shams that reproduced capitalist power relations. Notably, the Russian term for "show trial" was not pejorative, but rather signified the view that trials should be used to educate the public—a view with which, in its most generic sense, Americans would not have disagreed. Every civic proceeding can, in some sense, be viewed as having a secondary educative function. On the Soviet concept of "show trials" as it played out at Nuremberg, see Hirsch, "The Soviets at Nuremberg."

35. Alpers, *Dictators, Democracy, and American Public Culture*, 286. Alpers interprets Orwell as going further than Koestler, for Koestler's main character Rubashov retains some kernel of individual autonomy to the end, whereas Orwell suggests that the state can so thoroughly obliterate its subjects' individuality as to produce conformity of belief, not just speech (289).

36. The Vogeler episode is reconstructed and elucidated in Carruthers, *Cold War Captives*, 143–71. For another Cold War case study, see Seo, "Democratic Policing," 1285–90.

37. Langbein, *The Origins of Adversary Criminal Trial*, 338–43; see also Langbein, *Torture and the Law of Proof*.

38. Sklansky, "Anti-Inquisitorialism," 1635–36.

39. Watts v. Indiana, 338 U.S. 49, 54 (1949) (Frankfurter, J.) (plurality opinion).

40. Carruthers, *Cold War Captives*, 140. For American observers, Carruthers observes, the corruption of law helped to mark the Eastern bloc "as a 'brutally archaic' zone where law served to persecute, not protect—a sphere conceived as Asiatic in its cruelty and African in its barbarism." The Nazi regime, to be sure, also furnished examples of the worst-case scenarios of punishment unconstrained by law, but it had also already been defeated. Over time, the Soviet Union and its satellite states furnished an ever-growing catalog of examples of "show trials" against which American lawyers could continuously measure their own ideal procedures.

41. Neeley, *Report of Public Defender of Los Angeles County July 1, 1946 to June 30, 1948*.

42. Carruthers, *Cold War Captives*, 143; "Acheson Affirms Vogeler's Defense," *New York Times*, 16 February 1950.

43. "County Bar Backs Public Defenders," *New York Times*, 26 February 1954. Brownell presented indigent defense as part of a "two-pronged attack" on communism; the second prong "was vigorous and impartial enforcement of Federal laws against subversion and crime."

44. Douglas, "The Right to Counsel," 694.

45. Special Committee . . . , *Equal Justice for the Accused*, 45.

46. *Report of the Attorney General's Committee on Poverty and the Administration of Federal Criminal Justice* (hereafter Allen Report). On the Allen Commission, see Lewis, *Gideon's Trumpet*, 204–5.

47. Each of these two committees was composed of lawyers, law professors, and judges, most with elite pedigrees. George Nye, a former public defender in Oakland, California, also served on both committees.

48. For an overview and engaging study of legal realism's heyday at one elite law school, see Kalman, *Legal Realism at Yale*.

49. This quote is from a review of Rodell's work by the law professor Jerome Hall, who castigated Rodell's book *Woe unto You, Lawyers!* (which lampooned the Supreme Court as "full of hot air") as lacking "common sense." Hall, review, 359–60; on Hall as representative of midcentury legal thought, see Seo, "Democratic Policing." For other criticisms of Rodell as failing to grapple with totalitarianism, see Rosenberg, "Gideon's Trumpet," 115–16; on the wartime challenge to legal realism generally, see Purcell, *The Crisis of Democratic Theory*, 159–73.

50. Rodgers, *Atlantic Crossings*, 505.

51. Special Committee . . . , *Equal Justice for the Accused*, 34.

52. Allen Report, 11.

53. Allen Report, 10. For comparison, see the Restatement (Second) of Torts § 321 (1965): "If the actor does an act, and subsequently realizes or should realize that it has created an unreasonable risk of causing physical harm to another, he is under a duty to exercise reasonable care to prevent the risk from taking effect."

54. "Plan and Proposal for an Extension of the Work of The Voluntary Defenders Committee . . . ," 1953, box 1, folder 5, HLB. "When a man is arrested and is without funds . . . he is not a victim of passive neglect as would be the case if his community failed to provide him with fire protection and hospitals and sanitation; he is the victim of a society which has suddenly, and often rightfully, taken an active and positive action against him."

55. Allen Report, 9–10.

56. Kadish, "Francis A. Allen," 403.

57. Allen Report, 10. On the ideas and political imperatives that underwrote the War on Poverty, announced in January 1964, see Katz, *The Undeserving Poor*, chap. 3.

58. Dimock, "The Public Defender."

59. Steinberg and Paulsen, "A Conversation with Defense Counsel," 37.

60. Gideon v. Wainwright, 372 U.S. 335, 344 (1963). Richard Primus has highlighted this passage from *Gideon* as one of many examples of how American constitutional law was remade by "the desire to articulate principles that distinguished America from the Soviet Union and Nazi Germany." Primus, "A Brooding Omnipresence," 423, 445. On *Gideon* as "hardly startling" to lawyers at the time, see Israel, "Gideon v. Wainwright," 212; writing within a few months of *Gideon*, Israel notes that *Betts*'s "impending overruling was so obvious that it was predicted by computers" (212n6). Although unanimous as to the judgment, *Gideon* did yield two concurring opinions (by Justices Clark and Harlan) that reached the same result using different reasoning than Justice Black.

61. Newman, *Hugo Black*, 525; Kalman, *Abe Fortas*, 183.

62. Newman, *Hugo Black*, 525–26. Newman notes that prior cases that presented the issue were deemed too "unsavory" as vehicles for overruling *Betts*.

63. Lewis, *Gideon's Trumpet*, 1–11 (quote from 5).

64. Lewis, *Gideon's Trumpet*, 27–46, 50–58 (quote from 52); Kalman, *Abe Fortas*, 180–83.

65. See Lewis, *Gideon's Trumpet*, 137–38; the key scholarly research relied upon by the parties was later published as Kamisar, "The Right to Counsel and the Fourteenth Amendment." The figure of thirteen states is cited here because it is more accurate than the often-repeated statistic that only five Southern states—Alabama, Florida, Mississippi, North Carolina, and South Carolina—provided no right to appointed counsel in noncapital cases at the time of *Gideon*. As Lewis noted and as the underlying research by legal scholar Yale Kamisar also made clear, that statistic was something of a simplification, intended to capture the broad direction of legal change rather than provide a precise count. It captured Kamisar's finding that in eight of the thirteen states, there were organized efforts to provide lawyers for defendants in urban jurisdictions in noncapital cases; but even in those states, "there was no guarantee and the chances were not so good for rural defendants"; conversely, in Florida, some cities, including Miami, already had public defenders (Lewis, 138). This complex picture was later distilled in legal scholarship into a misleading claim that *Gideon* affected only five states, and *Gideon* therefore became widely remembered as a case targeting Southern outliers. For a more in-depth reconsideration of that interpretation, see Mayeux, "What *Gideon* Did."

66. Potter Stewart, quoted in Kalman, *Abe Fortas*, 183.

67. See Newman, *Hugo Black*, 526–28.

68. See Timbs v. Indiana, 139 S. Ct. 682, 687 (20 February 2019).

69. Gideon v. Wainwright, 372 U.S. 335, 344 (1963).

70. For the phrase (and an influential contemporaneous criticism of the development), see Friendly, "The Bill of Rights as a Code of Criminal Procedure."

71. For the major cases, see Mapp v. Ohio, 367 U.S. 643 (1961); Miranda v. Arizona, 384 U.S. 436 (1966); Duncan v. Louisiana, 391 U.S. 145 (1968). On Nixon's campaign, see, for instance, "Nixon Offers 4-Point Plan to Cut Crime," *Washington Post*, 30 September 1968.

72. Lewis, *Gideon's Trumpet*, 212–13. Describing *Gideon* as a "mandate to reevaluate the defense system in every jurisdiction," see Charles Decker and Arnold Trebach, "Status Report: The National Defender Project," 8 May 1964, grant #064000098, reel 2071, FFA.

73. Lewis, 209–10. As one New York judge observed, the decision "prompted the legal profession to reexamine the procedures by which [the right to counsel] is afforded to an indigent defendant." Schweitzer, book review, 184.

74. Quoted in Alschuler, "The Defense Attorney's Role in Plea Bargaining," 1220; Lynch and Goldberg, *The Dollars and Sense of Justice*, v.

75. NLADA, *The Other Face of Justice*, 164. Worden and Davies, "Protecting Due Process in a Punitive Era," 71, note that by the 1970s, the legal profession "agreed on the core components of a 'best practices' model for indigent defense." See also Goldberg, "Defender Systems of the Future," for a summary of national standards as of 1975.

76. NLADA, *The Other Face of Justice*, 159.

77. NLADA, *The Other Face of Justice*, 159; ISOJ, 20.

78. Lewis, *Gideon's Trumpet*, 205–6; U.S. Courts, "Defender Services."

79. Brief for the State of Alabama as Amicus Curiae, Gideon v. Cochran (No. 155), 20 December 1962, 11–12. More modestly but with the same gist, Florida's brief suggested that states "should not be required to equalize social and economic conditions among [their] citizens." Brief for the Respondent, Gideon v. Cochran (No. 155), 2 January 1963, 10.

80. Magliocca, *The Heart of the Constitution*, 46–57, 61–62. Magliocca's work provides a groundbreaking "biography" of the cultural life of the Bill of Rights from its origins through the twentieth century.

81. Magliocca, *The Heart of the Constitution*, chaps. 7–8. See also Kammen, *A Machine That Would Go of Itself*, chap. 12, for a discussion of how the Bill of Rights was "discovered" in the late 1930s and then "rediscovered" in the 1950s.

82. For an overview of how the Bill of Rights became central to judicial review, see Magliocca, *The Heart of the Constitution*, chap. 9.

83. Magliocca, *The Heart of the Constitution*, 110–14, 133–40.

84. Magliocca, *The Heart of the Constitution*, 136.

85. Truman, "Address Before the Attorney General's Conference on Law Enforcement Problems," 15 February 1950, in Peters and Woolley, *The American Presidency Project*, http://www.presidency.ucsb.edu/ws/?pid=13707. On Truman's frequent invocations of the Bill of Rights, see Magliocca, *The Heart of the Constitution*, 134–40.

86. Harry S. Truman, "Veto of Bill to Revise the Laws Relating to Immigration, Naturalization, and Nationality," 25 June 1952, in Peters and Woolley, *The American Presidency Project*, http://www.presidency.ucsb.edu/ws/?pid=14175.

87. Eisenhower also invoked the Bill of Rights on occasion, such as when he praised the federal government for prosecuting communists without sacrificing "our traditions and the Bill of Rights." Dwight D. Eisenhower, "Statement by the President Upon Signing the Communist Control Act of 1954," 24 August 1954, in Peters and Woolley, *The American Presidency Project*, http://www.presidency.ucsb.edu/ws/?pid=9998.

88. Auerbach, *Unequal Justice*, 192, 196–200.

89. Auerbach, *Unequal Justice*, 234–37; Rosenberg, "Gideon's Trumpet," 118–20.

90. Auerbach, *Unequal Justice*, 240.

91. Auerbach, *Unequal Justice*, 240–56.

92. Auerbach, *Unequal Justice*, 256–58; Kalman, *Legal Realism at Yale*, 194–95.

93. The defendants' convictions were upheld against First Amendment challenge in Dennis v. United States, 341 U.S. 494 (1951). The trial and the lawyers' subsequent tribulations are chronicled in detail in Kutler, *The American Inquisition*, chap. 6.

94. Sacher v. United States, 343 U.S. 1, 3 (1952); Frank, "The United States Supreme Court, 1951–52," 43.

95. *Sacher*, 343 U.S. at 15 (Black, J., dissenting).

96. *Sacher*, 343 U.S. at 89 (Douglas, J., dissenting).

97. Frank, "The United States Supreme Court, 1951–52," 44–45, 47n144.

98. *Sacher*, 343 U.S. at 28 (Frankfurter, J., dissenting).

99. *Sacher*, 343 U.S. at 15, 19, 18 (Black, J., dissenting).

100. Rodell, "For Charles Clark," 1328.

101. Kutler, *The American Inquisition*, 182; Kalman, *Legal Realism at Yale*, 194–95.

102. E.g., Joseph Hearst, "Court Extends Trial, Appeal Rights of Poor," *Chicago Tribune*, 19 March 1963.

103. Anthony J. Lewis, "Supreme Court Extends Ruling on Free Counsel," *New York Times*, 19 March 1963; see also "Supreme Court's Opinion on the Right of Counsel," *New York Times*, 19 March 1963 (reprinting Justice Black's opinion for readers).

104. J. M. Lawrence, "Gerald A. Berlin, 93, Wrote Brief for Landmark US Supreme Court Ruling," *Boston Globe*, 16 September 2012; Zanin, "Through the Skill of a Local Lawyer"; Lewis, interview by Geminiani.

105. Lewis, *Gideon's Trumpet*, 154.

106. One of the book's paperback editions bears the following cover text: "How one man, a poor prisoner, took his case to the Supreme Court—and changed the law of the United States."

107. Rosenberg, "Gideon's Trumpet," 107–9.

108. Lewis, *Gideon's Trumpet*, 125–32.

109. Ely, *Democracy and Distrust*. The dedication reads: "For Earl Warren. You don't need many heroes if you choose carefully."

110. Rosenberg, "Gideon's Trumpet," 107–8.

111. Paul Freund, "Justice Was Done for One and All," *New York Times*, 21 June 1964; on the book's warm reception, see also Rosenberg, "Gideon's Trumpet," 107. Partici-

pants in the case who were distant from Lewis's social and professional milieu, while praising the book overall, have disputed how he characterized certain facts in order to fit his narrative. See Jacob, "Memories of and Reflections about Gideon v. Wainwright."

112. Lewis, *Gideon's Trumpet*, 134–35. As Norman Rosenberg notes, the book merits examination as "a primary source for the study of cold war culture." Rosenberg, "Gideon's Trumpet," 109.

113. Lewis, *Gideon's Trumpet*, 229–30.

114. Lewis, *Gideon's Trumpet*, 107.

115. Lewis, *Gideon's Trumpet*, 6, 69.

116. See especially Lewis, *Gideon's Trumpet*, 101 (describing Gideon as an unlikely "subject of a great case," Panama City as a "dejected" setting, and the neighborhood of the pool hall that Gideon allegedly broke into as "a bitter, decayed parody of a movie set for a frontier town").

117. Lewis, *Gideon's Trumpet*, 218.

118. Rosenberg, "Gideon's Trumpet," 120.

119. On the history of NALAO, see Batlan, *Women and Justice for the Poor*, 147–53.

120. "Proposal for a Defender Development Project," 18 December 1961, grant #06400098, reel 3032, FFA.

121. Zunz, *Philanthropy in America*, 22, 26–43; on the work and power of the large foundations at midcentury, see chap. 5.

122. Zunz, *Philanthropy in America*, 146–47; O'Connor, *Poverty Knowledge*, 126–29. In one prominent example of this phenomenon, McGeorge Bundy left his post as national security adviser to take over the Ford Foundation in 1966.

123. Moynihan quoted in Zunz, *Philanthropy in America*, 211; on the scale of the foundation's resources, see 173–74.

124. Zunz, *Philanthropy in America*, 180–89; Ferguson, "Organizing the Ghetto," 83–84.

125. Quoted in Ferguson, "Organizing the Ghetto," 83. On "psychological warfare," see Zunz, *Philanthropy in America*, 147–49; on India, see Zunz, 156–57. The Ford Foundation coordinated with the State Department and the CIA on overseas efforts, though it declined an offer to serve as a direct conduit for CIA funds. See Zunz, 150–51. For a detailed study of the Ford Foundation's urban poverty and juvenile delinquency programs, see O'Connor, *Poverty Knowledge*.

126. Feeley, "Malcolm Feeley Reflects on Frank Remington, the ABF Survey, and Wisconsin"; Seo, "Democratic Policing," 1276–77.

127. Teles, *The Rise of the Conservative Legal Movement*, 46–51.

128. Teles, 48–49; for more background on tensions between the foundation's leadership and staffers, see O'Connor, "Community Action, Urban Reform, and the Fight against Poverty."

129. National Defender Project, "Basic Policy Statement and Application Guide," April 1965, grant #06400098, reel 2071, FFA; Lewis, *Gideon's Trumpet*, 211–12.

130. Clarence Faust to Henry Heald, "Grant Request—Public Affairs," 6 November 1963, grant #06400098, reel 2070, FFA; "Maj. General Decker Retires as Army Judge Advocate General"; "Gen. Decker Named Legal Aid Director," *Washington Post*, 29 December 1963.

131. In emphasizing the Cold War's significance for understanding *Gideon*, this chapter echoes scholarly findings across a number of contexts. Historians have highlighted the Cold War's significance for understanding other constitutional turning points, especially *Brown v. Board of Education* (1954). Truman's State Department urged the Supreme Court to order desegregation as a way to shore up the United States' international standing. Dudziak, *Cold War Civil Rights*, 90–114. This chapter does not argue that *Gideon* was motivated in a similarly direct way by diplomatic imperatives, although the relationship between foreign policy and criminal procedure is an intriguing question for future research. What is clear is that Cold War paradigms shaped how lawyers and jurists thought about the issue of indigent defense. In that sense, the Cold War's influence on *Gideon* resembles the way that anticommunist typologies shaped developments in the social sciences. Cohen-Cole, *The Open Mind*; Herman, "The Career of Cold War Psychology"; Wolfe, *Competing with the Soviets*, 55–73. For a precise discussion of the complex relationship between the Cold War and individual rights, see also Dudziak, *War Time*, 76–85.

132. On the rise of "poverty lawyering," see Davis, *Brutal Need*; Kalman, *Yale Law School and the Sixties*.

133. *Original Meaning Jurisprudence*, 59–61, 36. On the Reagan DOJ, see Teles, "Transformative Bureaucracy"; on the broader conservative legal movement, see Teles, *The Rise of the Conservative Legal Movement*.

134. Krash, interview by Geminiani, 18–19.

135. Anthony Lewis, "A Muted Trumpet," *New York Times*, 17 March 1988. Meese restated this view as recently as 2015. See Keller, "Prison Revolt."

136. Lewis, interview by Geminiani, 19–20. For a very recent sign that conservative jurists may now be turning on *Gideon*, see Garza v. Idaho, 139 S. Ct. 738, 759 (27 February 2019) (Thomas, J., dissenting), in which Justice Thomas describes *Gideon* and subsequent right-to-counsel cases as making "policy choices" that are "beyond our constitutionally prescribed role." Given Justice Thomas's idiosyncratic jurisprudence, it is too soon to tell whether his *Garza* dissent reflects his personal views only or prefigures a larger shift.

137. The film's production history illustrated the disconnect between its imagined South and the real South of the early 1960s. Plans to film on location in Alabama were dashed by the town's modern "commercial sprawl," so instead it was filmed in the facsimile small town of a Los Angeles studio lot. Crespino, *Atticus Finch*, 140.

138. Lee, *To Kill a Mockingbird*, Kindle loc. 281.

139. Crespino, *Atticus Finch*, 140. Crespino observes that the leading man, Gregory Peck, played Atticus Finch not as the novel's conflicted intellectual, but as a simple provincial "sage."

140. Freund, "Justice Was Done for One and All."

141. Lee, *To Kill a Mockingbird*, Kindle loc. 268, 275.

Chapter Four

1. Paul Reardon to LaRue Brown, "Re: New England Defender Conference," 25 September 1963; New England Law Institute, "The New England Conference on the

Defense of Indigent Persons Accused of Crime," 31 October 1963, both in box 5, folder 13, HLB. Although the closing dinner was held at the Parker House, the conference sessions were held at Harvard Law School. For examples of other meetings at the Parker House, see, e.g., Massachusetts Bar Association Committee on Criminal Law, "Agenda for Dinner Meeting," 27 October 1966, box 3, folder 5, HLB.

2. Kennedy, "The Department of Justice and the Indigent Accused," 182, 185.

3. Connell, *Lawyers' Committee for Civil Rights*, 48n24.

4. Connell, *Lawyers' Committee for Civil Rights*, 50. Connell finds no articles in the *ABA Journal* directly addressing African American civil rights organizing prior to 1963.

5. Quoted in Connell, *Lawyers' Committee for Civil Rights*, 39.

6. Frederick Norton Jr., "Speech Delivered to the Mid-Winter Meeting of the Lynn Bar Association," 5 March 1964, box 2, folder 5, HLB.

7. Paul Webb, "Report of Atlanta Bar Association Criminal Defense Committee," 1965, box 1, folder 86, CLD.

8. Buckley, *Public Defender of Los Angeles County Biennial Report 1969/70–1970/71*.

9. See Martin v. State, 51 Ga. 567, 568 (1874).

10. Friendly, "The Bill of Rights as a Code of Criminal Procedure"; "The Defense of Indigent Persons Accused of Crime: A Proposal for Atlanta and Fulton County," 23 October [1964?], box 1, folder 86, CLD.

11. For representative examples, see Friedman, *The Will of the People*, 273, which describes *Gideon* as imposing a national standard upon "five remaining states, all in the South"; Stuntz, *The Collapse of American Criminal Justice*, 222, which describes *Gideon* as having "mattered chiefly in the South." For a more in-depth discussion of scholarly assessments of *Gideon*, see Mayeux, "What *Gideon* Did."

12. Kamisar, "The Right to Counsel and the Fourteenth Amendment," 17–20; for subsequent citations to this tally, see, for example, Friedman, *The Will of the People*, 273n346.

13. Lewis, *Gideon's Trumpet*, 215–16.

14. On the rise and subsequent fate of the heroic image of the Warren Court, see generally Kalman, *The Strange Career of Legal Liberalism*.

15. Cover and Aleinikoff, "Dialectical Federalism," 1035.

16. Cover and Aleinikoff, "Dialectical Federalism," 1036, 1039.

17. Brown v. Board of Education (*Brown II*), 349 U.S. 294, 299–300 (1955). For *Brown I*, see Brown v. Board of Education, 347 U.S. 483 (1954).

18. See Cover and Aleinikoff, "Dialectical Federalism," 1038–39; the classic study is Fiss, *Injunctions*. On court-ordered desegregation and local dynamics, see, for instance, Lassiter, *The Silent Majority* (which provides case studies of Atlanta, Richmond, and Charlotte); for a general overview, see Driver, *The Schoolhouse Gate*, 256–84.

19. For a summary of assessments of *Brown II*, see Driver, *The Schoolhouse Gate*, 256–57.

20. See Cover and Aleinikoff, "Dialectical Federalism," 1041–43. To be sure, the Warren Court did expand habeas rules, so in that sense, it did engage in procedural creativity in the realm of criminal procedure. But the basic container of adjudication—judicial review of an individual criminal conviction—remained intact, as noninterference and abstention doctrines would be used to limit larger-scale intervention into

state courts. It should be emphasized that this discussion is limited to remedies for rights regarding criminal adjudication. For rights enforceable against the police, the courts arrived over time at a somewhat different (though still arguably inadequate) set of remedial frameworks, which is beyond the scope of this book.

21. Cover and Aleinikoff, "Dialectical Federalism," 1042n46, 1043. Recognizing these limits, litigators and scholars, in recent years, have developed new strategies and proposals for enforcing *Gideon* with structural reform litigation. See Drinan, "The Third Generation of Indigent Defense Litigation"; Primus, *Litigation Strategies for Dealing with the Indigent Defense Crisis*.

22. Cover and Aleinikoff, "Dialectical Federalism," 1044.

23. Cover and Aleinikoff, "Dialectical Federalism," 1066.

24. The Court specified that "appointment of counsel for an indigent is required at every stage of a criminal proceeding where substantial rights of a criminal accused may be affected," including sentencing. Mempa v. Rhay, 389 U.S. 128, 134 (1967). For an overview of the ineffective assistance of counsel cases (as of 1973), see Bazelon, "The Defective Assistance of Counsel."

25. Cover and Aleinikoff, "Dialectical Federalism," 1050–52.

26. Lewis, *Gideon's Trumpet*, 215–16.

27. Lewis, *Portrait of a Decade*, 286–87, 289–91.

28. For a precise taxonomy of Mississippi's rhetorical uses in midcentury culture, see Crespino, "Mississippi as Metaphor."

29. Lewis, *Portrait of a Decade*, 286–87.

30. Act of 5 August 1960, ch. 565, 1960 Mass. Acts 490, 490–91 (codified at Mass. Gen. Laws ch. 221, section 34D) (repealed in 1983); "At the State House: Senate Sends Furcolo Bill to Create 11-Member Public Defender Group," *Boston Globe*, 4 August 1960. For correspondence between Brown and Hollingsworth tracking the bill's passage, see box 1, folder 13, HLB.

31. Mass. Gen. Laws ch. 565, section 1 (1960). The statute was revised in 1962 to provide for appointment directly by the Massachusetts Supreme Judicial Court. Act of April 24, 1962, ch. 366, 1962 Mass. Acts (codified at Mass. Gen. Laws ch. 221, section 34D) (repealed in 1983).

32. For leftover stationery, see Wilbur Hollingsworth to LaRue Brown, 10 October 1960, box 1, folder 12, HLB.

33. LaRue Brown, "Memorandum for Mr. Hollingsworth Re: Appropriation," 23 March 1961, box 1, folder 14, HLB.

34. Frederick Norton Jr., "Speech Delivered to the Mid-Winter Meeting of the Lynn Bar Association," 5 March 1964, box 2, folder 5, HLB.

35. Transcript of LaRue Brown reminiscences on Voluntary Defenders, 1963, p16, box 16, folder 4, HLB; see also Brown to Rutherford, 10 December 1965, box 2, folder 10, HLB.

36. "Massachusetts Defenders Committee Budget Request for Fiscal Year 1966," 8 October 1964, box 2, folder 7, HLB.

37. David Hern, "Budget Slash for Defenders," *Boston Sunday Herald*, 7 March 1965. The MDC requested $709,000 for 1965–66, which Volpe slashed to $250,500.

38. Commonwealth v. O'Leary, 198 N.E.2d 403, 405 (Mass. 1964); Supreme Judicial Court Rule 10, 347 Mass. 808, 809 (1964).

39. "Study of the Impact upon the MDC of the Decision by the Supreme Court of the United States of Gideon v. Wainwright, 373 U.S. 335," April 1964, box 5, folder 3, HLB.

40. LaRue Brown to Permanent Charity Fund, draft letter, 16 April 1964, box 2, folder 1, HLB; Raynor Gardiner to LaRue Brown, 19 March 1964, box 2, folder 5, HLB.

41. Wilbur Hollingsworth to Samuel Wilkinson, 9 March 1964; Hollingsworth, draft budget, 12 September 1963, both in box 2, folder 4, HLB. In 1964, the MDC requested state funds to raise every attorney's salary to a floor of $5,000. That figure would, a few years before, have aligned defenders' pay with entry-level prosecutor salaries. But that same year, Massachusetts increased prosecutors' salaries and Boston prosecutors now earned between $10,000 and $20,000.

42. Samuel Wilkinson to Budget Director, draft letter, 20 March 1964, box 2, folder 7, HLB.

43. See Hollingsworth to Wilkinson, 9 March 1964, box 2, folder 4, HLB ("if Ways and Means wants to pay an assistant district attorney $9,400 for prosecuting motor vehicle violations . . . it should not complain if the Defenders Committee asks for more than $3,000 for a man to defend serious felonies").

44. Hollingsworth to Budget Sub-Committee, 12 September 1963, box 1, folder 17, HLB.

45. LaRue Brown to Wilbur Hollingsworth, draft letter, 13 September 1963, box 6, folder 12, HLB. It is not clear whether Brown sent this letter (or a similar letter) to Hollingsworth.

46. "The New England Conference on the Defense of Indigent Persons Accused of Crime. Reports on Discussions of Panel Topics 'A,' 'B,' and 'C,'" November 1963, p26, box 5, folder 14, HLB.

47. Clippings attached to MDC meeting minutes, 19 June 1964, box 2, folder 4, HLB.

48. Wilbur Hollingsworth to Edward Duggan, 9 July 1963, box 2, folder 4, HLB.

49. Clipping attached to MDC meeting minutes, 19 June 1964; see also "Hollingsworth Bids High Court Probe Defenders," *Boston Globe*, 14 June 1964; "Defenders Fire Hollingsworth," *Boston Globe*, 20 June 1964.

50. MDC, "Second Report to NLADA on Suffolk County Model Defender Project," October 1966, box 3, folder 6, HLB; "Huge Free Attorney Plan," *Boston Globe*, 25 January 1965. This grant was $138,000.

51. Press release, 21 July 1966, box 5, folder 3, HLB. The federal grant was $579,544.

52. See 42 U.S.C. 2809(a)(3) (1970) (precluding use of OEO funds or personnel "for the defense of any person indicted . . . for the commission of a crime").

53. MDC, "Second Report to NLADA on Suffolk County Model Defender Project," October 1966, box 3, folder 6, HLB.

54. MDC meeting minutes, 29 June 1967; James Crowley to William Homans Jr., 10 July 1967; Albert Kramer to LaRue Brown and Edward Duggan, 24 July 1967, all in box 3, folder 15, HLB.

55. MDC meeting minutes, 3 April 1968, box 4, folder 11, HLB; MDC meeting minutes, 8 August 1968, box 4, folder 12, HLB.

56. MDC meeting minutes, 16 November 1967, box 3, folder 13, HLB; Harris, "Annals of Law: In Criminal Court-II," 44, 58–60.

57. NLADA, "Evaluation Report of NLADA on the MDC," 90, 131; Richard Connolly, "Report Blasts Defender Unit on Pay, Case Load, Attitude," *Boston Globe*, 8 September 1972. In 1971, MDC salaries reportedly started at $7,935, compared to $12,000 for Boston law offices. "Case Crush Hits Public Defenders," *Boston Globe*, 9 April 1971.

58. [William Homans?], memorandum, 17 October 1966, box 3, folder 5, HLB.

59. Zinn, "Elijah Adlow's Court," 75–77; James K. Glassman, "A Day in Court," *Harvard Crimson*, 23 November 1968.

60. Harris, "Annals of Law: In Criminal Court-I," 45; Mayeux, "What *Gideon* Did," 63–64.

61. Alschuler, "The Defense Attorney's Role," 1237; Harris, "Annals of Law: In Criminal Court-I," 74.

62. MDC meeting minutes, 16 November 1967, box 3, folder 13, HLB.

63. Equal Opportunity Act of 1964, Pub. L. No. 88-452, 202(a)(3), 78 Stat. 508, 516.

64. Orleck, "Introduction: The War on Poverty."

65. For budgets, OEO grant materials, and plans for the grant, see especially the materials in box 3, folder 1; box 3, folder 4; box 3, folder 8; box 4, folder 1; box 4, folder 10; and box 4, folder 14, HLB. For discussion of how to fill the community slots, see Robert Spangenberg to William Homans Jr., 3 May 1966, box 3, folder 8, HLB; William Homans Jr., to James Nolan, 13 October 1966, box 3, folder 5, HLB. For minutes of meetings of the rump VDC, see box 4, folder 14. Most of the names listed appear to be lawyers recognizable from earlier iterations of the VDC and MDC boards, but it is possible that community members attended.

66. Susan Ross Stern and Stewart Dalzell, "Measuring Client Service of a Defender Organization: The Philadelphia Experience," May 1968, p1, box 10, folder 280, CLD; *In re Amendment to Articles of Incorporation of the Defender Association of Philadelphia*, 307 A.2d 906, 907–10 (Pa. 1973).

67. In fact, the state of Pennsylvania has continued to leave indigent defense funding up to local municipalities.

68. *In re Amendment*, 307 A.2d at 908–09.

69. *In re Amendment*, 307 A.2d at 907.

70. *In re Amendment*, 307 A.2d at 909n7, and at 918n4 (Roberts, J., dissenting); *In re Defender Association of Philadelphia*, 279 A.2d 240, 243 (Pa. Super. Ct. 1971) (Spaulding, J., dissenting). See also "Martin Vinikoor, 1918–1976."

71. Daughen and Binzen, *The Cop Who Would Be King*; Lombardo, *Blue-Collar Conservatism*; Countryman, *Up South*, 231–32, 312–17.

72. *In re Amendment*, 307 A.2d at 918n4 (Roberts, J., dissenting).

73. *In re Defender Association of Philadelphia*, 279 A.2d at 244–45 (Spaulding, J., dissenting).

74. *In re Amendment*, 307 A.2d at 909–12.

75. *In re* Amendment, 307 A.2d at 913, 917 (Spaulding, J., dissenting).

76. This description is based on the author's conversations with David Rudovsky, an attorney at the Defender Association during the time period described and a veteran of the Philadelphia defense bar.

77. Louis Schwartz to Charles Decker, 10 February 1967; John Cleary to Theodore Husted Jr., 6 December 1967, both in box 10, folder 280, CLD. For other correspondence regarding the grant, see box 10, folder 280, CLD. For reminiscences about the project, see "Transcript of Interview with Judge Stewart Dalzell."

78. Susan Ross Stern and Stewart Dalzell, "Measuring Client Service of a Defender Organization: The Philadelphia Experience," May 1968, pp. 4, 7-8, box 10, folder 280, CLD.

79. Stern and Dalzell, "Measuring Client Service of a Defender Organization," 26-27, 36; "Client Service in a Defender Organization," 468. Because of this procedure, only 17 percent of Defender Association cases ended with a plea, and only 27 percent in Philadelphia overall.

80. Stern and Dalzell, "Measuring Client Service of a Defender Organization: The Philadelphia Experience," 37-38, 1.

81. Louis Schwartz to Charles Decker, 8 July 1968, box 10, folder 280, CLD (Schwartz paraphrasing his sense of Decker's view); see also Decker to Schwartz, 4 November 1968, box 10, folder 279, CLD (suggesting "substantial redrafting" to revise "tone").

82. "University of Pennsylvania Study re Preparation for Trial," 10 February 1967, box 10, folder 280, CLD.

83. Charles Decker to Louis Schwartz, 7 June 1968, box 10, folder 280, CLD.

84. Decker to Schwartz, 4 November 1968, box 10, folder 279, CLD.

85. John Cleary to Louis Schwartz, 21 October 1968, box 10, folder 279, CLD; Susan Ross Stern and Stewart Dalzell, "Measuring Client Service of a Defender Organization: The Philadelphia Experience," May 1968, p25, box 10, folder 280, CLD.

86. Louis Schwartz to Charles Decker, 8 July 1968, box 10, folder 280, CLD; Schwartz to Decker, 7 November 1968, box 10, folder 279, CLD. Decker thanked Schwartz for advising him of the "severability of the editorial treatment." Decker to Schwartz, 12 July 1968, box 10, folder 280, CLD.

87. "Client Service in a Defender Organization," 469.

88. Student resumes, box 10, folder 280, CLD. One worked as a medical writer before law school, and the other for the NBC television network's business side. See also "Transcript of Interview with Judge Stewart Dalzell."

89. For an example, see Mayeux, "What *Gideon* Did," 68.

90. MDC, "Second Report to NLADA on Suffolk County Model Defender Project," October 1966, box 3, folder 6, HLB.

91. Feeley, *The Process Is the Punishment*, 3.

92. Feeley, *The Process Is the Punishment*, 30, 34.

93. Argersinger v. Hamlin, 407 U.S. 25, 26, 32-33, 37 (1972); see also Scott v. Illinois, 440 U.S. 367 (1979).

94. See Duncan v. Louisiana, 391 U.S. 145, 159 (1968).

95. *Argersinger*, 407 U.S. at 46 (Powell, J., concurring in the result).

96. *Argersinger*, 407 U.S. at 63–65 (Powell, J., concurring in the result).

97. *Argersinger*, 407 U.S. at 50 (Powell, J., concurring in the result).

98. *Argersinger*, 407 U.S. at 56–57, 58–59 (Powell, J., concurring in the result).

99. Feeley, *The Process Is the Punishment*, 81–82.

100. Feeley, *The Process Is the Punishment*, 82.

101. Feeley, *The Process Is the Punishment*, 268–69.

102. NLADA, *The Other Face of Justice*, 13; Goldberg, "Defender Systems of the Future," 723–24.

103. Decker and Lorigan, "Comment, Right to Counsel: The Impact of Gideon," 105–6.

104. Argersinger v. Hamlin, 407 U.S. 25 (1972). To be sure, this is not to suggest that states have continued to provide counsel in a robust way in low-level proceedings, only that many states attempted to do so after *Gideon* and *Argersinger*.

105. This is not to suggest that public defenders never appeared in courtroom dramas, only that they did not become widely featured characters to the extent that, for example, police did.

106. Mayeux, "What *Gideon* Did," 68.

107. Alschuler, "The Defense Attorney's Role," 1248.

108. Bing et al., *The Quality of Justice*, 32.

109. Bing et al., *The Quality of Justice*, 32.

110. Rimbold quoted in Harris, "Annals of Law: In Criminal Court-II," 45; Alschuler, "The Defense Attorney's Role," 1224.

111. Harris, "Annals of Law: In Criminal Court-II," 62.

112. Richard Connolly, "Report Blasts Defender Unit on Pay, Case Load, Attitude," *Boston Globe*, 8 September 1972; "Case Crush Hits Public Defenders," *Boston Globe*, 9 April 1971.

113. Harris, "Annals of Law: In Criminal Court-I," 80–81; Harris, "Annals of Law: In Criminal Court-II," 57.

114. Bing et al., *The Quality of Justice*, 31. Similarly, at the Vera Institute, the influential New York criminal justice think tank, an advocate complained that "legal-aid lawyers" too often saw themselves as "representing a docket—that is the system" rather than their clients. Harris, "Annals of Law: In Criminal Court-I," 82.

115. *The Challenge of Crime in a Free Society*, viii. For background on the commission and on the Johnson Administration's criminal justice policy generally, see Hinton, *From the War on Poverty to the War on Crime*. For a discussion of the continuing prevalence of the "assembly-line" metaphor, see Kohler-Haussmann, "Managerial Justice and Mass Misdemeanors," 619–20.

116. *Report of the National Advisory Commission on Civil Disorders*, 9.

117. MDC meeting minutes, 31 August 1967, box 3, folder 14, HLB.

118. Alschuler, "The Defense Attorney's Role," 1206n84, 1241n176.

119. E.g., Wilkerson, "Public Defenders as Their Clients See Them"; Arcuri, "Lawyers, Judges, and Plea Bargaining"; for a summary and bibliography of this literature, see Zeidman, "Gideon: Looking Back, Looking Forward," 939–40, 940n24.

120. Casper, "Did You Have a Lawyer," 6.

121. See Fisher, *Plea Bargaining's Triumph*.

122. Mather, "Some Determinants of the Method of Case Disposition," 200–201.

123. Harris, "Annals of Law: In Criminal Court-II," 74; "City/State: Law Appointment," *Boston Globe*, 18 August 1972; NLADA, "Evaluation Report," 12. Conversely, one National Defender Project visitor regarded Rimbold as a "fine leader[]" who inspired "trust, loyalty, and confidence" in his staff. "Field Evaluation Boston, Massachusetts 6–9 February 1968," 16 February 1968, box 7, folder 219, CLD.

124. Harris, "Annals of Law: In Criminal Court-II," 76 (quoting one of Schaefer's deputies).

125. Margo Miller, "Defenders to Pull out of Mass. Courts," *Boston Globe*, 21 April 1972; Harris, "Annals of Law: In Criminal Court-II," 74.

126. For a recent study, see Anderson and Heaton, "How Much Difference Does the Lawyer Make?"; for bibliographical discussion of this vein of research, see Mayeux, "What *Gideon* Did," 80n325.

127. *Playboy* interview with Eldridge Cleaver (December 1968), reprinted in Hentoff, "Eldridge Cleaver."

128. Blumberg, "The Practice of Law as Confidence Game," 15, 18, 39.

129. Feeley, *Court Reform on Trial*, 206.

130. ABA Standing Committee on Legal Aid . . . , *Gideon Undone*. The "volume representation" quote is from MDC, "Second Report to NLADA on Suffolk County Model Defender Project," October 1966, box 3, folder 6, HLB.

131. Spangenberg and Schwartz, "The Indigent Defense Crisis Is Chronic."

Chapter Five

1. "Field Evaluation Boston, Massachusetts 6–9 February 1968," 16 February 1968, box 7, folder 219, CLD. Describing Boston as "very cold" that month, see Posey, "The Weather and Circulation of February 1968," 332.

2. "Evaluation Visit Pascagoula Defender Project," 6 December 1968, box 8, folder 235, CLD.

3. "Field Visit—U. of Mississippi 28–30 April 1967," 3 May 1967, box 8, folder 233, CLD.

4. "Evaluation Visit Pascagoula Defender Project," 6 December 1968, box 8, folder 235, CLD. The report noted that a previous defender had "undertaken to appeal three cases" but the current incumbents "were at no time disposed to appeal" their cases; they had "taken no cases to the federal court" nor "followed any cases beyond the initial decision of the Circuit Court."

5. "Field Evaluation Boston, Massachusetts 6–9 February 1968," 16 February 1968, box 7, folder 219, CLD.

6. Cf. Rosenberg, *The Hollow Hope*.

7. Florida released 976 prisoners by 1964. Lewis, *Gideon's Trumpet*, 215.

8. For an example of a local court being described as "inquisitorial," see "Field Evaluation Boston, Massachusetts 6–9 February 1968," 16 February 1968, box 7, folder 219, CLD.

9. Ring, *The Problem South*.

10. ISOJ, ii, 124, 115–16.

11. See Thernstrom, *Poverty, Planning, and Politics*, 174–76.
12. ISOJ, 62–63, 116.
13. Quoted in Macdonald, *The Ford Foundation*, 118.
14. Thernstrom, *Poverty, Planning, and Politics*, 176.
15. ISOJ, 1–8.
16. Macdonald, *The Ford Foundation*, 101–2, 120. (The samples of foundationese are this author's own attempt at the genre after reading Macdonald's summary.)
17. Ferguson, *The Anti-Politics Machine*, xv. Ferguson's study focused on development discourse in Lesotho from 1975 to 1984.
18. Argersinger v. Hamlin, 407 U.S. 25, 44 (1972) (Burger, C. J., concurring in the result).
19. The National Defender Project's final report did, in an internal section, reference the debate between public and private defenders. The project's policy "was to support the machinery existent in a community . . . which seemed most likely to be able to continue," without regard to its public or private status. ISOJ, 60–62.
20. ISOJ, 127.
21. MDC meeting minutes, 21 October 1968, box 4, folder 14, HLB.
22. MDC meeting minutes, 8 August 1968, box 4, folder 12, HLB.
23. MDC meeting minutes, 21 October 1968, box 4, folder 14, HLB.
24. MDC meeting minutes, 21 October 1968, box 4, folder 14, HLB.
25. "No Negro as Defender Brings Summit Protest," *Atlanta Constitution*, 13 November 1967; "Pick Negro Defenders, Court Asked," *Atlanta Constitution*, 19 December 1967. According to the 1970 Census, the portion of the City of Atlanta within Fulton County was 50 percent black, while the portion within neighboring DeKalb County was 64 percent black. Fulton County's population overall was about 39 percent black.
26. ISOJ, 29–30.
27. I thank Jeffrey Gonda for suggesting and helping to formulate this point.
28. Sugrue, *Sweet Land of Liberty*, 357. These figures are for 1966.
29. MDC meeting minutes, 24 September 1968, box 4, folder 14, HLB.
30. MDC meeting minutes, 21 October 1968, box 4, folder 14, HLB.
31. MDC meeting minutes, 24 September 1968, box 4, folder 14, HLB.
32. O'Connor, "Community Action, Urban Reform, and the Fight against Poverty," 592. For the brochure, see "Basic Policy Statement and Application Guide," April 1965, grant #064000098, reel 2017, FFA. The brochure's first page consists of quotations from Magna Carta, the Sixth Amendment, and *Gideon*.
33. Paul Webb, "Report of Atlanta Bar Association Criminal Defense Committee," 1965, box 1, folder 86, CLD.
34. Thernstrom, *Poverty, Planning, and Politics*, 35; for an overview of political challenges to foundations throughout the twentieth century, see Zunz, *Philanthropy in America*. This contemporaneous criticism prefigured a growing political science literature that examines the antidemocratic implications of philanthropy, as well as the capacity of philanthropic giving to constrain social movements. For important examples, see Francis, "The Price of Civil Rights"; Reich, *Just Giving*. These issues are also explored in a large, and growing, historiography on philanthropy; for key studies ex-

amining the Ford Foundation in particular, see Ferguson, "Organizing the Ghetto"; Ferguson, *Top Down*; O'Connor, *Poverty Knowledge*.

35. By comparison, Americans in this same era increasingly demanded transparency from government agencies. During the 1960s and '70s, all levels of government became subject to new sunshine laws—including, at the federal level, the 1966 Freedom of Information Act—and watchdog journalism. For an overview of how disclosure became defined as a value in democratic governance, see Schudson, *The Rise of the Right to Know*.

36. ISOJ, 36.

37. This summary of the National Advisory Council is drawn from ISOJ, 36, which also states that the NLADA executive committee approved all grants. For the executive committee names, see, e.g., "Minutes of Meeting of Executive Committee Held on Wednesday, May 18, 1966, at the Mayflower Hotel, Washington, D.C.," grant #06400295, reel 2078, FFA.

38. ISOJ, iii, 33–38, 109–10.

39. ISOJ, chaps. 4–5.

40. National Defender Project of NLADA, "Basic Policy Statement," 5 May 1964; Charles Decker and Arnold Trebach, "Status Report: The National Defender Project," 8 May 1964, both in grant #06400098, reel 2071, FFA. Oakland was also a designated Gray Area, but Decker and Trebach's status report did not include it among the localities expected to apply for NDP funding.

41. O'Connor, "Community Action, Urban Reform, and the Fight against Poverty," 605.

42. Decker and Trebach, "Status Report."

43. ISOJ, 39, 37.

44. ISOJ, 116.

45. See Thernstrom, *Poverty, Planning, and Politics*, 35.

46. Quoted in Brown-Nagin, *Courage to Dissent*, 237.

47. Brown-Nagin, *Courage to Dissent*, 29; on this pattern generally in the South, see Klarman, *From Jim Crow to Civil Rights*, 155–57, 271–73.

48. Bibb County v. Hancock, 86 S.E.2d 511, 515 (Ga. 1955). In 1953, the Georgia legislature authorized attorneys' fees in capital cases, but the fees were quite low ($50–$150 in fees plus $500 for expenses). In addition, the top legal talent likely did not take appointed cases. Alan Rogers has traced how the quality of court-appointed legal representation declined precipitously in Massachusetts capital cases as the bar became more stratified; see Rogers, "'A Sacred Duty.'" Similar patterns likely held true in Southern states as well.

49. "The Defense of Indigent Persons Accused of Crime: A Proposal for Atlanta and Fulton County," [1964?], box 1, folder 86, CLD.

50. On "the city too busy to hate" strategy, see generally Kruse, *White Flight*, chap. 1. As evidence that boosterism pervaded every civic effort, even indigent defense, it is notable that one of Atlanta's grant proposals to the National Defender Project spent several pages describing the city's economy and extolling its recent growth. "The Defense of Indigent Persons Accused of Crime: A Proposal for Atlanta and Fulton County," [1964?], box 1, folder 86, CLD.

51. Paul Webb, "Report of Atlanta Bar Association Criminal Defense Committee," 1965, box 1, folder 86, CLD; Mears, *Brief History of the Georgia Indigent Defense Council*, 3.

52. Shepard, *Rationing Justice*, 2.

53. Charles Decker, "Comments of the Director on the Atlanta Defender Application," 2 June 1967, box 1, folder 86, CLD.

54. John Cleary to Paul Webb, 7 July 1967; "Atlanta Grant," 28 July 1967, both in box 1, folder 86, CLD.

55. "Atlanta Proposal," 19 June 1967, box 1, folder 86, CLD. For discussion of additional dynamics, see Nancy Cheves to Charles Decker, 20 July 1967, box 1, folder 86, CLD. Observing the commissioners' "niggardly attitude," see "Atlanta Visit, 1 March 1967," 6 March 1967, box 1, folder 86, CLD.

56. Nancy Cheves to Charles Decker, 20 July 1967; "Atlanta, Georgia," 5 November 1968; Michael Padnos to John Cleary, 13 November 1968, all in box 1, folder 86, CLD.

57. Shepard, *Rationing Justice*. For an illustration of Padnos's views, see his 1972 letter after he had entered private practice chastising the Legal Aid Society for having "sunk" into a "slough of mediocrity." Padnos to Emmet Bondurant, 24 February 1972, box 9, folder 2, ALAS.

58. "Atlanta, Georgia," 5 November 1968; Michael Padnos to John Cleary, 13 November 1968; "Atlanta Application," 18 November 1968; Decker to Cleary, 15 November 1968; Decker to Cleary, 22 November 1968; Cleary to Padnos, 26 November 1968; Cleary to Padnos, 20 February 1969, all in box 1, folder 86, CLD.

59. See Thernstrom, *Poverty, Planning, and Politics*, 175–76.

60. See McMillen, *Dark Journey*; Dittmer, *Local People*, 20–22.

61. Dittmer, *Local People*, 96. On Parchman generally, see Oshinsky, *Worse Than Slavery*.

62. Connell, *The Lawyers' Committee for Civil Rights*, 116.

63. Tatel, *The Lawyers' Committee*, 12–13.

64. Tatel, *The Lawyers' Committee*, 12–13.

65. Tatel, *The Lawyers' Committee*, 12–13; Dittmer, *Local People*, 264, 335–41.

66. Tatel, *The Lawyers' Committee*, 13–15, 28–29.

67. Quoted in Connell, *The Lawyers' Committee for Civil Rights*, 115–16.

68. See Dittmer, *Local People*, 14–20. Because of the Great Migration, the black share of Mississippi's population had fallen below a majority but remained 45 percent in 1950.

69. Crespino, "Mississippi as Metaphor," 100, 104.

70. White, *The Making of the President 1964*, 179, 178.

71. For histories of the Mississippi freedom struggle, see Dittmer, *Local People*; Payne, *I've Got the Light of Freedom*; Sanders, *A Chance for Change*.

72. White, *The Making of the President 1964*, 179; lawyer quoted in Connell, *The Lawyers' Committee for Civil Rights*, 116.

73. King, *The Autobiography of Martin Luther King, Jr.*, chap. 28.

74. Quoted in Connell, *The Lawyers' Committee for Civil Rights*, 116. On the Mississippi State Sovereignty Commission, see Crespino, *In Search of Another Country*.

75. "New Mood at Ole Miss," *Time*, 23 September 1966.

76. "New Mood at Ole Miss."

77. "New Mood at Ole Miss." On the curriculum, see also Landon, *The University of Mississippi School of Law*.

78. "Mississippi Application," 3 August 1965, box 8, folder 235, CLD; Gerald Blessey, "Ole Miss Corner: University Institutes Public Defenders Project in Wake of Gideon Case," *The Mississippi Lawyer*, June 1965, clipping in box 8, folder 235, CLD.

79. "Application to the National Defender Project of NLADA for a Grant-in-Aid to Establish the Mississippi Defender Aid Program," December 1965, box 8, folder 233, CLD.

80. "Mississippi Application," 2 February 1966, box 8, folder 235, CLD (internal memo noting "Mr. Marden's directions" to inquire about "the handling of 'civil rights cases'").

81. Harrison Tweed to Charles Decker, 8 February 1966, box 8, folder 235, CLD.

82. "Mississippi Application," 2 February 1966, box 8, folder 235, CLD.

83. The bar insisted that even the non-university components of the grant be administered through the university, ostensibly because the bar association had never received such a large donation and lacked the capacity to disburse the funds. "Mississippi Application," 26 January 1966, box 8, folder 235, CLD. Another red flag was that the grant application included only two letters of support from local judges, a smaller showing than was ordinarily expected. "Comments of the Director on the Application for Grant to Establish Mississippi Defender Aid Program," February 1966, box 8, folder 235, CLD.

84. White, *The Making of the President 1964*, 179n7.

85. "New Mood at Ole Miss."

86. "New Mood at Ole Miss"; for Decker's phone call to Morse, see handwritten notes, 31 August 1965, box 8, folder 235, CLD.

87. "New Mood at Ole Miss"; on Yale's reputation, see Kalman, *Yale Law School and the Sixties*, 32–38.

88. For positive reports and the approval vote, see "University of Mississippi Application," 13 December 1965; NLADA board minutes, 25 February 1966, both in box 8, folder 235, CLD. For announcements of the initiative, see *Jackson Clarion-Ledger* news clippings, box 8, folder 235, CLD, and National Defender Project press release, 9 March 1966, box 8, folder 233, CLD.

89. For examples, see "Field Visit—University of Mississippi—25–30 April 1966," 6 May 1966 (noting that grant was operating "contrary to proposal"); "Evaluation Visit, Pascagoula Defender Program," 11 March 1968 (recommending withholding of future funding unless changes are made); "Mississippi Finances," 15 March 1968 (describing program as "poorly administered"), "JJC and ARV visit to Oxford Mississippi on 20 September 1968," 23 September 1968 (listing problems and reporting "extensive discussions" about the need for better student supervision, recordkeeping, etc.); "Re: Mississippi (Oxford) Budget and how to cut it," 17 September 1968 (proposing substantial cuts and noting "erratic" nature of Pascagoula program), all in box 8, folder 235, CLD; and Cleary to Williams (withholding grant installment until financial statements are submitted), 27 April 1968, box 8, folder 233, CLD. Discussing changes to the Ole Miss curriculum as a result of the grant, see Dan Grove to General

Decker, "Re: Grants to the Mississippi Defender Project," 17 December 1969, box 8, folder 234, CLD.

90. For examples of administrative friction over disbursements, see "University of Mississippi," 5 April 1966 (noting "static" from the university accountant); "University of Mississippi Telephone Conversation," 11 April 1966 (describing further accounting conflicts); "Field Visit—U. of Mississippi 28–30 April 1967," 3 May 1967 (noting Pascagoula defenders' lack of careful timekeeping and data collection), box 8, folder 235, CLD. On doubts about local matching funds, see, for example, "Evaluation Visit, Pascagoula Defender Program," 11 March 1968, box 8, folder 235, CLD.

91. Quotation from "Field Visit to Pascagoula, Miss. on 6 Nov 67," 10 November 1967; for other examples of concerns about student supervision, see "Field Visit to the University of Mississippi on 7 Nov 67," 10 November 1967; "Evaluation Visit, Pascagoula Defender Program," 11 March 1968; "JJC and ARV visit to Oxford Mississippi on 20 September 1968," 23 September 1968, all in box 8, folder 235, CLD.

92. "Field Visit to Pascagoula, Miss. on 6 Nov 67," 10 November 1967, box 8, folder 235, CLD. For the persistence of concerns that defenders exaggerated their time on indigent cases, see "Evaluation Visit Pascagoula Defender Project," 6 December 1968, box 8, folder 235, CLD.

93. "Evaluation Visit Pascagoula Defender Project," 6 December 1968, box 8, folder 235, CLD.

94. "Field Visit to Pascagoula, Miss. on 6 Nov 67," 10 November 1967, box 8, folder 235, CLD. For the rearrest anecdote, see "Evaluation Visit Pascagoula Defender Project," 6 December 1968, box 8, folder 235, CLD.

95. It is also possible that they were willing to drop cases that involved crimes against black victims. In any event, one staffer observed that defenders were able to get cases settled so easily "in part due to the sloppy procedures of the prosecution" and in part due to defenders' disinterest in "push[ing] for trial." "Evaluation Visit Pascagoula Defender Project," 6 December 1968, box 8, folder 235, CLD.

96. "Evaluation Visit Pascagoula Defender Project," 6 December 1968, box 8, folder 235, CLD.

97. For examples of assurances that statewide defender legislation was underway, see "Evaluation Visit, Pascagoula Defender Program," 11 March 1968; memo, 20 March 1968; "Evaluation Visit Pascagoula Defender Project," 6 December 1968, all in box 8, folder 235, CLD.

98. Kenneth Robertson to Parham Williams, 19 September 1968, box 8, folder 235, CLD.

99. ISOJ, 116. In 1979, Mississippi authorized counties to establish public defenders instead of relying on court-appointed counsel, but few counties used this option. NLADA, "Mississippi: A Short Story."

100. Thompson, "Blinded by a 'Barbaric' South"; on the general phenomenon, see the introduction and essays collected in Lassiter and Crespino, eds., *The Myth of Southern Exceptionalism*.

101. Dan Grove to General Decker, "Re: Grants to the Mississippi Defender Project," 17 December 1969, box 8, folder 234, CLD.

102. Charles Decker to Orison Marden, 16 June 1967, box 8, folder 233, CLD.

103. Martha M. Wood, "Application for Grant for Public Defender," 25 July 1969, box 8, folder 233, CLD.

104. Dittmer, *Local People*, 177–78, 359–62; see also Payne, *I've Got the Light of Freedom*, 319, 360–61.

105. The Supreme Court declared "anti-miscegenation" laws unconstitutional in Loving v. Virginia, 388 U.S. 1 (1967).

106. The National Defender Project's initial response to Wood explained that the project was no longer awarding new grants, but that her letter would be passed along. Anton Valukas to Martha Wood, 28 July 1969, box 8, folder 233, CLD.

107. See note (OSM to "Ted"), 28 July 1969, box 8, folder 233, CLD. Other correspondence in box 8, folder 235, CLD, states that Wood was a former associate at White and Case, which perhaps explains Marden's interest or connection.

108. "Evaluation trip—re: Application of Fayette, Mississippi Public Defender (August 7–8, 1969)," 27 August 1969, box 8, folder 235, CLD.

109. Charles Decker to Charles Evers, 17 September 1969, box 8, folder 233, CLD.

110. "Fayette, Mississippi Grant," 14 October 1969, box 8, folder 235, CLD.

111. ISOJ, 57.

112. ISOJ, 57.

113. Harris, "Annals of Law: In Criminal Court-I"; Harris, "Annals of Law: In Criminal Court-II."

114. Ireland, "The Roxbury Defenders Committee," 153–55. Sherwood and Ireland had met through the Reginald Heber Smith Fellowship, a federally funded civil legal aid program.

115. Ireland, "The Roxbury Defenders Committee," 153.

116. Ireland, "The Roxbury Defenders Committee," 154.

117. Harris, "Annals of Law: In Criminal Court-II," 78.

118. Walt Haynes, "Roxbury Defenders Go beyond Just Legal Service," *Boston Globe*, 5 September 1971; Teri Agins, "Teenagers Learn the Law Is 'More than a Sword,'" *Boston Globe*, 31 July 1974; Washington and Hines, "Call My Lawyer"; Ireland, "The Roxbury Defenders Committee," 154.

119. Washington and Hines, "Call My Lawyer," 192, 194.

120. Haynes, "Roxbury Defenders Go beyond Just Legal Service"; Jerry Taylor, "Even Critics Feel Boston Police Doing Better Job," *Boston Globe*, 29 April 1977.

121. For background on LEAA and the larger policy shift, see Hinton, *From the War on Poverty to the War on Crime*.

122. General Accounting Office, "Justice and Law Enforcement."

123. Feeley and Sarat, *The Policy Dilemma*, 76–79, 137–38; Varon, "A Reexamination of the Law Enforcement Assistance Administration," 1307–9; Hinton, "'A War within Our Own Boundaries,'" 109–10.

124. General Accounting Office, "Justice and Law Enforcement," 95.

125. General Accounting Office, 2. This estimate referred to the years 1971–73.

126. Neuhard, oral history interview with Gottfried, 15.

127. Feeley and Sarat, *The Policy Dilemma*, 96.

128. Lynch and Goldberg, *The Dollars and Sense of Justice*.

129. Neuhard, oral history interview with Hartman; see Crime Control Act of 1973, Pub. L. No. 93-83, 87 Stat. 197, 216.

130. United States General Accounting Office, "Justice and Law Enforcement," 96. Within some states, the discrepancy was smaller. Taking a snapshot of 1975 LEAA allocations within Massachusetts, for example, police received $3.77 million, corrections $2.4 million, prosecutors $1.33 million, and defenders $1.27 million. Advisory Commission on Intergovernmental Relations, *Safe Streets Reconsidered*, 342.

131. Feeley and Sarat, *The Policy Dilemma*, 67.

132. Lynch and Goldberg, *The Dollars and Sense of Justice*, 24.

133. ISOJ, 115, 128n7.

134. The literature on the origins and dynamics of the "carceral state" is fast proliferating; of most relevance to this chapter's discussion, two recent studies that focus on mass incarceration's roots in 1960s and 1970s policy changes are Hinton, *From the War on Poverty to the War on Crime*, and Kohler-Haussmann, *Getting Tough*.

135. ISOJ, 114–16.

Epilogue

1. Strickland v. Washington, 466 U.S. 668 (1984).
2. Quoted in Gallini, "The Historical Case for Abandoning *Strickland*," 332.
3. Bazelon, "Defective Assistance of Counsel," 28–33 (quote at 29).
4. *Strickland*, 466 U.S. at 687–96 (quote at 688).
5. *Strickland*, 466 U.S. at 711–12 (Marshall, J., dissenting).
6. *Strickland*, 466 U.S. at 710 (Marshall, J., dissenting).
7. *Strickland*, 466 U.S. at 699–700.
8. For a bibliography of legal scholarship criticizing *Strickland*, see Mayeux, "Ineffective Assistance of Counsel before *Powell*," 104nn15–16.
9. King, Cheesman, and Ostrom, "Habeas Litigation in the U.S. District Courts."
10. *Columbia Jailhouse Lawyers' Manual*.
11. Murphy, "Indigent Defense and the U.S. War on Drugs."
12. Murphy, "Indigent Defense and the U.S. War on Drugs," 16.
13. Gottfried, oral history interview with Neuhard, 54.
14. Steinberg, "Heeding Gideon's Call," 979–80; Anderson, "Public Defenders in the Neighborhood."
15. See, e.g., Tracey Kaplan, "'Holistic' Criminal Defense Gains Footing in Bay Area," *Mercury News*, 21 March 2014.
16. Lefstein and Portman, "Implementing the Right to Counsel," 1084–87.
17. Murphy, "Indigent Defense and the U.S. War on Drugs," 18.
18. For example, the 2015 Law for Black Lives conference, sponsored by the Center on Constitutional Rights, included a panel on "Defending the Accused: Radical Approaches to Criminal Defense," with public defenders both on the panel and in the audience.
19. John Pfaff, "A Mockery of Justice for the Poor," *New York Times*, 29 April 2016; Carpenter, "The Gaping Hole in Clinton's and Sanders's Plans."

20. See, e.g., Jacob Gershman, "Koch Industries Funds Legal Defense for the Poor," *Wall Street Journal*, 22 October 2014; Alison Frankel, "Criminal Defense Lawyers' Group: No Reason to Shun Koch Industries' Money," *Reuters*, 23 October 2014.

21. Laurin, "Gideon by the Numbers," 349; Samaha, "Indefensible."

22. Bright, "Counsel for the Poor."

23. "Justice Department to Launch Indigent Defense Program," NPR Morning Edition, 26 February 2010, http://www.npr.org/templates/story/story.php?storyId=124094017.

24. For an overview of both representative articles and contrarian exceptions, a good introduction is the 2013 symposium issue of the *Yale Law Journal*, vol. 122, no. 8, available at https://digitalcommons.law.yale.edu/ylj/vol122/iss8.

25. For representative recent examples, see Furst, *A Fair Fight*; Richard Oppel Jr., and Jugal K. Patel, "One Lawyer, 194 Felony Cases, and No Time," *New York Times*, 31 January 2019.

26. Polk County v. Dodson, 454 U.S. 312, 315, 318, 321–22, 323n13 (1981).

27. *Polk County*, 454 U.S. at 318–19 (internal quotation marks omitted).

28. See Gilbert, "In Defense of Public Defenders."

Bibliography

Manuscript Collections

Atlanta Legal Aid Society Records, Kenan Research Center, Atlanta Historical Society, Atlanta, GA
Defenders Association Records, Urban Archives, Temple University Special Collections Research Center, Philadelphia, PA
Ford Foundation Archives, Rockefeller Archive Center, Sleepy Hollow, NY
Frederic H. Vercoe Papers, Department of Special Collections, Charles E. Young Research Library, University of California–Los Angeles, Los Angeles, CA
Fund for the Republic Records, Seeley G. Mudd Manuscript Library, Princeton University, Princeton, NJ
General Charles L. Decker Collection, Manuscripts Collection, Georgetown University Law Library, Washington, DC
Herman LaRue Brown Papers, Special Collections, Harvard Law Library, Cambridge, MA
John S. Bradway Papers, David M. Rubenstein Rare Book & Manuscript Library, Duke University, Durham, NC
Office of the Messrs. Rockefeller Archives, Rockefeller Archive Center, Sleepy Hollow, NY
Red Set Student Manuscript Collection, Special Collections, Harvard Law Library, Cambridge, MA
Rockefeller Foundation Archives, Rockefeller Archive Center, Sleepy Hollow, NY
United States Wickersham Commission Records, Special Collections, Harvard Law Library, Cambridge, MA

Cases, Statutes, and Treatises

Act of August 5, 1960, ch. 565, 1960 Mass. Acts 490 (codified at Mass. Gen. Laws ch. 221, section 34D) (repealed in 1983)
Adamson v. California, 332 U.S. 46 (1942)
Argersinger v. Hamlin, 407 U.S. 25 (1972)
Berger v. United States, 295 U.S. 78 (1935)
Betts v. Brady, 316 U.S. 455 (1942)
Bibb County v. Hancock, 86 S.E.2d 511 (Ga. 1955)
Brown v. Allen, 344 U.S. 443 (1953)
Brown v. Board of Education, 347 U.S. 483 (1954)
Brown v. Board of Education (Brown II), 349 U.S. 294 (1955)
Bute v. Illinois, 333 U.S. 640 (1948)
Chewning v. Cunningham, 368 U.S. 443 (1962)

Commonwealth v. O'Leary, 198 N.E.2d 403 (Mass. 1964)
Crime Control Act of 1973, Pub. L. No. 93-83, 87 Stat. 197
Criminal Justice Act of 1964 and 1970 Amendments, Pub. L. No. 91-447, 84 Stat. 916
Dennis v. United States, 341 U.S. 494 (1951)
Duncan v. Louisiana, 391 U.S. 145 (1968)
Equal Opportunity Act of 1964, Pub. L. No. 88-452, 78 Stat. 508
Garza v. Idaho, 139 S. Ct. 738 (27 February 2019)
Gideon v. Wainwright, 372 U.S. 335 (1963)
Griffin v. Illinois, 351 U.S. 12 (1956)
Habeas Corpus Act of 1867, 14 Stat. 385
Hurtado v. California, 110 U.S. 516 (1884)
In re Amendment to Articles of Incorporation of the Defender Association of Philadelphia, 307 A.2d 906 (Pa. 1973)
In re Defender Association of Philadelphia, 279 A.2d 240 (Pa. Super. Ct. 1971)
In re Hough, 24 Cal. 2d 522 (Cal. 1944)
Johnson v. Zerbst, 304 U.S. 458 (1938)
Loving v. Virginia, 388 U.S. 1 (1967)
Mapp v. Ohio, 367 U.S. 643 (1961)
Martin v. State, 51 Ga. 567 (Ga. 1874)
Mempa v. Rhay, 389 U.S. 128 (1967)
Miranda v. Arizona, 384 U.S. 436 (1966)
Moore v. Dempsey, 261 U.S. 86 (1923)
People v. Doyell, 48 Cal. 85 (Cal. 1874)
People v. Haun, 44 Cal. 96 (Cal. 1872)
Polk County v. Dodson, 454 U.S. 312 (1981)
Powell v. Alabama, 287 U.S. 45 (1932)
Quicksall v. Michigan, 339 U.S. 660 (1950)
Reynolds v. Sims, 377 U.S. 533 (1964)
Restatement (Second) of Torts (1965)
Sacher v. United States, 343 U.S. 1 (1952)
Scott v. Illinois, 440 U.S. 367 (1979)
Solesbee v. Balkcom, 339 U.S. 9 (1950)
Strickland v. Washington, 466 U.S. 668 (1984)
Supreme Judicial Court Rule 10, 337 Mass. 812 (1958)
Supreme Judicial Court Rule 10, 347 Mass. 808 (1964)
Timbs v. Indiana, 139 S. Ct. 682 (20 February 2019)
United States v. Ash, 413 U.S. 300 (1973)
United States v. Cronic, 455 U.S. 648 (1984)
Uveges v. Pennsylvania, 335 U.S. 437 (1948)
Watts v. Indiana, 338 U.S. 49 (1949)

Newspapers

Atlanta Constitution
Boston Globe
Boston Herald
Chicago Tribune

Christian Science Monitor
Harvard Crimson
Harvard Law Record
Los Angeles Times
Mercury News

New York Times
Quincy Patriot Ledger
Springfield Union
Wall Street Journal
Washington Post

Books, Articles, and Miscellaneous Sources

Adachi, Jeff. "10 Things Public Defenders Can Do to Stand Up for Racial Justice." *Medium*, 28 September 2015. https://medium.com/@sfdefender/10-things-public-defenders-can-do-to-stand-up-for-racial-justice-c8f508459c52

Adelman, Abram E. "In Defense of the Public Defender." *Journal of the American Institute of Criminal Law and Criminology* 5, no. 4 (November 1914): 494–97.

Advisory Commission on Intergovernmental Relations. *Safe Streets Reconsidered: The Block Grant Experience, 1968–1975*. Washington, DC: Government Printing Office, 1977.

Agee, Christopher. *The Streets of San Francisco: Policing and the Creation of a Cosmopolitan Liberal Politics, 1950–1972*. Chicago: University of Chicago Press, 2014.

Agyepong, Tara Eva. *The Criminalization of Black Children: Race, Gender, and Delinquency in Chicago's Juvenile Justice System, 1890–1945*. Chapel Hill: University of North Carolina Press, 2018.

Alschuler, Albert W. "The Defense Attorney's Role in Plea Bargaining." *Yale Law Journal* 84, no. 6 (May 1975): 1179–1315.

Alpers, Benjamin L. *Dictators, Democracy, and American Public Culture: Envisioning the Totalitarian Enemy, 1920s–1950s*. Chapel Hill: University of North Carolina Press, 2003.

"American Bar Association Medal: Harrison Tweed Received 1952 Award." *American Bar Association Journal* 38 (November 1952): 915.

American Bar Association. "Public Defense Summit to Examine Racial Justice and Role of Public Defender." 15 February 2017. https://www.americanbar.org/news/abanews/aba-news-archives/2017/02/midyear_2017_public/

American Bar Association Standing Committee on Legal Aid and Indigent Defendants. *Gideon Undone: The Crisis in Indigent Defense Funding*. 1983. http://www.americanbar.org/content/da/aba/migrated/legalservices/downloads/sclaid/indigentdefense/gideonundone.authcheckdam.pdf

Anderson, David C. "Public Defenders in the Neighborhood." *NIJ Program Focus*. Washington, DC: National Institute of Justice, 1997. https://www.ncjrs.gov/txtfiles/163061.txt

Anderson, James M., and Paul Heaton. "How Much Difference Does the Lawyer Make? The Effect of Defense Counsel on Murder Case Outcomes." *Yale Law Journal* 122, no. 1 (October 2012): 1–313.

Arcuri, Alan F. "Lawyers, Judges, and Plea Bargaining: Some New Data on Inmates' Views." *International Journal of Criminology and Penology* 4 (1976).

Auerbach, Jerold. *Unequal Justice: Lawyers and Social Change in Modern America*. New York: Oxford University Press, 1976.

Ayers, Edward L. *The Promise of the New South: Life after Reconstruction*. New York: Oxford University Press, 1993.

———. *Vengeance and Justice: Crime and Punishment in the 19th-Century American South*. New York: Oxford University Press, 1984.

Babcock, Barbara Allen. "Inventing the Public Defender." *American Criminal Law Review* 43, no. 4 (2006): 1267–1316.

———. *Woman Lawyer: The Trials of Clara Foltz*. Stanford, CA: Stanford University Press, 2011.

———. "Women Defenders in the West." *Nevada Law Journal* 1, no. 1 (2001): 1–18.

———. "Women's Rights, Public Defense, and the Chicago World's Fair." *Chicago-Kent Law Review* 87, no. 2 (2012): 481–502.

Balogh, Brian. *The Associational State: American Governance in the Twentieth Century*. Philadelphia: University of Pennsylvania Press, 2015.

Barak, Gregory. "In Defense of the Rich: The Emergence of the Public Defender." *Crime and Social Justice*, no. 3 (1975): 2–14.

Barrow, A. Mabel. "Public Defender. A Bibliography." *Journal of the American Institute of Criminal Law and Criminology* 14, no. 4 (February 1924): 556–72.

Batlan, Felice. *Women and Justice for the Poor: A History of Legal Aid, 1863–1945*. New York: Cambridge University Press, 2015.

Bazelon, David L. "The Defective Assistance of Counsel." *University of Cincinnati Law Review* 42, no. 1 (1973): 1–46.

Beaney, William M. *The Right to Counsel in American Courts*. Ann Arbor: University of Michigan Press, 1955.

Bellamy, Edward. *Looking Backward, 2000 to 1887*. Project Gutenberg, 1996. http://www.gutenberg.org/ebooks/624

Bennett, James V. "To Secure the Right to Counsel." *Journal of the American Judicature Society* 32, no. 6 (April 1949): 177–81.

Bernstein, Robin. *Racial Innocence: Performing American Childhood from Slavery to Civil Rights*. New York: New York University Press, 2011.

Bing, Stephen R., et al. *The Quality of Justice in the Lower Criminal Courts of Metropolitan Boston*. Boston: Lawyers Committee for Civil Rights Under the Law, 1970.

Blackmon, Douglas A. *Slavery by Another Name: The Re-Enslavement of Black Americans from the Civil War to World War II*. Reprint. New York: Anchor, 2009.

Blaustein, Albert P., and Charles O. Porter. *The American Lawyer: A Summary of the Survey of the Legal Profession*. Chicago: University of Chicago Press, 1954.

Bliss, Edward N. *Directory of Public Defenders 1957*. Springfield, IL: Charles C. Thomas, 1957.

Bloomfield, Maxwell. *American Lawyers in a Changing Society, 1776–1876*. Cambridge, MA: Harvard University Press, 1976.

Blumberg, Abraham S. "The Practice of Law as Confidence Game: Organizational Cooptation of a Profession." *Law & Society Review* 1, no. 2 (June 1967): 15–40.

Bodenhamer, David J. *The Pursuit of Justice: Crime and Law in Antebellum Indiana*. New York: Garland Publishing, 1986.

Boetticher, Budd, et al., dir. *The Public Defender*. Aired 1954–55 on CBS. Narberth, PA: Alpha Video Distributors, 2005. DVD.

Borchard, Edwin. *Convicting the Innocent: Errors of Criminal Justice*. New Haven, CT: Yale University Press, 1932.
Borstelmann, Thomas. *The Cold War and the Color Line: American Race Relations in the Global Arena*. Cambridge, MA: Harvard University Press, 2001.
Brickey, Kathleen F. "The Commerce Clause and Federalized Crime: A Tale of Two Thieves." *Annals of the American Academy of Political and Social Science* 543 (January 1996): 27-36.
Bright, Stephen B. "Counsel for the Poor: The Death Sentence Not for the Worst Crime but for the Worst Lawyer." *Yale Law Journal* 103, no. 7 (May 1994): 1835-83.
Brinkley, Alan. *The End of Reform: New Deal Liberalism in Recession and War*. New York: Vintage Books, 1996.
Brodin, Mark S. "What One Lawyer Can Do for Society: Lessons from the Remarkable Career of William P. Homans, Jr." *New England Law Review* 46, no. 1 (Fall 2011): 37-64.
Brown, LaRue. "Equal Justice Under the Law." *Massachusetts Law Quarterly* 50, no. 1 (June 1965): 57-62.
Brown-Nagin, Tomiko. *Courage to Dissent: Atlanta and the Long History of the Civil Rights Movement*. New York: Oxford University Press, 2012.
Buckley, Richard S. *Public Defender of Los Angeles County Biennial Report 1969/70-1970/71*.
Bureau of Justice Statistics. *Census of Public Defender Offices 2007*. Washington, DC: Department of Justice, 2007; revised 2010. https://www.bjs.gov/content/pub/pdf/pd007st.pdf
Bureau of Justice Statistics. Press release, 29 November 2000. https://www.bjs.gov/content/pub/press/iddcpr.cfm
Carle, Susan D. "Race, Class, and Legal Ethics in the Early NAACP (1910-1920)." *Law and History Review* 20, no. 1 (2002): 97-146.
Carpenter, Zoe. "The Gaping Hole in Clinton's and Sanders's Plans for Criminal Justice Reform." *The Nation*, 10 March 2016. https://www.thenation.com/article/the-gaping-hole-inclinton-and-sanders-plans-for-criminal-justice-reform/
Carruthers, Susan L. *Cold War Captives: Imprisonment, Escape, and Brainwashing*. Berkeley: University of California Press, 2009.
Carter, Dan T. *Scottsboro: A Tragedy of the American South*, rev. ed. Baton Rouge: Louisiana State University Press, 2007.
Casper, Jonathan D. "Did You Have a Lawyer When You Went to Court? No, I Had a Public Defender." *Yale Review of Law and Social Action* 1 (1971): 4-9.
Cebul, Brent, Lily Geismer, and Mason B. Williams, eds. *Shaped by the State: Toward a New Political History of the Twentieth Century*. Chicago: University of Chicago Press, 2019.
The Challenge of Crime in a Free Society: A Report by the President's Commission on Law Enforcement and Administration of Justice. Washington, DC: Government Printing Office, 1967.
Chappel, James. "The Catholic Origins of Totalitarianism Theory in Interwar Europe." *Modern Intellectual History* 8, no. 3 (2011): 561-90.

"Client Service in a Defender Organization: The Philadelphia Experience." *University of Pennsylvania Law Review* 117, no. 3 (1969): 448–69.

Cohen, Lizabeth. *Making a New Deal: Industrial Workers in Chicago, 1919-1939*. 2d ed. New York: Cambridge University Press, 2009.

Cohen-Cole, Jamie. *The Open Mind: Cold War Politics and the Sciences of Human Nature*. Chicago: University of Chicago Press, 2014.

Columbia Jailhouse Lawyers' Manual, 10th ed. http://blogs2.law.columbia.edu/jlm/viewprevioused/

Connell, Ann Garity. *The Lawyers' Committee for Civil Rights Under Law: The Making of a Public Interest Law Group*. Chicago: Lawyers' Committee for Civil Rights under Law, 2003.

Cortner, Richard. *A Mob Intent on Death: The NAACP and the Arkansas Riot Cases*. Middleton, CT: Wesleyan University Press, 1988.

Cover, Robert M., and T. Alexander Aleinikoff. "Dialectical Federalism: Habeas Corpus and the Court." *Yale Law Journal* 86, no. 6 (1977): 1035–1102.

Crespino, Joseph. *Atticus Finch: The Biography; Harper Lee, Her Father, and the Making of an American Icon*. New York: Basic Books, 2018.

———. *In Search of Another Country: Mississippi and the Conservative Counterrevolution*. Princeton, NJ: Princeton University Press, 2007.

———. "Mississippi as Metaphor: Civil Rights, the South, and the Nation in the Historical Imagination." In *The Myth of Southern Exceptionalism*, edited by Matthew D. Lassiter and Joseph Crespino, 99–120. New York: Oxford University Press, 2009.

Countryman, Matthew J. *Up South: Civil Rights and Black Power in Philadelphia*. Philadelphia: University of Pennsylvania Press, 2006.

Cuff, Ellery E. *Annual Report of Public Defender of Los Angeles County July 1, 1954 to June 30, 1955*.

———. "Public Defender System: The Los Angeles Story." *Minnesota Law Review* 45, no. 5 (1961): 715–35.

Cummings, Homer S. "The Lawyer Criminal." *American Bar Association Journal* 20, no. 2 (February 1934): 82–85.

Darrow, Clarence. *The Story of My Life*. New York: Scribner's Sons, 1932; Da Capo Press, 1996.

Daughen, Joseph R., and Peter Binzen. *The Cop Who Would Be King: The Honorable Frank Rizzo*. Boston: Little, Brown, 1977.

Davis, Martha. *Brutal Need: Lawyers and the Welfare Rights Movement, 1960-1973*. New Haven, CT: Yale University Press, 1993.

Davis Polk. "Historical Timeline." https://www.davispolk.com/history

Decker, John F., and Thomas J. Lorigan. "Comment, Right to Counsel: The Impact of Gideon v. Wainwright in the Fifty States." *Creighton Law Review* 3, no. 1 (1969–70): 103–34.

Dimock, Edward J. "The Public Defender: A Step Towards a Police State?" *American Bar Association Journal* 42, no. 3 (March 1956): 219–21.

———. "Reginald Heber Smith, 1889-1966." *American Bar Association Journal* 52, no. 12 (December 1966): 1138–39.

Dittmer, John. *Local People: The Struggle for Civil Rights in Mississippi*. Urbana: University of Illinois Press, 1994.
Dolan, Jay P. *In Search of American Catholicism: A History of Religion and Culture in Tension*. New York: Oxford University Press, 2001.
Douglas, William O. "The Right to Counsel: A Foreword." *Minnesota Law Review* 45, no. 5 (1961): 693–96.
Drinan, Cara H. "The Third Generation of Indigent Defense Litigation." *New York University Review of Law and Social Change* 33, no. 4 (2009): 427–78.
Dripps, Donald A. "Due Process: A Unified Understanding." In *The Cambridge Companion to the United States Constitution*, edited by Karen Orren and John W. Compton, 45–71. Cambridge: Cambridge University Press, 2018.
Driver, Justin. "The Constitutional Conservatism of the Warren Court." *California Law Review* 100, no. 5 (October 2012): 1101–68.
———. *The Schoolhouse Gate: Public Education, the Supreme Court, and the Battle for the American Mind*. New York: Pantheon Books, 2018.
Dudziak, Mary L. *Cold War Civil Rights: Race and the Image of American Democracy*. Princeton, NJ: Princeton University Press, 2000.
———. *Wartime: An Idea, Its History, Its Consequences*. New York: Oxford University Press, 2012.
Edwards, Laura F. *A Legal History of the Civil War and Reconstruction: A Nation of Rights*. New York: Cambridge University Press, 2015.
———. *The People and Their Peace: Legal Culture and the Transformation of Inequality in the Post-Revolutionary South*. Chapel Hill: University of North Carolina Press, 2009.
Ellis, Michael J. "The Origins of the Elected Prosecutor." *Yale Law Journal* 121, no. 6 (April 2012): 1286–1583.
Ely, John Hart. *Democracy and Distrust: A Theory of Judicial Review*. Cambridge, MA: Harvard University Press, 1980.
"Exterminate the Lawyer Criminal!" *American Bar Association Journal* 19, no. 11 (November 1933): 650–51.
Fabricant, Louis. "Voluntary Defenders in Criminal Cases." *The Annals of the American Academy of Political and Social Science* 205 (September 1939): 24–29.
Feeley, Malcolm M. *Court Reform on Trial: Why Simple Solutions Fail*. New York: Basic Books, 1983.
———. "Malcolm Feeley Reflects on Frank Remington, the ABF Survey, and Wisconsin." *New Legal Realism Blog*. 15 July 2019. http://newlegalrealism.org/2019/07/15/malcolm-feeley-reflects-on-frank-remingtonthe-afb-survey-wisconsin/
———. *The Process Is the Punishment: Handling Cases in a Lower Criminal Court*. New York: Russell Sage Foundation, 1979.
Feeley, Malcolm M., and Austin D. Sarat. *The Policy Dilemma: Federal Crime Policy and the Law Enforcement Assistance Administration*. Minneapolis: University of Minnesota Press, 1980.
Ferguson, Karen. "Organizing the Ghetto: The Ford Foundation, CORE, and White Power in the Black Power Era, 1967–1969." *Journal of Urban History* 34, no. 1 (2007): 67–100.

———. *Top Down: The Ford Foundation, Black Power, and the Reinvention of Racial Liberalism*. Philadelphia: University of Pennsylvania Press, 2013.

Ferguson, James. *The Anti-Politics Machine: "Development," Depoliticization, and Bureaucratic Power in Lesotho*. Minneapolis: University of Minnesota Press, 1994.

[Ferrari, Robert?]. R. F. "An Argument for the Public Defender." *Journal of the American Institute of Criminal Law and Criminology* 5, no. 6 (March 1915): 925–28.

Ferrari, Robert. "Analysis of New York and County Bar Reports on the Public Defender." *Journal of the American Institute of Criminal Law and Criminology* 6, no. 1 (May 1915): 18–27.

———. "The Public Defender: The Complement of the District Attorney." *Journal of the American Institute of Criminal Law and Criminology* 2, no. 5 (January 1912): 704–15.

Ferrari, Robert, et al., "On the Public Defender. A Symposium." *Journal of the American Institute of Criminal Law and Criminology* 6, no. 3 (September 1915): 370–84.

Fisher, George. *Plea Bargaining's Triumph: A History of Plea Bargaining in America*. Stanford, CA: Stanford University Press, 2003.

Fiss, Owen M. *Injunctions*. Mineola, NY: Foundation Press, 1972.

———. "A Life Lived Twice." *Yale Law Journal* 100, no. 5 (1991): 1117–29.

Flood, Edward H. "Bolshevism in the United States and Russia." 12 July 1919. Digitized scan available in ProQuest History Vault, U.S. Military Intelligence Reports: Surveillance of Radicals in the United States, 1917–1941. https://congressional.proquest.com/histvault?q=002371-014-0876&accountid=14816

Foltz, Clara Shortridge. "Public Defenders." *Chicago Legal News* 25 (12 August 1893): 431–32.

———. "Public Defenders." *American Law Review* 31, no. 3 (May–June 1897): 393–403.

Francis, Megan Ming. "The Price of Civil Rights: Black Lives, White Funding, and Movement Capture." *Law & Society Review* 53, no. 1 (March 2019): 275–309.

Frank, John P. "The United States Supreme Court, 1951–52." *University of Chicago Law Review* 20, no. 1 (Autumn 1952): 1–68.

Freedman, Estelle B. *Redefining Rape: Sexual Violence in the Era of Suffrage and Segregation*. Cambridge, MA: Harvard University Press, 2013.

Friedman, Barry. *The Will of the People: How Public Opinion Has Influenced the Supreme Court and Shaped the Meaning of the Constitution*. New York: Farrar, Straus and Giroux, 2010.Friedman, Lawrence. *American Law in the 20th Century*. New Haven, CT: Yale University Press, 2002.

———. *Crime and Punishment in American History*. New York: Basic Books, 1993.

Friedman, Lawrence M., and Robert V. Percival. *The Roots of Justice: Crime and Punishment in Alameda County, California, 1870–1910*. Chapel Hill: University of North Carolina Press, 1981.

Friendly, Henry J. "The Bill of Rights as a Code of Criminal Procedure." *California Law Review* 53, no. 4 (1965): 929–56.

Furst, Bryan. *A Fair Fight: Achieving Indigent Defense Resource Parity*. New York: Brennan Center for Justice, September 2019. https://www.brennancenter.org/publication/fair-fight

Gallini, Brian P. "The Historical Case for Abandoning *Strickland*." *Nebraska Law Review* 94 (2015): 302–54.

General Accounting Office. "Justice and Law Enforcement: Overview of Activities Funded by the Law Enforcement Assistance Administration." 29 November 1977. http://www.gao.gov/products/GGD-78-21

Gerstle, Gary. *Liberty and Coercion: The Paradox of American Government from the Founding to the Present*. Princeton, NJ: Princeton University Press, 2016.

———. "The Protean Character of American Liberalism." *American Historical Review* 99, no. 4 (October 1994): 1043–73.

———. "Race and the Myth of the Liberal Consensus." *Journal of American History* 82, no. 2 (September 1995): 579–86.

Gibbons, Don C. "Say, Whatever Became of Maurice Parmelee, Anyway?" *The Sociological Quarterly* 15, no. 3 (July 1974): 405–16.

Gilbert, Jeffrey C. "In Defense of Public Defenders: *Polk County v. Dodson*." *University of Miami Law Review* 36, no. 3 (1982): 599–613.

Gilfoyle, Timothy. "'America's Greatest Criminal Barracks': The Tombs and the Experience of Criminal Justice in New York City, 1838–1897." *Journal of Urban History* 29, no. 5 (2003): 525–54.

Goldberg, Nancy A. "Defender Systems of the Future: The New National Standards." *American Criminal Law Review* 12, no. 4 (Spring 1975): 709–38.

Goldman, Mayer C. "The Necessity for a Public Defender." *Journal of the American Institute of Criminal Law and Criminology* 5, no. 5 (January 1915): 660–65.

———. "The Need for a Public Defender." *Journal of the American Institute of Criminal Law and Criminology* 8, no. 2 (July 1917): 273–75.

———. "The Public Defender." *Journal of the American Institute of Criminal Law and Criminology* 11, no. 2 (August 1920): 280–83.

———. *The Public Defender: A Necessary Factor in the Administration of Justice*. New York and London: G. P. Putnam's Sons, 1917. http://archive.org/details/publicdefenderaoogoldgoog

———. "Public Defenders for the Poor in Criminal Cases." *Virginia Law Review* 26, no. 3 (January 1940): 275–83.

———. "Public Defenders in Criminal Cases." *Annals of the American Academy of Political and Social Science* 205 (September 1939): 16–23.

Goluboff, Risa. *The Lost Promise of Civil Rights*. Cambridge, MA: Harvard University Press, 2010.

Gordon, Robert W. "'The Ideal and the Actual in the Law': Fantasies and Practices of New York City Lawyers, 1870–1910." In *The New High Priests: Lawyers in Post-Civil War America*, edited by Gerard W. Gawalt, 51–74. Westport, CT: Greenwood Press, 1984.

———. "The Legal Profession." In *Looking Back at Law's Century*, edited by Austin Sarat, Bryant G. Garth, and Robert A. Kagan, 287–336. Ithaca, NY: Cornell University Press, 2002.

———. "Taming the Past: Histories of Liberal Society in American Legal Thought." In *Taming the Past: Essays on Law in History and History in Law*, edited by Robert W. Gordon, 317–60. New York: Cambridge University Press, 2017.

Gottfried, Ted. Oral history interview with Jim Neuhard. 14 November 1990. National Equal Justice Library Oral History Collection, Georgetown University Law Library. https://repository.library.georgetown.edu/handle/10822/711917.

Gray, R. S. "The Public Defender." *Journal of the American Institute of Criminal Law and Criminology* 4, no. 5 (January 1914): 650–54.

Green, Thomas A. "Freedom and Criminal Responsibility in the Age of Pound: An Essay on Criminal Justice." *Michigan Law Review* 93, no. 7 (1995): 1915–2053.

Grisinger, Joanna L. *The Unwieldy American State: Administrative Politics since the New Deal.* Cambridge: Cambridge University Press, 2014.

Grossberg, Michael. "Altruism and Professionalism: Boston and the Rise of Organized Legal Aid, 1900–1925 — Part I." *Boston Bar Journal* 22 (May 1978): 21–28.

———. "Institutionalizing Masculinity: The Law as a Masculine Profession." In *Meanings for Manhood: Constructions of Masculinity in Victorian America*, edited by Mark C. Carnes and Clyde Griffen, 133–51. Chicago: University of Chicago Press, 1990.

Gunther, Gerald, and Gerhard Casper, eds. *Landmark Briefs and Arguments of the Supreme Court of the United States: Constitutional Law.* Bethesda, MD: University Publications of America, 1997.

Haley, Sarah. *No Mercy Here: Gender, Punishment, and the Making of Jim Crow Modernity.* Chapel Hill: University of North Carolina Press, 2016.

Hall, Jerome. Review of *Woe Unto You O Lawyers!*. *Ethics* 51, no. 3 (April 1941): 359–60.

Halliday, Paul D. and G. Edward White. "The Suspension Clause: English Text, Imperial Context, and American Implications." *Virginia Law Review* 94 (2008): 575–714.

Harris, Richard. "Annals of Law: In Criminal Court — I." *The New Yorker*, 14 April 1973.

———. "Annals of Law: In Criminal Court — II." *The New Yorker*, 21 April 1973.

Hartog, Hendrik. "The Public Law of a County Court: Judicial Government in Eighteenth-Century Massachusetts." *American Journal of Legal History* 20, no. 4 (October 1976): 282–329.

Henderson, Dwight F. *Congress, Courts, and Criminals: The Development of Federal Criminal Law, 1801–1829.* Westport, CT: Greenwood Press, 1985.

Hentoff, Nat. "Eldridge Cleaver: A Candid Conversation with the Black Panther Leader." *Playboy Kinja.* 10 February 2014. http://playboysfw.kinja.com/eldridge-cleaver-a-andid-conversation-with-the-black-1518621816

Herman, Ellen. "The Career of Cold War Psychology." *Radical History Review* 1995, no. 63 (September 1995): 53–85.

Hill, Rebecca N. *Men, Mobs, and Law: Anti-Lynching and Labor Defense in U.S. Radical History.* Durham, NC: Duke University Press, 2008.

Hinton, Elizabeth. *From the War on Poverty to the War on Crime: The Making of Mass Incarceration in America.* Cambridge, MA: Harvard University Press, 2016.

———. "'A War within Our Own Boundaries': Lyndon Johnson's Great Society and the Rise of the Carceral State." *Journal of American History* 102, no. 1 (June 2015): 100–12.

Hirsch, Francine. "The Soviets at Nuremberg: International Law, Propaganda, and the Making of the Postwar Order." *American Historical Review* 113, no. 3 (June 2008): 701-30.

Hobson, Wayne K. *The American Legal Profession and the Organizational Society, 1890-1930*. New York: Garland Publishing, 1986.

Holt, J. C. *Magna Carta*. 3d ed. Cambridge: Cambridge University Press, 2015.

Horwitz, Morton. "The History of the Public/Private Distinction." *University of Pennsylvania Law Review* 130, no. 6 (June 1982): 1423-28.

Howard, A. E. Dick. *The Road from Runnymede: Magna Carta and Constitutionalism in America*. Charlottesville: University of Virginia Press, 1968.

Howard, A. E., Jr. Review of *The Public Defender*, by Mayer C. Goldman. *Yale Law Journal* 26, no. 7 (May 1917): 625-26.

Hurst, James Willard. *The Growth of American Law: The Law Makers*. Reprinted facsimile. Boston: Little, Brown, 1950; Clark, NJ: Lawbook Exchange, 2011.

Ireland, Roderick I. "The Roxbury Defenders Committee: Reflections on the Early Years." *Massachusetts Law Review* 95, no. 1 (2013): 153-62.

Israel, Jerold H. "Gideon v. Wainwright: The 'Art' of Overruling." *Supreme Court Review* (1963): 211-72.

Jacob, Bruce. "Memories of and Reflections about Gideon v. Wainwright." *Stetson Law Review* 33 (2003): 181-298.

Johnson, John W. *American Legal Culture, 1908-1940*. Westport, CT: Greenwood Press, 1981.

Kadish, Sanford H. "Francis A. Allen: An Appreciation." *Michigan Law Review* 85, no. 3 (December 1986): 401-5.

Kalman, Laura. *Abe Fortas: A Biography*. New Haven, CT: Yale University Press, 1990.

———. *Legal Realism at Yale, 1927-1960*. Chapel Hill: University of North Carolina Press, 1986.

———. *The Strange Career of Legal Liberalism*. New Haven, CT: Yale University Press, 1996.

———. *Yale Law School and the Sixties: Revolt and Reverberations*. Chapel Hill: University of North Carolina Press, 2005.

Kamisar, Yale. "The Right to Counsel and the Fourteenth Amendment: A Dialogue on 'the Most Pervasive Right' of an Accused." *University of Chicago Law Review* 30, no. 1 (1962): 1-77.

Kammen, Michael. *A Machine That Would Go of Itself: The Constitution in American Culture*. New York: Knopf, 1986.

Katz, Michael. *The Undeserving Poor: America's Enduring Confrontation with Poverty*. 2d ed. New York: Oxford University Press, 2013.

Keeffe, Arthur John. "Harrison Tweed—The 'Democratic Aristocrat.'" *American Bar Association Journal* 55, no. 11 (November 1969): 1094-97.

Keller, Bill. "Prison Revolt." *The New Yorker*, 29 June 2015.

Kennedy, Robert F. "The Department of Justice and the Indigent Accused." *Journal of the American Judicature Society* 47, no. 8 (1964): 182-85.

Kern, Stephen. *A Cultural History of Causality: Science, Murder Novels, and Systems of Thought*. Princeton, NJ: Princeton University Press, 2004.

Kessler, Amalia D. *Inventing American Exceptionalism: The Origins of American Adversarial Legal Culture, 1800–1877*. New Haven, CT: Yale University Press, 2017.

Keyssar, Alexander. *The Right to Vote: The Contested History of Democracy in the United States*, rev. ed. New York: Basic Books, 2009.

King, Martin Luther, Jr. *The Autobiography of Martin Luther King, Jr.* Edited by Clayborne Carson. New York: Warner Books, 1998. Reproduced in part at the website of the King Institute, Stanford University. https://kinginstitute.stanford.edu/king-papers/publications/autobiography-martin-luther-king-jr-contents/chapter-28-chicago-campaign

King, Nancy J., Fred Cheesman, and Brian Ostrom. "Habeas Litigation in the U.S. District Courts." SSRN Scholarly Paper. Rochester, NY: Social Science Research Network, 28 August 2007. http://papers.ssrn.com/abstract=1009640

Klarman, Michael J. *From Jim Crow to Civil Rights: The Supreme Court and the Struggle for Racial Equality*. New York: Oxford University Press, 2004.

——— . "*Powell v. Alabama*: The Supreme Court Confronts 'Legal Lynchings.'" In *Criminal Procedure Stories*, edited by Carol S. Steiker, 1–44. New York: Foundation Press, 2006.

——— . "The Racial Origins of Modern Criminal Procedure." *Michigan Law Review* 99, no. 1 (October 2000): 48–97.

Koch Newsroom. "NACDL Selected to Receive Significant Grant from Koch Industries." 21 October 2014. https://news.kochind.com/media-resources/multimedia/nacdl-selected-to-receive-significant-grant-from-k.

Kohler-Haussmann, Issa. "Managerial Justice and Mass Misdemeanors." *Stanford Law Review* 66, no. 3 (March 2014): 611–94.

Kohler-Haussmann, Julilly. *Getting Tough: Welfare and Imprisonment in 1970s America*. Princeton, NJ: Princeton University Press, 2017.

Kornacki, Steve. *The Red and the Blue: The 1990s and the Birth of Political Tribalism*. New York: Ecco, 2018.

Kornhauser, Anne M. *Debating the American State: Liberal Anxieties and the New Leviathan, 1930–1970*. Philadelphia: University of Pennsylvania Press, 2015.

Krash, Abe. Interview by Victor Geminiani, 17 March 1993. National Equal Justice Library Oral History Collection, Georgetown University Law Library. https://repository.library.georgetown.edu/bitstream/handle/10822/559570/krash.pdf

Kraus, Phillip. "The Office of Public Defender in Los Angeles County." MA thesis, University of California, Los Angeles, 1937.

Kruse, Kevin. *White Flight: Atlanta and the Making of Modern Conservatism*. Princeton, NJ: Princeton University Press, 2005.

Kutler, Stanley I. *The American Inquisition: Justice and Injustice in the Cold War*. New York: Hill and Wang, 1982.

Landon, Michael De L. *The University of Mississippi School of Law: A Sesquicentennial History*. Jackson: University Press of Mississippi, 2006.

Landsman, Stephan. "Rise of the Contentious Spirit: Adversary Procedure in Eighteenth Century England." *Cornell Law Review* 75, no. 3 (March 1990): 498–609.

Langbein, John. *The Origins of Adversary Criminal Trial*. Oxford: Oxford University Press, 2003.
Langbein, John. *Torture and the Law of Proof: Europe and England in the Ancien Regime*. Edition with a new preface. Chicago: University of Chicago Press, 2006.
Langum, David J. *Crossing Over the Line: Legislating Morality and the Mann Act*. Chicago: University of Chicago Press, 1994.
Laurin, Jennifer E. "Gideon by the Numbers: The Emergence of Evidence-Based Practice in Indigent Defense." *Ohio State Journal of Criminal Law* 12, no. 2 (Spring 2015): 325–70.
Lassiter, Matthew. *The Silent Majority: Suburban Politics in the Sunbelt South*. Princeton, NJ: Princeton University Press, 2006.
Lassiter, Matthew D., and Joseph Crespino, eds. *The Myth of Southern Exceptionalism*. New York: Oxford University Press, 2009.
Lears, Jackson. *Rebirth of a Nation: The Making of Modern America, 1877-1920*. New York: HarperCollins, 2009.
Lee, Harper. *To Kill a Mockingbird*. New York: Lippincott, 1960; Harper, 2002. Kindle.
Lefstein, Norman, and Sheldon Portman. "Implementing the Right to Counsel in State Criminal Cases." *American Bar Association Journal* 66, no. 9 (September 1980): 1084–87.
Lewis, Anthony. *Gideon's Trumpet*. New York: Random House, 1964.
———. Interview by Victor Geminiani, 18 March 1993. National Equal Justice Library Oral History Collection, Georgetown University Law Library. http://hdl.handle.net/10822/559582.
———. *Portrait of a Decade: The Second American Revolution*. New York: Random House, 1964.
Lichtenberger, J. P. Review of *The Public Defender*, by Mayer C. Goldman. *University of Pennsylvania Law Review* 66, no. 3 (February 1918): 187–88.
Lipow, Arthur. *Authoritarian Socialism in America: Edward Bellamy and the Nationalist Movement*. Berkeley: University of California Press, 1982.
Litwack, Leon F. *Been in the Storm So Long: The Aftermath of Slavery*. New York: Vintage Books, 1980.
Lombardo, Timothy J. *Blue-Collar Conservatism: Frank Rizzo's Philadelphia and Populist Politics*. Philadephia: University of Pennsylvania Press, 2018.
Lynch, Beth, and Nancy E. Goldberg. *The Dollars and Sense of Justice: A Study of the Law Enforcement Assistance Administration as It Relates to the Defense Function of the Criminal Justice System*. Chicago: National Legal Aid and Defender Association, 1973.
MacArthur Foundation. "Criminal Justice." https://www.macfound.org/programs/criminal-justice/strategy/
Macdonald, Dwight. *The Ford Foundation: The Men and the Millions*. 1955; reprint with new introduction. New Brunswick, NJ: Transaction Publishers, 1989.
Mack, Kenneth W. *Representing the Race: The Creation of the Civil Rights Lawyer*. Cambridge, MA: Harvard University Press, 2012.
Magliocca, Gerard N. *The Heart of the Constitution: How the Bill of Rights Became the Bill of Rights*. New York: Oxford University Press, 2018.

Maguire, John MacArthur. *The Lance of Justice: A Semi-Centennial History of the Legal Aid Society 1876-1926*. Photographic reprint. Cambridge, MA: Harvard University Press, 1928; Littleton, CO: Fred B. Rothman, 1982.

"Maj. General Decker Retires as Army Judge Advocate General." *Res Ipsa Loquitur* 16, no. 3 (Spring 1964): 4.

Mancini, Matthew J. *One Dies, Get Another: Convict Leasing in the American South, 1866-1928*. Columbia: University of South Carolina Press, 1996.

Marable, Manning. *Race, Reform, and Rebellion: The Second Reconstruction in Black America, 1945-2006*, 3d ed. Oxford: University of Mississippi Press, 2007.

Mars, David. "The Problem of the Indigent Accused: Public Defenders in the Federal Courts." *American Bar Association Journal* 45, no. 3 (March 1959): 272-75, 303-5.

"Martin Vinikoor, 1918-1976." *Temple Law Quarterly* 50, no. 1 (1976): 1-4.

Marx, Karl, and Friedrich Engels. *The Communist Manifesto*. 1848; New York: Pocket Books, 1988.

Mather, Lynn M. "Some Determinants of the Method of Case Disposition: Decision-Making by Public Defenders in Los Angeles." *Law & Society Review* 8, no. 2 (Winter 1974): 187-216.

Mayers, Lewis. "The Habeas Corpus Act of 1867: The Supreme Court as Legal Historian." *University of Chicago Law Review* 33, no. 1 (1965): 31-59.

Mayeux, Sara. "The Case of the Black-Gloved Rapist: Defining the Public Defender's Role in the California Courts, 1913-1948." *California Legal History* 5 (2010): 217-39.

———. "'An Honest but Fearless Fighter': The Adversarial Ideal of Public Defenders in 1930s and 1940s Los Angeles." *Law and History Review* 36, no. 3 (August 2018): 619-66.

———. "Ineffective Assistance of Counsel before *Powell v. Alabama*: Lessons from History for the Future of the Right to Counsel." *Iowa Law Review* 99 (2014): 2161-84.

———. "What *Gideon* Did." *Columbia Law Review* 116, no. 1 (January 2016): 15-104.

McConville, Michael, and Chester L. Mirsky. "The Origins of the Indigent Defense System." *New York University Review of Law & Social Change* 15 (1986-87): 592-631.

McDonald, William F. "In Defense of Inequality: The Legal Profession and Criminal Defense." In *The Defense Counsel*, edited by William F. McDonald, 13-38. Beverly Hills, CA: Sage Publications, 1983.

McIntyre, Lisa J. *The Public Defender: The Practice of Law in the Shadows of Repute*. Chicago: University of Chicago Press, 1987.

McLennan, Rebecca M. *The Crisis of Imprisonment: Protest, Politics, and the Making of the American Penal State, 1776-1941*. Cambridge: Cambridge University Press, 2008.

McMillen, Neil R. *Dark Journey: Black Mississippians in the Age of Jim Crow*. Champaign: University of Illinois Press, 1990.

Mears, Michael. *A Brief History of the Georgia Indigent Defense Council: A Twenty-Five Year Struggle to Provide Adequate Defense Counsel for the Poor*. 2d ed. Atlanta: Georgia Indigent Defense Council, 1996.

Menand, Louis. *The Metaphysical Club: A Story of Ideas in America*. New York: Farrar, Straus and Giroux, 2001.

Meras, Phyllis. "Kay Tweed." *Martha's Vineyard Magazine*, 12 November 2009. http://www.mvmagazine.com/news/2009/11/12/kay-tweed

Miller, James A., Susan D. Pennybacker, and Eve Rosenhaft. "Mother Ada Wright and the International Campaign to Free the Scottsboro Boys, 1931–1934." *American Historical Review* 106, no. 2 (April 2001): 387–430.

Miller, Jennifer M. *Cold War Democracy: The United States and Japan*. Cambridge, MA: Harvard University Press, 2019.

Miller, Justin. "Guilty or Not Guilty?" *North American Review* 227, no. 3 (March 1929): 361–69.

———. "Lawyers and the Administration of Criminal Justice." *American Bar Association Journal* 20, no. 2 (February 1934): 77–81.

Moley, Raymond. *Our Criminal Courts*. New York: Minton, Balch & Company, 1930.

Morgan, Arthur E. *Edward Bellamy*. New York: Columbia University Press, 1944.

Muhammad, Khalil Gibran. *The Condemnation of Blackness: Race, Crime, and the Making of Modern Urban America*. Cambridge, MA: Harvard University Press, 2011.

Murphy, Cait. *Scoundrels in Law: The Trials of Howe & Hummel, Lawyers to the Gangsters, Cops, Starlets, and Rakes Who Made the Gilded Age*. New York: Smithsonian Books, 2010.

Murphy, Timothy R. "Indigent Defense and the U.S. War on Drugs: The Public Defender's Losing Battle." *Criminal Justice*, September 1991.

National Legal Aid and Defender Association. "Evaluation Report of the National Legal Aid and Defender Association on the Massachusetts Defenders Committee." 1972. https://www.ncjrs.gov/pdffiles1/Digitization/26189NCJRS.pdf

———. "Mississippi: A Short Story." 2010. http://www.nlada.net/library/article/ms_ashortstory

———. *The Other Face of Justice: A Report of the National Defender Survey Funded by the Law Enforcement Assistance Administration of the U.S. Dept. of Justice*. Chicago: National Legal Aid and Defender Association, 1973.

The Necessity and Advisability of Creating the Office of Public Defender, being the Fifth Report of the Law Reform Committee of the Association of the Bar of the City of New York. 12 January 1915. https://archive.org/details/necessityadvisabooasso

Neeley, William B. *Report of Public Defender of Los Angeles County July 1, 1946 to June 30, 1948*.

Nelson, William E. *The Fourteenth Amendment: From Political Principle to Judicial Doctrine*. Cambridge, MA: Harvard University Press, 1988.

Neuhard, James. Oral history interview with Theodore "Ted" Gottfried, 30 August 1991. National Equal Justice Library Oral History Collection, Georgetown University Law Library. https://repository.library.georgetown.edu/handle/10822/711844.

———. Oral history interview with Marshall Hartman, 15 November 1990. National Equal Justice Library Oral History Collection, Georgetown University Law Library. https://repository.library.georgetown.edu/handle/10822/711826.

Newman, Roger K. *Hugo Black: A Biography*. 2d ed. New York: Fordham University Press, 1997.

Norris, Robert J. *Exonerated: A History of the Innocence Movement*. New York: New York University Press, 2017.

Novak, William. "Public-Private Governance: A Historical Introduction." In *Government by Contract: Outsourcing and American Democracy*, edited by Martha Minow and Jody Freeman, 23-40. Cambridge, MA: Harvard University Press, 2009.

O'Connor, Alice. "Community Action, Urban Reform, and the Fight against Poverty: The Ford Foundation's Gray Areas Program." *Journal of Urban History* 22, no. 5 (1996): 586-625.

———. *Poverty Knowledge: Social Science, Social Policy, and the Poor in Twentieth-Century U.S. History*. Princeton, NJ: Princeton University Press, 2001.

Oney, Steve. *And the Dead Shall Rise: The Murder of Mary Phagan and the Lynching of Leo Frank*. New York: Random House, 2003.

Orfield, Lester. *Criminal Appeals in America*. Boston: Little, Brown, 1939.

Original Meaning Jurisprudence: A Sourcebook. Washington, DC: United States Department of Justice, Office of Legal Policy, 1987. http://catalog.hathitrust.org/Record/002455032. Also available at https://www.ncjrs.gov/App/publications/abstract.aspx?ID=115083.

Orleck, Annelise. "Introduction: The War on Poverty from the Grass Roots Up." In *The War on Poverty: A New Grassroots History, 1964-1980*, edited by Annelise Orleck and Lisa Gayle Hazirjian, 1-28. Athens: University of Georgia Press, 2011.

Oshinsky, David. *Worse Than Slavery: Parchman Farm and the Ordeal of Jim Crow Justice*. New York: Free Press, 1996.

Ossei-Owusu, Shaun. "The Sixth Amendment Facade: The Racial Evolution of the Right To Counsel." *University of Pennsylvania Law Review* 167, no. 5 (April 2019): 1161-1239.

Parmelee, Maurice. "A New System of Criminal Procedure." *Journal of the American Institute of Criminal Law and Criminology* 4, no. 3 (September 1913): 359-67.

———. "Public Defense in Criminal Trials." *International Socialist Review* 6 (October 1905): 228-35.

———. "Public Defense in Criminal Trials." *Journal of the American Institute of Criminal Law and Criminology* 1, no. 5 (January 1911): 735-47.

Parrillo, Nicholas R. *Against the Profit Motive: The Salary Revolution in American Government, 1780-1940*. New Haven, CT: Yale University Press, 2013.

Payne, Charles M. *I've Got the Light of Freedom: The Organizing Tradition and the Mississippi Freedom Struggle*. Edition with new preface. Berkeley: University of California Press, 2007.

Peters, Gerhard, and John T. Woolley. *The American Presidency Project*. http://www.presidency.ucsb.edu/ws/?pid=14175

Phillips, Christopher J. "The New Math and Midcentury American Politics." *Journal of American History* 101, no. 2 (September 2014): 454-79.

Platt, Anthony M. *The Child Savers: The Invention of Delinquency*. 40th anniv. ed. New Brunswick, NJ: Rutgers University Press, 2009.

Pollak, Louis H. "Advocating Civil Liberties: A Young Lawyer before the Old Court." *Harvard Civil Rights-Civil Liberties Law Review* 17, no. 1 (Spring 1982): 1-30.

———. "Thomas I. Emerson: Pillar of the Bill of Rights." *Yale Law Journal* 101, no. 2 (1991): 321–26.
Pollock, Ellen Joan. *Turks and Brahmins: Upheaval at Milbank, Tweed; Wall Street's Gentlemen Take Off Their Gloves.* New York: Simon & Schuster, 1990.
Pollock, Herman I. "The Voluntary Defender as Counsel for the Defense." *Journal of the American Judicature Society* 32, no. 6 (April 1949): 174–76.
Posey, Julian W. "The Weather and Circulation of February 1968." *Monthly Weather Review* 96, no. 5 (1968): 330–36.
Pound, Roscoe. *Criminal Justice in America.* Cambridge, MA: Harvard University Press, 1945.
———. "Law in Books and Law in Action." *American Law Review* 44 (1910): 12–36.
Preyer, Kathryn. "Jurisdiction to Punish: Federal Authority, Federalism and the Common Law of Crimes in the Early Republic." *Law and History Review* 4, no. 2 (1986): 223–65.
Primus, Eve Brensike. "Litigation Strategies for Dealing with the Indigent Defense Crisis." *American Constitution Society Issue Brief*, September 2010: 1–19.
Primus, Richard. "A Brooding Omnipresence: Totalitarianism in Postwar Constitutional Thought." *Yale Law Journal* 102, no. 6 (1996): 423–57.
Purcell, Edward, Jr. *The Crisis of Democratic Theory: Scientific Naturalism and the Problem of Value.* Lexington: University Press of Kentucky, 1973.
Rakove, Jack N. *Original Meanings: Politics and Ideas in the Making of the Constitution.* New York: Vintage Books, 1997.
Rappaport, John. "The Structural Function of the Sixth Amendment Right to Counsel of Choice." *Supreme Court Review* (2017): 117–56.
Reich, Rob. *Just Giving: Why Philanthropy Is Failing and How It Can Do Better.* Princeton, NJ: Princeton University Press, 2018.
"The Reminiscences of Harrison Tweed." Transcription of interview conducted 1963. Oral History Research Office, Columbia University, 1972.
Report of the Attorney General's Committee on Poverty and the Administration of Federal Criminal Justice. Washington, DC: Government Printing Office, 1963. http://catalog.hathitrust.org/Record/001142663
Report of the National Advisory Commission on Civil Disorders. Washington, DC: Government Printing Office, 1968. https://www.ncjrs.gov/pdffiles1/Digitization/8073NCJRS.pdf
Rice, James D. "The Criminal Trial before and after the Lawyers: Authority, Law, and Culture in Maryland Jury Trials, 1681–1837." *The American Journal of Legal History* 40, no. 4 (October 1996): 455–75.
Richman, Daniel C., Kate Stith, and William J. Stuntz. *Defining Federal Crimes.* New York: Wolters Kluwer, 2014.
Ring, Natalie J. *The Problem South: Region, Empire, and the New Liberal State, 1880–1930.* Athens: University of Georgia Press, 2012.
Robertson, Stephen Murray. *Crimes Against Children: Sexual Violence and Legal Culture in New York City, 1880–1960.* Chapel Hill: University of North Carolina Press, 2005.
Rodell, Fred. "For Charles E. Clark: A Brief but Belated and Fond Farewell." *Columbia Law Review* 65, no. 8 (1965): 1323–30.

Rodgers, Daniel T. *Age of Fracture*. Cambridge, MA: Belknap Press of Harvard University Press, 2011.

———. *Atlantic Crossings: Social Politics in a Progressive Age*. Cambridge, MA: Belknap Press of Harvard University Press, 1998.

———. "In Search of Progressivism." *Reviews in American History* 10, no. 4 (1982): 113–32.

Rogers, Alan. "'A Sacred Duty': Court Appointed Attorneys in Massachusetts Capital Cases, 1780–1980." *American Journal of Legal History* 41, no. 4 (October 1997): 440–65.

Rosenberg, Gerald N. *The Hollow Hope: Can Courts Bring About Social Change?* 2d ed. Chicago: University of Chicago Press, 2008.

Rosenberg, Norman L. "Gideon's Trumpet: Sounding the Retreat from Legal Realism." In *Recasting America: Culture and Politics in the Age of Cold War*, edited by Lary May, 107–24. Chicago: University of Chicago Press, 1989.

Rothman, David J. *Conscience and Convenience: The Asylum and Its Alternatives in Progressive America*. Boston: Little, Brown, 1980.

Rovere, Richard H. *The Magnificent Shysters: The True and Scandalous History of Howe and Hummel*. New York: Grosset & Dunlap, 1947.

Ruth, David E. *Inventing the Public Enemy: The Gangster in American Culture, 1918–1934*. Chicago: University of Chicago Press, 1996.

Samaha, Albert. "Indefensible: The Story of New Orleans' Public Defenders." *BuzzFeed News*, 13 August 2015. http://www.buzzfeed.com/albertsamaha/indefensible-new-orleans-public-defenders-office#.vhKdxVRp

Sanders, Crystal R. *A Chance for Change: Head Start and Mississippi's Black Freedom Struggle*. Chapel Hill: University of North Carolina Press, 2016.

Savona, Francis. "Public Defender." *Journal of the American Institute of Criminal Law and Criminology* 7, no. 2 (July 1916): 274–76.

Schlesinger, Arthur M., Jr. *The Vital Center: The Politics of Freedom*. Boston, MA: Houghton Mifflin, 1949.

Schudson, Michael. *The Rise of the Right to Know: Politics and the Culture of Transparency, 1945–1975*. Cambridge, MA: Harvard University Press, 2015.

Schweitzer, Mitchell D. Book review. *Columbia Law Review* 65, no. 1 (January 1965): 183–86.

Shapiro, Karin. *A New South Rebellion: The Battle Against Convict Labor in the Tennessee Coalfields, 1871–1896*. Chapel Hill: University of North Carolina Press, 1998.

Seligman, Joel. *The High Citadel: The Influence of Harvard Law School*. New York: Houghton Mifflin, 1978.

Seo, Sarah A. "Democratic Policing Before the Due Process Revolution." *Yale Law Journal* 128 (2019): 1246–1302.

———. *Policing the Open Road: How Cars Transformed American Freedom*. Cambridge, MA: Harvard University Press, 2019.

Shea, Willard W. "Recollections of Alameda County's First Public Defender: An Interview Conducted by Miriam Feingold." In *Perspectives on the Alameda County District Attorney's Office, Vol. 1*. Regional Oral History Office, Bancroft Library, University of California, Berkeley, 1972. http://www.oac.cdlib.org/view?docId=kt9489p008&brand=oac4&doc.view=entire_text

Shepard, Kris. *Rationing Justice: Poverty Lawyers and Poor People in the Deep South*. Baton Rouge: Louisiana State University Press, 2007.

Simon, Jonathan. "Visions of Self-Control: Fashioning a Liberal Approach to Crime and Punishment in the Twentieth Century," in *Looking Back at Law's Century*, edited by Austin Sarat, Bryant G. Garth, and Robert A. Kagan, 109–50. Ithaca, NY: Cornell University Press, 2002.

Sklansky, David Alan. "Anti-Inquisitorialism." *Harvard Law Review* 122 (2009): 1634–1704.

Smith, Reginald Heber. "The English Legal Assistance Plan: Its Significance for American Legal Institutions." *American Bar Association Journal* 35, no. 6 (June 1949): 453–56, 526–28.

Smith, Reginald Heber. *Justice and the Poor, a Study of the Present Denial of Justice to the Poor and of the Agencies Making More Equal Their Position before the Law, with Particular Reference to Legal Aid Work in the United States*. New York: Carnegie Foundation for the Advancement of Teaching, 1919.

Spangenberg, Robert L., and Tessa J. Schwartz. "The Indigent Defense Crisis Is Chronic." *Criminal Justice*, Summer 1994.

Sparrow, James T. *Warfare State: World War II Americans and the Age of Big Government*. New York: Oxford University Press, 2011.

Sparrow, James T., William J. Novak, and Stephen W. Sawyer, eds. *Boundaries of the State in U.S. History*. Chicago: University of Chicago Press, 2015.

Special Committee of the Association of the Bar of the City of New York and the National Legal Aid and Defender Association. *Equal Justice for the Accused*. Garden City, NY: Doubleday, 1959.

Steinberg, Allen. "From Private Prosecution to Plea Bargaining: Criminal Prosecution, the District Attorney, and American Legal History." *Crime & Delinquency* 30, no. 4 (October 1984): 568–92.

———. *The Transformation of Criminal Justice, Philadelphia, 1800–1880*. Chapel Hill: University of North Carolina Press, 1989.

Steinberg, Harris B., and Monrad G. Paulsen. "A Conversation with Defense Counsel on Problems of a Criminal Defense." *The Practical Lawyer* 7, no. 5 (1961): 25–43.

Steinberg, Robin G. "Beyond Lawyering: How Holistic Representation Makes for Good Policy, Better Lawyers, and More Satisfied Clients." *New York University Review of Law & Social Change* 30, no. 4 (2006): 625–36.

Stevens, Mark. *Power of Attorney: The Rise of the Giant Law Firms*. New York: McGraw-Hill, 1987.

Stevens, Robert. *Law School: Legal Education in America from the 1850s to the 1980s*. Chapel Hill: University of North Carolina Press, 1983.

Stewart, James B. *The Partners: Inside America's Most Powerful Law Firms*. New York: Simon & Schuster, 1983.

Stewart, Wm. Scott. "A Criticism of the Public Defender System." *John Marshall Law Quarterly* 1, no. 3 (June 1936): 245–91.

———. "The Public Defender System Is Unsound in Principle." *Journal of the American Judicature Society* 32, no. 4 (December 1948): 115–17.

———. *Stewart on Trial Strategy: Practical Suggestions to the Young Lawyer on How to Obtain and Hold Clients, How to Prepare and Try Lawsuits*. Chicago: The Flood Company, 1940.

Stuntz, William J. *The Collapse of Criminal Justice*. Cambridge, MA: Belknap Press of Harvard University Press, 2011.

Sugrue, Thomas J. *Sweet Land of Liberty: The Forgotten Struggle for Civil Rights in the North*. New York: Random House, 2008.

Sutherland, Arthur E. *The Law at Harvard: A History of Ideas and Men, 1817–1967*. Cambridge, MA: Belknap Press of Harvard University Press, 1967.

Tani, Karen M. *States of Dependency: Welfare, Rights, and American Governance, 1935–1972*. Cambridge: Cambridge University Press, 2016.

———. "Welfare and Rights Before the Movement: Rights as a Language of the State." *Yale Law Journal* 122, no. 2 (2012): 314–83.

Tatel, Edith S. B. *The Lawyers' Committee: The First Twenty-Five Years*. Washington, DC: Lawyers' Committee for Civil Rights under Law, 1988.

Teles, Steven M. *The Rise of the Conservative Legal Movement: The Battle for Control of the Law*. Princeton, NJ: Princeton University Press, 2008.

———. "Transformative Bureaucracy: Reagan's Lawyers and the Dynamics of Political Investment." *Studies in American Political Development* 23, no. 1 (2009): 61–83.

Thaman, Stephen C. "The Good, the Bad, or the Indifferent: 12 Angry Men in Russia." *Chicago-Kent Law Review* 82, no. 2 (2007): 794–96.

Thernstrom, Stephan. *Poverty, Planning, and Politics in the New Boston: The Origins of ABCD*. New York: Basic Books, 1969.

Thomas, John L. *Alternative America: Henry George, Edward Bellamy, Henry Demarest Lloyd and the Adversary Tradition*. Cambridge, MA: Harvard University Press, 1983.

Thompson, Heather A. "Blinded by a 'Barbaric' South: Prison Horrors, Inmate Abuse, and the Ironic History of American Penal Reform." In *The Myth of Southern Exceptionalism*, edited by Matthew D. Lassiter and Joseph Crespino, 74–95. New York: Oxford University Press, 2009.

Tocqueville, Alexis de. *Democracy in America*, translated by Harvey C. Mansfield and Delba Winthrop. Chicago: University of Chicago Press, 2000.

"Transcript of Interview with Judge Stewart Dalzell." Biddle Law Library, University of Pennsylvania. https://www.law.upenn.edu/library/archives/other/oralhistory/interviews/transcripts/dalzell.php

Trout, Charles H. "Curley of Boston: The Search for Irish Legitimacy." In *Boston, 1700–1980: The Evolution of Urban Politics*, edited by Ronald P. Formisano and Constance K. Burns, 165–95. Westport, CT: Greenwood Press, 1984.

Tweed, Harrison. "The Lawyer as a Public Servant." *Practical Lawyer* 7, no. 7 (November 1961): 8–15.

———. *The Legal Aid Society New York City 1876–1951*. New York: The Legal Aid Society, 1954.

U.S. Courts. "Defender Services." https://www.uscourts.gov/services-forms/defender-services

Vale, Lawrence J. *From the Puritans to the Projects: Public Housing and Public Neighbors.* Cambridge, MA: Harvard University Press, 2000.

Varon, Jay N. "A Reexamination of the Law Enforcement Assistance Administration." *Stanford Law Review* 27, no. 5 (May 1975): 1303–24.

Waite, John B. Review of *The Public Defender*, by Mayer C. Goldman. *Michigan Law Review* 16, no. 4 (February 1918): 279–80.

Waldrep, Christopher. "War of Words: The Controversy over the Definition of Lynching, 1899–1940." *The Journal of Southern History* 66, no. 1 (February 2000): 75–100.

Walker, Anders. "The Anti-Case Method: Herbert Wechsler and the Political History of the Criminal Law Course." *Ohio State Journal of Criminal Law* 7 (2009): 217–46.

Wall, Wendy L. *Inventing the "American Way": The Politics of Consensus from the New Deal to the Civil Rights Movement.* Oxford: Oxford University Press, 2008.

Washington, Harold R., and Geraldine S. Hines. "Call My Lawyer: Styling a Community Based Defender Program." *Black Law Journal* 8 (1983): 186–97.

White, G. Edward. "From Sociological Jurisprudence to Realism: Jurisprudence and Social Change in Early Twentieth-Century America." *Virginia Law Review* 58, no. 6 (1972): 999–1028.

White, Morton Gabriel. *Social Thought in America: The Revolt against Formalism.* Boston: Beacon Press, 1957.

White, Theodore H. *The Making of the President 1964.* New York: Atheneum, 1965.

Wiebe, Robert H. *The Search for Order, 1877–1920.* New York: Hill and Wang, 1967.

Wigmore, John H. "Shall the Legal Profession Be Reorganized?" *Journal of the American Institute of Criminal Law and Criminology* 4, no. 5 (January 1914): 641–43.

Wilentz, Sean. *The Rise of American Democracy: Jefferson to Lincoln.* New York: Norton, 2005.

Wilkerson, Glen. "Public Defenders as Their Clients See Them." *American Journal of Criminal Law* 1, no. 2 (April 1972): 141–55.

Wilkinson, Dorothy B. "George Gordon Battle." *Dictionary of North Carolina Biography.* Chapel Hill: University of North Carolina Press, 1979. https://www.ncpedia.org/biography/battle-george-gordon

Willrich, Michael. *City of Courts: Socializing Justice in Progressive Chicago.* Cambridge: Cambridge University Press, 2003.

Wilmer, Hale. "Slice of History: Reginald Heber Smith and the Birth of the Billable Hour." 9 August 2010. http://www.wilmerhale.com/pages/publicationsandnewsdetail.aspx?NewsPubId=95929

Wolfe, Audra J. *Competing with the Soviets: Science, Technology, and the State in Cold War America.* Baltimore, MD: Johns Hopkins University Press, 2013.

Worden, Alissa Pollitz, and Andrew Lucas Blaize Davies. "Protecting Due Process in a Punitive Era: An Analysis of Changes in Providing Counsel to the Poor." In *Studies in Law, Politics, and Society: New Perspectives on Crime and Criminal Justice*, edited by Austin Sarat, vol. 47 (2009).

Worgan, David S., and Monrad G. Paulsen. "The Position of a Prosecutor in a Criminal Case—A Conversation with a Prosecuting Attorney." *The Practical Lawyer* 7, no. 7 (November 1961): 44–58.

Zanin, Krista. "Through the Skill of a Local Lawyer, Massachusetts Is Part of Gideon's Legacy." *Massachusetts Bar Association Lawyers Journal*, March 2003. http://www.massbar.org/publications/lawyers-journal/2003/march/through-the-skill-of-a

Zeidman, Steven. "Gideon: Looking Back, Looking Forward, Looking in the Mirror." *Seattle Journal for Social Justice* 11 (2013): 933–62.

Zinn, Howard. "Elijah Adlow's Court." In *Justice in Everyday Life: The Way It Really Works (Radical 60s)*, vol. 6, 75–77. Boston: South End Press, 2002.

Zunz, Olivier. *Philanthropy in America: A History*. Princeton, NJ: Princeton University Press, 2014.

Index

ABA Journal, 52, 118
Acheson, Dean, 95
Action for Boston Community Development (ABCD), 128
Adlow, Elijah, 129–30
adversarialism, 40–41
Alabama, 104, 120
Alameda County. *See* California
Aldrich, Winthrop, 87
Aleinikoff, Alexander, 122–23
Allen, Francis, 96
Allen, Jr., Ivan, 165
Allen report. *See Poverty and the Administration of Federal Criminal Justice*
American Association of Law Schools, 67
American Bar Association (ABA): advertising and, 34; American Bar Foundation and, 112; civil rights and, 118; creation of, 11–12, 87; federal public defender legislation and, 75, 185–86; Goldman and, 55; Harvard and, 67; indigent defense funding and, 150; the New Deal and, 106; NLADA and, 17; *Sacher v. United States* and, 107–8; Smith, Reginald Heber and, 52. *See also* bar associations
"American Way of Life," 1–2, 5, 88–90, 99, 193n4–193n5
Anderson, Ruben, 173
anticommunism, 16, 88–90, 105–6, 113
anti-totalitarianism, 105, 113, 197n48, 219n23
Arendt, Hannah, 91
Argersinger v. Hamlin, 140–42, 158, 178–79
associationalism, 11–12, 19

Atlanta, 160–61, 164–65
Auerbach, Jerold, 106

bar associations: anticommunism and, 106; Association of the Bar of the City of New York, 47–50; elite lawyers and, 47; as gatekeepers, 47; legal aid and, 53; Mississippi State Bar, 167, 170; negative stereotypes of lawyers and, 44; professional ethics and, 34; state and local, 12. *See also* American Bar Association (ABA); elite lawyers; lawyers
Batlan, Felice, 52–53
Bellamy, Edward, 26–29
Berlin, Gerald, 108–9
Betts, Smith, 76–80
Betts v. Brady, 76–81, 83, 95, 99–100, 140, 157, 182, 215n114, 215n118, 221n60
Bill of Rights, 46, 74–75, 78, 101, 104–6, 119
Black, Hugo, 71, 75, 78, 101–2, 107, 182
Black Lives Matter movement, 186
Blumberg, Abraham, 149
Boston. *See* Massachusetts
Boston Globe, 59, 64, 144, 176
Boston Lawyers' Committee for Civil Rights, 143–44
Bradway, John, 42, 53
Bright, Stephen, 186–87
Brown, LaRue, 60–61, 63, 68, 81, 125, 127, 148
Brownell, Herbert, 95, 106
Brown II, 122
Brown v. Board of Education, 118, 121–22, 130, 225n131
Bundy, McGeorge, 112, 224n122

263

Burger, Warren, 103, 158, 183
Burger Court, 122

California, 8, 30, 44, 61–62, 85, 92, 119, 184–85
capitalism, 9–10, 17, 26–27, 70, 84, 87–88
capital punishment, 186–87
Carroll, Lewis, 179
Carruthers, Susan, 90
The Challenge of Crime in a Free Society (report), 144
Chicago, 30, 35
Cincinnati, 50
Civil Rights Act of 1964, 160, 165
civil rights movement, 118, 167
Cleaver, Eldridge, 149
Cohen, Benjamin, 79–80, 95
Cold War: criminal justice and, 94–95; democracy and, 90–92, 197n51; *Gideon's Trumpet* and, 109–10; national identity and, 89–90, 92, 105; public defender concept and, 1–2, 88–89, 94–95, 98, 113–15; race and, 14
Commonwealth v. LaPlante, 57–59, 64–65
communism, 88–90, 95, 105
Communist Party, 72
community chest, 63–64, 83, 125, 131, 133
compulsory public defense, 11, 44–47, 55
Connecticut, 30, 145
the Constitution (U.S.): *Argersinger* and, 140; *Betts* and, 77; Fifth Amendment and, 69; Fourteenth Amendment and, 69–72, 78, 212n77; *Polk County* and, 188–89; public defense and, 41, 104; rights of the accused and, 14; Sixth Amendment and, 6, 78; the Warren Court and, 130. *See also* Bill of Rights; Supreme Court
Cover, Robert, 122–23
Crespino, Joseph, 168
criminal bar, 33, 39, 41, 53, 68
Criminal Justice Act of 1964, 103
criminal law: adversarial format and, 40–41, 97; the Cold War and, 98; elite lawyers and, 12, 33; expansion of, 20;

Journal of Criminal Law and Criminology, 35; *Justice and the Poor* and, 53; legal reformers and, 35; local control and, 122; mass incarceration and, 178; the poor and, 8; *The Process is the Punishment* and, 139; race and, 14, 124, 154, 167, 176; review of criminal convictions and, 184; role of lawyers and, 26; state encroachment and, 10
Cuff, Ellery, 1–2, 85

Darrow, Clarence, 33
Decker, Charles "Ted," 113, 130, 137–38, 163, 166, 171, 173
the deep south: civil rights and, 118; local power structures and, 151–54; National Defender Project and, 163–66; racism and, 124–25; resistance to public defenders and, 186; Southern exceptionalism and, 172–73
Defender Newsletter, 163
The Defense of Indigent Persons Accused of a Crime (conference), 117
democracy, 90–94, 97
Democracy and Distrust (Ely), 109
Dennis v. United States, 223n93. *See also Sacher v. United States*
Department of Justice, 187
Dewey, John, 91
dialectical federalism, 123
Dimock, Edward, 99
dissidents, 107–8
Douglas, William, 95, 107, 140
due process: the Cold War and, 88, 93; the Constitution and, 69; dissidents and, 108; public defender as a violation of, 41, 62; Supreme Court and, 59, 70–74, 78–81, 102, 182, 189. *See also Gideon v. Wainwright*; Supreme Court

elite lawyers: African American lawyers and, 161; as the aristocracy, 86–87; bar associations and, 47; corporate capitalism and, 87; criminal courts and, 33–34, 68, 149; embrace of public

264 Index

defender concept and, 6–8, 16–18, 22, 88–89, 95, 108, 149, 179; fee-for-service advocacy and, 36; as gatekeepers, 32, 47; *Gideon* myth and, 19–22; indigent defense and, 8, 41, 49, 67, 148, 187; influence of, 13–15, 86; legal aid movement and, 52; National Lawyers Guild and, 106; private charitable aid and, 26, 50–55, 62, 81–83; resistance to public defender concept and, 2–5, 12, 15–16, 19, 23, 26, 47–49. *See also* lawyers

Ely, John Hart, 109
Emerson, Thomas, 106
Engels, Friedrich, 70
Equal Justice for the Accused (NLADA), 88, 95–97
Evarts, William Maxwell, 87
Evers, Charles, 173–74

fascism, 15, 90–91
federalism, 75, 77, 108, 123
Feeley, Malcolm, 139, 141, 150
Ferguson, James, 158
Florida, 100, 104, 120, 153
Foltz, Clara, 25, 29–30, 179
Ford, Edsel, 112
Ford, Henry, 112
Ford Foundation: communism and, 16–17, 82; creation of, 112; creation of the National Defender Project and, 82, 113; foundationese and, 157–58; governance of, 161–62; interests of, 112. *See also* National Defender Project
Ford II, Henry, 112
Fortas, Abe, 100–101, 109–10
foundationese, 157–58
Frank, Leo, 42
Frankfurter, Felix, 92, 94, 101, 107
Franko, Selma, 30–31
Fund for the Republic, 82–83, 111

Gardiner, Raynor, 126, 162
Gardner, Erle Stanley, 58
Georgia, 118–19, 164–65

Georgia Supreme Court, 85, 119
Gideon, Clarence Earl, 100, 110, 115–16
Gideon myth, 19–22
Gideon's Trumpet (Lewis), 20, 109–10, 115–16, 120–21, 124
Gideon v. Wainwright: antitotalitarianism and, 105, 111; *Argersinger* and, 140–42; case facts and decision, 99–104; caseload increases after, 136–42; foreign policy and, 225n131; guidance on compliance with, 120–23, 127–28, 141, 149; Kennedy, Robert F. and, 117–18; local courts resistance to, 129–30, 179; Massachusetts Defenders Committee and, 125–30; National Defender Project final report and, 178–79; Philadelphia Defender Association and, 131–36; as a product of the Cold War, 113–15; response to, 5, 16–17, 102–4, 108, 119–20, 125–30. *See also Gideon's Trumpet* (Lewis); National Defender Project; Supreme Court
Gilfoyle, Timothy, 31
Goldman, Mayer C., 24, 30–32, 36, 39, 41–43, 45, 47, 49–56
Gordon, Robert, 48
Gossett, William T., 162
Griffin v. Illinois, 81, 216n133
Griswold, Erwin, 57, 67–68, 79–80, 84, 95

habeas corpus, 33, 70–71, 77, 119, 122–23, 153, 181–84, 212n77, 227n20
Hadley, Reed, 85
Harvard Law School, 67–68
Holder, Eric, 187
Hollingsworth, Wilbur, 57–59, 63, 66, 68, 82–83, 125–27, 143
Holmes, Jr., Oliver Wendell, 70
Homans, Jr., William, 148
Hoover, Herbert, 25
Howe, William, 32
Howe and Hummel, 32
Hughes, Charles Evans, 50

Index 265

Hummel, Abraham, 32
Hurst, James Willard, 84, 194n17

Illinois, 81
immigrants, 41, 52
indigent defense: African American lawyers and, 160–61, 175–76, 202n51; Allen report and, 96; *Betts v. Brady* and, 77; California and, 42, 85; as a career, 66–68, 127, 148, 161; due process and, 79; elite lawyers and, 15, 17–19, 49, 52, 108; *Equal Justice for the Accused* and, 97; federal, 76, 95, 103, 163; funding and, 2, 20, 130, 132, 135, 138, 150, 154–55, 159, 178–79, 185–86; *Gideon v. Wainwright* and, 111–13; *Griffin v. Illinois* and, 81; Griswold, Erwin and, 67; indigent defense crisis and, 154–55, 187; LEAA outlays and, 177–78; Manhattan and, 59–60; private charitable aid and, 26, 50–55, 81–83, 111, 128; public defender concept and, 8, 18, 103–4; race and, 14, 33, 65, 84, 154–55, 159–61, 166–70, 193n4, 196 n43, 210n49; Roxbury Defenders Committee and, 185; spectrum of local arrangements for pre-*Gideon*, 85; voluntary defenders and, 57–63; war on poverty and, 99; Wickersham Commission and, 25. *See also* public defenders (in practice); voluntary defenders
The Indigent Defense Crisis Is Chronic (ABA report), 150
individualism, 1–2, 9, 12–14, 16, 28, 38, 41, 45, 49–50, 60–61, 90, 92, 109–10, 146–47, 197n51, 218n19, 219n23, 220n35
individual rights, 2–3, 12, 19, 28–29, 45–47, 60, 82, 105, 109, 149, 153. *See also* the Constitution (U.S.); right to counsel
industrial capitalism, 9–10
International Labor Defense, 72, 194n20, 213n84

Ireland, Roderick, 175–76

Jim Crow, 14, 69, 72, 88, 115, 163
Johnson, John, 75
Johnson, Lyndon, 128
Johnson v. Zerbst, 75–77, 96, 102
Journal of Criminal Law and Criminology, 35, 202n69
judges: assignment of counsel and, 29, 83–85, 101, 140; the deep south and, 124, 169; federal indigent defense and, 103; *Gideon's Trumpet* and, 109–11; legal reform and, 35; penalizing defendants who invoke their rights and, 151, 153; political trials and, 107; resistance to public defenders and, 48, 129–30, 153, 187; role of, 34, 45; *Sacher v. United States*, 106–8
judicial reforms, 30, 35
juries, 72
Justice and the Poor (Smith), 51–54, 159

Kane, Francis Fisher, 60
Kelley, Florence, 67, 162
Kennedy, Robert F., 117–18, 187
Kennedy, Ted, 185
Kerner Commission, 144
King Jr., Martin Luther, 168
Kirchwey, George, 43, 212n70
Koch Industries, 186
Krash, Abe, 114

LaPlante, Richard, 57–59, 64–65, 85
Law Enforcement Assistance Administration (LEAA), 176–78, 185–86
law firms, 12, 33, 48, 87, 152. *See also* elite lawyers
lawyers: adversarial legal culture and, 40–41, 93, 97, 147; as agents of their clients, 12–13, 38–39, 48, 61, 146; American Bar Association and, 11–12; associationalism and, 11–12; de Tocqueville on, 86; due process and, 71–75; Jim Crow and, 69; lawyer-criminals and, 32–33, 44, 65;

modernity and redefinition of, 9–10; negative stereotypes and, 44; poverty lawyers and, 114; the Smith Act and, 106; totalitarianism and, 92; Tweed on, 86–87; women as, 29–30; younger cities and, 30. *See also* elite lawyers; indigent defense
Lawyers' Committee for Civil Rights under Law, 88, 167, 170
Lee, Harper, 116
legal aid organizations: Atlanta Legal Aid Society, 165–66; Bronx Defenders, 185; Committee for Public Counsel Services (Massachusetts), 185; Criminal Courts Branch (New York), 50, 59, 63–64, 66, 88; Defender Association (Philadelphia), 60–61, 63, 66, 77, 131–38; Harvard Voluntary Defenders, 67–68; Legal Aid Society of New York, 50, 59, 63–64, 66, 68; Legal Aid Society of Pittsburgh, 65–66; Massachusetts Defenders Committee, 125–31, 139, 142–44, 148–49, 159–61, 185; Neighborhood Defender Service of Harlem, 185; Roxbury Defenders Committee and, 174–76, 185; Voluntary Defenders Committee (Boston), 57–60, 63–64, 66, 80–85, 111, 125. *See also* voluntary defenders
legal aid societies, 50–51, 59
Legal Aid Society of New York. *See under* legal aid organizations
legal realism, 96, 221n48–221n49
Lewis, Anthony, 20, 68, 108–11, 114–16, 120–21, 124
liberal democracy: anti-totalitarianism and, 197n48, 219n23; fair trials and, 89, 155; lawyers role within, 15–16; political extremes and, 91; public defenders and, 1–3, 19, 149
liberalism: Cold War, 1–2, 112; consensus, 193n4; *Gideon* and, 114; laissez-faire classical, 9; lawyers role within, 15, 20–21; midcentury, 156; Northern elites and, 88; postwar, 90; progressivism and, 9; public defenders and, 5, 97
Lipow, Arthur, 28
local courts: as assembly lines, 143–50; equal justice and, 151–55; local power structures and, 152–53, 155; public defender caseloads and, 136–42, 148; white supremacy and, 124
Looking Backward (Bellamy), 26–28
Los Angeles. *See* California
Lumet, Sidney, 93
lynching, 69, 71–72

Macdonald, Dwight, 157
Magliocca, Gerard, 105
Manhattan, 50, 59–60. *See also* New York; the Tombs
Mapp v. Ohio, 102, 114
Marden, Orison, 162, 170, 173
Marshall, Thurgood, 182
Marx, Karl, 70
Massachusetts: Committee for Public Counsel Services, 185; judges resistance to public defenders and, 130; Massachusetts Defenders Committee and, 125–31, 139, 142–44, 148–49, 159–61, 185; post-*Betts* concerns, 80–81, 118; praise for *Gideon* implementation and, 130; requirement for counsel in felony cases and, 83; Roxbury and, 159–61; Roxbury Defenders Committee and, 174–76, 185; Voluntary Defenders Committee (Boston), 57–60, 63–64, 66, 80–85, 111, 125
mass incarceration, 2, 23, 178, 239n134
McReynolds, James Clark, 71
Meese, Edwin, 114
Meredith, James, 118
Michigan Law Review, 43
Miranda v. Arizona, 102, 114
Mississippi, 120, 124, 151–54, 166–74
Mississippi State Sovereignty Commission, 169
Missouri, 156

Moore v. Dempsey, 70–71
Morse, Joshua, 171
Moynihan, Daniel Patrick, 112

NAACP Legal Defense Fund, 167
The Nation, 35, 186
National Advisory Commission on Criminal Justice Standards and Goals, 103
National Association of Legal Aid Organizations, 53, 111. See also National Legal Aid and Defender Association (NLADA)
national defender initiative, 111–13
National Defender Project: amount spent by, 177; Atlanta and, 163–66; Boston and, 151; creation of, 113; final report, 155–56, 178–79; governance of, 162; Massachusetts Defenders Committee and, 128–30, 159; matching funds requirement and, 165–66; Mississippi and, 151–52, 169–74; national reach of, 162–63; observation of local courts and, 136–37, 151–53; organized defense delivery systems and, 157, 159; Philadelphia and, 132; race and, 161; results of private investment and, 155–56, 186. See also Ford Foundation
national identity: Bill of Rights and, 104–6; the Cold War and, 89–90, 92, 94; *Gideon's Trumpet* and, 110; public defender concept and, 1–2, 5, 15–16; right to counsel and, 99
Nationalism, 28–29
National Lawyers Guild, 14, 106, 167, 197n47
National Legal Aid and Defender Association (NLADA), 17, 88, 103, 111–13, 129–30, 144, 150, 170, 177–78. See also National Association of Legal Aid Organizations
New England Defender Conference. See The Defense of Indigent Persons Accused of a Crime (conference)

The New Nation, 28
New York, 31–32, 50, 59, 63–64, 66, 88, 185
New Yorker, 130, 174–76
New York Times, 20, 24–25, 30, 79, 108, 186
Nineteen Eighty-Four (Orwell), 93
Nixon, Richard, 102
North Carolina, 120

Oakland. See California
obiter dicta, 74
O'Connor, Sandra Day, 182–83
Office of Economic Opportunity, 128–29, 131
organized defense delivery systems, 157, 159
originalism, 114
The Origins of Totalitarianism (Arendt), 91
Orwell, George, 93

Padnos, Michael, 166
Parker House Hotel, 117
Parmelee, Maurice, 25–26, 36–37, 45
Pascagoula. See Mississippi
Pennsylvania Supreme Court, 133–35
Philadelphia, 50, 59, 61, 131–36
philanthropy, 51, 55, 64, 82, 159
Pittsburgh, 50, 65–66
police, 57–58, 177
Polk County v. Dodson, 187–89
Pollak, Walter, 72–73
Pollock, Herman, 61–62, 67
Portrait of a Decade, 124
Poverty and the Administration of Federal Criminal Justice, 96–99
Powell, Jr., Lewis, 140–41, 188
Powell v. Alabama, 72–75
President's Commission on Law Enforcement, 144
Primus, Richard, 92, 221n60
The Process is the Punishment, 139–41, 150
progressivism, 9–11, 195n27
The Public Defender (Parmelee), 25
The Public Defender (TV show), 85

public defenders (as a concept): Allen report and, 96, 98–99; Bellamy and, 28; compulsory public defense and, 11, 44–47, 55; effect on criminal trials and, 39–40; elite lawyers embrace of, 16–18, 22, 99; elite lawyers resistance to, 2–4, 12, 15–16, 47–49; *Equal Justice for the Accused* and, 96–97; Foltz and, 29–30; *Gideon* myth and, 19–22; the immigrant poor and, 41; indigent defense and, 8, 18; *Justice and the Poor* (Smith), 51–52; lack of a fixed meaning for, 23; national defender initiative and, 111–13; national identity and, 1–2, 5, 15–16; problems with, 8–9, 12–13, 60; as a reform project, 5, 7–8, 35–43, 45–46, 189; right to counsel and, 6–7; separation of state and defense counsel and, 60–62; socialism and, 3–4; as a state-building project, 7. *See also* Goldman, Mayer C.; indigent defense

public defenders (in practice): antitotalitarianism and, 92–93; California and, 8, 30, 42, 44; caseloads and, 136–44, 148, 150; the Cold War and, 94–95, 113–15; defendants lack of faith in, 144–45, 149–50, 155, 160–61; definition of, 6; establishment of public defender offices and, 30, 142, 153; Ford Foundation and, 111–13, 128; funding and, 2, 17–18, 20, 60, 88–89, 125–36, 145–46, 154–55, 176–79; *Gideon v. Wainwright* and, 5, 111–13; independence from the state and, 135–36, 187–89; institutional legitimacy and, 146–48; legal reform and, 23; Massachusetts Defenders Committee and, 125–31; Mississippi and, 171–74; National Defender Project and, 113, 128, 132, 136–37, 151–52, 155–59; Philadelphia Defender Association and, 131–38; plea bargaining and, 143–46; *Polk County v. Dodson*, 187–89; response to *Gideon* and, 102–4, 119–20, 125–30; Roxbury Defenders Committee and, 174–76; salaries and, 126–27, 129; statistics for, 2, 142–43, 155–56, 193n9; *Strickland v. Washington* and, 181–84; War on Drugs and, 184–85. *See also* indigent defense

Quicksall v. Michigan, 80

race/racism: African American lawyers and, 160–61, 167, 175–76; Black Lives Matter movement and, 186; *Brown v. Board of Education* and, 118, 121–22; Cold War and, 14; criminal law and, 8, 14, 33, 129–30, 152–55; the deep south and, 124–25, 166–74; Georgia courts and, 164; indigent defense and, 14, 33, 65, 84, 154–55, 159–61, 166–70, 193n4, 196n43, 210n49; Jim Crow and, 69–70; riots and, 70–71; Roxbury and, 159–61; Roxbury Defenders Committee and, 175–76; voluntary defenders and, 65; voting rights and, 91

radical leftism, 70. *See also* dissidents; International Labor Defense; National Lawyers Guild

reactionaries, 71

red feather agencies, 63

reform liberalism, 9

Rhode Island, 30

right to counsel: Allen Report and, 97–98; civil proceedings and, 6; constitutional provisions and, 46; criminal process and, 123; criticisms of *Betts* and, 79–80; effective counsel and, 181–84; effect on funding for indigent defense and, 84; elite lawyers and, 1, 17–18; *Equal Justice for the Accused* and, 96–97; fair trials and, 94–95, 140; *The Process is the Punishment* and, 150; public defenders and, 7, 16; race and, 14, 33, 65, 84, 154–55, 159–61, 166–70, 193n4, 196

Index 269

right to counsel (cont.)
  n43, 210n49; total incorporation
  theory and, 78. *See also Argersinger v.
  Hamlin*; the Constitution (U.S.);
  Gideon v. Wainwright; *Johnson v. Zerbst*;
  Supreme Court; individual rights
Rimbold, Edgar, 128, 139, 143, 145, 148, 161
Rizzo, Frank, 133–34, 136
Roberts, Owen, 60, 77–79
Rockefeller Jr., John D, 50
Rockefeller lawyers, 50, 54
Rodell, Fred, 96, 107
Rodino, Peter, 185
Roosevelt, Franklin, 105
Rosenberg, Norman, 110, 198n56
Roxbury. *See* Massachusetts

Sacher v. United States, 106–8
Safe Streets Act of 1968, 176
San Francisco. *See* California
Satterfield, John, 118
Schaefer, Gerard, 148
Schlesinger, Jr., Arthur, 90
Schwartz, Louis, 136, 138
Scottsboro prosecutions, 72–74
Second Bill of Rights, 105
sexism, 29–30, 33
Sherwood, Wally, 175–76
show trials, 89, 93, 220n34, 220n40
Smith, Reginald Heber, 51–55, 159
Smith Act, 106
socialism, 3–4, 15–16, 25, 60, 88–89, 95, 98, 105, 155
Socialist Party, 4
sociology, 34–35
South Carolina, 120
Southern Center for Human Rights, 186–87
Southern exceptionalism, 172–73
Soviet communism, 15, 89
Spangenberg, Robert, 150, 159
Specter, Arlen, 134
Stewart, William Scott, 41
Strickland v. Washington, 181–84, 240n8

Supreme Court: *Argersinger v. Hamlin*, 140–42, 158, 178–79; *Betts v. Brady*, 76–81, 83, 95, 99–101, 140, 157, 182, 215n114, 215n118, 221n60; Bill of Rights and, 104–5; *Brown II*, 122; *Brown v. Board of Education* and, 118, 121–22, 130, 225n31; code of criminal procedure and, 102; due process and, 59, 70–74, 78–81, 102, 182, 189; *Griffin v. Illinois*, 81, 216n133; *Johnson v. Zerbst*, 75–77, 96, 102; *Mapp v. Ohio*, 102, 114; *Miranda v. Arizona*, 102, 114; *Moore v. Dempsey*, 70–71; originalism and, 114; petitions to, 100; *Polk County v. Dodson*, 187–89; *Powell v. Alabama*, 72–75; *Quicksall v. Michigan*, 80; on the role of the prosecutor, 38; *Sacher v. United States*, 106–8; Sixth Amendment and, 75, 101–2; state courts and, 76–77, 101–2; *Strickland v. Washington*, 181–84, 240n8; total incorporation theory and, 78, 101. *See also* the Constitution (U.S.); due process; *Gideon v. Wainwright*; right to counsel; Warren Court
Sutherland, George, 74

Tate, James, 132
Taylor, Frederick Winslow, 37
Through the Looking Glass (Carroll), 179
Time, 170
To Kill a Mockingbird (Lee), 115
Toll, Maynard, 162
the Tombs, 31–32
total incorporation theory, 78, 101
totalitarianism, 3, 90–95, 105, 219n23
trial by jury, 46, 72
Truman, Harry S., 105
Tweed, Harrison, 1–4, 12, 17, 55–56, 86–89, 162, 170
12 Angry Men (film), 93

United Community Services, 83
United States attorneys, 103

University of Mississippi Law School, 169, 171
University of Pennsylvania Law Review, 43, 137

Vercoe, Frederic, 42
Vinikoor, Martin, 133
The Vital Center (Schlesinger), 90
Vogeler, Robert, 93–95
Volpe, John, 126
voluntary defenders: allocation of assistance and, 64–66; associationalism and, 19; benefits of, 57–63; due process and, 84–85; funding and, 63–66; hierarchies in the legal profession and, 66–68; justifications for, 62; Rockefeller lawyers and, 50. See also indigent defense; legal aid organizations; public defenders (in practice)
voting rights, 91

War on Crime, 176, 178
War on Drugs, 184–85
War on Poverty, 99, 113, 128, 166, 176
Warren, Earl, 20, 81, 100, 102–3
Warren Court, 20, 81, 101–2, 113–14, 116, 119–23, 183, 186, 227n20. See also *Gideon v. Wainwright*; Supreme Court
Washington, David Leroy, 181–84
White, Theodore, 168, 170
white supremacy, 8, 69–70, 124–25, 167–69, 173–74
Wickersham Commission, 25
Wiebe, Robert, 11
Wigmore, John, 9–10
Willrich, Michael, 35
women, 29–30
Wood, Martha, 173
wrongful convictions, 58

Yale Law Journal, 43
Yale Law School, 96, 106–7, 109, 122, 171, 198n57, 208n7
Ylvisaker, Paul, 163

Zinn, Howard, 130

Index 271

www.ingramcontent.com/pod-product-compliance
Lightning Source LLC
Chambersburg PA
CBHW031802220426
43662CB00007B/497